THINKING OF THE MEDIEVAL

The mid-twentieth century gave rise to a rich array of new approaches to the study of the Middle Ages by both professional medievalists and those more well-known from other pursuits, many of whom continue to exert their influence over politics, art, and history today. Attending to the work of a diverse and transnational group of intellectuals – Hannah Arendt, Erich Auerbach, W. E. B. Du Bois, Frantz Fanon, Erwin Panofsky, Simone Weil, among others – the essays in this volume shed light on these thinkers in relation to one another and on the persistence of their legacies in our own time. This interdisciplinary collection gives us a fuller and clearer sense of how these figures made some of their most enduring contributions with medieval culture in mind. *Thinking of the Medieval* is a timely reminder of just how vital the Middle Ages have been in shaping modern thought.

R. D. PERRY is Assistant Professor of English and Literary Arts at the University of Denver.

BENJAMIN A. SALTZMAN is Associate Professor of English at the University of Chicago.

THINKING OF THE MEDIEVAL

Midcentury Intellectuals and the Middle Ages

EDITED BY

R. D. PERRY
University of Denver

BENJAMIN A. SALTZMAN
University of Chicago

Shaftesbury Road, Cambridge CB2 8EA, United Kingdom

One Liberty Plaza, 20th Floor, New York, NY 10006, USA

477 Williamstown Road, Port Melbourne, VIC 3207, Australia

314–321, 3rd Floor, Plot 3, Splendor Forum, Jasola District Centre, New Delhi – 110025, India

103 Penang Road, #05–06/07, Visioncrest Commercial, Singapore 238467

Cambridge University Press is part of Cambridge University Press & Assessment, a department of the University of Cambridge.

We share the University's mission to contribute to society through the pursuit of education, learning and research at the highest international levels of excellence.

www.cambridge.org
Information on this title: www.cambridge.org/9781108748766

DOI: 10.1017/9781108781565

© R. D. Perry and Benjamin A. Saltzman 2023

This publication is in copyright. Subject to statutory exception and to the provisions of relevant collective licensing agreements, no reproduction of any part may take place without the written permission of Cambridge University Press & Assessment.

First published 2023
First paperback edition 2025

A catalogue record for this publication is available from the British Library

Library of Congress Cataloging-in-Publication data
NAMES: Saltzman, Benjamin A., editor. | Perry, R. D., 1979– editor.
TITLE: Thinking of the Middle Ages : midcentury intellectuals and the Middle Ages / edited by Benjamin A. Saltzman, University of Chicago, R.D. Perry, University of Denver.
OTHER TITLES: Midcentury intellectuals and the Middle Ages
DESCRIPTION: Cambridge, United Kingdom ; New York, NY : Cambridge University Press, 2022. | Includes bibliographical references and index.
IDENTIFIERS: LCCN 2022022856 | ISBN 9781108478960 (hardback) | ISBN 9781108781565 (ebook)
SUBJECTS: LCSH: Civilization, Medieval. | Middle Ages – Historiography. | BISAC: LITERARY CRITICISM / European / English, Irish, Scottish, Welsh
Classification: LCC CB351 T45 2022 | DDC 909.07–dc23/eng/20220614
LC record available at https://lccn.loc.gov/2022022856

ISBN   978-1-108-47896-0   Hardback
ISBN   978-1-108-74876-6   Paperback

Cambridge University Press & Assessment has no responsibility for the persistence or accuracy of URLs for external or third-party internet websites referred to in this publication and does not guarantee that any content on such websites is, or will remain, accurate or appropriate.

For Kenneth "Satch" Head, who first got me thinking about philosophy – R. D. P.

For Oliver William Saltzman, in memoriam *William Saltzman* – B. A. S.

Contents

List of Contributors	*page* ix
Acknowledgments	xii
About the Cover	xiv

Introduction: Directions of Thought – The Middle Ages at the Midcentury   1
R. D. Perry and Benjamin A. Saltzman

PART I: POLITICS   33

1 Outside History: Fanon's Negative Manicheism   35
 D. Vance Smith

2 "The Noblest Blood God Ever Made": W. E. B. Du Bois's Medievalism in the Contexts of the World Wars   68
 Cord J. Whitaker

3 Ernst Kantorowicz, Carl Schmitt, and the University of California Regents   88
 Nancy van Deusen

4 Hannah Arendt's Middle Ages for the Left   106
 R. D. Perry

PART II: ARTS   129

5 Curtius and Jung: Commonplaces, Archetypes, and Literature's Collective Unconscious   131
 Emily V. Thornbury

6 Old English at the Midcentury: Poetry, Scholarship, and Fiction in Britain in the 1940s and 1950s   147
 Clare A. Lees

7 Erwin Panofsky's Neo-Kantian Humanism and
   the Purported Relation between Gothic
   Architecture and Scholasticism   167
   C. Oliver O'Donnell

8 "Are Women Human?": Authority, Gender,
   and Dante in Dorothy L. Sayers's Scholarship   190
   Helen Brookman

PART III: EPOCHS   213

9 Periodization Trouble: Auerbach, Huizinga, and
   the Question of Medieval Realism   215
   Jane O. Newman

10 Medieval Mysticism and the Making of Simone Weil   239
   Anna Kelner

11 Hermeneutics and the Medieval Horizon: Zumthor,
   Jauss, Barthes, and Gadamer   255
   Benjamin A. Saltzman

   Afterword   273
   Martin Jay

Bibliography   301
Index   337

Contributors

HELEN BROOKMAN is Professor of Liberal Arts & Interdisciplinary Education and Vice-Dean (Education) in the Faculty of Arts and Humanities at King's College London. Her interests lie in innovative and co-creative pedagogies and knowledge production. She focuses on the functions of gender, embodiment, space, and authority within humanities scholarship, particularly in relation to women medievalists in the nineteenth and twentieth centuries.

MARTIN JAY is Sidney Hellman Ehrman Professor Emeritus of History at the University of California, Berkeley. Among his works are *The Dialectical Imagination* (1973 and 1996), *Marxism and Totality* (1984), *Adorno* (1984), *Permanent Exiles* (1985), *Fin-de-Siècle Socialism* (1989), *Force Fields* (1993), *Downcast Eyes* (1993), *Cultural Semantics* (1998), *Refractions of Violence* (2003), *La Crisis de la experiencia en la era post-subjetiva*, ed. Eduardo Sabrovsky (2003), *Songs of Experience* (2004), *The Virtues of Mendacity: On Lying in Politics* (2010), *Essays from the Edge* (2011), *Kracauer: l'Exilé* (2014), *Reason after Its Eclipse* (2016), *Splinters in Your Eye: Frankfurt School Provocations* (2020), and *Genesis and Validity: The Theory and Practice of Intellectual History* (2022).

ANNA KELNER received her Ph.D. from Harvard in English in 2021, where she specialized in women's visionary writing. She is currently an independent scholar based in Los Angeles, where she continues to teach and study medieval literature.

CLARE A. LEES is Professor of Medieval Literature, Director of the Institute of English Studies and Vice Dean, School of Advanced Study, University of London. She is a fellow of the English Association and a fellow of King's College London. Clare's research interests include early medieval literatures, languages, and cultures of Britain and Ireland, gender and sexuality studies, and histories of place and belief. Her most recent work explores how modern and contemporary poets, writers, and artists engage with early medieval cultures.

JANE O. NEWMAN is Professor of Comparative Literature at the University of California, Irvine. She discusses the German seventeenth century in *Pastoral Conventions* (1990) and *The Intervention of Philology* (2000). Her third book, *Benjamin's Library: Modernity, Nation, and the Baroque* (2011), addresses the political implications of periodization in the early twentieth century. Newman's new translation of a collection of Erich Auerbach's essays, *Time, History, and Literature: Selected Essays of Erich Auerbach*, was published in 2014. She has held Fulbright, Guggenheim, and Humboldt fellowships, and was a fellow at the National Humanities Center (2015–16) and at the American Academy in Berlin (2017). She is currently completing the book *Auerbach's Worlds: Early / Modern Mimesis between Theology and History*.

C. OLIVER O'DONNELL is a historian of modern art and intellectual history currently based at the Warburg Institute of the University of London, where he is a member of the Bilderfahrzeuge Project. His first book, *Meyer Schapiro's Critical Debates: Art Through a Modern American Mind* (2019), was awarded the 2019 Willibald Sauerländler Prize from the Zentralinstitut für Kunstgeschichte in Munich. Recent articles of his have appeared in the *Art Bulletin*, *Word & Image*, *History of Humanities*, and the *Zeitschrift für Ästhetik und Allgemeine Kunstwissenschaft*.

R. D. PERRY is Assistant Professor of English and Literary Arts at the University of Denver. He is completing his first book, *Chaucerian Coteries and the Beginnings of the English Literary Tradition*, and has begun a second one, *The Complete Canterbury Tales*, on the aesthetics of incompleteness. He is also the co-editor of two other collections of essays: *Charles d'Orléans' English Aesthetic: The Form, Poetics, and Style of Fortunes Stabilnes*, with Mary-Jo Arn (2020), and *The Hundred Years War and European Literary History*, with Daniel Davies (forthcoming).

BENJAMIN A. SALTZMAN is Associate Professor of English at the University of Chicago and author of *Bonds of Secrecy: Law, Spirituality, and the Literature of Concealment in Early Medieval England* (2019). He has received fellowships from The American Council of Learned Societies and the National Endowment for the Humanities.

D. VANCE SMITH is Professor of English at Princeton University and a former director of the Program in Medieval Studies. He is the author of several books on medieval literature – most recently *Arts of Dying: Literature and Finitude in Medieval England* (2020) – and two

African cultural studies, and he is completing a book on Africa and the Middle Ages.

EMILY V. THORNBURY is Associate Professor of English at Yale University, specializing in Old English and Anglo-Latin poetry and poetics. Her first book, *Becoming a Poet in Anglo-Saxon England* (2014), explored pre-Conquest poetry as a fundamentally social practice; her second monograph, *The Virtue of Ornament*, will consider theories of labor and value in early medieval literature and art. Before moving to Yale, she taught at the University of California, Berkeley.

NANCY VAN DEUSEN is Professor of Music and Louis and Mildred Benezet Professor of the Humanities at Claremont Graduate University, and is Director of the Claremont Consortium in Medieval and Early Modern Studies, Claremont Colleges and Graduate University. She has received American Philosophical Society, Mellon, National Edowment for the Humanities, and Fulbright grants. She has published on music within the medieval city of Rome; music, liturgy, and institutional structure within the medieval cathedral milieu of Nevers, France; the medieval sequence within its Latin codicological and paleographical contexts, 900–1600, as well as its significance for the history of ideas; and music as a medieval discipline and its "ministry" as exemplification within the curriculum of the early university. Since 1997 she has been a fellow of the Medieval Academy of America.

CORD J. WHITAKER is Associate Professor of English at Wellesley College. He works on the development of racial ideology, medieval rhetorical theory, and the roles of popular and scholarly medievalisms in modern racial politics. The author of *Black Metaphors: How Modern Racism Emerged from Medieval Race-Thinking* (2019), he is currently writing on African-American writers' radical uses of the Middle Ages in the Harlem Renaissance. Whitaker edited the award-winning *postmedieval* special issue "Making Race Matter in the Middle Ages" (2015) and he has received awards from the Institute for Advanced Study, the Ford Foundation, and the National Endowment for the Humanities, among other organizations.

Acknowledgments

This volume, and many of the ideas collected in it, originated as a series of panels sponsored by the Program in Medieval Studies at the University of California, Berkeley. These panels took place at the International Congress of Medieval Studies at the University of Western Michigan, running for four years, from the 49th Congress of 2014 to the 52nd Congress of 2017. We would like to thank, first, Katherine O'Brien O'Keeffe for the initial impetus to run the panels, and for deputizing us to do with them as we wished. This volume would not have been possible without her guiding spirit. We would also like to thank the community at Berkeley who made the series possible, including Fred Dulson, Christopher Hench, Jasmin Miller, Maureen Miller, Michelle Ripplinger, and Spencer Strub. Several of the chapters in this volume began in those panels, and we would like to express our deep appreciation to those panelists and for all the others who presented at one of the most invigorating series of conversations in which we have had the pleasure of participating. In addition to the editors and contributors, our other panelists were as follows: on Arendt, Stephanie Batkie and Tara Mendola; on Auerbach, Tracy Cummings and Niklaus Largier; on Curtius, C. Stephen Jaeger and David Wallace; on Gilson, Jack H. Bell, Fred Dulson, and Francesca Murphy; on Huizinga, Peter Cibula and Lukas Ovrom; on Kantorowicz, Robert Pawlik; on Panofsky, Elizabeth Sears and Laura Hatch; on Zumthor, Seeta Chaganti and David F. Hult. Our sincere thanks to them all.

In the spring of 2020, Benjamin Saltzman ran a Ph.D. seminar at the University of Chicago titled "The Middle Ages in Midcentury Thought." We owe the students in that seminar our utmost gratitude: Danica Cao, Rowanne Dean, Cole Donovan, Heather Glenny, Shariq Khan, Hunter Koch, Matthew Neumann, Gabriel Ojeda-Sague, Shay Swindlehurst, and Mary Kemp Thornberry. As our lives were upturned by the pandemic, you all managed to show up week after week with compelling insights and original perspectives on the intellectual circumstances with which this volume attempts to recon. Your energy, curiosity, and ideas helped bring this volume to fruition during a time of crisis in its own right.

For conversations and feedback at various stages and on various parts of this project, we would like to thank Sophia Azeb, Timothy Harrison, Tom O'Donnell, Julie Orlemanski, Adam Rovner, Joe Stadolnik, and Mo Pareles. We are also indebted to Natalia McCormick, Kashaf Qureshi, and Josephine Dawson for their meticulous and expert assistance. To Emily Hockley at Cambridge University Press, we thank you for seeing the value in this book from the start, for your patience in awaiting its completion, and for your guidance of it into print. For the anonymous reader through Cambridge University Press, our profound appreciation for your enthusiasm for the book and for seeing what we did in it. And Martin Jay: it was always an honor merely to imagine your willingness to write an afterword. You have given us not only a sharp and illuminating reflection on the chapters in this volume, but a true lesson in intellectual generosity.

About the Cover

"Cathedral" (1966, 2 of 12) is a woodblock print by my grandfather, the American artist William Saltzman. His work ranges in scale and medium, from dramatically abstract watercolors to precisely angular stained glass, from intimate pen-drawn studies of the human body to massive copper installations in banks and churches and synagogues across the Midwest. The idea for "Cathedral" was perhaps first sparked in Europe during World War II, where he served in the US Army 604th Engineer Camouflage Battalion. His photographs from that period alternate between the workshop where they painted faux signage and built other objects of deception, to the friends and landscapes that caught his eye, to some of the great Gothic cathedrals and more modest medieval churches of France. He visited Brussels on March 17th (I can't read the full year) and wrote a postcard back to his wife, Muriel Saltzman: "Dearest – All these buildings and monuments are untouched by war – just drab in appearance – very interesting examples of early Gothic – classical – and Romanesque – plus Baroque." On the back of another postcard from the Cathedral of St Gudule, he wrote, "This Cathedral is not half as inspiring as Notre Dame in Paris, Rheims – in Rheims or Chartres in Chartres." Then again, "Cathedral" could have just as well been inspired by the glorious year he relocated his family from Minnesota to Italy (1960–1961). Yet there's something about the energy of the print – the way the lines of coppered light burst forth from the black structure and gray-blue underbrush – that seems to move between his two encounters with the cathedrals of Europe, between the dark and gloomy, yet massively uplifting structures, enveloped in the dust of war, and the brightly rekindled encounter with a Europe fifteen years later.

BENJAMIN A. SALTZMAN, Chicago, IL
March 29, 2022

Introduction
Directions of Thought – The Middle Ages at the Midcentury

R. D. Perry and Benjamin A. Saltzman

> I have heard the key
> Turn in the door once and turn once only
> We think of the key, each in his prison
> Thinking of the key, each confirms a prison
> – T. S. Eliot

In the decades following the end of World War II, the medieval reemerged as a category freighted with the weight of the past, ready to carry new significance. Its historical status, sociological properties, and artistic creations were taken up at this pivotal moment by intellectuals in radically novel and divergent ways that not only would influence the narrow field of scholarship on the Middle Ages itself, but at a much deeper level would also shape the future of humanistic enquiry more widely.[1] The essays in this book are interested in those midcentury writers whose enduring scholarship and criticism touched on the medieval: the ways these intellectuals were thinking of the Middle Ages and the ways the Middle Ages served as a point of intellectual departure and connection between them.

Many of the thinkers whose paths cross in the pages of this book are not, strictly speaking, known as medievalists: Kingsley Amis (1922–1995),

---

[1] To a certain extent, we will use the Middle Ages and the medieval period as synonymous terms, with the understanding that both phrases are, necessarily, the product of later intellectual periods (see also Jay's Afterword on this issue). That said, we are also cognizant of the fact that the adjectival form "medieval" serves as a base for the nominalization "medievalism," a term on which we have much more to say. For this volume, we are primarily interested in thinkers who are engaged with the culture of the Middle Ages and the way that influences their understanding of "the medieval" as a conceptual formation produced from that direct engagement, rather than an understanding of the period produced at a remove, a reaction to an already metabolized version of the Middle Ages that one would call "medievalism." The lines between the two are never clear cut, and the way that thinkers understand the Middle Ages will always be in conversation with the medievalism of their own moment, but nevertheless we believe there is something to be gained by considering those writers who are using medieval material in formulating their own thoughts, the fruits of which are borne out by the essays collected here.

Hannah Arendt (1906–1975), Roland Barthes (1915–1980), Bryher (1894–1983), Simone de Beauvoir (1908–1986), Ernst Bloch (1885–1977), W. E. B. Du Bois (1868–1963), Frantz Fanon (1925–1961), Hans-Georg Gadamer (1900–2002), Antonio Gramsci (1891–1937), Carl Jung (1875–1961), Henri Lefebvre (1901–1991), Dorothy Sayers (1893–1957), Carl Schmitt (1888–1985), Simone Weil (1909–1943), and Angus Wilson (1913–1991). Of others, such as Erich Auerbach (1892–1957), Ernst Robert Curtius (1886–1956), Johan Huizinga (1872–1945), Hans Robert Jauss (1921–1997), Ernst Kantorowicz (1895–1963), Erwin Panofsky (1892–1968), and Paul Zumthor (1915–1995), we might more accurately say that they were not *only* medievalists. And yet the European Middle Ages holds a crucial and often underappreciated place in the work of every member of this transnational, widely influential, and by no means exhaustive group.

In this respect, the present book shares similar aims with two recent books that demonstrate the significance of the Middle Ages in modern thought.[2] Bruce Holsinger's *The Premodern Condition: Medievalism and the Making of Theory* attends to the influence of medieval studies upon French theory, covering figures such as Georges Bataille (1897–1962), Pierre Bourdieu (1930–2002), Jacques Derrida (1930–2004), Jacques Lacan (1901–1981), and Emmanuel Levinas (1906–1995). Andrew Cole's and D. Vance Smith's edited collection of essays, *The Legitimacy of the Middle Ages: On the Unwritten History of Theory*, cuts a longer and larger swath through theory's history – covering figures such as G. W. F. Hegel (1770–1831), Karl Marx (1818–1883), Martin Heidegger (1889–1976), and Theodor Adorno (1903–1969) – and argues for the centrality of the Middle Ages in its account of modernity. The present book, in contrast, focuses on a narrower period (the mid-twentieth century) but in other ways ranges more widely, addressing figures that are not normally covered by that loose categorization of Theory with a capital T (such as Sayers, or even Curtius) as well as those who are (such as Barthes or Fanon). Our purpose in considering this wider purview over a shorter period of time is to show how endemic the medieval as a conceptual object was for intellectuals of all

---

[2] Despite being concerned with the lives of individual thinkers, this volume is not one of those biographies of the "great" twentieth-century medievalists, such as Norman Cantor's highly problematic *Inventing the Middle Ages* and J. Aurell Cardona's *Rewriting the Middle Ages in the Twentieth Century*, which focus their attention on the lives of scholars within the field of medieval studies. Nor is this volume specifically concerned with the rapid growth and development of new movements within medieval studies itself, such as the emergence of the *Annales* School; on that topic, see, for example, Burke, *The French Historical Revolution*. For a representative critique of Cantor, see Howe, "Review of Norman F. Cantor," discussed later.

different stripes at a shared moment in history. That is, instead of tracing an intellectual genealogy of Theory over the *longue durée*, we are mapping a *mentalité* of the medieval at the midcentury, as it were, and demonstrating its importance for our own thinking today. The essays in this volume illustrate how the Middle Ages served as an object of thought: how mid-twentieth-century thinkers used different aspects of medieval literature, art, history, and culture to think through contemporary political and philosophical problems. Taken together, these essays reveal a nexus of influences, illuminating these thinkers genealogically in relation to one another and in light of their own contemporary moments, offering a fuller and clearer sense of the lasting contributions that each of these figures has made to so much of today's scholarly work in literature, philosophy, and the humanities more broadly.

Each of the thinkers explored in this volume has shaped our understanding of the Middle Ages and many other critical methodologies in use today: literary, historical, philological, political. Auerbach's *figura* and Curtius's book of nature, Kantorowicz's two bodies and Arendt's political action, Fanon's manicheanism and Zumthor's naive historicism are now commonplace concepts widely employed. Often disconnected from the thinkers who first mobilized them, they nevertheless carry particular meanings precisely because of the work done by these thinkers and their medieval points of reference. Paradoxically, as citations of their work by medievalists have declined steadily since the 1980s, their ideas have become ever more ingrained in scholarly assumptions about the Middle Ages and how we come to approach the study of the literary and artistic cultures of this period. It is now, therefore, an ideal time to revisit these ideas and directly address the intellectual contexts in which they were formed.

At the same time, the fundamental and broad influence that these figures have had on a range of other and later fields of study, especially within the province of critical theory, is well recognized. Auerbach's theory of representation, for instance, lies behind Fredric Jameson's (he was, after all, Auerbach's student).[3] Kantorowicz's work has recently motivated a debate among such diverse thinkers as Giorgio Agamben, Victoria Kahn, Simon Critchley, and Eric Santner.[4] Arendt's writings on political action as a manifestation of the will (indebted to St Augustine of Hippo [354–430] and John Duns Scotus [*c.* 1266–1308]) continue to shape her

---

[3] See Bill Brown, "The Dark Wood of Postmodernity."
[4] E.g., Agamben, *Homo Sacer*, 57–62; Critchley, *The Faith of the Faithless*; Kahn, *The Future of Illusion*, 55–82; Santner, *The Royal Remains*.

reception by J. M. Bernstein, Wendy Brown, and Judith Butler among others.[5] Panofsky's homology between the structures of scholastic thought and the architecture of the Gothic cathedral stressed the importance of habitus, a concept that influenced the oeuvre of his early French translator, Pierre Bourdieu, and has continued to be an important concept in sociology and discourse analysis.[6] The debate between Karl Löwith (1897–1973) and Hans Blumenberg (1920–1996) abides as a faint backdrop to recent studies of secularization by, say, Talal Asad and Charles Taylor.[7] And Paul Zumthor's engagement with French poststructuralism underlies many current debates in literary studies about formalism and historicism.[8]

But the Middle Ages have also often served as a darker catalyst. In our own contemporary intellectual and political moment, as the medieval is being dangerously appropriated by the alt-right and white supremacists, it can be helpful to remember that this kind of political misappropriation has a long history, as do strategies for its resistance.[9] To take one of too many possible examples from the twentieth century, the medieval historian Percy Ernst Schramm (1894–1970) had worked in the Warburg Library in the 1920s and 1930s alongside Erwin Panofsky and other influential art historians. He would go on to become the official diarist of the Nazi High Command between 1943 and 1945. These two commitments were not unconnected in the least and coalesced in the serialized biography of Hitler he would eventually publish in the 1960s. Schramm's study of medieval portraiture, according to Eliza Garrison, forced the artworks to "serve as models for his own time," and with the rise of National Socialism he "saw an opportunity for the modern realisation of political ideals visualised in medieval images." In other words, for Schramm and likeminded German intellectuals of the period, "the clear goal was to construct the history of their own time as an answer to and a fulfilment of events and ideas set in motion in the eighth through early eleventh centuries by people who were perceived as the first 'Germans'."[10] His biography of Hitler, as Garrison demonstrates, was thus unmistakably modeled on Einhard's (c. 770–840)

---

[5] For example, Bernstein, "Promising and Civil Disobedience;" Wendy Brown, *Manhood and Politics*, 23–31; Wendy Brown, *Edgework*, 101–2; Butler, *Notes Towards a Performative Theory of Assembly*; Butler, "Hannah Arendt's Death Sentences."
[6] On Bourdieu, see Holsinger, *The Premodern Condition*, 94–113.
[7] Asad, *Formations of the Secular*, 191; Taylor, *A Secular Age*, 114.
[8] See Chapter 2 in this volume, Saltzman, "Hermeneutics and the Medieval Horizon."
[9] See, for example, Kim, "White Supremacists"; and see n. 36.
[10] Garrison, "Ottonian Art and Its Afterlife," 209–10. One of Schramm's collaborators, Hans Sedlmayr (1896–1984), had similar ideological entanglements, on which see Männig, *Hans Sedlmayrs Kunstgeschichte*.

early ninth-century *Life of Charlemagne* in its opening description of the leader's physical appearance.[11] Panofsky, for one, despised this ideological position of his former colleague, and in 1967 when deciding whether to accept an award from Schramm, apparently told his wife he had no interest in "letting Hitler's Thucydides hang a medal around [his] neck."[12]

Figures such as Ernst Kantorowicz illuminate a more complicated picture of how the ideologies of the early twentieth century could become wrapped up in the study of the Middle Ages. Panofsky's principles, for instance, influenced not only his view of Schramm, but also his view of Kantorowicz, whose appointment at the Institute for Advanced Study was "by no means predetermined, for until the spring of 1950 Panofsky had associated him with right-wing positions he abhorred."[13] His 1927 *Habilitationsschrift* on the Emperor Frederick II (1194–1250) is accordingly famous for its powerful praise for the German despot, and its message was embraced in bourgeoning Nazi discourses.[14] The swastika on its cover made this connection particularly visible, even though it was originally an apolitical signet for the book series published by Georg Bondi (1865–1935) – also a Jew – which preceded Nazi usage by a decade.[15] And yet Kantorowicz publicly protested the Nazi regime, refused to sign a Nazi loyalty oath, and as a Jewish academic fled Germany, eventually taking up a position at the University of California, Berkeley. In 1950, he was fired from the University of California for refusing, once again, to sign a loyalty oath – the decision that would convince Panofsky to recommend his appointment at the Institute of Advanced Study.[16] Then in 1957, he published his most well-known work, *The King's Two Bodies* – a study of medieval kingship that Giorgio Agamben would decades later engage with as "one of the century's great critical texts on the state and techniques of power."[17] Even this most cursory account of this one scholar's life serves as an important reminder of how scholarly engagements with the Middle Ages can become politically charged in unpredictable ways.

---

[11] Garrison, "Ottonian Art and Its Afterlife," 220–21; Schramm, *Hitler*, 17–18.
[12] Garrison, "Ottonian Art and Its Afterlife," 221; for more on the Nazi interest in the Middle Ages, see Diebold, "The Nazi Middle Ages"; Johnson and Caputo, "The Middle Ages and the Holocaust." For a biographical survey of medieval studies during the 1930s, see Wallace, "Medieval Studies in Troubled Times."
[13] Lerner, *Ernst Kantorowicz*, 331. On the events of Spring 1950, see Chapter 3 in this volume, van Deusen, "Ernst Kantorowicz, Carl Schmitt, and the University of California Regents."
[14] Kantorowicz, *Kaiser Friedrich der Zweite*.
[15] Lerner, *Ernst Kantorowicz*, 2, 113–14.
[16] See Chapter 3 in this volume, van Deusen, "Ernst Kantorowicz, Carl Schmitt, and the University of California Regents."
[17] Agamben, *Homo Sacer*, 91.

The postwar period saw a variety of responses to such ideological misappropriation of the Middle Ages.[18] Hannah Arendt's critique of totalitarianism – in taking up medieval thinkers such as Augustine to imagine a progressive politics of willed and thoughtful neighborly love – is perhaps one of the most overt, if also the most controversial and complex.[19] But even amidst the rise of National Socialism in the 1930s, a period when "one frequently heard that the Nazis wished to turn the clock back to the 'dark' Middle Ages" (as Salo W. Baron [1895–1989] put it in his report on the Eichmann Trial),[20] thinkers such as Ernst Bloch, in his 1935 examination of the rise of National Socialism and Nazi uses of history, made the case against the idea that anyone gets to own the Middle Ages.[21] And indeed, writing in 1962, Baron himself was arguing that this common pejorative sentiment about Nazi medievalism unfairly "maligned the Middle Ages, which tried to establish the reign of morality and order.... The unprecedented character of Nazi racial antisemitism could not be camouflaged by references to the Middle Ages."[22] But as the medieval is so susceptible to misappropriation – even to this day – it is often employed as a source of historical authority just as easily as it is pejoratively deployed as a regressive attribute.

Looking back to the nineteenth century, we can easily see where these paradoxical tactics originate and how they then become dangerously exacerbated in the early twentieth century. "The Heroic Age of medieval scholarship,"[23] to borrow Emily Thornbury's befitting characterization of the nineteenth century, witnessed a shift in the study of the Middle Ages from romantic and antiquarian interests to the emergence of new "scientific" approaches in the disciplines of, say, philology and art history. But that romantic inheritance was never fully displaced. As Paul Zumthor mused in *Speaking of the Middle Ages*, its quest for mythical origins, its "well-ordered dreams," its "nostalgias for epochs full of meaning," its "naive historicism," all became "cross-bred with positivism."[24] These scientific

---

[18] For a sense of this range, see the 2014 *postmedieval* special issue on "The Holocaust and the Middle Ages," ed. Johnson and Caputo. See also Hart, "Modern and Genuine Mediaevalism."

[19] See Chapter 4 in this volume, Perry, "Hannah Arendt's Middle Ages for the Left."

[20] Baron, "The Eichmann Trial," 37. A Columbia University professor, Baron was making this argument in relation to his recent testimony at the Eichmann Trial, but he had already been making these arguments in 1935; see his essay, "Germany's Ghetto."

[21] Ernst Bloch, *Heritage of Our Times*. A similar kind of critique has been employed more recently in, for example, Albin et al., eds., *Whose Middle Ages?*

[22] Baron, "The Eichmann Trial," 37.

[23] Thornbury, *Becoming a Poet*, 1.

[24] Zumthor, *Speaking of the Middle Ages*, 43–45. In many ways, Zumthor's little book also provides a helpful introduction to the midcentury trends in medieval studies. See Chapter 2 in this volume, Saltzman, "Hermeneutics and the Medieval Horizon."

approaches to the Middle Ages in the nineteenth century by the so-called Fathers of medieval studies thus embraced "the romantic myth of continuity, appropriated but displaced," which, especially after the European revolutions of 1848 and the Franco-Prussian War (1870–1871), facilitated medieval scholarship's enmeshment in nationalist politics.[25] At the same time, many nineteenth-century investments in the Middle Ages – literary, architectural, scholarly, artistic, economic – also worked to reimagine the present and the future as a kind of new Middle Ages, a nostalgic return to the pre-industrial, pre-capitalist past.[26] The two modes of appropriation went hand in hand.

By the twentieth century, this nationalist mythologization of the Middle Ages, as we have seen, reached a crest in emerging totalitarian ideologies. But even after the wave of totalitarianism had broken, the same fundamentally romantic approach to tracing the origins of the present back to the medieval would still occasionally persist, as it does, for instance, in Ernst Robert Curtius's magisterial – or "magnificent," as his sometime interlocutor T. S. Eliot (1888–1965) deemed it – *European Literature and the Latin Middle Ages*. Published in 1948, Curtius's book replaced the nationalist frame with a pan-Europeanism: a postwar philological recuperation of European unity and continuity through its shared legacy of Latinity.[27] In Curtius's own words, the book "grew out of a concern for the preservation of Western culture.... [and it] attempts to illuminate the unity of that tradition in space and time by the application of new methods. In the intellectual chaos of the present it has become necessary, and happily not impossible, to demonstrate that unity."[28] Such heroic unification amidst the intellectual – and

---

[25] Zumthor, *Speaking of the Middle Ages*, 46. For a wider overview of the association between nationalisms and medieval studies, see Evans and Marchal, eds., *The Uses of the Middle Ages*.

[26] See Saltzman, "Towards the Middle Ages to Come." That is not to say that such modes of medievalism did not continue into the twentieth century. Framed by the medieval legend of Saint Eustace, for example, Russell Hoban's post-apocalyptic novel *Riddley Walker* seems to take its cue from nineteenth-century novels such as Richard Jefferies' *After London, or Wild England* (1885) or William Morris's *News from Nowhere* (1890) (we thank Gabriel Ojeda-Sague for bringing Hoban to our attention). One could also point, in a different vein, to the midcentury growth of Disney and Disneyland (which opened in 1955); see Pugh and Aronstein, eds., *The Disney Middle Ages* (we thank Heather Glenny for her insights on the midcentury medievalism of Disneyland). To countless individual and amateur forms of medievalism; see Dinshaw, *How Soon Is Now?* And on twentieth-century literary medievalism, see Chapter 6 in this volume, Lees, "Old English at the Midcentury."

[27] See Chapter 5 in this volume, Thornbury, "Curtius and Jung." Curtius and T. S. Eliot had several intellectual exchanges (Curtius even translated *The Wasteland* into German in 1927), on which see Burrow, "Introduction," xiv.

[28] Curtius, *European Literature and the Latin Middle Ages*, xxiv. On this Eurocentric mode of "civilizational survival" shared by Auerbach and Curtius (but unheeded by the emergent field of comparative literature), see, Said, *Culture and Imperialism*, 47.

political – chaos of the 1940s sounds perfectly magnificent. Indeed, for Leo Spitzer (1887–1960), the book conveyed the sensation of being "aroused precisely by the realization of the historical continuity of our European civilization" such that "one feels as though the world-clock stood still: man appears here as a being consisting in continuity."[29]

But for Spitzer, Curtius's project could not merely have been a political reaction to the idea "that under the Nazi regime a European point of view on cultural questions was dangerous"; Curtius's project was about deploying philology as a response to the very "irrationalism" that engendered "a barbarous movement such as Hitlerism":

> With his flair for the duty of the hour, Curtius turned toward "solid philology." ... It was logical that an aristocratic mind such as Curtius' should, before the onslaught of the plebian hordes, retreat into the Latin past of Germany, into a difficult subject matter, inaccessible to the minds of the Rosenberg stamp, and should limit itself to strictly rational methods that could have a sobering effect on the ideology- and world-drunken Germans, thus avoiding the pitfalls of a Karl Vossler [1872–1949] whose vague irrational or idealistic categories ... seemed ironically enough, dangerously close to those of Hitlerism.[30]

Could "solid philology" rescue Europe from its ideological maelstrom, stirred up as it had been by ideologues such as Alfred Rosenberg?

Spitzer had his doubts, for he concludes his review by noting the conspicuous "bias against French classicism" and Curtius's other lingering "resentments," which "seem to include the German emigré scholars in Romance who have worked before him in the same direction: there is no mention in his book of Auerbach."[31] Auerbach's study of prefiguration, notes Spitzer as a fellow Jewish emigré to Istanbul, would have fit well in Curtius's account of medieval topoi had he thought to include it.[32] In other respects, Auerbach's

---

[29] Spitzer, "Review of Ernst Robert Curtius," 428.
[30] Ibid., 426. In his Foreword to the English translation of *European Literature and the Latin Middle Ages*, Curtius explains that the "tradition of thought and art" from Homer to Goethe "was severely shaken by the war of 1914–18 and its aftermath, especially in Germany. In 1932 I published my polemical pamphlet *Deutscher Geist in Gefahr*. It attacked the barbarization of education and the nationalistic frenzy which were the forerunners of the Nazi regime. In it I pleaded for a new Humanism, which should integrate the Middle Ages, from Augustine to Dante.... When the German catastrophe came, I decided to serve the idea of a medievalistic Humanism by studying the Latin literature of the Middle Ages. These studies occupied me for fifteen years. The result of them is the present book" (xxiii–xxiv).
[31] Spitzer, "Review of Ernst Robert Curtius," 431.
[32] Zakai and Weinstein, in "Erich Auerbach and His 'Figura'," argue that Auerbach's approach to *figura* was in fact a sharp rejection of Nazi philology that sought to demonstrate Christianity's opposition to Judaism, rather than (as Auerbach's essay shows) its indebtedness.

Mimesis is a similar kind of project, taking up a long stretch of European literary history in which the Middle Ages holds a pivotal place. Yet it employs a different mode of philological inquiry: its focus is placed on the individuality of literary examples, rather than on generalizable commonplaces and continuities of the sort that interest Curtius.[33] *Mimesis* signaled another kind of break as well. After its publication in 1946, Auerbach found himself fending off criticism, not only from Curtius, but also from those accusing the book of being "especially pro-French" and "unjust toward German literature" (a noticeable inversion of the critique of Curtius by Spitzer). Other readers accused the book more generally of being "all too much determined by the present."[34] Auerbach embraced this charge: "in the end I asked: How do matters look in the European context? No one today can see such a context from anywhere else today than precisely from the present, and specifically from the present that is determined by the personal origin, history, and education of the viewer. It is better to be consciously than unconsciously time-bound."[35]

Through Auerbach's words one begins to sense a sea change around the necessity of acknowledging one's own historicity in relation to the past. And as we will consider again in a moment, scholars after World War II increasingly began thinking of the medieval less as a source of continuity than as a detached object of study. The medieval has long been (and still is) a contested period: ripe for mythologizing, heritage-making, and the bolstering of nationalisms and white-supremacy.[36] So readily appropriable, so easily drawn into the ideological or the political, is it ever possible for the period to be a neutral object of study? Is it possible to draw the uncomfortable line between medievalism and appropriation?

With the postwar rupture of historical distance came entirely new ways of thinking of the Middle Ages. Perhaps therefore the most important word in the title of this present book is actually the preposition. What does thinking *of* the Middle Ages entail? What relation does it insinuate between the thinker and the medieval past? The process implied in thinking *of* is distinct from that implied in thinking *with* or thinking *about* or thinking *through* or thinking *for*. Less entangled, less objective, less penetrative, the preposition *of* suggests a casual yet productive relation,

---

[33] See Zakai, *Erich Auerbach*, 54–56.
[34] Auerbach, "Epilegomena zu *Mimesis*," 13 and 17; "Epilegomena to *Mimesis*," 570 and 573.
[35] Auerbach, "Epilegomena zu *Mimesis*," 17–18; "Epilegomena to *Mimesis*," 573–74.
[36] See Miyashiro, "Our Deeper Past;" Symes, "The Middle Ages between Nationalism and Colonialism"; Whitaker, "Race-ing the Dragon"; and Cohen and Steel, "Race, Travel, Time, Heritage."

aimless yet full of possibility. Indeed, *of* etymologically suggests detachment, related as it is to an Indo-European root shared by Latin *ab-* and Greek *apo-* and their senses of removal and separation. We therefore want to distinguish the practice of *thinking of* from a practice of *appropriation*, which is about taking ownership (*proprius*), bringing the object towards and into one's own position (a movement implied by the prefix *ad-*).[37] The thinking catalogued in this volume is therefore largely, though not entirely, in the mode of distinction, of thinking *away from*, rather than grabbing toward.

The term "medievalism," however, has tended to describe the latter mode of thinking, though it is used in reference to all manner of engagements with the medieval world, from the amateur to the professional, from the scholarly to the fictional and fantastical. When the term "medievalism" was first used to refer to a way of being (in the mid-nineteenth century), its sense was primarily pejorative: retrograde, backwards, feudal, anti-industrial.[38] Over the course of the nineteenth century, this retrogression gave way to nostalgia in cultural movements that sought to imagine a future that would resemble the Middle Ages (or at least a nineteenth-century futuristic fantasy of the Middle Ages). The term "medievalism" reached its peak in the 1920s and 1930s, often referring back to various earlier forms of medievalist engagement: early modern antiquarianism, the Gothic revival, the Arts and Crafts movement. And then in the 1940s and 1950s its usage dropped off considerably and was rarely applied to contemporary intellectual activities.[39] Given the trajectory of the term "medievalism" during the

---

[37] To be sure, forms of appropriation (and the meaning of the term) vary widely. While commonly applied to describe cultural theft from subjugated peoples, instrumentalized to gain additional power over them, the "appropriation of the Middle Ages" as we use it here follows the work of scholars who have called attention to and fought against the continued "appropriation" and "misappropriation" of the Middle Ages by white supremacists: see, for example, Lomuto, "Public Medievalism"; Lomuto, "White Nationalism"; Kim, "White Supremacists"; Hsy, "Antiracist Medievalisms"; and Gabriele and Rambaran-Olm, "The Middle Ages Have Been Misused." Many of these questions were addressed at the 2020 RaceB4Race conference on "Appropriations" at the Arizona Center for Medieval and Renaissance Studies, especially in Sierra Lomuto's talk, "Antiracism or Appropriation?" and Adam Miyashiro's talk, "Appropriating the Crusades." See also Ashley and Plesch, "The Cultural Processes of 'Appropriation'."

[38] *Oxford English Dictionary Online*, s.v. "medievalism." See the longer discussion in Matthews, "From Medieval to Medievalism."

[39] Google N-Gram Viewer, s.vv. "medievalism" and "mediaevalism." Indeed, one might have expected J. R. R. Tolkien's (1892–1973) writing to be described with such language, but it rarely was: one review of *The Lord of the Rings* (by a professor of nineteenth-century American history in the *Princeton Alumni Magazine*), notes that Tolkien "keeps his characters and incidents partly within a tone like that of nineteenth-century medievalism"; Calhoun, "Review of J. R. R. Tolkien."

mid-twentieth century, we hesitate to use it in describing what we understand to be a radically different mode of engaging with the medieval past. As most of the twentieth-century intellectuals in this volume tended instead to register the alterity of the Middle Ages and are not medievalists (in the sense that they have devoted their careers to the study of the Middle Ages), they are intellectuals who happen to be thinking of the medieval.[40]

What will therefore become especially apparent in the chapters that follow is that to each of these intellectuals the Middle Ages means something slightly different. To some it is a delimited period of time, a particular geography, a single poet or author, or a set of cultural forms. To others, the Middle Ages is constituted less by concrete historical topographies and more as a conceptual marker for the antecedent of modernity, particularly European modernity. In many ways, around the midcentury the feedback loop between modern Europe and medieval Europe further propped up the very narrow conception of the Middle Ages *as* European, against which so much work in medieval studies today is now working to correct.[41] And yet Simone Weil's medieval differs from Zumthor's; Du Bois's medieval differs from Arendt's; Kantorowicz's differs from Fanon's. Mystics, manuscripts, Africa, Augustine, oaths, and the manichean bonds of colonialism – these are a few of the terms that constitute the medieval as it is broadly conceived in this book.

* * *

Insofar as it is possible to capture the intellectual climate and commitments of a given era, there seem to be four – by no means exclusive or universal – features of the midcentury moment that shaped these approaches to the Middle Ages: educational practices and scholarly training at the turn of the century that produced the thinkers this volume studies, the various crises and wars of modernity (1914–1945), widespread decolonization and the Civil Rights movement (1945–1962), and the first phase of the Cold War and the accompanying pressures on the intellectual commitments of the left and the right (1945–1975). Further events could certainly be adduced. Bruce Holsinger, for instance, has pointed out the importance of the Second Vatican Council (1962–1965) in influencing French intellectuals to

---

[40] One of the most explicit interrogations of this question is by Jauss, "The Alterity and Modernity of Medieval Literature." See Chapter 2 in this volume, Saltzman, "Hermeneutics and the Medieval Horizon."
[41] See Heng, "The Global Middle Ages"; Lomuto, "Becoming Postmedieval."

consider medieval culture anew even as the Church was deciding to modernize itself.[42] In terms of representing the transnational group of thinkers covered in this volume, though, these four aspects of midcentury culture seem to have the farthest reach. In addition to their widespread impact, each of these major historical events and political movements provided an intellectual framework for thinking of the Middle Ages at a moment when thinking of the past could no longer so easily be divorced from or appropriated into the contemporary moment. These events not only served as a backdrop, but also conditioned the very approaches documented throughout the essays in this volume. As Auerbach wrote of *Mimesis*, so any one of the thinkers in this book could have said, *mutatis mutandis*, of their own work, that "it is quite consciously a book that a particular person, in a particular situation, wrote at the beginning of the 1940s."[43]

Education at the Turn of the Century

One of the first things that a person might notice when encountering any one of the authors covered in this volume is just how impressive their education is, even for those without advanced degrees. The educational system in which these authors were raised, be it in America, Britain, France, Germany, or elsewhere, was very different from our own, both for better and worse. The problems with that system are well known, the most significant of which was the overrepresentation of white male authors as objects of study. And though not unrelated, the system also prepared these thinkers to access the vast riches of medieval writings by emphasizing training in Greek and Latin early and throughout their secondary education.[44] Their chance to explore those riches would come during their tertiary schooling. The fact that the universities were themselves a product of the Middle Ages would have not escaped notice. Prior to World War II, many university towns would have still looked medieval, as much of Oxford does today, having escaped Hitler's bombing campaign. And the educational and social structures were still beholden to medieval traditions – including the deplorable fact that women were not permitted to take degrees at Oxford

---

[42] Holsinger, *The Premodern Condition*, 152–94.
[43] Auerbach, "Epilegomena zu *Mimesis*," 18; "Epilegomena to *Mimesis*," 574. Likewise, Curtius, *European Literature and the Latin Middle Ages*, xxvi, said his own book "grew out of vital urges and under the pressure of a concrete historical situation."
[44] For a brief history of the persistence of this language training, and the effect its discontinuation had on the study of the classics – which is easily extrapolated to include its effect on medieval studies – see Forrest, "The Abolition of Compulsory Latin."

until 1920 and not until 1948 at Cambridge. Class, too, would have been a barrier, as the world of higher education during the period in which the authors studied here were pursuing their educations had not yet expanded outside the privileged few – a change that really only came to pass during the period covered here and only after structural changes made possible by things such as the GI Bill (1944) in the United States or the Education Act of 1962 in the United Kingdom, which codified funding practices that had been going on since the mid-1940s and the close of the war.

Within such an exclusionary context, those let past the front gate would have met university professors who would have been trained in the discipline of philology as it was practiced in Germany, spreading outward from there throughout the nineteenth century.[45] These were the professors who largely created medieval studies as a disciplinary field, although they were also the ones, as mentioned earlier, deeply enmeshed in the process of legitimizing the nation-state.[46] Indeed, it was not until the early twentieth century that something like a coherent field of medieval studies first began to emerge.[47] For those thinkers who became medievalists, this was a propitious moment; they benefited from the educational training in the methods and materials of the older generation, but they could take their learning in different directions. Some, such as Kantorowicz in his book on Frederick II, seemed to continue the work of defining and memorializing the nation-state and the heroes of its past, although in this instance overlaid with a romanticism inspired by Stefan George (1868–1933); both the affinity with George and the political ramifications of the first book would eventually be tempered by Kantorowicz's later biography and work.[48] Others, such as Auerbach in *Mimesis*, stretched beyond the national concerns of their teachers in order to conceptualize a trans-European culture, an artistic forerunner to the European Union.[49]

---

[45] On this history, see Momma, *From Philology to English Studies*.

[46] Often in ways that make appropriation by contemporary white nationalist not as surprising as it might have otherwise been; see Ellard, *Anglo-Saxon(ist) Pasts*.

[47] From where he stood in the mid-1940s, Curtius lamented the lack of such a field: "the Middle Ages is dismembered into specialties which have no contact. There is no general discipline of the Middle Ages – a further impediment to the study of European literature" (*European Literature and the Latin Middle Ages*, 13). In 1925 and out of similar motivations, the Medieval Academy of America was founded around the newly formed field of Medieval Latin Studies; see Coffman, "The Mediaeval Academy of America."

[48] In addition to Chapter 3 in this volume, van Deusen, "Ernst Kantorowicz, Carl Schmitt, and the University of California Regents," see Lerner, *Ernst Kantorowicz*.

[49] Auerbach's work shares this quality with Curtius's *European Literature and the Latin Middle Ages*; see the discussion in Wallace, "General Introduction."

Even those thinkers who did not become medievalists were beneficiaries of this educational system. Carolyn Dinshaw has drawn our attention to the importance of amateur medievalists and the way they construct the Middle Ages as an object of desire.[50] The thinkers in this volume who are not professional medievalists join the ranks of Dinshaw's amateurs, although it must be said that, with their educational background, these are some of the most highly trained (and famous) amateurs one is likely to encounter. Individual essays will necessarily cover the engagement that these amateurs had with the Middle Ages, but one might note here that any one of these thinkers could serve as a nodal point to trace out multiple and overlapping attachments to medieval writings that are more professionally academic. A few examples will suffice. A particularly robust set of connections exists among the German intellectuals of the midcentury. Hannah Arendt wrote her dissertation on Augustine under the supervision of Karl Jaspers (1883–1969).[51] Jaspers, who started his career as a psychologist, came to philosophy as a result of his contact with Max Weber (1864–1920) and under the influence of other thinkers associated with Weberian thought, such as Ernst Bloch, Georg Simmel (1858–1913), and György Lukács (1885–1971). Weber had earned his law doctorate in 1889, writing a dissertation titled *Zur Geschichte der Handelsgesellschaften im Mittelalter* (*The History of Commercial Partnerships in the Middle Ages*). And while his 1891 *Habilitationsschrift* – *Die römische Agrargeschichte in ihrer Bedeutung für das Staats- und Privatrecht* (*Roman Agrarian History and Its Significance for Public and Private Law*) – took him further back into history, one can understand his most famous work, *The Protestant Ethic and the Spirit of Capitalism* (1905), as predicated specifically on a medieval/modern periodization that situates the medieval Catholic backdrop against which the Protestant ethic broke away.[52] Of course, Arendt was also deeply influenced by Martin Heidegger, her early mentor and – infamously – her lover. Heidegger's *Habilitationsschrift* was on *Duns Scotus's Theory of the Categories and of Meaning* (*Die Kategorien- und Bedeutungslehre des Duns Scotus*, 1916), though the actual tract that Heidegger discusses is by a different medieval author, Thomas of Erfurt (fl. early fourteenth century).[53] Arendt would also edit a collection of essays by her dear departed friend, Walter

---

[50] Dinshaw, *How Soon Is Now?*
[51] See Chapter 4 in this volume, Perry, "Hannah Arendt's Middle Ages for the Left."
[52] For Weber's life, see Radkau, *Max Weber*.
[53] That tract is Thomas of Erfurt, *De modis significandi*. On Heidegger's medievalism, see Knapp, "Medieval Studies."

Benjamin (1892–1940), who had written his failed *Habilitationsschrift* on the German *Trauerspiel* and the ways its approach to allegory differed from the medieval allegory that preceded it.[54]

Two shorter examples give a sense of the ubiquity of medieval culture in the educational system of the late nineteenth and early twentieth centuries outside Germany, although the first is a story explicitly about the spread of German scholarly methodologies. W. E. B. Du Bois, as detailed in Cord Whitaker's essay here, explores the formal possibilities of medieval romance in a story that involves a Black man who flees the United States for self-imposed exile in Germany.[55] Du Bois had spent some time in Germany himself, not romancing an Indian princess, but doing graduate work. While at Harvard earning his Ph.D. in sociology, Du Bois would spend 1892 abroad at the University of Berlin, learning from those associated with the then ascendant historical school of economics, particularly Gustav von Schmoller (1838–1917). Schmoller, like others in the historical school, insisted that economics can only be understood in relation to its historical context and, along with various studies in mercantilism, had published *Strassburg zur Zeit der Zunftkämpfe* (*Strasbourg during the Guild Fights*, 1875) on fourteenth-century disputes that ended in revolution and the guilds seizing control of the city. Schmoller's reputation was at its height when Du Bois studied with him: the important English economist William Ashley (1860–1927) had dedicated to Schmoller his inaugural lecture as the Professor of Political Economy and Constitutional History at the University of Toronto in 1888, the same year Ashley published his *An Introduction to English Economic History and Theory, Part 1: The Middle Ages*. Part two, on "the end of the Middle Ages," appeared in 1893, by which time he had moved to Harvard – where Du Bois had also returned – in order to become the first Professor of Economic History.

An even briefer example from France: Simone Weil, as discussed in Anna Kelner's essay, imagined her mysticism in response to medieval examples. In her early education at the renowned secondary school Lycée Henri-IV, she was influenced by the famous teacher Émile-Auguste Chartier (1868–1951), who insisted on being called "Alain," in homage to the medieval French writer Alain Chartier (*c.* 1385–1430).[56] This twentieth-century Chartier seemed to have a knack for inspiring some interest in

---

[54] Benjamin, *Origin of the German Trauerspiel*.
[55] For more on Du Bois's medieval imagination, see Vernon, *The Black Middle Ages*, 19–22.
[56] See Bédé, "Alain," 10.

the Middle Ages among his pupils: at that same time as Weil, he also taught Simone de Beauvoir, who would write of Christine de Pizan (1364–c. 1430) in *The Second Sex* that her "L'Epistre au Dieu d'amours" was "the first time a woman takes up her pen to defend her sex," and who would defend the importance of historical thinking, including a healthy respect of cathedrals, in *The Ethics of Ambiguity*.[57]

It is often difficult to discern and appreciate the particular avenues of influence, the university hallways, as it were, that molded the thinkers in this volume. Some belong to distinct academic lineages that render their knowledge of medieval culture at least traceable, while others would have absorbed such knowledge in less direct ways. In either case, the centrality of medieval texts and history in the academy at the turn of the century begins to explain the residual commitments that animate the thinking of so many important intellectuals in the subsequent decades.

A Period of Crisis

The turbulence of the early twentieth century and the widespread sense of crisis that emerged with the two world wars called into question the belief in the rapid, unimpeded, foregoing progress of modernity.[58] This interruption served as a crucial catalyst for intellectual reflections on that earlier "dark age." Before World War I (1914–1918), Europe had experienced growth on numerous fronts: colonial, scientific, industrial. The rate of expansion was unprecedented. As Auerbach wrote in the final chapter of *Mimesis*, "The widening of man's horizon, and the increase of his experiences, knowledge, ideas, and possible forms of existence, which began in the sixteenth century, continued through the nineteenth at an ever faster tempo – with such a tremendous acceleration since the beginning of the twentieth that synthetic and objective attempts at interpretation are produced and demolished every instant."[59] Over the course of the second decade of the twentieth century, Filippo Tommaso Marinetti (1876–1944) would lead the Futurists in their rejection of the past and admiration of speed, technology, mechanization; moving even faster and more chaotically by the middle of the decade, Ezra Pound (1885–1972) and Wyndham Lewis (1882–1957) would energetically reject

---

[57] de Beauvoir, *The Second Sex*, 117; *Ethics of Ambiguity*, 92; see Cole and Smith, "Introduction," 20–21.
[58] On crisis as an impetus for humanistic thinking, see Dumitrescu, "Introduction," in *Rumba under Fire*.
[59] Auerbach, *Mimesis*, 549.

Futurism in favor of Vorticism: "We stand for the Reality of the Present – not the sentimental Future, or the sacripant Past," "AUTOMOBILISM (Marinetteism) bores us."[60]

Then before the end of the decade, the sudden devastation brought by World War I – life and landscape, rendered bleak by modernity's technological advancements – gave way, in Auerbach's words, to "a Europe unsure of itself, overflowing with unsettled ideologies and ways of life, and pregnant with disaster."[61] The uncertainty of this future – in what Arendt would call an "atmosphere of disintegration" – was met with initial attempts to grapple with the past: as early as 1919 and with growing disillusionment over modernity itself, T. S. Eliot would famously urge poets and readers to be perceptive "not only of the pastness of the past, but of its presence."[62] Economic depressions in Germany and America, the easy rise of fascism, the failures of Western liberalism, and the catastrophes of World War II with the barbarous cruelty and inhumanity it brought to the surface, further shifted perspectives on the status of the modern era, and, more crucially, about its relation to history. In 1947, Simone de Beauvoir could reflect on the naive futurism of the first decades of the century and declare that "if the world behind us were bare, we would hardly be able to see anything before us but a gloomy desert."[63] For many, it was a gloomy desert indeed. A growing pessimism was evident, for instance, in the "bleak radicalism" of the Frankfurt School as it trained its attention on the historical conflict between man and nature.[64] And like the members of the Frankfurt School, which relocated to Columbia University in New York City as those associated with it scattered even more broadly, many of

---

[60] Wyndham Lewis, ed., *BLAST*, 1–2.
[61] Auerbach, *Mimesis*, 551. In many ways, Auerbach puts it better than we could: "In Europe this violent clash of the most heterogeneous ways of life and kinds of endeavor undermined not only those religious, philosophical, ethical, and economic principles which were part of the traditional heritage and which, despite many earlier shocks, had maintained their position of authority through slow adaptation and transformation; nor yet only the ideas of the Enlightenment, the ideas of democracy and liberalism which had been revolutionary in the eighteenth century and were still so during the first half of the nineteenth; it undermined even the new revolutionary forces of socialism, whose origins did not go back beyond the heyday of the capitalist system. These forces threatened to split up and disintegrate. They lost their unity and clear definition through the formation of numerous mutually hostile groups, through strange alliances which some of these groups effected with non-socialist ideologies, through the capitulation of most of them during World War I, and finally through the propensity on the part of many of their most radical advocates for changing over into the camp of their most extreme enemies" (550).
[62] Arendt, *Origins*, 268; Eliot, "Tradition and the Individual Talent," 14.
[63] de Beauvoir, *Ethics of Ambiguity*, 92.
[64] The phrase is from Anderson, *Bleak Liberalism*, 102; for background, see Jay, *The Dialectical Imagination*, esp. "Toward a Philosophy of History," 253–80.

the thinkers in this volume were writing from a state of exile having been forced to flee Nazi Germany. The Middle Ages served their intellectual needs in ways we can often only speculate about, but certainly in their attempts to theorize precisely this transhistorical desert of the present and grapple with the meaning of cultural decline, crisis, catastrophe.

Most of all, the Middle Ages played an essential role in the very question of modernity's legitimacy, which emerged in the debate over secularization most famously articulated between Karl Löwith and Hans Blumenberg. In his widely influential book *Meaning in History* (1949), Löwith advanced the so-called "secularization thesis," arguing that the idea of progress that runs through modern philosophies of history, starting with Voltaire (1694–1778) through Hegel and Marx, is actually a secularized form of pre-Enlightenment "Judeo-Christian" eschatology and thus operates paradoxically as mere faith disguised through claims of reason.[65] Progress, for Löwith, is therefore always thought of as inevitable, and certain relapses (such as the Dark Ages or incidents of mass killing) are understood as unavoidable preparation for the ongoing forward momentum of history. "Hope and faith," in other words, "are justified in interpreting present events and catastrophes in the light of an *eschaton*, as a prefiguration of an ultimate outcome."[66] The appeal of this logic at a time when the world was just recovering from two wars and losing faith in modernity's promise of progress should be obvious. But Löwith's theory also implicitly meant that modernity's own conception of its historicity and progress – like many of its institutions – was basically medieval.[67]

Modernity needed a good defense. It began as a lecture in 1962 and eventually would be published in 1966 as *Die Legitimität der Neuzeit*

---

[65] Beginning in the late 1920s, Carl Schmitt had formulated a similar kind of argument with respect to modern statehood, which he posited as a secularized form of theological concepts. But by the time Löwith published *Meaning in History*, Schmitt's theory of political theology would become quite different. As George Schwab puts it in the introduction to Schmitt, *The Concept of the Political*, "the rapid succession of momentous events – World War I, Versailles, the Communist victory in Moscow, and the Nazi victory in Berlin about a year after the publication of the 1932 text of Schmitt's essay – halted the broad course of development of the epoch of the European sovereign state and also soon showed that the traditional European sovereign state was no longer a politically viable entity in a rapidly changing world" (10). On the significance of Blumenberg-Löwith debate for how we understand the Middle Ages, see Cole and Smith, "Introduction," 2–11; and Ingham, *The Medieval New*, 172–75.

[66] Löwith, *Meaning in History*, 205.

[67] Löwith was, of course, not alone in making such an argument about modernity's secularization of medieval institutions, which is a central piece in the political theology of Schmitt and later in the work of Kantorowicz; see Chapter 3 in this volume, van Deusen, "Ernst Kantorowicz, Carl Schmitt, and the University of California Regents."

(*The Legitimacy of the Modern Age*), Blumenberg's formidable response to the secularization thesis. Blumenberg argued that the modern idea of progress works towards a future through an immanent process of human action rather than from a transcendent authority or fate.[68] In particular, he sought to divorce modernity from the Middle Ages – a break he locates, for example, between Nicholas of Cusa (1401–1464; the medieval) and Giordano Bruno (1548–1600; the modern) – by contending, among other things, that the very idea of the Middle Ages was a modern invention:

> The modern age was the first and only age that understood itself as an epoch and, in so doing, simultaneously created the other epochs. The problem of legitimacy is latent in the modern age's claim to carry out a radical break with tradition, and in the incongruity between this claim and the reality of history, which can never begin entirely anew. Like all political and historical problems of legitimacy, that of the modern age arises from a discontinuity, and it does not matter whether the discontinuity is real or pretended. The modern age itself laid claim to this discontinuity vis-à-vis the Middle Ages.[69]

Blumenberg's defense of the modern age registers modernity's invention of itself in relation to the medieval, and in this respect it shares with Löwith what Kathleen Davis notes as one of the most important contributions of his work: "its insistence that conceptions of historical time must be understood as political strategy – and, in the case of periodized, progressive history, as a means of aggression."[70] In other words, after the crises of the early twentieth century, there was no way to think of the Middle Ages without also thinking of the period of crisis just past.

Stages of Decolonization

Of course, the world outside Europe had been in the midst of crises for quite some time. Over the course of the nineteenth century and into the early twentieth century, "Western civilization" had advanced in a perceived state of peace. Crucially, though, this peace was only perceived and experienced "in Europe and between Europeans," as Du Bois observes, for in fact "there was not a single year during the nineteenth century when the world was not at war, chiefly, but not entirely, these wars were waged to

---

[68] Blumenberg, *The Legitimacy of the Modern Age*, 27–36.
[69] Ibid., 116. Cole and Smith, eds., *The Legitimacy of the Middle Ages*, conceived of their volume as a rebuke to Blumenberg, by demonstrating the vital role that the Middle Ages played in modern thought and theory.
[70] Davis, "The Sense of an Epoch," 45. See also *Periodization and Sovereignty*.

subjugate colonial peoples."[71] During this period, the idea of the medieval continued to be deeply enmeshed with racism, slavery, and the enterprise of colonialism (inseparable as it is from the politics of capital).[72] Indeed, it continues to be so enmeshed. But in the postwar era, these colonial enterprises were violently collapsing. In 1947, India gained independence from the United Kingdom; in 1962, Algeria had gained independence from France; and between these years, almost forty states across Africa and Asia were decolonized, securing autonomy and claiming their independence from colonial rulers. In this context, the medieval takes on complicated and contradictory roles not only in reinforcing colonial ideology, but also within the discourses of resistance, especially under thinkers such as Fanon and Du Bois.

The colonial rationale, Du Bois observes, persisted in Europeans' belief "that they were spreading civilization."[73] The Middle Ages were at the heart of this civilizing business, offering the British in India, to use Ananya Jahanara Kabir's example, "a way out of the ontological shock generated by the colonial encounter."[74] As such, medieval history played a paradoxical role. On the one hand, the Middle Ages cemented a European sense of cultural superiority, a heritage validated by a particular vision of the past and one that could claim the crusades, for instance, as a model of imperialism. But on the other hand, the Middle Ages were conceived as a precivilized, preindustrial period, and thus easily deployed as a pejorative characterization of the colonized subjects' retrogression, their "barbarity," and their potential to become civilized under colonial rule.[75] As Aimé Césaire puts it, this "incarnation of human progress" was realized by bringing back tortures "from the depths of the Middle Ages!"[76]

---

[71] Du Bois, "Color and Democracy," 16.

[72] For the history of the affiliation between colonialism and the rise of English studies (especially medieval English studies), see Momma, *From Philology to English Studies*; on colonialism and English studies, see Viswanathan, *Masks of Conquest*, a classic; on colonialism and the history of medieval studies, see Miyashiro, "Our Deeper Past;" see also Dagenais and Greer, "Decolonizing the Middle Ages." But cf. Hsy, "Antiracist Medievalisms," for a fascinating account of how around the turn of the century, some "Chinese Americans expressed resistance to discrimination and rerouted [medievalist] notions of nobility, chivalry, and virtue to antiracist ends;" Hsy expands on this tendency in *Antiracist Medievalisms*.

[73] Du Bois, "Color and Democracy," 17. Vernon, *Black Middle Ages*, shows how this kind of colonial rhetoric also gets upturned, for example, by Du Bois's analogy of "Belgium's ruthless rule over Congo" as a "questing knight who achieves the Holy Grail" (20).

[74] Kabir, "Analogy in Translation," 184.

[75] See, for example, Davis, *Periodization and Sovereignty*, 34; "The Sense of an Epoch," 59.

[76] Césaire, *Discourse on Colonialism*, 67 and 48.

Colonialism, in other words, sought to civilize the colonized out of the Middle Ages. But it did so by importing Gothic architecture to colonies, by adopting the structures of feudalism, and by using – in Césaire's account – methods of cruelty fit for the Middle Ages.[77] Feudalism in particular gained new forms of attention as a colonial concept in the mid-twentieth century.[78] In addition to the central role it played in Marxist historiography and its accompanying discourses of periodization, discussed later, it emerged as an object of serious study under the *Annales* School, well suited to their motto of doing history from the ground up.[79] Partly under the influence of Marxism as well as the early work of the *Annales* School (especially Marc Bloch [1886–1944] and Lucien Febvre [1878–1956]), Norbert Elias (1897–1990) wrote *The Civilizing Process*. It was first published in 1939 but with little audience, then republished to great acclaim in 1969, thus straddling this period of decolonization: it is hard not to read it differently in light of the events of the intervening years.[80] Feudalism is central to Elias's exploration of the sociogenesis of the European state and thus becomes not only fundamental – in his view – to a history of Western civilization, but also as a symbol of colonial primitivism. Early in the book, Elias thus invites his readers into a little thought experiment:

> If members of present-day Western civilized society were to find themselves suddenly transported into a past epoch of their own society, such as the medieval-feudal period, they would find there much that they esteem 'uncivilized' in other societies today. Their reaction would scarcely differ from that produced in them at present by the behaviour of people in feudal societies outside the Western world.[81]

As Kathleen Davis has observed more broadly, feudalism was bound to the Middle Ages, and yet permitted "to roam across time and space, but always as a temporal marker, a tick on the clock of development."[82]

Colonists ingrained this logic in the minds of the colonized. Ventriloquizing the colonizer, Franz Fanon could thus proclaim: "If you want

---

[77] On colonial Gothic architecture, see Biddick, *The Shock of Medievalism*, 19–57; Niell and Sundt, "Architecture of Colonizers." From its beginnings in the sixteenth century, the historiography of feudal law facilitated European colonialism feudalism; see Davis, *Periodization and Sovereignty*, esp. chapters 1 and 2.
[78] See Davis, *Periodization and Sovereignty*, 67–69, for a discussion of Ranajit Guha's use of the term "quasi-feudal" in his 1963 book, *A Rule of Property*.
[79] See, for example, Marc Bloch, *Feudal Society*.
[80] See Goudsblom, "Norbert Elias."
[81] Elias, *The Civilizing Process*, ix.
[82] Davis, *Periodization and Sovereignty*, 24.

independence, take it and return to the Dark Ages."[83] Or the young factory worker arriving in France in the mid-1960s from Réunion Island could thus declare: "It's like I came from the Middle Ages."[84] History plays a powerful role in these statements as it becomes a tool of colonialism. As Fanon puts it, "The colonist makes history and he knows it."[85] But for Fanon, decolonization is a historical process, too: "The immobility to which the colonized subject is condemned can be challenged only if he decides to put an end to the history of colonization and the history of despoliation in order to bring to life the history of the nation, the history of decolonization."[86] As D. Vance Smith argues in his contribution to this book, the Fanonian "petrification of the peasantry" is a historical petrification, which stands in the way of the colonized writing their own history, their own movement and maturation, towards decolonization; it keeps history written in stone, the history of the colonist.[87] One is reminded here, imperatively, of Gayatri Chakravorty Spivak's (b. 1942) observation that "The subaltern as female cannot be heard or read."[88]

Decolonization is clearly fundamental to the work of Fanon and Du Bois. But colonialism itself is a significant – if often dangerously unstated – ideological background behind many references to the Middle Ages during this period. To think of the Middle Ages without explicitly thinking of the colonized onto whom the medieval was projected, then, is a move that reinforced precisely those dominant history-making discourses against which revolutions were being fought.

But the effects of colonialism and decolonization were not evenly impressed upon all twentieth-century minds. The Eurocentrism of the emerging field of comparative literature allowed Auerbach to comment on

---

[83] Fanon, *The Wretched of the Earth*, 53. This is one of several such moments in the text. For additional discussion, see Chapter 1 in this volume, Smith, "Outside History."

[84] Quoted and discussed in Warren, *Creole Medievalism*, xi. Warren shows how "On one level, the Middle Ages support conservatives who invoke 'ancient France' to defend cultural and religious hegemony; they also tend to champion the 'positive' value of French colonialism. On another level, the Middle Ages can signify a 'savage' time before civilization, denying access to culture altogether.... In this perspective, the medieval conspires with colonialism to delegitimize those not from continental France. On yet another, more optimistic, level, the fact that the Middle Ages predate modern colonialism can facilitate thinking outside colonialism's rigid binaries.... From this perspective, the medieval can trace a counter-intuitive path toward decolonization. Appropriations of the Middle Ages ... thus weave together various contradictory tendencies – affirmations of traditional pasts, postcolonial alienation, and dreams of radical futures" (194–95).

[85] Fanon, *The Wretched of the Earth*, 15 (see also 2). See Chapter 1 in this volume, Smith, "Outside History."

[86] Fanon, *The Wretched of the Earth*, 15.

[87] Fanon, *The Wretched of the Earth*, 65.

[88] Spivak, "Can the Subaltern Speak?" 308; see also Chatterjee, "Reflections," 83.

the existence of so many "other" literatures in a gesture of naiveté criticized by Edward Said (1935–2002): these "other" literatures appear "as if from nowhere: he makes no mention of either colonialism or decolonization."[89] By the 1980s, the emerging field of subaltern studies would come into its own, drawing the term "subaltern" from Gramsci's study of Italian peasantry and, as Bruce Holsinger has shown, borrowing some of its methodological approaches from the *Annales* School and other medievalist work from earlier in the century: "The result is an eclectic historical methodology that refuses to abandon so-called traditional methodologies even as it seeks to dethrone the institutional privilege of traditional history writing and to revise its official narratives of colonialism."[90] But those medievalist methodologies, borrowed though they may have been by the subaltern studies collective, were themselves being developed precisely in the decades when the violence of colonialism's historicity was being called out by thinkers such as Fanon, fighting at the forefront of the independence movements.

The Medieval Cold War

Concurrent with decolonization and certainly related, as World War II passed into a Cold one, the responses to the Middle Ages from those on the political left and right did not so much cease but instead entered into a new form of antagonism. The result was something akin to the "domino theory" – the theory in international relations, articulated most prominently by US president Dwight D. Eisenhower (1890–1969) in 1954, whereby the fall of one country to communism would result in the fall of neighboring countries – but applied to historical epochs. That such a front could open up during the Cold War was due to the importance that Marxism has always given the medieval: Marxist historiography maintains a strict periodizing logic by which the feudalism of the Middle Ages is transformed into modernity's capitalism. As Karl Marx himself puts it in the *Grundrisse* (written 1857–1858), "only in the period of the decline and fall of the feudal system but where it still struggles internally – as in England in the fourteenth and the first half of the fifteenth centuries – is there a golden age for labour in the process of becoming emancipated."[91] For Marx, this emancipation of labor allows the feudal mode of production

---

[89] Said, *Culture and Imperialism*, 45.
[90] Holsinger, "Medieval Studies," 1215.
[91] Marx, *Grundrisse*, 510. For a broader discussion of Marx on this issue, see Katz, "Karl Marx on the Transition."

to become capitalist, but by the mid-twentieth century, other possibilities were evident, unnervingly for those concerned about the spread of Marxism. In an instance of what contemporary Marxist theory now calls "uneven development," feudalism persisted longer in some places than in others, as indeed Andrew Cole has shown in regards to Hegel's experience of feudalism in early nineteenth-century Germany as opposed to Marx's capitalist England.[92] What V. I. Lenin (1870–1924) had attempted after the revolution of 1918 was to take an agrarian, largely feudal society and make it into a socialist one without going through the intervening stage of capitalism, a feat that Mao Zedong (1893–1976) replicated following the 1949 establishment of the People's Republic of China with the Great Leap Forward (1958–1962). Regardless of what one thinks about the efficacy or persistence of Russian or Chinese communism, the transition of feudalism into capitalism (as it occurred at the end of the Middle Ages) or feudalism into something else (as Chairman Mao was attempting at that moment) was a concern with clear contemporary importance in the middle of the twentieth century.[93]

In midcentury Marxist theory, the salient position afforded to the medieval is clear in a variety of ways. Most obviously, the transition from feudalism to capitalism at the end of the Middle Ages was the site of concern for a number of Anglo-American historians.[94] The "transition debate" began in earnest with Maurice Dobb's (1900–1976) *Studies in the Development of Capitalism* (1946) and Paul Sweezy's (1910–2004) "A Critique" (1950). It culminated with what is known more specifically as the "Brenner Debate" – the response occasioned by Robert Brenner's "Agrarian Class Structure and Economic Development in Pre-Industrial Europe" (1976) – and the status of what was called "Political Marxism."[95] That the latter appellation (in opposition to "economic Marxism") was

---

[92] On this uneven development, see Harvey, *Spaces of Global Capitalism*; on Hegel's feudalism, see Cole, *The Birth of Theory*, 65–85.

[93] On the contemporary status of Maoism in China, see Sorace, Franceschini, and Loubere, eds., *Afterlives of Chinese Communism*. For an overview of Hegel and Marx's influence on Lenin, see Anderson, *Lenin, Hegel, and Western Marxism*.

[94] There has been some concern both about the accuracy of feudalism presented in the following models and about the implicit understanding of Marxism they represent; our focus here is on the visibility of the Middle Ages in Marxism, which is amply demonstrated in these models regardless of their accuracy.

[95] Dobb, *Studies in the Development of Capitalism*. Sweezy's essay, "A Critique," originally appeared in *Science and Society* and was later collected with responses and comments in *The Transition from Feudalism to Capitalism*. The Brenner Debate has been usefully anthologized in Aston and Philpin, eds., *The Brenner Debate*. A more recent and fuller articulation of the "Political Marxism" position is Wood, *The Origin of Capitalism*.

coined by Guy Bois (1934–2019), a French Marxist historian, testifies to the fact that the debate captured the interest of a range of Marxist thinkers.[96] At around the same time, elsewhere in France, the way that the Middle Ages built upon preexisting structures and then served as the basis for capitalist architectural forms was inspiring a different sort of Marxist thinker: Henri Lefebvre would write that "there is no doubt that medieval society – that is, the feudal mode of production, with its variants and local peculiarities – created its own space" and that "medieval space built upon the space constituted in the preceding period, and preserved that space as a substrate and prop for its symbols; it survives in an analogous fashion itself today."[97] Like Marx before him, albeit with slightly different concerns, Lefebvre understands the wealth generated by medieval peasant communities, and the formations of space they subsequently produce, as the necessary precursor to capitalism: "manors, monasteries, cathedrals – these were the strong points anchoring the network of lanes and main roads to a landscape transformed by peasant communities. This space was the take-off point for Western European capital accumulation, the original source and cradle of which were the towns."[98] A great deal more could be said here, including everything from the influence of the Middle Ages on Antonio Gramsci – who helped define the way that intellectuals function in society by reference to the medieval clergy and said that "the peasant was no less cheated by the Church than by the feudal lords" – to the way that Mao's transformation of China and Maoism influenced debates within French Marxism, but this is not the space for an endless enumeration of examples.[99]

It is the space, though, to point out that this well-established Marxist interest in the Middle Ages produced its own sort of counterreaction. One would need look no further in the Anglo-American sphere than the work of Michael Postan (1899–1991), himself a refugee from the Russian revolution, in order to find an oppositional viewpoint to the transition debate. Postan's "passionately anti-communist" sentiment is not necessarily overt in his work, but he gives a vision of economic history that eschews the Marxist narrative about the development – and linked exploitations and

---

[96] See Bois, "Against the Neo-Malthusian Orthodoxy." For a different overview and critique of the debate, see Anievas and Nişancioğlu, *How the West Came to Rule*, 22–32.
[97] Lefebvre, *The Production of Space*, 53.
[98] Ibid.
[99] Gramsci, *Further Selections from the Prison Notebooks*, 10. Colleen Lye is currently working on the response to Maoism around the globe and has published some early thoughts in "Maoism and the Air We Breathe"; see also Bourg, "The Red Guards of Paris."

inequalities – of capitalism, from his early collaboration with his wife Eileen Power (1889–1940) in *Studies in English Trade in the 15th Century* (1933) to his later *Medieval Economy and Society* (1972).[100] Other responses to Marxism's interest in the Middle Ages were decidedly more reactionary, a kind of medieval studies McCarthyism. One can identify this tendency at work with Norman Cantor (1929–2004), who had come to prominence with his *Medieval History* (1963) and who was a student of Joseph R. Strayer (1904–1987), the Princeton professor and sometime CIA consultant.[101] Nicholas Howe (1953–2006) points out Cantor's extremism in his review of a later work, *Inventing the Middle Ages* (1991):

> those whom Cantor suspects of holding a grimmer view of the medieval world are dismissed, especially if they are French and might by a very long stretch be termed Marxists. As a contributor to the neoconservative New Criterion, Cantor can spot contaminations of Marxism even in those who never thought themselves Marxists. He wildly misrepresents Marc Bloch by calling him a Marxist and likening him to Theodore [sic] Adorno (p. 143). Bloch's writing, particularly after 1939, suggests that his politics were classically liberal, even somewhat old-fashioned for the time. That he learned from Marx about economic and agrarian history hardly makes him a Marxist, only a product of his time. Nor does it make those who followed him in the *Annales* school into Marxists, as if the father's politics were a mutant gene passed on to his intellectual children, most especially to Fernand Braudel.[102]

That the *Annales* School is pulled into the paranoia surrounding Marxism, starting in the midcentury but still very much alive today, is a salient reminder of two points. First, the Marxist interest in the Middle Ages is an important impetus for a broad reception of medieval thought for both those on the left and the right throughout the twentieth century. Second, as Kantorowicz's life had done, Howe's critique of Cantor's *Annales* School is a crucial reminder that scholarly work is necessarily a product of its time and, as such, has political resonances whether one wants it to or not. And so these midcentury intellectuals thought of the Middle Ages with their own moment in mind, creating a vision of the medieval that – just as we

---

[100] Postan and Power, eds., *Studies in English Trade*; Postan, *Medieval Economy and Society*. The characterization is from Hobsbawm, *Interesting Times*, 283. Eric Hobsbawm (1917–2012), who sat in Postan's lectures, actually retained a great deal of respect for him. Hobsbawm was not the only Marxist who felt this way: Perry Anderson, in his own account of the end of the Middle Ages published two years before the Brenner debate began, preferred Postan's writings about the crises of feudalism to Dobb's; see Anderson, *Passages from Antiquity to Feudalism*, 198, n. 3.

[101] Cantor, *Medieval History*. On Strayer as a CIA consultant, see Hutchings, "Introduction," 19, n. 24.

[102] Howe, "Review of Norman F. Cantor," 182.

inherited the world they left to us – continues to inform the understanding of the medieval today.

* * *

Organized into three sections – *Politics, Arts, Epochs* – the essays in this volume each take a unique approach to an individual figure or group of figures, yet together they engage in a dialogue over a set of common concerns. The essays under *Politics* engage with the ways that considerations of the Middle Ages shaped aspects of midcentury political life, from Kantorowicz's refusal to sign a loyalty oath to Du Bois's use of medieval romance to reflect on questions of racial identity and internationalism. Under *Arts*, the essays are concerned with the ways the Middle Ages inspired artistic work, conceptualization, and interpretation across the field of poetics, the visual arts and architecture, and literary history. Finally, *Epochs* is about the different modes of temporality, historicity, and periodization that emerge in the intellectual movement between the present and the medieval past.

Opening the *Politics* section, D. Vance Smith's "Outside History: Fanon's Negative Manicheism," reconsiders the role that Manicheism plays in Fanon's thought. Far from the starkly binary and oppositional way it is posited in some of the postcolonial criticism after Fanon, Smith argues that Manicheism allowed him to engage in a project of historical remembering, which Fanon accomplishes by thinking through what the term meant for Augustine. Fanon's Augustinianism is aided in part by midcentury French scholars who also opposed the war in Algeria. Fanon's exploration of Manicheism, filtered through Augustine, ultimately reveals him to be a complex sort of Hegelian thinker, critiquing the logic of colonialism for its calcifying effects as it attempts to lock in a certain interpretation of history. Rather than disavowing all historical thinking, Fanon champions a vision of history as vitally complex, preserving possibilities with the potential to exist outside the stultifying categories of colonialism.

Colonialism in a broad perspective remains a central concern of the work of W. E. B. Du Bois, the subject of Cord Whitaker's "'The Noblest Blood God ever Made': W. E. B. Du Bois's Medievalism in the Contexts of the World Wars." Whitaker follows Du Bois through four moments in his engagement with the Middle Ages. First, Du Bois is interested in the medieval under the influence of a Hegelian Middle Ages, in a way that has recently been explained by Andrew Cole, even as it also shares in some of the existential Hegelianism of Jean-Paul Sartre (1905–1980) or Alexandre

Kojève (1902–1968). Du Bois uses that Hegelian-infused Middle Ages in his early twentieth-century short story, "The Princess Steel," which imagines a feudal lordship as an ideal form of self-determination. Such control of oneself is extended into a control over one's history in Du Bois's novel *Dark Princess*, which sets him on a path made explicit in some of his postwar lectures: that the colonial subjects across the globe must unite and, using their own role in the construction of European society from the Middle Ages to the present, claim a new relationship to history and to the world. Whitaker ends by pointing out the way that Du Bois's engagement with the Middle Ages prefigures some of the important work happening now, work meant to combat the white-supremacist vision of the Middle Ages in our own moment, just as Du Bois had to contend with it in his.

From the atrocities of colonial history to the paroxysms of US history at the midcentury, Nancy van Deusen's "Ernst Kantorowicz, Carl Schmitt, and University of California Regents" shows how those domestic controversies affected Kantorowicz's thought. The University of California Regent's decision to make employees sign a loyalty oath – and the protests, resignations, and firings that followed in its wake – caused Kantorowicz to consider the tensions between one's individual existence and one's official role, a tension instantiated in the concept of the king's two bodies. The loyalty oath crisis, moreover, raised issues associated with the sovereignty of the state, the exceptional event, and the emergency decision, all concerns that led Kantorowicz to engage with the work of Carl Schmitt and his theory of political theology. Schmitt's work guided Kantorowicz not only in his exploration of the political and theological aspects of medieval kingship, but also in his own personal emergency and the decision it required of him.

R. D. Perry's "Hannah Arendt's Middle Ages for the Left" addresses both an earlier emergency and our own political moment, recognizing that the current fascist appropriation of the Middle Ages follows the same logic of the earlier Nazi appropriations. Perry argues that we can learn something from the earlier midcentury resistance to this fascist takeover of the past, especially from the work of Hannah Arendt. Arendt turns to the Middle Ages to address the ills of modernity, both politically and phenomenologically. Augustine allows Arendt to imagine an alternative to a modern political order predicated on Thomas Hobbes's (1588–1679) war of all against all, countering that Hobbesian individualism with an Augustinian love of one's neighbor. This capacity to create a new community is predicated on the capacity of the human will to start a new series of events, a vision of the will that she finds in Augustine and in John Duns Scotus. What

Arendt finds in the Middle Ages, then, is a world that operates under quite different philosophical assumptions than our own, and the alterity of the Middle Ages, as a critical alternative to the modern condition, has the capacity to invigorate our own political commitments in the present.

The political concerns of the midcentury follow us into the section on *Arts*, where we explore attempts to rebuild conceptually the damage that war had wracked on the entire European continent. Emily Thornbury's "Curtius and Jung: Commonplaces, Archetypes, and Literature's Collective Unconscious" freshly uncovers Ernst Robert Curtius's indebtedness to Carl Jung's theories of the human psyche. Curtius's magisterial and foundational *European Literature and the Latin Middle Ages* is rarely read today for its overall argument and instead persists as the source of how we understand and map so many commonplace tropes of medieval literature. So influential has it been in this respect that even as such tropes have widely come to be understood as givens, Curtius's book is rarely cited. What underlies Curtius's individual accounts of literary topoi is an effort to find unity in European literature, which he locates in the Latin Middle Ages and also in the form of a collective literary unconscious akin to Jung's collective unconscious of the human psyche. Thornbury urges us to take inspiration from the ambitions of Curtius's project as a recuperative effort to heal the torn world through the study of literature.

Rather than unity, Clare A. Lees's "Old English at the Midcentury: Poetry, Scholarship, and Fiction in Britain in the 1940s and 1950s" finds a great deal of diversity in the cultural engagement with Old English poetry. Lees asserts that the dominance of J. R. R. Tolkien (1892–1973) in our understanding of midcentury British scholarly and literary understandings of early medieval English writings, and – to a somewhat lesser extent – Kingsley Amis's satirical portrait of midcentury medievalist scholarship in his *Lucky Jim*, obscure other modes of medieval appropriation from the period. The essay turns to Amis's lesser-known poem "Beowulf," as well as the work of several other authors, including Alexander Scott's (1920–1989) and Gavin Bone's (1903–1942) translations of Old English poetry and two popular novels, Bryher's *Beowulf* and Angus Wilson's *Anglo-Saxon Attitudes*. Amis's poem critiques Tolkien and Bone, even as it draws inspiration from Bone especially, a potent reminder that these scholars and writers, associated with Oxford, are only part of the picture – a picture transformed, for instance, by Scott's appropriation of Old English elegies for a project of Scottish nationalism. Lees then turns to the inspirational potential offered by Old English writings, observing how Bryher's and Wilson's novels deploy the status of Old English in order to articulate the workings of the queer communities that their novels depict. Lees ends, then, by encouraging us to consider other modes of engagement with Old English, ones that promote queer and racial inclusion in the scholarly and literary traditions.

From a diversity of opinion during a brief period of time to a single controversy over an extended period of time, C. Oliver O'Donnell's "Erwin Panofsky's Neo-Kantian Humanism and the Purported Relation between Gothic Architecture and Scholasticism" centers on the controversy addressed within, and which subsequently follows, Panofsky's *Gothic Architecture and Scholasticism*. The relationship between these quintessentially medieval forms of art and philosophy were already a famous and controversial topic by the time Panofsky came to write his treatment of the problem, and O'Donnell suggests that Panofsky was inspired to address this contentious issue owing to his own philosophical commitments. O'Donnell argues that Panofsky's thought evinces a persistent debt to the form of Kantian thought taught at Marburg and associated most famously with Ernst Cassirer (1874–1945). Panofsky shares with Cassirer, and with Marburgian neo-Kantianism in general, a belief in a systematic and mathematical description of nature as a key to providing foundational knowledge of the world. Such a belief undergirds Panofsky's understanding of Scholasticism, and therefore its applicability to Gothic architecture as a representation of this schematic understanding of nature. Panofsky's assumptions about the capacity of mathematical models to represent life help explain why his work has been less inspirational in art history than in the more statistically informed social sciences, following the example of Pierre Bourdieu.

If O'Donnell's essay follows the resonances of one work, Helen Brookman's "Fantasies of Authority: The Dantean Desires of Dorothy Sayers" shows the way that a variety of writings by one author intertwines with the changing world of the mid-twentieth century. Dorothy Sayers is best known as a mystery writer, but she is also an author of feminist essays and a popular – and learned – translation of Dante's (*c.* 1265–1321) *Divine Comedy*. Brookman is interested in the ways those different modes of writing inform one another, as she identifies a quality they all share: an attempt to reach the common reader. As her feminist writings demonstrate, Sayers was invested in breaking down the patriarchal structures of her own moment. In opposition to the oppressive expectations of those structures, she constructs an affective relationship to Dante, one that theorizes literary authority and the process of literary inheritance differently, allowing Sayers to present herself as Dante's surprising twentieth-century heir.

The untimely resonances of medieval art in the work of twentieth-century thinkers, exemplified in the essays collected under *Arts*, also serve as a fitting introduction to the section we have titled *Epochs*, which addresses the issue of periodization directly. Jane O. Newman's "Periodization Trouble: Auerbach, Huizinga, and the Question of Medieval Realism" is exemplary of the complications caused by modernity's attempt to cordon itself off from its medieval past. Newman ponders whether the lack of representation of the medieval period in Auerbach's monumental *Mimesis*, while it is somewhat addressed by his later work, actually belies a discomfort with the way that the Middle Ages and the Renaissance were then distinguished from one another. Newman finds that Auerbach's is greatly influenced by the thought of – and perhaps even a meeting with – Johan Huizinga, especially his *The Autumn of the Middle Ages*. Huizinga inspires Auerbach to disrupt the progressivist tendencies in the story of mimetic representation, and Auerbach does so by positing a kind of "creaturely realism," inspired by the figuration of the person of Christ, and which would be available in any time period.

While Newman shows us the difficulty of conceptualizing strict period distinctions, Anna Kelner's "Medieval Mysticism and the Making of Simone Weil" reveals the process of anachronism that attends any periodizing attempt, as we try to use our own categories to the lived experience on an earlier period. Weil is often understood to be a kind of modern version of a medieval mystic, and Kelner points out that the association is no accident. As the writings of female mystics in the Middle Ages were often shaped and promulgated by male clerics, who attempted to guide their reception, so too were Weil's works shaped by the editorial work and critical apparatuses of her editors: men associated with the Catholic Church. Weil, of course, attempted her own self-fashioning, one that was ambivalent about institutional religion and certain sacramental practices, such as baptism. Weil's complex relationship to the Church, then, was one of the things that her editors had to smooth out in their presentation of her work. Mysticism gave these editors a chance to make sense of Weil's idiosyncrasies, and so they were at pains to present Weil as a mystic according to the understanding of medieval mystical practice as it was then being formulated by French scholars of the Middle Ages.

A complex retrospective conceptualization likewise characterizes the work explored in Benjamin Saltzman's "Hermeneutics and the Medieval Horizon: Zumthor, Jauss, Barthes, and Gadamer." As the concluding essay, Saltzman's essay details Zumthor's appreciation – at the end of the period with which this volume is concerned – of those scholars that made up the generation that preceded him. Zumthor particularly engages with the field of hermeneutics, especially as practiced by Hans-Georg Gadamer and Hans Robert Jauss, and which has long been concerned with the way that understanding is constructed across historical distances. Zumthor understands the earlier medieval studies as characterized by a romantic impulse to fill in the gaps and fissures of history, whereas the task of those following Zumthor – inspired by his own moment in history – was to explore those very same interstices, even as these contemporary medieval scholars must also confront their own fragmentation and their own distance from the medieval past.

Finally, in his afterword, Martin Jay engages in the temporal exercise of intellectual reflection. Jay is astutely aware of the preposterous temporality – a mode of understanding that tries to take into account both a "before" and "after" at the same time – that characterizes the concerns of the essays in this volume as well as his own retrospective attention to them. It is a temporality that has been stretched through a global pandemic that has altered the way all of us see the world and the place of our work in it: most of the essays were finished just before the pandemic of 2020 began, some were written through its early stages, and Jay's afterword was completed midway through it (though it still continues in 2022 as this book makes its way through production). Such double vision allows Jay to characterize the essays collected here as points in a chain of understanding, placing the medieval past in conversation with the midcentury attempt to conceptualize it, even as we are also trying to understand that midcentury moment and the medieval past that it too was after. As distinct points in time, each moment reveals itself to us in its unique richness, both a testament to the persistence of the past even as the world changes into something new. Such change should serve, finally, as a reminder of our own limitations of understanding the world we inherit; that, while we may be able to conceptualize different moments in time, our own thought about them remains persistently preliminary, something to be revised and expanded as we proceed through life. In this way, Jay's afterword ultimately shows us that there will always be much more work to be done in thinking of the Middle Ages.

PART I
Politics

CHAPTER I

Outside History
Fanon's Negative Manicheism

D. Vance Smith

When I look for man in European techniques and styles I see a succession of negations of man, an avalanche of murders.[1]

Without responsibility, straddling Nothingness and Infinity, I began to weep.[2]

—Frantz Fanon

It is because of Frantz Fanon (1925–1961) that an esoteric gnostic religion that was last popular in Late Antique North Africa became an important part of the lexicon of postcolonialism. Manicheism, probably best known to medievalists because of its formative and then adversarial role in the thinking of Augustine of Hippo (354–430), provided Fanon with an analogy for white supremacism in his massively influential 1952 book *Peau noire, masques blancs* (*Black Skin, White Masks*). For the person of color, the world is divided into the stark oppositions of "Good-Evil, Beauty-Ugliness, White-Black," and for Fanon this is a "genuinely Manichean concept of the world."[3] Fanon uses the term only twice in *Black Skin, White Masks*, although he underscores its importance, asking his readers to commit it to memory: "the word [Manichean] has been spoken, it must be remembered."[4] But what kind of remembering are we asked to do? The answer, as often with Fanon, is both immediate and more complicated than it seems: "white or black, that is the question." It's an answer that is literally a question, and it's a question that really does not demand an answer, because, and this is Fanon's whole point, the answer is predetermined, already decided: once the question is even asked, the

---

[1] Fanon, *Damnés*, 302 (translation mine).
[2] Fanon, *Black Skin*, 108.
[3] Ibid., 141 and 31. I will use lower-case "manichean" when I talk about Fanon's use of the concept, upper-case "Manichean" when I refer to the late antique religion. In the French originals, Fanon typically writes it in lower case, although English translations are inconsistent.
[4] Fanon, *Black Skin*, 31.

answer is "white." So why bother to remember, and remember something as arcane as Manicheism? In an important sense, Fanon does just that kind of remembering when he comes back to the concept of Manicheism in his incendiary *Les damnés de la terre* (*The Wretched of the Earth*), published in 1961, nine years after *Black Skin, White Masks*. He not only refines the concept of manicheism, but he also seems to have engaged in historical remembering of the late antique phenomenon of Manicheism. It is not incidental that the last important arena of Manicheism was the part of North Africa where Fanon was living, and that the most important conduit was through the writing of another North African thinker: Augustine.

Much of the manicheism of *The Wretched of the Earth* seems informed by a deeper knowledge of Augustine's anti-Manichean polemic. It was Fanon's presence in Algeria, and his involvement in the struggle for Algerian independence, that seems to have activated the latent metaphors that manicheism already held in his writing. In fact, one of Fanon's colleagues in the resistance was to become one of the most important Augustine scholars of the twentieth century: André Mandouze (1916–2006), whose writings on both Augustine and the Algerian struggle are almost equally voluminous. Mandouze published two resistance journals, *Consciences algériennes* and *Consciences maghrébines*, that printed Fanon's articles. And Fanon's wife, Josie Fanon (1929–1989), attended Mandouze's seminars on Augustine at the University of Algeria at the same time.[5]

At the very least, I want to show that Fanon's use of the concept of manicheism in *The Wretched of the Earth* is extraordinarily attuned to the work of remembering, as well as to the historical and Augustinian resonances of Manicheism, resonances that have been overlooked in the assimilation of the term to a general, globalized, and vague theory of postcolonialism. Perhaps more than any single work, Abdul JanMohamed's important 1983 book *Manichaean Aesthetics: The Politics of Literature in Colonial Africa* made manicheism part of the necessary kit of tropes in postcolonial theory, but that book quotes Fanon on manicheism in just one place and does not discuss what Fanon might have meant by manicheism beyond a superficial paraphrase.[6]

Fanon's ironic fate, although it is one he predicted, is that his own thinking has tended to be confused with the absolute polarizations that he identified in the colonial world. This misreading has been a common way to

---

[5] See Macey, *Frantz Fanon*, 258.
[6] In a single paragraph, JanMohamed, *Manichean Aesthetics*, 3–4, quotes two passages from *The Wretched of the Earth*.

dismiss Fanon's critique in general. Malvern van Wyk Smith, using mostly secondhand quotations of Fanon, criticizes Fanon's "naive dramaturgy of racial conflict" and his "morality-play version of racial contestation."[7] But deeper, more sophisticated, readers of Fanon also misread him in this way. Paul Gilroy's *Against Race*, which places an epigraph from Fanon at the beginning of each section, and which acknowledges the complexity and subtlety of Fanon's thought, also argues that "his thinking remains bound to a dualistic logic" and a "binary code almost as pernicious as the manichean dualism that he sought to supplant."[8] In what follows, I hope it will become clear that, while Fanon certainly thinks in terms of oppositions, his thinking should not be confused with the erstwhile object of colonial racism. With devastating rigor and honesty, he shows how, again and again, experience in the colonial world is reduced to the subjugation of the colonized by the colonizer, of Black by white. But part of his horror over this situation, if only a somewhat detached and abstract part, is motivated by his distaste for the implacable but sophistical logic of this reduction, its refusal to move beyond a primary – yes, even primitive – confrontation.

It might help to think of Fanon as a deeply Hegelian thinker, for whom oppositions, denials, and negations are not just the way thought works, but a part of thought itself (G. W. F. Hegel [1770–1831] said that the negative is the power of thinking). What is horrifying for a Hegelian is the obduracy of an opposition that cannot move beyond itself, that never admits to an opposition that opens onto something bigger than itself. Fanon's Hegelian loathing of colonialism centers on its fixity, what Fanon referred to as petrification or "substantialisation," the past as a frozen statue, a "stagnation where gradually dialectic has changed into the logic of equilibrium."[9] At the end of *Black Skin, White Masks*, Fanon rails against the past, to which Black people, he says, are slaves. Another part of Fanon's contempt is reserved for bourgeois culture, but precisely because of its fixation on the

---

[7] van Wyk Smith, *The First Ethiopians*, 19–20.
[8] Gilroy, *Against Race*, 253, 248. Gilroy's main criticism of Fanon is that his racism is outdated, and that contemporary "race-thinking" contaminates the possibilities of liberal democracy: "Today, in Europe, at least, there is less justification for this stark dualistic diagnosis" (249). One of the ironies of Gilroy's book is that it is difficult now, given the state of U.S. politics, to imagine that we live in anything remotely approaching a postracial world. A more recent example of the attribution of stark dualism to Fanon is Jefferess, *Postcolonial Resistance*, 185: although his discussion is more nuanced elsewhere, he closes the book by characterizing "Manichean or binary thought" (implicitly, Fanon's own) as calling for a "simply reversed ... structure of material relations of power and identities."
[9] Fanon, *Damnés*, 303 ("ce mouvement immobile où la dialectique, petit à petit, s'est muée en logique de l'équilibre"); *Wretched*, 237 (translation modified). Unless otherwise noted, all translated text from *Wretched* will be quoted from the Philcox translation.

past: it is "rigidified in predetermined forms, forbidding all evolution, all gains, all progress, all discovery."[10]

While this might sound as if Fanon is rejecting any orientation toward the past – and there are many passages in both of his major books that do, indeed, sound like that – his work is shot through with references to history. While he might say that "the past can in no way guide me in the present moment," or that he does not have the "right" to allow himself "to be mired in what the past has determined," he does indeed draw from it throughout his work.[11] He certainly draws from it in order to critique that bourgeois, colonialist "petrification," but he also draws from it as an active thinker himself, steeped in Hegelian ways of conceiving history as an active, creative, synthetic phenomenon – as change itself.[12] At the end of *Black Skin, White Masks* he seems to embrace a kind of humanist universalism that he does not necessarily countenance, at least not as directly, in *Wretched*, in which the possibility of future action lies in a reconfiguration of a past that is exterior, somehow, to the petrified history given to us by the pedagogy of colonialism. "I am a man," he states in one moment, "and what I have to recapture (*reprendre*) is the whole past of the world."[13] In another, he declares "I am not the slave of the Slavery (*l'Esclavage*) that dehumanized my ancestors."[14] The echo of Hegel's *Phenomenology* here, amplified by the capitalization of "l'Esclavage" in the French edition, is not accidental. These two sentences read as a virtual restatement of the crux of the most influential reading of Hegel's "master/slave" dialectic in Fanon's day, Alexandre Kojève's (1902–1968) *Introduction a la lecture de Hegel* (orig. pub. 1958, based on lectures in 1933–39): "in transforming the world through his work, the slave (*l'Esclave*) transforms himself and thus creates the new conditions which allow him to recapture (*reprendre*) the liberation struggle."[15] Where Kojève is full of optimism about recapturing the struggle for liberation, Fanon only holds out the possibility that there is a past that has, thus far, escaped the machine of "l'Esclavage," although

---

[10] Fanon, *Black Skin*, 175. This condemnation applies not just to the "petrification of … colonial meanings and institutions" but also to the "*anticolonial* practico-inert"; decolonization is every bit as much subject to petrification unless it takes a critical relation to history. The postindependence leader, in Fanon's words, "*brings the people to a halt and persists in either expelling them from history or preventing them from taking root in it*": Ficek, "Reflections on Fanon and Petrification," 83; quoting Fanon, *Wretched of the Earth*, 136 (emphasis in original).
[11] Fanon, *Black Skin*, 175, 179.
[12] Ibid., 179.
[13] Ibid., 176; Fanon, *Peau noire*, 183.
[14] Ibid., 179; Fanon, *Peau noire*, 186.
[15] Kojève, *Introduction à la lecture de Hegel*, 34 (translation mine).

the past that could be recaptured (*reprendre*) is nothing less than the past of the entire world.

Fanon is full of surprising reversals and demurrals like this, reversals that seem to turn into a corner where only bitter despair lies yet which are also open onto possibilities far beyond the mere recuperation of the moment. Notice that Fanon remembers the passage from Kojève not for its celebration of the inevitable renewal of the struggle for revolution, but for its endorsement of the underlying vitality of history – for the possibility that a history beyond the enforced polarizations of manichean colonialism can still be recaptured.

Nevertheless, *The Wretched of the Earth* begins with an infamous chapter on violence, which seems to reject resoundingly the kind of optimism for a universal humanity that Fanon imagines at the end of *Black Skin, White Masks*. Perhaps more than his deployment of the term manichean, this chapter has been responsible for Fanon's reputation as an uncompromising, polarized, binary thinker. The first copies of *The Wretched of the Earth* were confiscated because of it, and Fanon's former assistant in Tunis said that after its publication even those supposedly close to him regarded him as a "bloodthirsty maniac."[16] Even almost a decade later, Hannah Arendt (1906–1975) acknowledges the complexity of Fanon's theory of violence, and points out (although in a footnote) that "Fanon himself ... is much more doubtful about violence than his admirers" and that "only the book's first chapter, 'Concerning Violence,' has been widely read."[17] Yet the prominence of that first chapter of *Wretched* seems to pull her irresistibly toward a cruder characterization of Fanon's total theory. She puts Fanon together with thinkers who "glorify violence for violence's sake," a position manifestly different from her more balanced assessment of Fanon in her book's notes.[18] Jean Paul Sartre's (1905–1980) own reading of Fanon, and his preface to the first edition of *Wretched*, may have

---

[16] For the first, see Bhabha, "Forward: Framing Fanon," in Fanon, *Wretched*, viii; for the second, see the interview with Manuellan, "Dans l'ombre de Fanon."

[17] Arendt, *On Violence*, 14, n. 19. Moten, *The Universal Machine*, suggests that "to reread *Les damnés de la terre* against the grain of Arendt's nonreading of it is to consider that we don't and can't either know or fight the murderous brutality of the settler's weakness with our own; rather, we think and struggle from and with our own potency" (184). In glossing potency, Moten notes that it is not, "contra Arendt, a political thing; that her relegation of the social in favor of a regulated and specifically political publicness is, in fact, inseparable from her commitment to an already given structure of power in which both acknowledged and unacknowledged constituents subsist in a shadow they cast but cannot control" (265–66, n. 50). For more on Arendt, see Chapter 4 in this volume, Perry, "Hannah Arendt's Middle Ages for the Left."

[18] Arendt, *On Violence*, 65.

helped to shape Arendt's cruder version of Fanon – and that of many in her wake. Sartre's preface, Arendt implies, has reduced Fanon's argument to a simpler but even more pungent version: "'Violence,' he now believes, on the strength of Fanon's book, 'like Achilles' lance, can heal the wounds it has inflicted.'"[19] Even if Sartre has simplified Fanon's argument, Arendt's rhetoric suggests that Fanon's theory of violence exerts a malevolent influence, a "strength" that implicitly exculpates Sartre from total responsibility for the more totalizing violence he advocates in that preface. Elsewhere, Arendt implies that Fanon's theory of violence necessitates an ontology of primal *agon*, the notion that "where we have life we have struggle and unrest."[20] She links this worldview to the French right-wing thinker Georges Sorel (1847–1922), whose vision of uncompromising struggle, she implies, sprang out of his disillusion with the supporters of Alfred Dreyfus (1859–1935) and his subsequent disgust with democracy and his embrace of anti-Semitism. Arendt attributes Fanon's immediate acceptance of the possibility of violence to his involvement in the Algerian war, which is what seems to have given him "an infinitely greater intimacy with the practice of violence."[21] What is surprising, given Arendt's deployment of the language of cosmological struggle here, and her own sympathy for intellectual history, is that she does not mention, in her genealogy of the Fanonian theory of violence, the primal importance of struggle in Manichean cosmology.

All but one of Fanon's invocations of manicheism in *The Wretched of the Earth* come in the initial chapter on violence, and the link between the manicheism and violence is tacit, if not always spelled out plainly, as when he says that the colonialist's slogan – "it's them or us" – is the result of the "organization of a Manichean world."[22] In "classical" Manicheism, the battle between light and dark began even before the creation of the world, and the most fundamental fact about the world they lived in was that the elemental struggle still continued.[23] As it happens, one of the best sources for this information is Augustine, who was a Manichean disciple for a time, and who spent a large part of his career debunking Manicheism. It is possible to see the entirety of Augustine's work as a response to his

---

[19] Ibid., 20. In her preface to Fanon, *Damnés*, Alice Cherki argues that Sartre was responsible for shaping the interpretation of Fanon as an advocate of violence, noting that "Sartre justifie la violence alors que Fanon l'analyse" (11).
[20] Arendt, *On Violence*, 69.
[21] Ibid., 71.
[22] Fanon, *Wretched*, 43.
[23] See, for example, Augustine, *Contra epistulam Manichaei quam uocant fundamenti*, cap. 14 and 15.

earlier dalliance with Manicheism, as scholars such as Johannes van Oort and Jason BeDuhn have argued.[24] In what follows, I would like to explore the possibility that Fanon's use of manicheism, especially in his late work *The Wretched of the Earth*, is bound up with Augustine's own struggle with Manicheism, and the not irrelevant fact that much of this struggle happened just about where Fanon was engaged in his own struggle, in modern-day Algeria and Tunisia.[25]

I have already suggested that Fanon's manicheism is more complicated and elusive than the static dualism he is credited with in postcolonial shorthand. One of the many ironies of this fate is that Fanon's use of the term "manichean" is deceptively complex, hedged around with qualifications that make it difficult to pin down what, exactly, manicheism actually is. Fanon writes in a seductively simple style, and many of his sentences come as virtually ready-made apothegms. Yet almost every one of them contains depths that betray his intense engagement with intellectual history. Read properly, Fanon's texts prompt the reader to pause frequently, to think about the layers of irony that wrap a sentence, or about the way in which Fanon invokes a complex aspect of the Hegelian dialectic. So, when Fanon uses the term "manichaean" to describe what only seems to be a simple polarization, a straightforward binary, the death-struggle of white and Black race relations in the colonial era, that simple opposition is rapidly subsumed.[26]

---

[24] See van Oort, *Mani and Augustine*; and BeDuhn, *Augustine's Manichaean Dilemma, 1: Conversion and Apostasy*; *Augustine's Manichaean Dilemma, 2: Making a 'Catholic' Self*; and a third volume is projected.

[25] Ney, "Teleology and Secular Time," finds analogies between the anti-Manichean strain of Augustine's *City of God* and the manicheism described by (largely) JanMohamed.

[26] Only two major readings of Fanon that I know of fully express this aspect of Fanon's work. Ato Sekyi-Otu's scintillating and profound excavation of the analogy of drama in Fanon's work insists on the contingent, propaedeutic nature of almost every statement in his work, which can only be grasped as an unfolding totality – or as unfolding toward an already ruined totality. What he describes as the spatialization of dialectic in Fanon is another aspect of the "stagnation" of dialectic in Europe generally (*Wretched*, 237): "the critique of domination becomes an analysis of the spatial structuring of positions" (Sekyi-Otu, *Fanon's Dialectic of Experience*, 80). I choose to believe that Fanon's dialectic works more as a chordal, interposed *negation* of dialectic. It insists both on the irresistible, diremptive, scopic regime of dialectic, *and* on the force – the violence – of negation, and the immanent destruction of a dialectical *skopos*. The other brilliant and essential reading is Fred Moten's, in *The Universal Machine*. His is also attuned to the multimodal nature of Fanon's dialectic, but I would argue is a doubly *symptomatic* reading: first, it is founded on Fanon's attention to the physical and psychic symptoms of the oppressed; and, second, it leaves us with a symptomatic Fanon, one who unwittingly comes up against aporia rather than one who, as I argue here, dwells cannily and forcefully in the negative.

Indeed, his description of this supposed binary unravels even as he writes:

> The people who in the early days of the struggle had adopted the primitive Manicheism of the colonizer—Blacks versus Whites, Arabs versus *Roumis*—realize en route that some Blacks can be whiter than the Whites, and that the prospect of a national flag or independence does not automatically result in certain segments of the population giving up their privileges and their interests. The people realize that there are indigenous populations like themselves (*des indigènes comme lui*) who, far from missing the chance (*lui ne perdent pas le nord*), seem to take advantage of the war to better their material situation and reinforce their burgeoning power. These profiteering elements realize considerable gains from the war at the expense of the people (*Les indigènes trafiquent et réalisent de véritables profits de guerre aux dépens du peuple*) who, as always, are prepared to sacrifice everything and soak the national soil with their blood.[27]

Note that Fanon describes this colonizer's perspective as "primitive" manicheism. He seems to define it as a kind of manicheism different from an evolved, sophisticated, or complex manicheism, a manicheism that has nothing to do with the people (as yet), a colonial import. But it also bears the sense of "original," a sense that becomes increasingly ironic in the next two sentences. Fanon talks about the dawning realization on the part of the "people" that some of their own exploit others during crises, becoming "whiter than the Whites." Yet these exploiters, initially part of the people, are distanced as "des indigènes comme lui," sharing an identity but somehow different precisely because of the need to compare them with the rest of the people. It is a phrase, too, that makes clear that these are not "people" in general, but the *indigènes* of the *Code de l'indigénat*, excluded in perpetuity as a group "inapt for politics," in the words of the Algerian philosopher Sidi Mohammed Barkat.[28] Reinforcing this sense, Philcox translates the phrase as "indigenous elements in their midst," while the 1963 English translation uses the word "natives" for *indigènes*, retaining some of the reactionary flavor of the word but losing the French connotations of legal status and, ultimately, of autochthonous identity.[29] The irony that emerges in these three sentences is that the part the "Whites" played in the first "primitive Manicheism" is now played by *indigènes*, by people who come to occupy the place of the primitive, in every sense, in the dynamic of exploitation. These exploitative *indigènes* reinscribe the narrative that domination is originary, that colonization is legitimate because domination

---

[27] Fanon, *Damnés*, 138; *Wretched*, 93–94 (translation modified).
[28] Barkat, *Le corps d'exception*, 40.
[29] Fanon, *Wretched*, trans. Farrington, 144; trans. Philcox, 93.

is an indigenous phenomenon. It is not just that "Blacks" now do it, so the culpability is diffused, but that their emergence as a dominating class creates the fiction that exploitation itself is an indigenous phenomenon. It is a much subtler version of the argument that colonization is justified by the strife that preceded it, but it is the same argument. What I want to call attention to, however, is the way in which Fanon twists the connotations of the word *indigène* here. It first appears as a synonym *for* "people" – a people that is not *all* the people. It next appears as a term that differentiates itself *from* the people ("Les indigènes trafiquent et réalisent de véritables profits de guerre aux dépens du peuple"). Indigeneity, in Algeria both the marker of autochthonous identity and of subjugated status, *is also*, in this passage, ultimately the marker of a colonized mentality. When war came along, these emergent indigenous oppressors, he sarcastically says, "ne perdent pas le nord" (translated in 1963 as "did not lose sight of the main chance" and more recently by Philcox as "far from being at loose ends").[30] The literal sense of the French ("they did not lose the north") idiomatically suggests that they maintained their sense of direction. But the devastation of the irony lies in their emergence, in this passage, as the "true" *indigènes* who are oriented (so to speak) away from Algeria, north toward France.

This passage shows how rich Fanon's critique of colonialism is. It does not just argue that colonialism takes away a people's identity; it shows how that identity gets taken away within the unfolding of language itself. It is almost impossible to write about the phenomenon of the colonial mentality from the outside, precisely because it is so inescapable a phenomenon that it shapes perception itself. But this passage also reveals how diegetic, diachronic, and historical Fanon's indictment of colonialism can be. Not only does it account for the ways that the perception of the colonized and colonizers changes according to the unfolding of the historical dialectic – that is, Fanon's is also a phenomenological account of domination – but it continually refers, points back to, the deep historical roots of colonial domination.

From the outset of this passage, Fanon makes it impossible to think of this "primitive manicheism" as a simple binary outside time. There are "les Blancs et les Noirs," yes, but there are also, immediately and inseparably from them, "les Arabes et les Roumis" (the 1963 English translation called this last group "Christians," the more recent translation by Philcox opts for "Infidel").[31] It is not clear how the two groups relate to each other: are

---

[30] Ibid.
[31] Ibid.

they simply two opposing pairs, or in apposition? Is there no difference between them? Is the second group a subset of the first, a more particularized, Maghrebian version? If so, where do the people who are neither Arab nor Christian, the people who were imagined by colonial ethnographers to be the true *indigènes* of Algeria, the Berbers, belong? There is also a complex play of deterritorialization behind the word *Roumis*: usually identified as an Arabic word originally, it arrived in Arabic from Ottoman Turkish, and was originally used to describe members of the Byzantine Empire (who were not, to confuse things further, *Italian* Romans). Fanon's point here is, of course, that this manicheism might be primitive, but it is not simple. It is adaptable but contradictory and immensely versatile at hiding those contradictions. That is, it does not stand outside history – in fact, it is a certain aspect of the writing of history itself. Fanon's sly exposure of the rootedness of manicheism in history is a way of calling attention to its very reinscription of history. Indeed, as I will argue, the very term "manicheism" is an example of Fanon's insistence on colonialism's entanglement in history.

The term *Roumis* hints at the historical force of manicheism for Fanon. As the first English version of Fanon attests, its primary sense in Algeria is "Christian," but French colonial historiography believed that the term survived from the Roman colonization of North Africa. Henri Leclerq (1869–1945), an eminent historian of the early Church in Africa, argued that the ruined churches of Late Antiquity had not just an archeological significance, but also a political use (*utilité politique*). Those whom the *indigènes* have named the *Roumis*, he says, "are in their eyes, and must be in reality, the descendants and the inheritors of those who so long ago so glorious and so efficiently governed the land."[32] The *perception* of this connection by the *indigènes* is partly what legitimates the rule of these new masters, but, as Leclerq goes on to say, so does the reappropriation of the Roman past by the new colonizers. It is the very respect that these successors of the Romans have for the ancient monuments of Christian North Africa that legitimates their larger cultural work, which is to restore "l'oeuvre de civilisation" itself.[33] The opposition between Arabs and *Roumis* is thus, like

---

[32] Cabrol and Leclerc, *Dictionnaire d'archéologie chrétienne et de liturgie*, s.v. Lambèse, vol. 8, 1073 ("Ceux que les indigènes nomment les *roumis* sont à leurs yeux et doivent être en réalité les descendants et les héritiers de ceux qui ont si longtemps, si glorieusement et si utilement gouverné le pays"). I was pointed to this passage by Kaegi, *Muslim Expansion*, 22.

[33] Cabrol and Leclerc, *Dictionnaire d'archéologie chrétienne et de liturgie*, s.v. Lambèse, vol. 8, 1073 ("Y ont restauré l'oeuvre de civilisation, et ont montré dans leur intelligence et leur respect pour les anciens monuments leurs titres de propriété, leurs droits à les ramener à la lumière et à ne pas souffrir qu'on les détruise").

all of Fanon's manichean oppositions, the product of an historical narrative. But it is a narrative that doubles back on itself: the new colonizers are the *Roumis*, who are called that because they are the inheritors of the old colonizers, who preceded the Arabs, the people they now colonize. To compound the complexity, the *indigènes* are not even a term in that opposition: the Berbers are neither Arab nor *Roumi*, unless one considers the isolated testimony of colonial-era travelers that the Kabylé occasionally saw themselves as *Roumis*.[34] The opposition is hardly dualist, or at least not the same intractable colonial opposition that Fanon is primarily talking about. What is "primitive" about this manicheism, according to the fantasized historiography that Fanon is critiquing, is that it now seems to be an *original* manicheism, a dualism that existed before the Arabs arrived and thus so antique that it has begun to edge into an ontology.

This process of making history more solid and certain than it actually was is what Fanon refers to as petrification. It is not just history, strictly speaking, but a politics that shapes the present in the image of a supposed past, even – and especially – when national parties are attempting to break free of the colonial past. The urban elites, says Fanon, act on the assumptions they have inherited from the colonizers about the rural masses: they have only the *impression* that the rural masses are "bogged down in their inertia and futility (*s'enliser dans l'inertie et dans l'infécondité*)."[35] It is not so much, speaking precisely, that the elites put in place policies to reinforce the backwardness, the atavism, of the countryside, but that colonization has already subjugated the rural populace "by an organized petrification of the peasantry."[36] The countryside, then, is not just backward; it is an historical artifact, although it remains one only because it is actively preserved. Colonial officials are thus like a frame around the rural masses they supervise. Fanon's word for supervision is *encadrer*, which also means "framing": the metaphor implies that colonial officials are a defensive barrier that, like a new frame around an old picture, sets off the quaint antiquity of the countryside.[37] Historicity, then, is something that is both exhibited and actively maintained and guarded. The colonial frame of the past guards both inside and outside: it keeps those within its borders in a suspended state of development – it keeps them "historical" – and it

---

[34] See the examples quoted in Greenhalgh, *The Military and Colonial Destruction of the Roman Landscape of North Africa*, 33. The Kabylé are the largest Berber/Amazigh group in Algeria.
[35] Fanon, *Damnés*, 109; *Wretched*, 65 (translation modified).
[36] Fanon, *Damnés*, 109; *Wretched*, 65.
[37] Ibid.

reassures the urban elite, the national parties, of their place, by contrast, in the outside of modernity.

* * *

It is precisely the opposition between modernity and premodernity that is at stake for Fanon, an opposition that colonialism stages as a recapitulation of the Marxist development of urban capitalism out of, and beyond, rural economies. The rural and the medieval merge inside the frame. The masses of the countryside, in Fanon's words, "still live in a feudal state (*stade féodal*)" in an all-powerful "medieval structure (*structure moyenâgeuse*)."[38] Although Fanon does not spell this out explicitly, the "feudal" and "medieval" quality of the countryside is an invention, a back-formation of the whole colonial enterprise. The economic and cultural history of the European Middle Ages is written onto the Algerian landscape, the rigid lines of its discourse enforced at every level of administration. These "feudal overlords" defend their power by keeping the countryside feudal, by resisting the modernity represented by the "young Westernized nationalists" of the towns and cities because it will "threaten the fundamental sustainability of feudalism (*le principe même de la pérennité des féodalités*)."[39] The enemy is not, ultimately, the colonial occupier, but an historical one; or, rather, the forces of history themselves: the *modernistes* who intend to dismantle *la société autochtone*, the autochthonous, true indigenous society that, in this alternative history, has not been altered by the arrival of colonialism. Yet it is colonialism itself that designates its members as *indigènes*, people who have both a primary claim to the land and virtually none, precisely because their historical status has made them, so to speak, miss out on modernity.

Fanon's lucid summary of the historical dialectic of colonialism hides, at almost every turn, dizzying contradictions and reversals like this. It is precisely the simplicity of his prose that leads readers into thinking that manicheism is a straightforward process. We tend to think: yes, it is; it's simply a matter of dividing the world into black and white. But having identified that division, with Fanon's help, as the primary process of colonialism, we also discover that there is no other process. Once we divide the world, it is too late to think of other divisions, or of a world without any. The *masses rurales* become the backward agrarian populace of the

---

[38] Fanon, *Damnés*, 109; *Wretched*, 65.
[39] Fanon, *Damnés*, 110 (translation mine); *Wretched*, 65.

capitalist, urban revolution; the original people become the indigenous excluded from full legal representation; the nationalist leader becomes a mere bourgeois disrupter of tradition. The horror of colonialism is not just that it is a dualistic world, in which everything is cruelly and irrevocably divided between white and black by one event or one decree, but a world in which thought itself seems always to bend back to that original division and confirm it. In *Black Skin, White Masks*, the delirium of manicheism is described with something of the detached perspective of the clinician describing what a person in the throes of the pathology tends to do. But in *Wretched* the delirium infects – no, it *is* – the writing of the critique of colonialism itself. It is not the description of a pathology, but the very language of the pathology itself, inside the delirium, that it is also attempting to deactivate.

In *The Wretched of the Earth*, manicheism has become a world-transforming system, not just the pathological effect of colonialism but the very logic of the machine of domination. Unlike some later critics of colonialism, however, Fanon is always clear that the work of domination is psychic as much as anything else, that it depends upon a transformation of worldview and not just of the world itself. It may be that this interior dimension is missing from later uses of the term in postcolonial studies, which ironically treats the binaries of colonial racism as essentially lodged in the world (although Achille Mbembe introduces Lacan to Fanon in his *Critique of Black Reason*). Part of the force of Fanon's critique of the manichean world, however, is the tone of bemused outrage with which he describes the imposition of this worldview and the acquiescence to it of the colonized: "when we consider the resources deployed to achieve the cultural alienation so typical of the colonial period, we realize that nothing was left to chance and that the final aim of colonization was to convince the indigenous population it would save them from darkness."[40] Fanon's point is not just that colonialism presents itself as a system of intellectual enlightenment and spiritual salvation, but that the very concept of the "darkness" that colonialism illuminates and from which the indigenous are being saved exists only within the narrative of colonial domination. The myth is that this narrative is like a Hegelian determination: before it comes into being, there is no way of understanding what its opposite is, and the darkness before colonialism anticipates, or even demands, the light that colonialism brings. But that light is always the *fulfillment*

---

[40] Fanon, *Wretched*, 149.

of the darkness, the reason that can explain away and dispel the night of unreason. The belief that colonialism demands is a belief that there was no belief before it arrived.

Why does Fanon's use of manicheism become so subtle and complex in *The Wretched of the Earth*? Part of the reason is because Fanon's own understanding of it has moved from the universal to the particular. In *Black Skin, White Masks*, it was a pathology, or an ancient view of the cosmos. It described, in psychiatric literature, someone who divides the world into absolutes. The psychiatric manual that Fanon drew from, Maurice Dide (1873–1944) and Paul Guiraud's (1882–1974) *Psychiatrie du médecin praticien* (1922), begins by summarizing the belief held by the "Sect of the Manicheans" in an eternal struggle between "the principle of Good and that of Evil, between God and the Devil."[41] Yet the struggle could be between almost anything, depending upon the "color of delirium": between revolutionaries and counter-revolutionaries, Freemasons and Jesuits, entire nations.[42] In the complex unfolding of Fanon's analytic, the terms of manicheism do seem occasionally to change – for example, the pairings "Good–Evil, Beauty–Ugliness" – but they are always subordinated to the originary dualism: "white and black represent the two poles of a world, two poles in perpetual conflict."[43]

Fanon's manicheism seems haunted by the historical content of the practice of Manicheism in the period of Late Antiquity, with its recurrent emphasis on light and dark, terms that Fanon treats as refractions of that primal dualism. The colonized, for instance, begin life in "opacity," but with the arrival of the colonist discover a "great thirst for light." Indeed, the whole enterprise of colonialism is designed to convince the *indigènes* that colonialism came to "snatch them from the night (*arracher à la nuit*)."[44] The archives of historical Manicheism are full of the same imagery. For instance, take this passage from Mani (*c.* 216–274), quoted, of course, by Augustine:

> In one direction, on the border of this bright and holy region, there was a land of darkness (*tenebrarum terra*), deep and vast in extent, where abode fiery bodies, destructive races. Here was boundless darkness flowing from the same source in immeasurable abundance, with the productions properly belonging to it. Beyond this were muddy, turbid waters, with their

---

[41] Dide and Giraud, *Psychiatrie du médecin praticien*, 164.
[42] Ibid.
[43] Fanon, *Black Skin*, 31.
[44] Fanon, *Damnés*, 201; *Wretched*, 149 (translation mine).

inhabitants .... And similarly inside of this, a race full of smoke and gloom, where abode the dreadful prince and chef of all, having around him innumerable princes ... Such are the five natures of the region of corruption.[45]

The Wretched of the Earth echoes the topography of this Manichean vision quite closely. Fanon describes the towns (which he refers to as both "zones" and "villes") of the colonizers as "a sector of lights," the towns of the colonized as "hungry for ... light," opposed but not complementary to the town of the colonizers.[46] Fanon is describing not an ideal, abstract set of oppositions, but the real world of colonial Algeria, where one town is tarmacked and its inhabitants wear shoes, while the other is starved of coal, bread, and shoes. In one sense, writing about the manichean world in Algeria brought Fanon, quite literally, down to earth. The very oppositions of colonialism are made visible in and on the landscape: the difference is apparent even if you don't know anything about Manicheans or colonialism or theories of mastery. One town is well fed, the other hungry; one town is spacious and built to endure, the other is cramped and shoddy.

Yet even as Fanon gets down to earth there is another register, another kind of reference, hovering behind his text. The very notion that two towns represent two consequences of governance echoes the basic opposition of Augustine's *The City of God* (426), which pits the earthly against the heavenly city, the opposition framed in terms reminiscent of the Manichean opposition of light and dark. The earthly city is "dark, beclouded," while the heavenly city is the "light of the Lord."[47] Fanon's ironic appropriation of Augustine's trope makes the town of the *indigènes* the all-too-earthly city, squalid in its materiality, all matter without form; the town of the colonizers is a parodic heavenly city, where the inhabitants' "feet can never be glimpsed," as if, like angels, they float from point to point.[48] Indeed, Fanon's next paragraph sounds almost like a bald restatement of Augustine's central argument: "This compartmentalized world, this world cut in two (*coupé en deux*), is inhabited by different species."[49] An important difference between the two texts, of course, is that Augustine is writing about the eschaton, about the difference between the here and now and the afterlife; Fanon is writing about a deeply riven here and now. But Fanon's language is unmistakably

---

[45] Augustine, *Against the Epistle of Manichaeus Called Fundamental*, trans. Dods, cap. 15, p. 113; Augustine, *Contra epistulam Manichaei quam uocant fundamenti*, ed. Zycha, cap. 15, p. 212.
[46] Fanon, *Wretched*, 4.
[47] van Oort, *Jerusalem and Babylon*, 118–23.
[48] Fanon, *Wretched*, 4.
[49] Fanon, *Damnés*, 41; *Wretched*, 5 (translation modified).

eschatological, bordering on the kind of language that Mani uses in the passage quoted earlier, which is ultimately about the difference between the land of light and the land of darkness, the *tenebrarum terra*.

The paradox of Fanon's use of manicheism is that when he moves from Europe, where he wrote *Black Skin, White Masks*, to a colony (Algeria), when he moves from a theory about colonialism from a distance to a praxis of resistance on the ground, his rhetorical, philosophical, and historical use of manicheism gets more complex. As I have suggested, this is partly because Fanon realizes that manicheism has already done this work, and on the same terrain. Its historical alterity, the very strangeness of using an arcane term taken from Late Antique religious history to analyze the contemporary colonial world, is part of what gives it its affective force: it renders a phenomenon, a psychosis, that its adherents almost by definition overlook, through an objectifying term that makes it at least partially apprehensible. Ultimately, of course, it *is* a psychosis, as Dide and Guiraud had classified it in the psychiatric handbook where Fanon first encountered it, and an analysis of its logic is as relevant to reality as the conspiracy maps of *A Beautiful Mind*. But the rootedness of manicheism in North Africa, and Augustine's powerful and sustained contempt for it, give Fanon's deployment of the term the dimension of a genealogical critique not yet possible in *Black Skin, White Masks*. Manicheism is not just a psychiatric pathology but a recurrent, historically inflected phenomenon.

Fanon demonstrates the same kind of historical attunement with his appropriation of other systems of thought that he uses, in turn, to think through manicheism. Take Hegel, for instance. The colonial master that Fanon talks about is different from Hegel's master. For Fanon, the master/slave opposition is not a dialectical one because one term is always contained within the other. The bondsman has no opportunity for the self-consciousness that would allow him to recognize himself as a term in an opposition; he is simply the deprivation of the self-consciousness of the master. In Hegel – especially in Hegel according to his first great French popularizer, Jean Hyppolite (1907–1968) – the struggle for recognition gives the bondsman recognition of his other, his opposite, his negation in various ways, each of which allows him to recognize different abstractions of which he is part. In the opposition to death, the primal fear, he recognizes life – not quite his life, but a life given to him by "external thingness."[50] He knows that there is an abstraction called "life" that makes him

---

[50] Hyppolite, *Genesis and Structure*, 173.

different from the material world around him. But he does not fully know, or experience, this life as his because the object of his "life" is to labor for the sake of others who can enjoy the things he makes fully, and so experience life fully. Their life is a continual demonstration that they have the ability to turn the things that have "independent being" for the bondsman into things that no longer have being because they are fully enjoyed, used up, in fulfilling their desire.

For Hegel, Hyppolite, Kojève, and Sartre (Fanon's most important sources for the dialectic of servitude), work is precisely what will liberate the bondsman.[51] He notices the power of his instrumentality in the world, and discovers how fully he shapes the world, and in doing so discovers the fuller extent of his being-in-the-world. "In the product of the work," says Hyppolite, "he finds himself."[52] This stage (or "moment," as Hegel calls it) is exactly where Fanon argues that the colonial subject's struggle for recognition peters out. In an important footnote in *Black Skin, White Masks*, Fanon spells out precisely why work cannot be the road to self-consciousness, and ultimately liberty, for the colonial subject. The Hegelian slave ("esclave") "loses himself in the object and finds in his work the source of his liberation."[53] His work allows him to discover his own power and independent being in the objects he transforms. Because they once represented for him the independence of being as an abstraction, his capacity to alter them proves to him his *own* independence, and his own capacity to make the independence of being, in a sense, his own independence. Work makes the recognition of this liberatory idea possible, and, by strengthening the slave's engagement with the independence of being, is also the way in which he can realize that idea. But because the "Negro wants to be like the master," says Fanon, he does not ultimately find his identity in what he does, but in what he is told. Of course, every slave begins working because he is told to, but for Hegel the slave's work is the first step away from the interanimation of the master–slave relationship. But as a result of the Black man's desire to be like the Master, in Fanon's view,

> Therefore he is less independent than the Hegelian slave.
> In Hegel the slave turns away from the master and turns toward the object.
> Here the slave turns toward the master and abandons the object.[54]

---

[51] For more on Fanon's engagement with Kojève's and Sartre's versions of Hegel, see Sekyi-Otu, *Fanon's Dialectic of Experience*, 32, 73 (Kojève); 61–70 (Sartre).
[52] Hyppolite, *Genesis and Structure*, 176.
[53] Fanon, *Black Skin*, 221, n. 8.
[54] Ibid.

Fanon's argument asks us to rethink the way in which capitalism alienates the worker from the product of their labor. The worker's own involvement in the process of production is what ultimately causes their alienation from the product: because they submit themselves to the process of specialization, they are a part of an abstract labor machine in which their labor is measured in abstract units and in which the thing they make is not their own. The question of how liberation can come about in these circumstances is largely the story of how Karl Marx (1818–1883) has been understood and used. This is not the place to explore how Marx understands Hegel's dialectic of liberation and applies it to the moment of capitalism. What I want to emphasize is that the subjection of the worker in the capitalist West is fundamentally different from subjugation in the colony. Indeed, as Ato Sekyi-Otu argues, Marx's is simply one of the many Western narratives of domination and subjugation that fail in the colony because they are "predicated on relations of reciprocity, benign or malignant, [that] are incapable of capturing the 'originality of the colonial context.'"[55] The alienation of the worker, which is both the result and the consequence of the specialization of labor, also produces multiple spheres of social relations in which specialization becomes a form of identity.

In an oblique and ingenious way, the very title of *Les damnés de la terre* underscores this difference. Most of Fanon's readers, and certainly those who fell more on the *colon* side of the equation than on the *colonisé* side, would have assumed that the title alludes to *L'Internationale*, the stirring communist hymn that celebrates the universal worker. The supposed allusion of Fanon's book to the first line of *L'Internationale* ("Debout! les damnés de la terre!") has misleadingly suggested that Fanon is engaging with a kind of universal colonial subject. But this is a book that ends with a devastating critique of the recourse to universalism by the colonial subject, which Fanon argues is only a capitulation to the colonial obliteration of distinctive local histories and cultures. In fact, the title comes through Jacques Roumain's (1907–1944) "Sales nègres," a poetic litany of places and races that is a vociferous denial of a universalism that would only be racist.[56] It devastatingly parodies the slippage between *terre* as a specific (piece of) land and *terre* as "Earth." The colonist insists, according to Fanon, that he has made the *terre*: he is the "absolute beginning," and without him the *terre* would return to the Middle Ages. "We made (*faite*) this land ... If we

---

[55] Sekyi-Otu, *Fanon's Dialectic of Experience*, 62.
[56] See Macey, *Frantz Fanon*, 175–76, who suggests that, while the phrase originates in *L'Internationale*, that reference is mediated through Roumain's poem. See also Mellino, "The *Langue* of the Damned."

leave, all will be lost, and this land will return to the Dark Ages (*cette terre retournera au Moyen Âge*)."⁵⁷ Indeed, "The colonist makes (*fait*) history and he knows it."⁵⁸ Land and history: the very elements of Marxist economic historiography are marshaled against the colonized subjects cut off from the land that now acquires a history from which they are removed.

Or the decision is made that there was no history before the colonizers came. The abstract version of this decision is Hegel's infamous declaration that Africa "is no historical part of the world; it has no movement or development to exhibit."⁵⁹ The brutally pragmatic version of this argument holds that the land was vacant before Europeans occupied it. It did not matter whether people were, in fact, occupying it. If the land was not possessed in accordance with the rules of the French Civil Code it was declared "terre vacante et sans maître." The decision of "terre vacante" makes opposition to the master a vacant space; the worker is doubly annulled. The dialectic of recognition can't even commence because no term is the negation of the master. This manicheism only *appears* to be the emergence of two opposites; it really is the establishment of a single category, which, in Aristotelian fashion, can be known by its accidents: whiteness, the master, the colonizer. The colonized, by contrast, is not a category, so what appear to be the accidents of an underlying substance are really an impossibility.

In the section of *The Wretched of the Earth* where Fanon makes the famous, and notoriously misunderstood, pronouncement that the colonial world is "cut in two," he also makes it quite clear that he is not talking about dueling binaries, each of which has a chance to become the term that dominates the other.⁶⁰ The kind of "cutting" that he means is more radical than that: it creates a split in which only one part can have the attribute

---

⁵⁷ Fanon, *Damnés*, 53; *Wretched*, 15. Medievalization is the threat that the colonist also makes against independence movements: "If you want independence, take it and return to the Dark Ages (*retournez au Moyen Âge*)" (*Damnés*, 94; *Wretched*, 53). And what he uses to justify the use of corporeal punishment: "We need to use the lash if we want to take this country out of the Dark Ages (*sortir ce pays du Moyen Âge*)" (*Damnés*, 116; *Wretched*, 72). In fact, references to *Le Moyen Âge* are always only in the voice of the colonist. A slight exception appears in the very last sentence of the chapter on "The Grandeur and Weakness of Spontaneity," but even here it is used as an adjective and sardonically placed in quotation marks: "All that is left is a slight readaptation, a few reforms at the top, a flag, and down at the bottom a shapeless, 'medieval' mass, which continues in its perpetual movement (*Un minimum de réadaptation, quelques réformes au sommet, un drapeau et, tout en bas, la masse indivise, toujours 'moyenâgeuse', qui continue son mouvement perpétuel*)" (*Damnés*, 141; *Wretched*, 96; translation modified).
⁵⁸ Fanon, *Damnés*, 53; *Wretched*, 15.
⁵⁹ Hegel, *The Philosophy of History*, 99. On Du Bois's theory of African History, by contrast, see Chapter 2 in this volume, Whitaker, "'The Noblest Blood God ever Made'."
⁶⁰ Fanon, *Damnés*, 41; *Wretched*, 5 (translation modified).

of existence. The "'native' sector" cannot vie with the "European sector," because the former is not really an alternative to the latter.[61] As Fanon says, both sectors are "governed by a purely Aristotelian logic," and both "follow the dictates of mutual exclusion."[62] In the language of Aristotle, the opposition between them is not that of "relation." The European is not afraid that the native town will supplant his town, but that the natives "want to take our place."[63] There is only *one* place, and only one party can occupy it. But, as I have suggested, the logic is even more existential: if one party (the European party) does not occupy that place, it does not exist.

The Aristotelian text behind Fanon's analysis here is the fundamental handbook of the Aristotelian system, the *Categories*. Its main purpose is to set out the ten principal ways in which being can be analyzed (substance, quantity, quality, relation, location, time, position, possession, doing, undergoing). Fanon's reading of Aristotle here makes the issue of the relation between black and white not just one of political rights but of the *right to be* in the first place.[64] Under colonialism – that is, under racist regimes of occupation – the question never arises. The Aristotelian logic that Fanon invokes makes it quite clear that the issue is not whether the native is defined as a set of attributes that does not fit into one of the ten categories of being. It is crueler than that. The cut that divides the world in two is the cut that creates racial difference, the opposition between Black and white. Once this cut is made, Fanon argues, it can only be understood as the Aristotelian principal of "mutual exclusion."[65] This principle is quite specific, and is spelled out in one small section of the *Categories*. It is clear, too, that Fanon is referring to just one condition of this Aristotelian principle. Aristotle says that "with contraries it is not necessary if one exists for the other to exist too."[66] To apply this logic to Fanon's argument, it is possible that the category "black" could exist independently of the category "white." It is possible that "white" could be inferred from the existence of "black." But that seems like a speculative exercise. What Fanon means is that one category has *made* the existence of the other category impossible. It is possible, even likely, that Fanon was attracted to Aristotle's discussion

---

[61] Fanon, *Wretched*, 4.
[62] Ibid.
[63] Ibid., 5.
[64] For a crucial reading of Fanon's Aristotelian logic here, see Sekyi-Otu, *Fanon's Dialectic of Experience*, who argues that Fanon "avers that it is in the formal logic of Aristotle's *Categories*, not in the dialectical logic of Hegel's *Phenomenology*, that we will find the open secret of the colonial relation" (72).
[65] Fanon, *Wretched*, 4.
[66] Aristotle, *Categories*, §11, p. 24.

of reciprocal exclusivity by the example that Aristotle uses of one category's existence making the other's impossible. I will quote from the French translation of the *Categories* made by J. Tricot in 1936 and in print ever since: "si tous les *êtres* sont blancs, la blancheur *existera*, à l'exclusion de la noirceur."[67] What is at stake here is not just white or Black people, but being (*l'être*), existing as white or Black. More than that: it is not a question of white beings and Black beings existing, but of the abstract qualities of *blackness* and *whiteness* existing, *as a category of being* on its own terms. Thus, in a sense, it is not white people in the colony who exclude Black people – though that is certainly true – but whiteness itself that makes the existence of blackness impossible. That is one reason why the only kind of imaginary identification possible for the native seems to be the place of the settler. But Aristotle is talking about an extreme instance, the limit cases of these categories. Fanon is talking about precisely the extreme instance, the limit case, that Aristotle uses as a mere example. The difference is that, in Fanon's world, the "reality" of being itself, becoming white, has actually come about.

The possibility that whiteness could become an abstraction that makes it impossible to attach being to blackness is not a recent one, nor is it restricted to the colony. It is the result of a centuries-long habituation to thinking of color as abstract that begins with passages like this one from Aristotle. The most common example used in analyses of logical problems throughout the high Middle Ages was that of Socrates himself (sometimes Plato) "becoming white."[68] One of Aristotle's recurrent examples of qualities that imply their opposites is – along with heat and cold, and, to a lesser extent, health and sickness – white and black. Although his ultimate point is not that whiteness is a self-subsisting entity, Thomas Aquinas says that a "white man" can be understood as a man *and* something "composed of itself and another, just as a white thing is composed of that which is white and whiteness."[69] Nicholas Oresme uses "whiteness and perhaps some flavors (*albedo et forte quidam sapores*)" as the primary example of one of the few qualities that follow from one of the four primary qualities.[70] The analysis of whiteness makes its way outside the intramural limits of Scholasticism: Dante compares justice to whiteness (although as something that cannot

---

[67] Aristotle, *Catégories*, trans. Tricot, §11, p. 77 (emphasis mine).
[68] See the numerous examples in Newton, ed., *Medieval Commentaries on Aristotle's Categories*.
[69] Thomas Aquinas, *Quodlibet* II, §2.1, p. 80.
[70] Nicholas Oresme, *Questiones super Physicam*, bk. II, §5, lines 193–94, p. 203 (quoted in Robert Pasnau, "Scholastic Qualities," 48).

have degrees), and the Middle English poem *Pearl* concerns an object that refers to varying degrees of whiteness.[71] Not only is the difference between white and black one of the most common subjects of research into the nature of the qualities that make up bodies, but it is also, again and again, whiteness that is used as the primary and often exclusive example. I am not arguing that the analysis of *albumen* in Scholasticism created racism in Europe on its own.[72] I just want to suggest one of the ways in which whiteness was treated as an abstract, self-subsisting category, and one frequently without relation to its opposite, blackness. In the colony, says Fanon, the European is defined by this abstract quality, which not only reinforces – or, rather, legitimates – itself but impoverishes other categories: "you are rich because you are white, you are white because you are rich."[73]

I think this is what Fanon means when he says that the received version of the Hegelian dialectic of the master and bondsman works differently in the colony, or that Marxist analysis "should always be slightly stretched."[74] Hegel's master is not defined or transformed by his relation with the slave because, as with the "white thing" of Scholasticism, it is composed out of itself "and another" – except the other ("whiteness," in the case of the "white thing") is its own abstraction. Fanon's comment about Marxist analysis may be a little more straightforward, because (as he does not do with his Hegelian use of the master/slave dialectic) he states succinctly what would be involved, what would need stretching. The abstract force of whiteness is what compartmentalizes the world, and so what is usually regarded as the epiphenomenon, the superstructure of the underlying economic activities that actually alter the world, becomes more important than the substructure. The validity of a critique of the superstructure was one of the points of contention in French academic Marxism after the war, and the success of this critique can be gauged by the outsized influence of figures such as Fredric Jameson today. It is arguable that the reason that it becomes acceptable to use the superstructure as an object of analysis is related to the conditions that Fanon describes in the colony. The logic of white mastery, and its cost in the Algerian War, perhaps made the domination of the symbolic a phenomenon that needed to be addressed outside purely economic conditions. It may be significant that one of the earliest thinkers to treat the superstructure as an "instituting institution," and one

---

[71] Dante, *De Monarchia*, bk. I, §11, p. 53.
[72] See Whitaker, *Black Metaphors*, 79–104.
[73] Fanon, *Wretched*, 5.
[74] Ibid., 5.

of the earliest to be criticized for his focus on symbolic capital, was the anthropologist Pierre Bourdieu (1930–2002), whose main work concerned the Kabylé of Algeria, and who supported the struggle for Algerian independence in many ways. But Fanon at this point is not primarily concerned with the future of Marxist analysis. His argument conveys the insistence of history – not the protocols that Marxist analysis has established, but the problem of dealing with the historiography that Marxism itself has created: "It is not just the concept of the precapitalist society, so effectively studied by Marx, which needs to be reexamined (*repensé*) here."[75]

On the one hand, colonialism "petrifies" medieval governing structures; on the other, a return to the Middle Ages is the threat that the colonizer makes when the colonized threatens insurrection.[76] It legitimates the governing structures of the colony, and also is what the colonies will collapse into without those governing structures. The arrival of the Middle Ages signals the imminence of modernity, but the Middle Ages is also the negation of modernity. In at least one moment of *The Wretched of the Earth*, the medieval gives Fanon a way of imagining a history that unfolds outside the Marxist materialist historical dialectic. It is not strictly true that Fanon is such a committed Marxist that, to keep him relevant, one must first jettison (or, to be kinder, "bracket") his commitment to Marxist dialectic. He certainly hews close to it throughout his work, but even in such a crucial place as his chapter on revolutionary violence, he says that it is inadequate to account for the phenomenon of colonial domination. A strictly economic account of colonialism does not work, he says, because race is an even more fundamental category. It calls for nothing less than a reconfiguration of Marx's concept of the precapitalist moment: that is, it calls for a reconfiguration of the way that Marx has taught us to think about the place of the medieval in the modern, that is to say colonial, world. The fabled relation of the master and the bondsman (*chevalier* and *serf*), so central to Hegel's and Marx's placement of the genesis of modern economic history in the European Middle Ages – as Andrew Cole has argued – is simply irrelevant in the colony.[77] The problem is that there is no intimacy, no relation in the physical, familial, or philosophical senses. The *serf* is "essentially different from the knight," for they are "different species (*espèces différentes*)."[78] Fanon underscores the *serf*'s lack of economic and

---

[75] Fanon, *Damnés*, 43; *Wretched*, 5.
[76] Fanon, *Wretched*, 53; 72.
[77] See Cole, *The Birth of Theory*.
[78] Fanon, *Damnés*, 43; *Wretched*, 5.

political substance by describing him only in relation to the colonizer's *essence*. The colonized lacks being, in a fundamental sense, in the colony.

A simple, "allegorical" manicheism might map out a distinction between the "people of the shadows" (the evil of Manichean opposition) and those who dwell in the light. But Fanon's point is both less and more than that. On the one hand, even the people of the shadows possess being in the original, historical, Manichean system, a kind of substantiality that weighs against those in the light: in modern colonial manicheism the colonized lack even the attribute of being. But on the other hand, of course they do not. Fanon's point here is that it is really the entire philosophical delirium that lacks being. Or, to bring closer to the surface the metaphor that Fanon is using in this passage, the other is really the one that imagines the colonized as other: no matter what the colonizer does, despite all his work of *l'appropriation* (a word that folds into one the theft of property and the assertion of self-identity), he will remain always a stranger. The ruling "species" will remain one that comes from elsewhere, and the fundamental incoherence – the real delirium – of the system will never change: that there will never be a true relation, a real resemblance, between the ruling species and the "autochthones, 'les autres.'"[79] Those last words wreck the extended irony that Fanon has been tracing; they close the bracket that colonialism first opened. The earth that the colonized first inhabited is no longer theirs. They are the other of their own territory. Fanon's ultimate point is not just that the colonized lack being, but that the entire system is a vast delusion, ludicrous precisely because people still believe in its supposed substance despite its patent and derisory contradictions.

* * *

Augustine and Manicheism turn out to be far more significant in the struggle against colonialism than Fanon's *Black Skin, White Masks* had intimated. Fanon may have discovered all of these resonances himself in his wide reading, although the remaining books in his library do not include any by Augustine, except for the popular 1940 biography of Augustine by Gustave Bardy.[80] A likelier nexus for information about Augustine and Manicheism is probably the occasion of the Algerian war itself. Two of France's greatest Augustine scholars were deeply involved in opposing the war, one from France and another as a leading leftist, Catholic intellectual in Algeria.

---

[79] Fanon, *Damnés*, 43.
[80] Khalfa, "Frantz Fanon's Library," 726.

The first of these is Henri-Irénée Marrou (1904–1977) from the Sorbonne, still the greatest authority in education in Late Antiquity. Although Marrou was a critic of Marxism, he opposed France's conduct of the war in Algeria on moral, political, and religious grounds. He and Fanon even published articles in the same issue of the leading journal opposed to the Algerian war, *Esprit*, in February 1955. Marrou's most visible intervention was an editorial published in *Le Monde* on April 5, 1956 ("France, ma patrie…"), which blasted the French government's use of torture in conducting the Algerian war. It was not until September 2018, when President Emmanuel Macron acknowledged that torture had been used in at least one case, that anyone in the French government admitted to its widespread use in Algeria. While Marrou was motivated by a sense of outraged morality, he was not exactly a revolutionary. The heart of his column argues that absolute good and evil cannot easily be separated in the real world, and in those terms he seems to reject the dualist world that Fanon had three years before seemed to portray in *Black Skin, White Masks*. Marrou says that as an historian he must reject all "Manichean classifications."[81] But while he may have opposed Marxism and Marxist-Leninist revolutionary action, he does not reject Fanon's critique as bluntly as it might seem. After all, Fanon does not exactly argue that we ought to accept "Manichean classifications" either – just that they are imposed by colonialism. Part of Marrou's point, to be sure, is that Fanon's revolutionary violence is predicated on a conviction that it is virtually impossible to overturn the division of the world into black and white. But in 1956 Fanon had not yet written the chapter on revolutionary violence in *The Wretched of the Earth*. Marrou's invocation of "Manichean classifications" is therefore inspired, most immediately, by Fanon's analysis in *Black Skin, White Masks*.

But as Marrou says, he is speaking as an historian and, to be specific, one who studies *Augustine*. His rejection of "Manichean classifications" is also a deliberate echo of Augustine's own rejection of Manicheism. Indeed, when he describes what the Manicheism to be rejected in Algeria and France looks like, he turns not to Fanon but to Augustine himself, drawing from precisely the passage I discussed earlier. Marrou does not believe that there has ever really been a party of the Pure confronting the "Puissances des Ténèbres," the powers of darkness or the *gens tenebrarum*.[82] Instead,

---

[81] "Historien, je me refuse à toute classification manichéenne." Quoted in Mandouze, *Mémoires d'outre-siècle*, 243.

[82] Marrou, "France, ma patrie…." The latter phrase is Augustine's, used throughout *Contra epistolam Manichaei quam vocant fundamenti* (§§ 18, 20, 24, 25, 32).

like his teacher Augustine, Marrou believes that we have always lived in an inseparable jumble of the City of Good and the City of Evil. The immense difference between Marrou and Fanon lies partly in the ease with which Marrou sets aside a fissure in the world so profound that Fanon sees violence as the only truly effective response. Marrou's Enlightenment confidence in the virtues of French republicanism (he appeals throughout his *Le Monde* editorial to the importance of the ideals of "la patrie") is the kind of confidence that Fanon attacks as a symptom of Manichean delusion. To believe either that we must accept colonial manicheism because we live in a mixed world, or to believe that we can improve the situation, is ultimately to be trapped within that delirium. What is perhaps most important about Marrou's editorial for the elaboration of that critique of colonial manicheism, however, is that Marrou, like other Augustine scholars who opposed the war in Algeria, sees a profound historical connection between the world of Augustine and the world of the anti-colonial movement. For Marrou, the Augustine who opposed the delusional division of the world into light and dark is a contemporary *indigène*, "ce Berbère," *this* Berber, as if he is standing right there before him.

During his time in Algeria, Fanon also had continual contact with André Mandouze, mentioned earlier, one of the other leading scholars of Augustine, who would go on to publish in 1968 *Saint Augustin: l'aventure de la raison et de la grâce* and would eventually compile the indispensable archive of North African Christians, the *Prosopographie de l'Afrique chrétienne* with a preface by Marrou. He was also a committed and active anti-colonialist, engaged with the resistance in Algeria throughout the war, advising, organizing, and publishing two anti-colonial journals, *Consciences algériennes* and *Consciences maghrébines*, for which Fanon wrote a number of articles. He and Fanon met frequently to discuss strategies of resistance, and as noted earlier, Fanon's wife, Josie, attended his seminars on Augustine. For Mandouze, the war in Algeria against French colonialism was an extension of the resistance to the Nazis during the war, in which he had also been an active participant. The title of the first volume of his memoirs attests to the deep continuity he saw between the struggle against fascism and the struggle against colonialism: *D'une résistance à l'autre*. But as an Augustine scholar, for him Algeria also irresistibly summoned up the particular struggles of Late Antique North Africa. In his memoirs, Mandouze laments that his plan to commemorate the 1,600th anniversary of Augustine's birth was interrupted by the beginning of the Algerian war. His complaint is not about his interrupted scholarly career, of course. It is about the misery that the war brings, a misery that has the shape of historical irony. Not only did the war break out exactly 1,600 years after Augustine's birth, it also broke out in the same month and, above all, "dans son pays," in his own land, the "malheureuse terre de saint Augustin."[83] For Mandouze, Augustine haunts the war like a specter. "Wherever the war is, there Augustine is also," he says at one point in his memoirs.[84] As it happens, these words come from Mandouze's recollection of his reaction to Marrou's famous 1956 editorial in *Le Monde*. Wherever the war is, there Manicheans were also. And there was Fanon, too, writing about the land that the Manicheans themselves inhabited. Manicheism is not just a remote and arcane theology, but the worldview of a large number of the people who lived where Fanon was writing, and the *terre* in which he wished to be buried (and was: his body was flown from Bethesda, Maryland, where he died, to Tunis, from which it was covertly taken across the border and buried just inside Algeria).[85] In some ways Fanon may have seen Manicheism as a forerunner of colonialism, with its imposition of foreign belief; in some ways it represents a form of belief prior to the arrival of modern colonialism, a belief that is, or becomes, characteristically African. François Decret's great study of Manicheism in North Africa argues that it survived so long as an African "church" precisely because it dropped features of Manicheism that seemed alien to North African culture: it "became indigenous."[86]

But indigenity is not simple. Where "indigenization" now is virtually synonymous with decolonization, and where the first cultural push of the postindependence FLN Government of Algeria was a deliberate strategy of indigenization, Decret's use of the term implies a colonial context. It echoes, indeed, the long rule of France over Algeria, and the attempt to imagine a white settler identity that was French while also distinctly Algerian, expressed, for example, in a literary movement sometimes called *Algérianisme*. This attempt sometimes exposed the desire for a phantasmatic foundational legitimacy among the settlers, a desire that leaped right over the work of becoming *like* an indigenous population to the invention of a myth of originary presence. The Association des Ecrivains Algériens thus awarded Paul Achard's (1897–1962) novel *L'Homme de Mer* (1931) its

---

[83] Mandouze, *Memoires d'outre siècle*, 1.226, 242.
[84] Ibid. 1.243: (*encore une fois, si la guerre est là, Augustin l'est aussi*).
[85] See Macey, *Frantz Fanon*, 6.
[86] Decret, *L'Afrique manichéenne*: "la grande originalité des Africains dans l'Eglise de mani est d'avoir ecarté, autant que possible, tout particularisme qui les ferait se singulariser parmi les populations de leur pays.... Il est hors de doute aussi que cette 'indigénisation' du manichéisme africain explique sa longue survie" (1.210).

Grand Prix Littéraire de l'Algérie for its celebration of France's millennium of domination over North Africa: Achard imagines modern France as the inheritor of Rome, recreating "a new France" in Algeria "from the debris of the Roman Empire."[87] But the real importance of this historical fantasy is that it forges a narrative of legitimacy from the earth: the French are, as the descendants of the Romans, autochthonous Algerians, not invaders. As Achard says, the "land of Africa was therefore not new for them."[88] But neither was France: the settlers of Algeria derived their political legitimacy precisely from their status as simultaneously French citizens, although known as "Latins d'Afrique" or "Français de'Algerie."[89]

Decret's observation about the indigenization of Manicheism may also carry with it a completely antithetical sense, a trace of the deprecation implied by the "Code d'Indigenat," under which non-white residents of Algeria were second-tier citizens. White settlers in colonial Algeria have been described as oscillating between "the need, on one hand, to maintain the privilege of the coloniser, and the appeal, on the other, of a process of indigenisation."[90] The final irony of Fanon's life is that despite, and because of, what Homi Bhabha calls his "consummate self-fashioning of himself as an Algerian," he died in the United States and his body had to be smuggled across the Algerian border to be buried. His final wish, as reported by the ALN commandant who spoke the final words at the funeral, was to lie with his brothers "en terre algérienne."[91] He performed in death the most radical act of indigenization: to share the earth with the damned of the Algerian colony, the earth that had long been the resting place of the original Manicheans.

Like Fanon, Manicheism originated elsewhere, yet became African once it arrived. It precedes Islam and the modern form of Christianity, but in its spread throughout Northern Africa it also anticipates some of the ductile adaptability of the system of colonial belief. However Fanon would have mapped the historical phenomenon of Manichean religion onto his topography of the dualistic colonial world, he would have absorbed from his most likely sources two things: that Manicheism was a powerful explanatory tool and that it demanded such a suspension of credulity that Augustine spent a large part of his career marveling over how thoroughly he had been deceived by it.

---

[87] Quoted in Cummings, "Civilising the Settler," 177.
[88] Ibid., 178.
[89] Ibid., 181.
[90] Barclay, Chopin, and Evans, "Introduction," 119.
[91] Belkacem, "Frantz Fanon, notre frère," 648; the phrase was repeated on several other occasions, for example, Juminer, in "Hommages à Frantz Fanon," 129.

If recent arguments that Augustine remains entangled in Manichean epistemological modes are accurate, it is not enough simply to name, and to repudiate, heretical (or racist) ontologies. Augustine's anti-Manichean polemic also shapes his Christian apologetics, which is summoned, across the course of his conversion, by the need to resolve, and then repudiate, incoherencies in Manichean metaphysics. In Augustine's work, Christian theology is what Hegel would call a determinate negation, a truth that is discernible only in the ruination of a previous belief, because it is the truth that both destroys it and, in doing so, brings itself about. For Augustine, determinate negation led to a Christian orthodoxy; for Fanon, or rather according to Fanon's critique of the colonial world, it led to the articulation of the supposedly primitive superstitions that colonization was meant to bring to an end. The myths of the colonized, says Fanon, "are the very mark of … indigence and innate depravity."[92] The attribution of mythic immediate experience to the colonized serves three functions simultaneously: it annuls the modernity of the colonized as potential participants in modern liberal democracy; it performs a coercive and inhibitory function, allowing the colonized to redirect their urge for reciprocal violence into fantasized powers of far greater malevolence – and force – than those of the colonizers; and, most consequentially, it continues to articulate and produce forms of counterviolence. The symbolic machines of colonial domination, says Fanon, "serve not only as inhibitors but also as stimulants … under certain emotional circumstances an obstacle actually escalates action."[93] Because the colonizer forces the colonized to dwell in the negative, in other words, the colonized have at their disposal the tremendous power of the negative.

In Fanon's intellectual heritage – and in the biographical trajectory of *Black Skin, White Masks* and *The Wretched of the Earth* – the negative does the work of what Manicheism does for Augustine: it contains the negation of the beliefs he inherits, and out of it emerges his radically contingent forays into the intelligibility of a reality that is neither directly experienced nor comprehensible because of the wreckage of present experience. In many ways, Fanon's earlier book, which is founded on the personal trauma of being a Black person in a world dominated by "Whites" and whiteness, narrates the ruination of the knowledges and self-certainty that he may at one point have believed that he could hold fast. *Black Skin, White*

---

[92] Fanon, *Wretched*, 7.
[93] Ibid., 17.

Masks holds out the possibility, perhaps outlined a bit more firmly in *The Wretched of the Earth*, that this experience of negation could be an act of ethical cleansing and of radical beginning (e.g., the absolute night). For Augustine, the utter speciousness and fantasmatic content of Manicheism is also the means to drive thought forward, out of the night of ignorance.

What is vastly different about Fanon's work, of course, is that rather than write about the slow recuperation from a world of *darkness* and superstition, as Augustine does, he is writing about the formation of a world of phantasms and nightmares by the totalitarian machinery of colonization. Turning the ideology of the civilizing mission of colonization on its head, Fanon argues that, rather than bring modernity and post-Enlightenment reason into the world, colonization produces, instead, a reenchantment of the world. Fanon is not describing the mere inversion of the process by which Max Weber (1864–1920) says industrialization displaces older, "enchanted" modes of belief. He means something more like what Theodor W. Adorno (1903–1969) and Max Horkheimer (1895–1973) describe in *The Dialectic of Enlightenment* (1944). They argue that the vestiges of primeval superstition, magic, or religious belief have not disappeared, and that these vestiges explain why it is that we so willingly accept relations of domination that we might otherwise find intolerable: "justified in the guise of brutal facts as something eternally immune to intervention, the social injustice from which those facts arise is as sacrosanct today as the medicine man once was under the protection of his gods."[94] What is powerful in Fanon's critique is the exposure of the magical world behind the discourse of enlightened, colonial domination: it really is founded not on rationality but on a primitive fear of the other, on the mythical, mystified, structure of race, which masquerades as race science, but also as the rational apparatus of colonial administration generally. The mythmaking of the colonized is a critique – and an exposure – of the dominations that global capital employs, but above all, of the demonization that fuels the engine of colonization.

In Fanon's account, superstition and myth are produced by a determinate negation that is the reflex action of the colonized. This particular act of negation, however, is the result of the prior acts by which the colonizers have negated their right to exist. Reasserting that right can only be by means of that first act of negation, not by a simple act of opposition: "Yes, I have the right to exist" can only be said once you acknowledge that the right to

---

[94] Horkheimer and Adorno, *Dialectic of Enlightenment*, 21.

say that – the very concept of rights and of political self-assertion – is a part of the juridical operations of European sovereignty. The right to exist can therefore only become a primordial right in the form of ancestral, indigenous prohibition. The right to exist is expressed *as* the threat of annihilation, a threat made tolerable only by a negative guarantee of existence in a world that is the determinate negation of the colonizer's ontology.

Determinate negation, however, is simply a way of describing the unintelligible and intolerable situation of the colonized, and therefore another way of framing the necessity – because it is the only action that is left – of violence. What makes the situation of the colonized intolerable, at least outside the sphere of violence, is that it cannot be repudiated. The colonized cannot simply walk away, or decide to choose another belief system. That is the difference from historical Manicheism, which was not a machine of total domination. Augustine did not have to contemplate violence because he could use debate and polemic in a public sphere that was actually Manichean, in the sense that one opposite could in fact overcome the other – which is what Augustine and his followers believed was the outcome of Augustine's public disputations. But mere opposition and contradiction are meaningless as strategies for the colonized; they are constitutive annulments of Aristotelian categories of being, not transitional moments in a dialectic. Unlike Augustine's, Fanon's *remains* a manichean world – except that white and Black, colonizer and colonized, are not true antagonists, struggling against each other. In the history that colonization writes over the land it appropriates, the colonizer is always already transcendent.

But Fanon argues that there is a price for this transcendence: it is achieved by a determinate negation ("a *systematic negation* of the other person and a *furious determination* to deny the other person all attributes of humanity").[95] Although this transcendence is not a resolution, synthesis, or *Aufhebung* in the movement of a Hegelian dialectic, it preserves one important feature: the negative, which Hegel associates, in fact, with the work of preserving ("something *preserves* itself in the negative determinate being").[96] In the course of a normative logic that would unfold outside the manichean world of colonialism, negations would continue to imply all of the previous moments that have been passed over, transcended, left

---

[95] Fanon, *Wretched*, 250. My italics.
[96] Hegel, *Science of Logic*, trans. Miller, 119. Miller's 1969 translation is something of a gloss, though accurate: George di Giovanni's more recent translation has "The something *preserves* itself in its non-being" (Hegel, *The Science of Logic*, trans. Giovanni, 92).

behind. But in the colonial world even the *implied content* of the negative is utterly annulled. What does remain, ineradicable and powerful, is negation itself, which, for Fanon, is not nothing; far from it. Lurking behind or, rather, outside the text of colonialism is an absolute negative, a negation that can only be invoked in terms that themselves demand further cancellations and negations, names of what cannot, in the text of colonialism, fully be named. The most provocative term, provocative in every sense of the word, is of course, violence. But another is death, a condition and an act that, in a fragment by Aimé Césaire (1913–2008) that Fanon quotes, is the apprehension of both hate and love, "evil and pernicious" but also "verdant and sumptuous."[97]

Readings of Fanonian violence that reduce it to mere murder cannot account for the multitudes in Césaire's vision of death, partly because it is the only mode of being left to the colonized, the one that Fanon calls their "absolute praxis (*praxis absolue*)."[98] The strange adjective *absolue* points to what cannot be named (why would Fanon not refer to praxis as final, or only, or necessary?): violence as a praxis of death. To put this in different terms, but terms that are haunting Fanon's text on violence, the absolute is precisely an absolute (as opposed to a determinate) negation, what Hegel in the Preface to the *Phenomenology* calls the "tremendous (*ungeheuer*) power of the negative."[99] It is unnamable, and Hegel is slightly coquettish about what to call it (spoiler alert: he calls it death): "Death, if that is what we want to call *this non-actuality*, is of all things the most dreadful, and to hold fast to what is dead requires the greatest strength."[100] The story of violence in *The Wretched of the Earth* is the story of a continually deforming agent, one that first produces the nonreality of (as both a subjective and objective genitive) the colonized, and then turns a transformed violence against that agent. In the opening pages of *The Wretched of the Earth*, Fanon says that the manichean world of colonization produces the colonized as the mere "quintessence of evil," "absolute evil (*mal absolu*)."[101] But the force that produces this determinate negation of the colonized becomes, in turn, an absolute negation, a form of pure, uncontained force. The colonized, Fanon says, is "an agent (*dépositaire*) of malevolent powers,

---

[97] Fanon, *Wretched*, 45.
[98] Ibid., 44; *Damnés*, 82. Two recent accounts of the "absolute" version of afropessimism are Wilderson, *Afropessimism*; and Mbembe, *Necropolitics*. Also see Calvin Warren's recent intervention, *Ontological Terror*, which, in part, challenges the metaphysical investments of afropessimism.
[99] Hegel, *Phenomenology*, 19; *ungeheuer* can also mean "monstrous" or "atrocious."
[100] Ibid.
[101] *Wretched*, 6; *Damnés*, 44.

an unconscious and incurable instrument of blind forces."[102] There is a revocable ambiguity here, a glimpse behind the scenes of the tremendous power of the negative itself: *depositaire* means "agent," but its literal sense is someone who receives, someone with whom something is deposited. The colonized is demonized by the unfathomable forces that stand outside the modern machine of colonialism (presumably forces of darkness, superstition, antiquity), yet forces that are themselves, of course, the fantasized deposit of white supremacy. In the manichean world that the colonizer has forced into being, these forces cannot be contained as merely backward, superstitious customs; they are the tremendous power of the absolute negative, what the colonizer immediately experiences as unconscious, implacable, blind force: violence.

---

[102] *Wretched*, 6; *Damnés*, 44.

CHAPTER 2

"The Noblest Blood God Ever Made"
W. E. B. Du Bois's Medievalism in the Contexts of the World Wars

Cord J. Whitaker

Among W. E. B. Du Bois's (1868–1963) early engagements with medievalism – or the interest in, study of, and deployment of the Middle Ages in modernity in popular and academic contexts – is his absorption of the philosophy of Georg Wilhelm Friedrich Hegel (1770–1831). Hegel, as Andrew Cole has shown, is more indebted to medieval forms of life, especially European feudalism, than was previously thought. More than forty years later, Du Bois's medievalism responds to another product of Germany: the highly institutionalized and militarized racism of Hitler and his National Socialist Party, and the global war that resulted. This essay examines Du Bois's medievalism in the contexts of the world wars, focusing on several moments: Du Bois's engagement with Hegel, his *c.* 1910 short story "The Princess Steel," his 1928 novel *Dark Princess*, and the political medievalism of his post-World War II thought. Du Bois finds in medievalism a tool for the political reorganization of the modern world into one in which global governance is shared among postimperial powers and postcolonial nations alike, without regard to race, culture, or former hierarchical position. As the twentieth century presents social, political, and economic upheaval after upheaval, Du Bois uses medievalism to interpret a topsy-turvy world and to assert how history might set it right.

The Princess Steel and Black Medievalism at the Turn of the Twentieth Century

Du Bois's documented engagement with the Middle Ages begins innocently enough. He likely read G. W. F. Hegel's *Phenomenology of Spirit* (1807) in German under George Santayana (1863–1952) at Harvard in 1889–90.[1] He

---

[1] Zamir, *Dark Voices*, 113, 248–49, n. 2. Siemerling, "W. E. B. Du Bois, Hegel, and the Staging of Alterity," 326.

drew much of his inspiration for his own master-slave or, for this essay's purposes, lord–bondsman dialectic and his theory of double consciousness from Hegel. The concepts appear in Du Bois's 1903 "Of Our Spiritual Strivings," the first chapter of his *Souls of Black Folk*. Indeed, the essay "constitutes itself as a narrative structure by reference to key sections from Hegel's *Phenomenology*."[2] This means that Du Bois was influenced, if indirectly, by the European Middle Ages, for, as Andrew Cole has argued, Hegel's eighteenth-century Germany would have been experienced in ways quite similar to its medieval past.[3] Hegel's position, medieval and modern at once, reveals the mirage of discrete periodization to be illusory, and is the conduit by which the Middle Ages initially influenced Du Bois's thought.

Through Hegel, then, Du Bois's early thought is influenced by the Middle Ages and the medievalism of Hegel's experience and philosophy. Du Bois's comportment toward labor has everything to do with the Hegelian approach in which the lord-and-bondsman offers "a dialectical scenario that pointedly emphasizes the central problem of any feudal formation" in which each party desires and depends on the recognition of its rights by the other.[4] As Cole has argued, "feudalism presents a struggle between ownership by legal right and military force (that of the lord) and effective possession via labor (that of the bondsman). Each could claim ownership of the same parcel of land by different means."[5] Du Bois's lord-and-bondsman resolves in the revelation that the master is indeed the dependent in that he must have his power recognized by the bondsman. Otherwise, his is no power at all. The servant, were he to realize his own will, becoming fully at one with his own consciousness by remerging the split consciousness that has been torn and doubled, has the power to become no servant at all; rather, it is he who may hold all the cards. Indeed, as Shamoon Zamir argues, Du Bois's reworking of Hegel "is closer to Marx's, Sartre's, and Alexandre Kojève's existentialist and materialist commentaries on Hegel than any other accounts of Hegel."[6] Kojève (1902–1968), famous for his lectures throughout the 1930s

---

[2] Zamir, *Dark Voices*, 114.
[3] Cole, *The Birth of Theory*, 66. For further discussion of Hegelian medievalism, see chapter 5 of my *Black Metaphors*, titled "Separate and Together: Strife, Contrariety, and the Lords and Bondsmen of Julian of Norwich, G. W. F. Hegel, and W. E. B. Du Bois," especially 131–32.
[4] Cole, *Birth of Theory*, 73.
[5] Whitaker, *Black Metaphors*, 132.
[6] Siemerling, "W. E. B. Du Bois, Hegel, and the Staging of Alterity," 332, n. 6.

and his writings interpreting Hegel, claims that, for Hegel, work "forms, transforms the World, humanizes it by making it more adapted to Man."[7] Hegel's lord–bondsman dialectic is, of course, a phenomenological study supremely focused on labor – and one that I have argued elsewhere has roots not only in the heldover feudalism of Hegel's experience but also in the metaphorization of feudal power dynamics seen in actual medieval, fourteenth-century theological writing such as that of Julian of Norwich (*c.* 1342–post-1416).[8] For medieval people, the lord–bondsman relationship could be a platform for examining the inner workings of sin and condemnation, forgiveness and salvation, and suffering and redemption. For Julian in particular, it was a way of considering why God allows those who serve Him to suffer. Du Bois's investment in the dialectic may help explain why, in the early years of the twentieth century, he turns to *medievalizing* forms – expressions of medieval life and culture that have occurred in modernity, whether or not they explicitly call attention to their medieval provenance – and in particular to romance – the short, narrative form popular in the West since the later Middle Ages and that regularly features power and identity reversals. Medievalizing romance provides Du Bois the perfect platform on which to consider the roles of labor in social development and financial accumulation in his own day.

Du Bois's medievalism also should be taken in the context of African-American medievalism more generally. Black American authors and intellectuals had identified and deployed medievalism in matters concerning their social and political milieus, and racial justice in general, since long before Du Bois. Matthew X. Vernon registers the utility of medievalism to Black American politics when he writes that

> African-Americans throughout the late nineteenth and twentieth centuries have utilized the critical matrix of meaning bound up within the Middle Ages—its association with individual nobility, the cultural reconciliation and hybridization implied by the Anglo-Norman period, theories of feudal land attachments, the sociolinguistic implications of speaking and writing in English, even the notion of Anglo-Saxon slavery—to expose the fantasy that underpinned discourses of citizenship and to suggest alternative terms of belonging within the nation.[9]

Black medievalism shows remarkable breadth. Examples range from early nineteenth-century poetry to post-Civil War tournament reenactments

---

[7] Kojève, *Introduction to the Reading of Hegel*, 52.
[8] See again chapter 5 of my *Black Metaphors*.
[9] Vernon, *The Black Middle Ages*, 18.

"The Noblest Blood God Ever Made" 71

to mid-twentieth-century novels. Take, for instance, the 1833 poetry of African American Dr. James McCune Smith (1813–1865), who wrote "To the River Clyde" while studying medicine at Glasgow:

> And such art thou my bonnie Clyde
> Nor Roman steel nor Norman [y]ell
> Nor Saxon craft nor England's pride
> Could fling around thee slavery's spell.[10]

Black medievalism likewise inspires the ring tournaments of Black clubs such as the Colored Tournament Club of Aiken, South Carolina in the latter decades of the nineteenth century.[11] It appears in the ring tournament scene of Charles Chesnutt's (1858–1932) *House Behind the Cedars* (1900).[12] Even in *Invisible Man* (1952), one of the most canonical novels by an African American author of the mid-twentieth century, Ralph Ellison (1913–1994) makes significant, if often overlooked, use of medievalism to criticize modern racism in the glaring light of American medievalizing notions of liberty and freedom.[13] For Du Bois, in particular, medievalism enables the control and organization of history; such epistemic control over the past offers, in turn, self-determination in the present and future.

The use of medievalism as an epistemic lever for self-determination is on display in Du Bois's pre-World War I deployment of romance to address the concerns of labor. The recently discovered short story "The Princess Steel" was written between 1908 and 1910. Described as a "medieval allegory of primitive accumulation" written within the generic confines of "speculative romance," "The Princess Steel" depicts a sociologist's and a young couple's examination of the social and economic forces that govern the world.[14] A newlywed couple who studied sociology in college come

---

[10] Smith, "To the River Clyde (Scotland)," 39.
[11] Colored Tournament Club, "Grand Tournament."
[12] Chesnutt, *The House Behind the Cedars*, 45–58.
[13] Vernon, 15–17, has noted how Ellison's novel "evokes the historical teleology of Marx, its charting of progress from feudal economic relationships to modern capitalist ones" and that, in Ellison's view, "African Americans were uniquely positioned to understand and critique the idea of moving towards modernity from feudalism, as they were acutely subject to the harsh transition between the two." Black Americans, Ellison argued could experience the transition simply by moving across the Mason-Dixon line. See also my "We were outside history," where I argue that considering how the novel deploys the Middle Ages can facilitate strategic developments in the struggle for racial justice: "When *Invisible Man* invokes feudalism, African and European military methods, and an elegiac non-linear temporality, the Middle Ages offers the epistemological off-ramp from the strict hierarchies, spatial and temporal, that inform a modernity defined by racial ideology" (438).
[14] The story was recently discovered in the Du Bois archives at the University of Massachusetts-Amherst and edited by Adrienne Brown and Britt Rusert. Thoughout this chapter, parenthetical page numbers correspond to this edition.

to New York on their honeymoon. Once there, they see a newspaper advertisement in which a sociology professor invites interested parties to experience "the results of his great experiments in Sociology by the aid of the megascope at two tomorrow." What follows is a multilayered narrative examining race, interdisciplinarity, technology, and, according to the story's editors, the aforementioned "primitive accumulation." The young couple is shocked that the professor is Black. They are surprised by the stunning view from the top of the new Whistler Building – based on the forty-plus-story Singer Building, a new technological feat soaring over lower Manhattan in 1908 – and perplexed by the complexity of his machines. They think he is a quack, until his machine offers the husband a virtual-realityesque experience. Through the megascope, he views a medievalizing battle that serves as a thinly veiled allegory for ethical questions about the extraction of wealth from advances in the use of steel – the very uses that have made the construction of the Singer Building, or fictional Whistler Building, possible.

"The Princess Steel" represents an early example of Du Bois's use of the medieval past as an epistemic tool. Quite literally, the story is about forms of knowledge accumulation. The text's only explicit mention of the Middle Ages comes from the old professor. When he introduces the young couple to his apparatus, with its stunning crystal orb, he states: "You know in the Middle Age they used to use spheres like this—of course smaller and far less perfect—but that was mere playing with science just as their alchemy was but the play and folly of chemistry" (823). He refers, it seems, to the astrolabe – that astronomical tool from classical antiquity that was, in the Middle Ages, preserved in and further developed in the Islamic world. Western Europeans were in awe of these tools. For instance, Geoffrey Chaucer (*c.* 1340–1400), famously interested in matters of physical science, wrote a *Treatise on the Astrolabe*, ostensibly to his five-year-old son Lewis, on how to use one. The professor tells them that his apparatus is far better than a mere medieval "sphere." Yet the comparison to the Middle Ages is how he expects his new students to *know*. The Middle Ages are, for the professor, the metric by which modernity is to be discerned.

The story's approach characterizes Du Bois's early medievalism: immersion in the Middle Ages reveals experiential knowledge about the dynamic motions of the world and the humans in it. The immersed subject gets to *feel* the push and pull of history on the whole. The professor has improved upon tools such as the astrolabe, so bound by the physical world, by making observable the "Over-world of Steel and its

Over-men" (824). This "Over-world" and "Over-life" he describes by defining its "Over-men": "field marshalls of the Zeit-geist, who today are guiding the world events and dominating the lives of men. It is a Life so near ourselves that we think it is ourselves, and yet so vast that we vaguely identify it with the universe" (823). "Over-men" are living lives that direct regular human lives without humans' knowledge. Though the professor protests that he "means nothing metaphysical or theological" (823), this is precisely what he offers. The "Over-men" occupy roughly the same position as the Greco-Roman deities of classical antiquity. As if to underscore his disingenuity, the professor reinvokes the spiritual when he proclaims that "I will not merely know this Over-life. I will see it with my *Soul*" (823).[15] When the husband begins to see it as well, the apparent spirituality of these "Over-men" gives way to their generic and temporal situation, to their medievalism. When the husband sees "one of the Over-men – his deeds, his world, his life, or rather Life of lives" (823) he sees a castle, which is also a sort of "mill" (824). At the portcullis, he sees a knight on horseback, with visor down: Sir Guess of Londonton is an "An Over-man – Immortal – All Powerful" (825). We soon learn that he is on a quest to find the Golden Sword which he must use to strike the African Queen of Iron in the arm. This will expose her daughter, the Princess Steel. The daughter is at first inanimate, and he will have to fling her into the fires of hell – to forge her – in order to produce the beautiful creature he seeks. No quest worth reading about, however, is simple: he teams up with the Lord of the Golden Way, the owner of the Golden Sword. They strike a deal that Sir Guess will gain the princess as his lady and Golden Way will have her treasure. When it becomes clear that her body and her treasure are one and the same, an epic battle worthy of medieval romance ensues. To the extent that these "Over-men's" lives are meant to dictate the world's motions, there is little difference between their roles and those of the classical gods, whose contests over beauty, for instance, were used to explain the Trojan Wars.

The knights and their battle, their armor, with visors, and settings at castles with portcullises evoke the Middle Ages. So do the story's transformations. For the princess to spring forth from the stricken queen's arm evokes not only the deific births among the classical gods – Athena springing forth from Zeus's head, for instance; but it also mimics medieval romance themes, such as the so-called lump-child motif that appears in the late thirteenth- or early fourteenth-century romance *King of Tars*. In that

---

[15] My emphasis.

text, a Muslim sultan and a Christian princess marry. Their offspring is a lifeless, faceless, boneless lump of undifferentiated flesh. When the sultan converts to Christianity, his black skin miraculously turns white as a condition of conversion and the lump-child miraculously transforms into a beautiful little white baby boy.[16] Whether Du Bois read *Tars* is immaterial, though a scholarly edition of the text had become available by 1882;[17] his invocation of the motif establishes that he knew of similar transformations in premodern literature, whether in the *Tars* or in Arthurian texts such as *The Turke and Sir Gawain* (c. 1500). The transformational nature of Du Bois's tale cements its medievalizing provenance.

The knights' positions as Over-men, and that their experiences comprise Over-life, means that the Over-life of the modern world, in which the professor and his new students sit some forty-stories up in a bustling, modern, technologically advanced New York, is in fact medieval and chivalric. That history influences contemporary life is no surprise, but "The Princess Steel" suggests that history is playing itself out contemporaneously with modernity. History, inasmuch as the medievalism of the narrative allows it to stand in for history, *directs* modernity. Two events in particular emphasize the contemporaneous and directive nature of the chivalric story. The knights battle for the princess when Golden Way realizes that her body is her treasure: "'her hair is silver and her eyes are golden, and,' he whispered 'mayhap there be jewels crusted on her heart'" (823). Aware that Golden Way would murder his bride, Sir Guess defends her. In the battle, Guess is mortally wounded. The princess keeps watch over his body, offering mystical incantations meant to heal him. The husband hears her proclaim,

> I watch and ward above my sleeping
> lord till he awake and then woe World! when
> I shake my curls a-loose. (829)

The old professor then asks her "What then? O Princess?" She responds by pulling a single curl and flinging it. It hurtles past Chicago, past Omaha, over the Great Plains, and it plunges into San Francisco. There "the world whirled," and the Great San Francisco earthquake of April 1906 occurs. In it, some 3,000 were killed. She flings another, and "far down in Valparaiso the earth sighed and sank and staggered" (829). In

---

[16] For more on the *King of Tars'* investments in identity and transformation, see Whitaker, *Black Metaphors*, 20–47.

[17] The Vernon and Simeon version (VS) of the *King of Tars* appears in Krause, ed. "Kleine Publikationen aus der Auchinleck-hs, XI: The King of Tars."

the Valparaiso, Chile earthquake, also of 1906, nearly 4,000 people were killed and some 20,000 injured. According to the professor's megascope, the most pressing events of the modern day are directly dictated by a medievalizing romance playing out in the Over-life, on a higher and usually inscrutable plane of existence.

Du Bois posits the Middle Ages as a tool for examining human sovereignty in all three periods here discussed – before World War I, between the world wars, and after World War II. But they are deployed with signal differences that illumine the many facets of medievalism. The Over-life's implications for sovereignty in "The Princess Steel" are rather exclusive: the Over-men are free, constrained by nothing other than their attempts to assert their wills over one another. The humans – the husband, the wife, the professor, and all New York – are not sovereign. Their fates are instead controlled by events occurring on a plane that most of them, save the husband and the professor, do not know exist. In Du Bois's prewar period, when his medievalism was shaped mainly by his encounters with Hegel, the denizens of the Middle Ages exhibit a god-like freedom that is not yet available to regular humans. In fact, the Over-life's freedom and human freedom are mutually exclusive; the former constrains the latter. The bondsman has not yet realized that he can obtain the Over-life.

Dark Princess and the Interwar Period

In Du Bois's 1928 novel *Dark Princess: A Romance*, the Black American protagonist Matthew Towns comes of common stock. At the end of the text, he consummates his relationship with Kautilya, the princess of Bwodpur on the Indian subcontinent. The novel concludes on Matthew's mother's farm in Virginia, where they celebrate their son's birth, along with jubilant attendees representing Christianity, Buddhism, Islam, and Hinduism. The ending has been called by Claudia Tate a "messianic masque," and it would be easy to take the conclusion as a culmination of Du Bois's dialectic: it might seem that the story's main characters attain something like lordship via others' recognition of their power.[18] The novel offers instead a kind of god-like power, an achievement of the Over-life in its characters, that disables the dynamics of double consciousness. The novel resolves in a unification of the split subject that offers a way forward toward the unification of the collective human spirit torn asunder by World War I.

[18] Tate, *Psychoanalysis and Black Novels*, 62.

Dark Princess is every bit a medievalizing romance. Matthew follows a pattern common to several subgenres of medieval romance – most notably Arthurian and *family* romances. In those subgenres, a text begins with a chivalric hero or heroine who is presented a seemingly insurmountable obstacle. In *Gawain and the Green Knight* (c. 1390s), for instance, Sir Gawain is obliged to quest for the green knight's green chapel in order to receive an axe blow that will likely be fatal. He finds the green knight, survives the blow, and triumphs in other adventures along the way. He returns victorious to King Arthur and his fellow knights of the Round Table. For the part of family romance, take the narratives that make up the literary "family" known as the Constance Group, which includes the *King of Tars* and Chaucer's *Man of Law's Tale* (c. 1390s). In Chaucer's version, a beautiful Christian princess sets out from Rome in order to marry the Muslim Sultan of Damascus for political reasons. She ultimately creates a new nuclear family in Northumbria, a kingdom in pagan Britain, and then combines her new English family with her family of origin when she returns to Rome. In both forms of romance, a hero/ine must leave their home and family, have an adventure in which they travel significant distances and overcome impossible odds, and then return to that family or group in which they started.[19] Matthew's masculinity, the novel's concern with family relations and the creation of new family groups, and the extensive travels Matthew undertakes after he leaves his home places of the United States and medical school, make it a modern variation that features elements of traditional chivalric and Arthurian as well as family romance.

Though it never mentions the "Over-men" or the "Over-life," Matthew's story continues to engage the themes that animate "The Princess Steel." The tale begins with Matthew's inability to continue his medical training at the University of Manhattan. The dean informs him that he cannot register for his rotation in obstetrics because it would require that he, a Black man, deliver the babies of white patients. "Well, what did you expect?" the dean sneers at him. After throwing "his certificates, his marks and commendations straight into the drawn white face of the Dean," Matthew boards a ship to Antwerp and to new adventures

---

[19] Family romances, according to Heng, *Empire of Magic*, "feature women, and sometimes, children" and "offer conventional feminine performance" (185). They concern "family relations" and "explore the central taboos identified by Freud many centuries later," including erotic lineaments and sexual politics such as but not limited to incest, "while still retaining a specifically medieval contextuality" (387, n. 3).

in Europe (4).[20] Like the heroes of romance, Matthew leaves home. After the landing in Antwerp, he does not know where he will go next: France, Germany, Russia, the Near or Far East (4–5). All are options. The dean is much like the Over-men of Du Bois's earlier text. The direction of Matthew's life, if not his exact choices, are controlled by him. The dean's choices dictate Matthew's motions. They dictate that he sets off in motion.

Much of *Dark Princess* is about Matthew's attempts to take matters into his own hands, to become an Over-man himself. Sitting in a café in Berlin, he laments that, "in leaving white, he had also left black America – all that he loved and knew." "God!," he pines, "he never dreamed how much he loved that soft, brown world which he had so carelessly, so unregretfully cast away" (7). Then he sees Princess Kautilya. Her skin is "darker than sunlight and gold … lighter and livelier than brown" (8). "Slim and lithe, gracefully curved," she bears a regal air and is "radiantly beautiful" (8). Matthew begins his hero's journey in earnest when a white American approaches her disrespectfully. Matthew punches him and, with the princess, flees in a taxi. The rest of the novel features Matthew making his way in the world as, first, a porter who nearly perpetrates a terrorist act when he plans to blow up a train specially chartered by the Ku Klux Klan. Uncomfortable with the act and surprised to find the princess is on the train, he foils the plot and spends time in prison as a result. In another endeavor to take control, he enters political life in Chicago. Finally, he enters a romantic relationship with the princess and achieves a happy ending worthy of a family romance. The novel's conclusion offers a scene that seems designed to position Matthew as an Over-man. When Matthew travels to his mother's farm in Virginia, it is by aircraft. At the princess's behest, he is to arrive on the first of May, an auspicious date in the romance tradition – May is the month in which medieval romances' action often begins. Matthew has not flown before and he is fearful, but soon "the whole thing became symbolic." Matthew is "riding Life above the world." He rides "triumphant over the universe. He was the God-man, the Everlasting Power, the eternal and undying Soul. He was above everything – Life, Death, Hate, Love" (305). On his way home to his mother, and to Kautilya, Matthew becomes an Over-man who is, at least until he lands, in control of everything.

The idea of the Over-man is medievalizing, but it is also fitting for the high modernism associated with Du Bois's time. The spirit of modernism – the directive to "make it new" in words attributed to Ezra Pound

---

[20] Pages cited parenthetically.

(1885–1972) – was integral to Harlem Renaissance-era art and literature.[21] In 1926, Du Bois registers a sort of Black modernism when he publishes his address "The Criteria of Negro Art" in *The Crisis*. Blacks, he proclaims:

> have within us as a race new stirrings; stirrings of the beginning of a new appreciation of joy, of a new desire to create, of a new will to be; as though in this morning of group life we had awakened from some sleep that at once dimly mourns the past and dreams a splendid future; and there has come the conviction that the Youth that is here today, the Negro Youth, is a different kind of Youth, because in some new way it bears this mighty prophecy on its breast, with a new realization of itself, with new determination for all mankind.[22]

Du Bois's emphasis on novelty and innovation was of a piece with the sentiments of white thinkers and artists such as Pound. Indeed, Du Bois's writing simply registers an impulse he saw in the writers of his day, including those Black writers he names in the address: Countee Cullen (1903–1946), Langston Hughes (1901–1967), Jessie Redmon Fauset (1882–1961).[23] What has been termed Afromodernism forms when Black artists, working across the African diaspora, "meshed black art forms emerging from lived experience into the art of Europe and the United States to create new forms while retaining their own distinctive styles."[24] Du Bois's Over-men similarly endeavor to create – or at least discover and reveal – something new in the object of steel and the modernity it facilitates. When they collapse time – their European-style medievalizing figures, accoutrements, and chivalry with the Africanizing mythology, which seems timeless – they bring together, like Afromodernists, materials and ideas from the past that together form something new, even as they remain distinct.

Modernism's function in Black American literature is different than its function for white America, and it has been understood through the lens of the debate about whether racial equity is better achieved through "propaganda" or something closer to "art for art's sake."[25] The debate's two sides have been typified by the approaches of Du Bois and Black philosopher, activist, and patron of the arts Alain LeRoy Locke (1885–1954).

---

[21] The slogan "Make it New" appears in a footnote of Pound's 1928 translation of *Da Xue*, the first of the four books of Confucian moral philosophy; see North, "The Making of 'Make It New'."
[22] Du Bois, "Criteria of Negro Art," 292.
[23] Ibid., 294.
[24] Lawson, "Afterword," 233. The term "Afromodernism" emerges from the work of Sweeney and Marsh, "Afromodernism."
[25] Du Bois, "Criteria," 296; and Locke, "Art or Propaganda?"

In "Criteria," Du Bois famously exclaims that "all Art is propaganda and ever must be," and implies that "gaining the right of black folk to love and enjoy" is a worthy propagandistic cause.[26] He points out how white American literary and artistic tastes are propagandistic in the direction of "racial pre-judgment which deliberately distorts Truth and Justice, as far as colored races are concerned."[27] In 1928, Locke responds with "Art or Propaganda?", opining that Blacks have had "little sustained art unsubsidized by propaganda" which "perpetuates the position of group inferiority even in crying out against it." Locke's commitment to "free and purely artistic expression ... as a tap root of vigorous, flourishing living" was well established in the 1920s and would only continue to grow in the early 1930s.[28] Locke biographer Jeffrey C. Stewart writes that Locke "returned repeatedly to the temple of high modernism trying to claim an art tradition all but destroyed by European colonialism, then hijacked by European modernists, and now claimed as the intellectual property of American curators and art historians..."[29] African artistic traditions, it seemed, may have grown out of free and artistic expression, but in the hands of white modernists they had certainly become what Du Bois would have viewed as *white* racial artistic propaganda.

As Bill E. Lawson has put it, the question central to "the great debate" can be distilled down to "What is the role of the black artist and art in advancing the status of black people?"[30] Both Du Bois and Locke register the centrality of this question. The difference between them might be reduced to whether art ought to show the ravages – psychological, spiritual, material – of racial inequality explicitly; for Du Bois, such a demonstration ought to be quite explicit, while for Locke, such "protest" could only produce "the most degraded forms of art possible."[31] Art, for Locke, ought to rise above the quotidian concerns of the artist, including racial experiences, and speak to or even beyond the universal human experience in ways "rooted in self-expression," "self-contained" and without being bogged down by the specifics of everyday material experience, and that evince "a deep realization of the fundamental purpose of art."[32] What's more, the question is especially central to Black thought in the

---

[26] Du Bois, "Criteria," 296.
[27] Ibid., 297.
[28] Locke, "Art or Propaganda?"
[29] Stewart, *The New Negro*, 717.
[30] Lawson, 233.
[31] Stewart, *The New Negro*, 720.
[32] Locke, "Art or Propaganda?"

period between the world wars, "becoming the focus of both blacks and whites."[33] In order to understand Du Bois's medievalism, it is also necessary to understand the role of medievalism within modernism and within Afromodernism in particular.

Medievalism is integral to modernism as the background from which some of modernity's most traditional notions emerge. An age of chivalry and an "age of faith," supplanted by capitalism and reason in early modernity, the period is at once antiquated and charmingly innocent. The quests of its romances are considered honorable and pure, while, for literary critics, modernism is defined by "the collapse of traditional orders ... the corrosion of conventions ... the loss of the social and aesthetic codes" that provided order and narrative coherence."[34] Jonathan Ullyot expounds that "the disintegration of previous aesthetic models ... is the work of modernity" and modernity "*is* that very breaking down."[35] It makes sense, then, that an innocent and pure – and internally coherent – Middle Ages is a platform on which modernism can perform its disunifying work. Ullyot argues that "modernist 'impossible' quest narratives," such as T. S. Eliot's (1888–1965) *The Waste Land* (1922) and Franz Kafka's (1883–1924) *The Castle* (1926), are "indebted to the medieval Grail romance as it was revealed by nineteenth- and twentieth-century philology."[36] These and similar modernist texts are "failed or 'stalled' versions of the Grail romance;" they conform to modernism in a "failure aesthetics" comprising the collapse of previous aesthetic models and the conservation, or continual representation, of the collapse.[37] The unified coherence that medieval literature is supposed to represent is the straw man upon which modernism demonstrates its power.

For Afromedievalism, the Middle Ages does not offer the same backdrop against which to show modernity's incoherence. For Black Americans, access to the Middle Ages is itself a "collapse of traditional orders." The enslavement of Blacks in the United States brought with it the strategic denial of Blacks' history before early modernity and chattel slavery in the United States. I have called this dynamic "the denial of medieval coevalness" and, more broadly, Orlando Patterson has discussed it as "natal alienation," in which the enslaved is denied "all claims on, and obligations to, his parents

---

[33] Ibid.
[34] Hamacher, "The Gesture in the Name," 294.
[35] Ullyot, *The Medieval Presence in Modernist Literature*, 2.
[36] Ibid., 1.
[37] Ibid., 1–9, esp. 1–2.

and living blood relations" and "all such claims and obligations on his more remote ancestors and on his descendants."³⁸ The "genealogical isolate" is "desocialized and depersonalized" and is made devoid of history.³⁹ On Blacks' lack of access to the Middle Ages in particular, Maghan Keita writes that "[i]n much of contemporary Europe, the perception remains that Africans ... have no history of which to speak, and to many it therefore seems self-evident they have no history within premodern Europe."⁴⁰ Positioning Black heroes and heroines within medievalizing narratives, as Du Bois does, is modernist at its very core. To do so disrupts traditional narratives of Black exclusion from the Middle Ages and premodernity. It also disrupts their exclusion from all the positive valences of premodernity: chivalry, honor, purity, innocence. At the same time, it is also modernist in that it asserts the value of incoherence – not that incoherence is something new, as modernism by white authors might be, but that new or previously ignored insights, specifically Black Americans' insights, reveal the inherent incoherence and inaccuracy of traditional historical narratives that assert premodern homogeneity and hegemonic whiteness.

Between the wars, Du Bois's Afromedievalism is defined by thinking on World War I that takes a shape similar to the Hegelian "drama of alterity" and double consciousness. World War I had laid bare and exacerbated the psychic torment of those who strove to be fully "Negro" and fully "American" at once. Chad L. Williams has limned the history of Du Bois's relationship with the war, from his support of Black participation to his doubt about and rejection of the war in 1920 and beyond.⁴¹ In 1918, in a controversial *Crisis* editorial, Du Bois offers a call to arms, writing "Let us, while this war lasts, forget our special grievances and close our ranks shoulder to shoulder with our own white fellow citizens and the allied nations that are fighting for democracy."⁴² By 1924, in what was supposed to be the opening chapter of the book he sought to write on the role of Black American soldiers, he calls the war "a Scourge, an evil, a retrogression to Barbarism, a waste, a wholesale murder."⁴³ In 1930, he

---

[38] Patterson, *Slavery and Social Death*, 5.
[39] Ibid., 38. See Whitaker, "Race-ing the Dragon," 6.
[40] Keita, "Race: What the Bookstore Hid," 130.
[41] Williams, "The Wounded World."
[42] Du Bois, "Close Ranks," 111.
[43] Du Bois, "The Black Man and the Wounded World." Williams, "World War I in the Historical Imagination of W. E. B. Du Bois," 17–18, discusses at length Du Bois's argument, an extension of his 1915 essay, that wealthy individuals, or the "Dominant Wills," misused the war to subvert democracy and redouble their suppression of the world's non-white peoples. Williams, "The Wounded World," also quotes Du Bois's condemnation of the war.

continues in a letter to the pacifist Disciples of Christ minister and editor of *The World Tomorrow* Kirby Page (1890–1957), "Instead of a war to end war, or a war to save democracy, we found ourselves during and after the war descending to the meanest and most sordid of selfish actions, and we find ourselves today nearer moral bankruptcy than we were in 1914."[44] All the while, foremost on Du Bois's mind was the conflict and confluence of Black and American identities.[45] As early as 1915, Du Bois argues that World War I had its roots in European competition and jealousies over "the exploitation of the wealth of the world mainly outside the European circle of nations … in Asia, and particularly in Africa."[46] Such exploitation and the resulting war are animated by a "new democratic despotism" in which laborers and "average" citizens of Western democracies were promised a share of imperialist wealth. Capital and labor were, he argued, united in order to provide "wealth, power, and luxury for all classes on a scale the world never saw before."[47] Nevertheless, such opportunity brings with it jealousies and competitions enough to produce a global war. The only solution, for those who "desire peace and the civilization of all men," he contends, is to "extend the democratic ideal to the yellow, brown, and black peoples."[48] In other words, the cause of the war is the oppression of the world's non-white people while the white world sought, at least nominally, to include its laboring class in the amassment and enjoyment of wealth. Since that inclusion increases the wealth required, competition and racialized exploitation grows more fierce until world war is inevitable. Only the inclusion of all the world's people can drive an equity that resists, even obviates, warfare. It is only the reunification of all humanity under democracy and wealth-sharing – a reunification akin to the imagined solution to the Black American's double consciousness – that might put an end to the psychic and material torments of war.

Indeed, *Dark Princess* demonstrates the potential of Afromedievalist modernism when it uses Du Bois's interwar thought to propose an answer

---

[44] Du Bois, Letter to Kirby Page, June 24, 1930 (quoted in Williams, "The Wounded World," and Williams, "World War I in the Historical Imagination of W. E. B. Du Bois," 20.
[45] Williams, "World War I in the Historical Imagination of W. E. B. Du Bois," treats at length Du Bois's disappointment at the treatment of Black soldiers during and after the war, and at his own inability to complete a book-length study that would establish the greatness of their accomplishments.
[46] Du Bois, "African Roots of War," 711.
[47] Ibid., 709.
[48] Ibid., 712.

to the problem of double consciousness. In asserting the incoherence of white hegemonic understandings of the Middle Ages, Du Bois also asserts that unification of the Black subject, and with him all humanity, is possible. Though "The African Roots of War" is published thirteen years before *Dark Princess*, the essay lays out the character and adventures of Matthew Towns. It presages the plot of the novel when it asserts that in order to achieve lasting peace, "[r]acial slander must go," and asks who can make that happen:

> In the Orient, the awakened Japanese and the awakening leaders of New China; in India and Egypt, the young men trained in Europe and European ideals … But in Africa? Who better than the 25 million grandchildren of the European slave trade, spread through the Americas and now writhing desperately for freedom and a place in the world? And of these millions, first of all the ten million black folk of the United States, now a problem, then a world salvation.[49]

In *Dark Princess*, the World Coalition of Darker Peoples that Towns confronts comprises representatives from precisely these regions: The princess brings him to a meeting of representatives including a "Japanese, faultless in dress and manner;" "two Indians, one a man grave, haughty and old," and another "a young man, handsome and alert;" "two Chinese, a young man and a young woman;" "an Egyptian and his wife;" and "a rather stiff Arab who spoke seldom" (18). In their discussion of how to combat European domination and global racism, they question "the ability, qualifications, and real possibilities of the black race in Africa or elsewhere" (21). Much as Du Bois asks in 1915, the coalition asks, to the question of how to relieve oppression: "but who will do it?" Towns responds: "American blacks … come out of the depths – the blood and mud of battle. And from just such depths, I take it, came most of the worth-while things in this old world … some of the noblest blood God ever made is dumb with chains and poverty."[50] Towns, like Du Bois in "African Roots," makes precisely the argument that American Blacks are up to the task. His adventures depict him as one who strives to do this work – in and through his subject position as a Black American man – and the messianic ending offers a vision of interreligious, interracial, and global salvation. Matthew, now an Over-man, is a unified subject who has overcome double-consciousness. Madhu, Matthew's child with Kautilya, extends that unification unto one of all humankind.

---

[49] Ibid., 714.
[50] Du Bois, *Dark Princess*, 18–23.

"Color and Democracy" after the Wars

In the immediate aftermath of World War II, Du Bois continues to lament the problem of colonized peoples as he did in 1915, and he is direct about the fact that World War II has done little to address their plights. In his *Color and Democracy*, published in 1945, as the war is ending, he argues that European civilization, whose merits the war has thrown into question and whose stability has been proven contingent, must no longer be the gold standard for global aspirations. He leaves intact the notion that democracy should be that gold standard when he prefaces the book: "Henceforth the majority of the inhabitants of earth, who happen for the most part to be colored, must be regarded as having the right and the capacity to share in human progress and to become copartners in that democracy which alone can ensure peace among men."[51] He criticizes 1944's Dumbarton Oaks accords for expecting "a peace resting on force [to] ensure the defense and rebirth of civilization" and for ignoring the extent to which World War II was "the result of race hate, and of colonial might based on racial repulsions."[52] Indeed, he argues, to properly ensure a world of peace will require attention to the situation – especially economic disadvantage – of colonized and formerly colonized peoples. It requires attention to race and racial disparagement. As Carter G. Woodson puts it, "What the author is demanding is the destruction of the European empires; for exploitation, trade and subordination of weaker peoples constitute the foundations upon which the European empires are built."[53] Ultimately, to ensure world peace requires the presence of colonized nations and their peoples as equals at the bargaining table with the Great Powers.

Equality requires not only the extension of economic power nor merely the extension of democracy unto the "yellow, brown, and Black peoples" of the world. It also requires an equal share of access to, and ownership of, history. In many ways, *Color and Democracy* is a continuation of the thoughts and themes that had long dominated Du Bois's work: racism, inclusion, the political implications of cooperation between allied states, and specifically between what he presented in *Dark Princess* as a World Coalition of Darker Peoples. Though the Middle Ages do not figure heavily in *Color and Democracy*, the text offers insight into its writer's thoughts on humans' freedom vis-à-vis history, and how to deploy that relationship

---

[51] In Du Bois, *The World and Africa and Color and Democracy*, ed. Gates, 241.
[52] Ibid., 246.
[53] Woodson, "Color and Democracy," 343.

in order to influence the future; the medieval period rates only one mention in that text, and that is in order to compare modern colonialist land hoarding with aristocratic land accumulation and the disempowerment of peasant farmers in the later Middle Ages.[54] That tenant farming elicits a mention of the European Middle Ages signals that the period remains important to Du Bois's thought on one of the most central components of colonial power and postcolonial negotiation: the production of wealth and its implications for claims to sovereignty.

Though Du Bois's nonfiction works – *Souls* or "The Criteria of Negro Art," for instance – had long mentioned the Middle Ages, his interest in medieval literature, history, and culture finds its fullest expression in the genres, characters, and plotlines he employs in his fictional work, including the "The Princess Steel" and *Dark Princess*;[55] that is, until after World War II and the publication of *Color and Democracy*. Though *Color and Democracy* itself gives the Middle Ages short shrift, an identically titled 1947 speech delivered to the George Washington Carver Society in Schenectady, New York, gives a full-throated scholarly and activist voice to Du Bois's Afromedievalist modernism. While Du Bois's earlier medievalism had been interested in the intersection of medieval notions of chivalry and honor with the technological promise of modernity and eventually how the postwar reunifications of the Black and human subjects might be catalyzed by the tropes of medieval romance, the post-World War II iteration found in the "Color and Democracy" speech directly and explicitly addresses the uses, misuses, and implications of history for Black people's sovereignty and self-determination.

Near its beginning, the speech offers an historical survey of blackness's place in classical antiquity through modern day, in order to show how aberrant are modern racist views of blackness and Black people. After opening with the nineteenth-century provenance of the idea that it was "scientific fact that colored peoples did not have the ability to share in

---

[54] Ibid., 267. The Middle Ages figure more heavily in Du Bois's *The World and Africa*, published only a year after *Color and Democracy*, but in that text they mainly appear in the vein of comparing Africa's social and economic achievements in the later Middle Ages, the fourteenth and fifteenth centuries, with Europe's. Late medieval West Africa "had a more solid politico-social organization, attained a greater degree of internal cohesion and was more conscious of the social function of science than Europe" (Du Bois, *The World and Africa and Color and Democracy*, ed. Gates, 103).

[55] In his 1926 "Criteria of Negro Art," written in praise of Carter G. Woodson upon his receipt of the Springarn medal, Du Bois registers his reliance on the Middle Ages for negotiating the contemporary world, writing "We are remembering that the romance of the world did not die and lie forgotten in the Middle Age [sic]; that if you want romance to deal with you must have it here and now and in your own hands" (326).

modern civilization and particularly in modern political democracy," he talks about Greek veneration of classical Ethiopia and then moves on to discuss medieval European "romantic respect" for the "black world."[56] He discusses three medieval European matters: The first is the life and depiction of Saint Maurice, a third-century CE Egyptian military commander – Du Bois terms him a "prince" – in the Roman army who became the patron saint of the Holy Roman Empire. Maurice was depicted with undeniably Black African features from the mid-thirteenth century onward in the environs of the seat of the Empire in Germany, especially at Magdeburg. Du Bois then turns to the popular medieval romance *Parzival*, by the German Wolfram von Eschenbach, in which the chivalric Arthurian knight Parzival's half-brother Fierefiz shares his white European father with Parzival while his mother is a Black African queen. Fierefiz is spotted, black and white, to denote his heritage, and he is also shown to be a fully courageous and worthy chivalric knight. Finally, Du Bois cites the Black Madonnas – he calls one a "Black Virgin Mary" – popularly venerated at Chartres and other cathedrals.[57] He positions the Middle Ages as a period whose race-thinking is more advanced than, and an aspirational model for, modernity. The story of Fierefiz and Parzival "points toward the bridging of the gaps between creeds and races and is of great significance in revealing the thought of enlightened and civilized society of Europe in the thirteenth century."[58] The era ushered in by European colonialism in the New World, and with it the mass enslavement of African people, brings the degradation of and disrespect for labor: "The result of the African slave trade and slavery on the European mind and culture was to degrade the position of labor and the respect for humanity as such."[59] The early modern period might have, according to Du Bois, brought "a new realization of beauty, a new freedom of thought and religious belief," had not "the temptation to degrade human labor [been] made vaster and deeper by the incredible accumulation of wealth based on slave labor."[60] The Middle Ages, for Du Bois, represents a time when double-consciousness and the splitting of the racialized subject had not yet occurred. The period offers a model of "enlightenment" and "civility" that promises the full humanization and sovereignty of Black subjects.

---

[56] Du Bois, "Color and Democracy," 2–3.
[57] Ibid., 3–4.
[58] Ibid., 4.
[59] Ibid.
[60] Ibid., 7.

In 2021, more than seventy years after Du Bois's speech, the reverse might seem to be true as the United States, Europe, and the world deal with the growth of far-right, fascist, white nationalist, and white supremacist groups who seek to make the United States and Europe into white ethnostates. These groups argue that whiteness should be the criteria for inclusion in these nations, and that their supposed homogeneous whiteness in the Middle Ages serves as the model.[61] Groups promoting the white ethnostate run the gamut from Matt Heimbach's Traditionalist Worker Party, which gained some fame during the U.S. presidency of Donald Trump and after the deadly 2017 "Unite the Right" rally in Charlottesville, Virginia, to The Base, which has been actively working to create such white ethnostates in the U.S. Midwest and recruits in Europe and globally.[62] Their white supremacist manipulation of history is highly erroneous because medieval Europe was diverse.[63] It is born of natal alienation and the denial of medieval coevalness to Blacks and other people of color. And it is precisely what Du Bois argued against all those years ago. From Du Bois's engagement with Hegelian medievalism through the narrative medievalism of "The Princess Steel" and *Dark Princess* through the explicitly political medievalism in Du Bois's post-World War II speech, the imbrication of the Middle Ages with race and labor politics grows only stronger and more explicit. As Du Bois struggles with first the causes and then the legacies of global war, the Middle Ages are an epistemic tool through which to know history, its receptions and manipulations, and its effects. Du Bois's historical and contemporary political thought posits the Middle Ages as a site of comfort, a home place, in which Black people can be at one with premodern history and the modernity it has engendered.[64] At home in the Middle Ages, they may be no longer self-divided between their knowledge of themselves as a people grounded in history and others' perceptions that they are "genealogical isolates" unmoored from relation and free for exploitation.

---

[61] Dickson, "The Neo-Nazi Has No Clothes."
[62] De Simone and Winston, "Neo-Nazi Militant Group Grooms Teenagers;" Oosting, "FBI: Neo-Nazi Leader Sought 'White Ethno-State' in Michigan's Upper Peninsula."
[63] See work on diversity in medieval London from bioarchaeologist Rebecca Redfern and colleagues: Redfern, et. al., "Written in Bone"; Redfern and Hefner, "Officially Absent but Actually Present."
[64] For more on the Middle Ages and medievalism as a site of comfort and belonging for African Americans, see Whitaker, "B(l)ack Home in the Middle Ages."

CHAPTER 3

Ernst Kantorowicz, Carl Schmitt, and the University of California Regents

Nancy van Deusen

The King's Two Bodies

Immediately recognized for its seminal importance, Ernst H. Kantorowicz's (1895–1963) *The King's Two Bodies: A Study in Medieval Political Theology* has been acclaimed and criticized ever since it first appeared in print in 1957.[1] But the acknowledgment was not universal. The French, at the time, mostly ignored the work, and Kantorowicz would be deceased for over two decades before it was translated into German.[2] Nor was the work itself an expected step in Kantorowicz's career. As Kantorowicz himself admitted in the preface to his study, he had "swerved again" (as in his previous *Laudes regiae*) from "the normal tracks of the mediaeval historian and broke through the fences, this time, of mediaeval Law, for which he was not prepared by his training."[3] What provoked this swerve, I will suggest here, was the immediate questions of the sovereignty of the state, the logic of the exceptional event, and the nature of the emergency situation that requires

---

[1] Reception of *The King's Two Bodies* included, for example, a trenchant discussion by Smalley, "Review Article," 32 and 34, who observed that the book was "like a diet of jam without bread," referring especially to the footnotes being "even more dense and impenetrable than the main text." See Leyser, "Introduction," ix; and Jordan, "Preface," xxv–xxvii. For a longer introduction to this topic, see van Deusen, "Assembled in the Presence of God," 79–81, which shares with this paper passages relating to Kantorowicz's description of his project.

[2] *The King's Two Bodies* was translated into German only in 1990. For the German reception of Kantorowicz, see Fischer, "Ernst Kantorowicz," 103–18. Leyser, "Introduction," observes that "*The King's Two Bodies* is still revered as a classic: translated into several languages, reprinted, commemorated on every conceivable anniversary" (ix). Indeed, the French reception of Kantorowicz increased around the same time as in Germany: see, for example, Boureau, *Histoires d'un historien*; and Cantillon, "Ernst Kantorowicz," which addresses anew the "ignorance" concerning the reality of Kantorowicz's "person" as separated from the "personage" that he fashioned for himself (his personal papers and documents were destroyed). In addition to *The King's Two Bodies*' primary focus on English sources, it may have received a muted reception in Europe because its "theological" arguments had already been covered by Marc Bloch's (1886–1944) study of the significance of the anointment, based on the Old Testament, as a sacral, empowering, event; see Raulff, *Ein Historiker im 20. Jahrhundert*, esp. 15–30, 268–370, and 372–92.

[3] Kantorowicz, *The King's Two Bodies*, xxxv.

a decision, all of which were shaped by events in Kantorowicz's life – the University of California Oath Crisis of 1949–50 – and by his likely engagement with the work of political theorist, Carl Schmitt (1888–1985). As I will show, these questions have continued relevance to this day.

Hoping to avoid the "dangers customary with some all-too-sweeping and ambitious studies in the history of ideas: loss of control over topics, material, and facts; vagueness of language and argument; unsubstantiated generalizations; and lack of tension resulting from tedious repetitions,"[4] Kantorowicz used the fiction of the "king's two bodies" as a unifying principle and crafted a study that brought together the history of a concept, its interpretation, and the relevant texts as documentation within a narrative structure.[5] Moving from the creeds of the early Christian Church to William Shakespeare's (1564–1616) *Richard* II (*c*. 1595) and back again to medieval treatises and iconography, "the king's two bodies" was the one cohesive factor within a study that has been criticized as diffuse and often confusing – though consistently deemed "great." If there was one overriding internal consolidating agent, it was the issue of sovereignty: "How is it that rulers, humans like the rest of us, are able to hold sway? What kind of fictions are in place to enable some to commend the allegiance, even the worship, of others?"[6]

In *The King's Two Bodies*, Kantorowicz explores the invisible nature of corporate office – the corporate body and the visible, physical, body of the king himself, with his normal bodily routines that would fuse him in obvious ways to the generality of other human beings alive at that specific place and time. As the concept was explained in the sixteenth century:

> For the King has in him two Bodies, *viz*., a Body natural, and a Body politic. His Body natural ... is a Body mortal, subject to all Infirmities that come by Nature or Accident, to the Imbecility of Infancy or old Age, and to the like Defects that happen to the natural Bodies of other People. But

---

[4] Kantorowicz, *The King's Two Bodies*, xxxv. Kantorowicz was not trained as a jurist or legal historian, nor was he trained as a political philosopher.

[5] The discovery of the concept of the king's two bodies did not belong to Kantorowicz, but in fact had been studied during the previous century by, for example, F. W. Maitland (1850–1906), whom Kantorowicz refers to as a "Great mediaevalist" and notes that "From his admirably stocked garner of juridical *exempla* Maitland was able to produce case after case illustrating the absurdity of that doctrine" (*The King's Two Bodies*, 5 and 3).

[6] Leyser, "Introduction," x. Kantorowicz, likewise, seems to have been obsessed with similar things in fashioning the fiction of himself. That he was successful is evidenced by the physical design of his *Selected Studies*, collected and edited by his closest disciples (Michael Cherniavsky [1922–1972] and Ralph E. Giesey [1923–2011]) in impressive large format with EK in gold on the cover as a visual indicator of the *figura* Kantorowicz fashioned for himself amongst devoted students.

his Body politic is a Body that cannot be seen or handled, consisting of Policy and Government, and constituted for the Direction of the People, and the Management of the public weal, and this Body is utterly void of Infancy, and old Age, and other natural Defects and Imbecilities, which the Body natural is subject to, and for this Cause, what the King does in his Body politic, cannot be invalidated or frustrated by any Disability in his natural Body.[7]

The relation between these two bodies relied upon, as Kantorowicz states, "truly mysterious forces which reduce, or even remove, the imperfections of the fragile human nature."[8] Because of these mysterious forces, "in sixteenth-century England, by the efforts of the jurists to define effectively and accurately the King's Two Bodies, all the Christological problems of the early Church concerning the Two Natures once more were actualized and resuscitated in the early absolute monarchy."[9]

Absorbed as Kantorowicz was with this pivotal relationship between physical body and office, he drew out this relationship from his own life experience. He reacted to the extraordinary event of the loyalty oath as a historian of the Middle Ages – in contrast with his distinguished Berkeley colleague and friend, a scholar of the Italian Renaissance, Leonardo Olschki (1885–1961). We will examine the force of this reaction beginning first with a few of the aspects of medieval theology most influential to his thinking on the concept of the king's two bodies, followed by Carl Schmitt's (1888–1985) concept of political theology, and finally the emergency situation requiring a decision, the Oath Crisis at the University of California, Berkeley.

Medieval Theology

The king occurred in experiential time while his office was outside time. This situation brings to mind a parallel in Augustine's treatise on free will to the effect that some laws occur in delimited time (as one experiences time in the world), while other laws are untimed and eternal.[10] This dual temporality was an important and intriguing idea that corresponded to a reality that everyone who had lived under a monarchy could appreciate, but the

---

[7] Kantorowicz, *The King's Two Bodies*, 7.
[8] Ibid., 9. "Body politic" and "mystical body" seem to be used without differentiation.
[9] Ibid., 17.
[10] Augustine, *De libero arbitrio*, bk. I, cap. 6, §14–15. For a summary of this seminal topic, see van Deusen, "*Ubi Lex?*"

concept of "the king's two bodies" was also, as Kantorowicz noticed, valid for many centuries, reaching a culmination within political discussions of the fifteenth and sixteenth centuries, particularly in England.

Another conceptual background for "the king's two bodies" would have been available throughout the medieval period to nearly everyone who could read – and even many who could not.[11] The Book of Psalms within the Old Testament makes much of rulership, as well as the office and conduct of a king, especially within his own household. Periodically, throughout the Book of Psalms, the topos of kingship, especially, the spirit of a capacity for rulership, for leadership and decisiveness are all addressed. During the weeklong sequence of medieval liturgical offices, the subject of kingship was addressed as the Psalms were said and sung. These kingship psalms (e.g., Psalms 5, 21, 29, 45, 48, 57, 66) often emphasized or presupposed the dual nature of the king: personal–private–temporal and official–dynastic–eternal.[12]

Similar context for the concept of "the king's two bodies" also occurs in Cassiodorus's (died c. 585) *Commentary on the Psalms*, especially in his attention to the matter of the invisible "body" of the church (*ecclesia*) signified by a crown (*corona*) placed within and encircling the entire world.[13] The visible, immediately apparent, *ecclesia*, here is coterminous with the body of all believers from all times and places, gathered together within the conceptual *figura* of the crown, *corona*. This comparison brings to mind not only the "king's two bodies," but also our bodies, living in time *and* timelessness, in normal daily life as well as in an office: Kantorowicz, for example, held a professorship beyond the tenure of the individual professor, and he made just such a comparison in the pamphlet he published concerning his reaction to the Berkeley Oath Crisis to be discussed later. These significant medieval influences, evident in the documents collected by Kantorowicz for his study of "the king's two

---

[11] Because of this familiarity with the Psalms, formulations from the Psalter seeped into education, as well as political discourse, well into the sixteenth century, see van Deusen, ed., *The Place of the Psalms*.

[12] See van Deusen, "*Laudes regiae*" (some essential background from this article is included in the present study). The *Laudes regiae* incipit (*Christus vincit, Christus regnat, Christus imperat*) introduced a liturgical acclamation customarily sung at the *Gloria* during festive masses when the bishop was present. See Kantorowicz's earlier study, *Laudes Regiae*, which includes an extensive list of manuscripts containing the *Laudes regiae* compiled and interpreted by his colleague, the Berkeley musicologist, Manfred F. Bukofzer (1910–1955).

[13] For more on Cassiodorus's commentary, see van Deusen, "Assembled in the Presence of God," 82. Cassiodorus, *Expositio psalmorum*, Psalm 20, line 74, vol. 1, pp. 183–84. See "Corona visibilis et invisibilis" in Kantorowicz, *King's Two Bodies*, 336–38.

bodies" as well as for his previous study of the *Laudes regiae*, demonstrate that this concept of "the king's two bodies" was by no means new, even in the sixteenth century.

Is this conception of the political (namely, the body politic of the entirety of Christian believers) together with its theological implications (namely, the duality of the two "bodies" of Christ) the basis for Kantorowicz's subtitle that unites the political with the theological? Although Kantorowicz includes no discussion of Cassiodorus in *The King's Two Bodies*, three points should be made about the so-called kingship psalms. First, they had historical validity: that medieval rulers were considered to have received the power to rule – a spirit of leadership – from God. Secondly, they established a connection between temporal rulers and the eternal rule of God, both legitimated by and founded on the structure and normative function of the law. There are timed laws and untimed laws, without measure or terminus. Thirdly, as Cassiodorus does in his commentary on Psalm 20, the abstraction of power becomes a network, a relationship based on leadership that is not bound to a specific place and time. This conceptualization of "corporate identity" is abstract. "Where are the sources of power?" one is tempted to ask. This is a question that was to become personally relevant for Kantorowicz. Where is the network? What are the boundaries and what is the reality of the relationship, especially in the case of perceived network as far-flung, *in absentia*, throughout the whole world, yet nowhere? In other words, *where is* what is not present to the physical eye?

The kingship psalms, the Old Testament David with his kingly figure as well as a human body and personality, the invisible "crown" and corporate identity of Christian believers united from all times and places: all of these were certainly well established and familiar topics when Kantorowicz began collecting material for his study. "The king's two bodies" had received a great deal of discussion and multisided interpretation from Edmund Plowden (1518–1585), whose assembled papers constitute the enormous collection of Frederic Maitland upon which Kantorowicz based a good deal of his footnote apparatus.[14] So, in fact, this topic had been worked over

---

[14] A problem, overall, alluded to in both introductory essays to the 2016 edition is a lack of clarity concerning dates, writers, editions, and reprinted editions, particularly related to Maitland (*Selected Essays*, 1936) and Plowden, *Commentaries or Reports* (London, 1816). This is not, as some have suggested, a school for the writing of history – for future historians – but a mise-en-scène in which Maitland sets Plowden up to provide a frame onto which quotations could be hung. Maitland's papers are extensive. A careful chronology of sources is needed to give an overall sense of organization; for example, one is beguiled throughout the work by Kantorowicz's "mysticism."

very well indeed by the time Kantorowicz began to bring together the gigantic weight of quotations, primarily from Maitland's collection. Often the quotations overwhelm Kantorowicz's discussion, which also frequently lacks directionality and focus. This material and Kantorowicz's reflections upon it – possibly already begun in Germany during in the early years of his career in the 1920s – would eventually concentrate his stance toward and decision concerning what became known as the University of California Loyalty Oath Controversy.

The Oath Controversy

At the beginning of the new academic year, 1949–50, the Regents of the University of California required all faculty to sign the following loyalty oath:

> I do solemnly swear (or affirm) that I will support the Constitution of the United States and the Constitution of the State of California, and that I will faithfully discharge the duties of my office according to the best of my ability; that I am not a member of the Communist Party or under any oath, or a party to any agreement, or under any commitment that is in conflict with my obligation under this oath.[15]

The statement adopted by the Regents on June 24, 1949, explained that "At its birth the University of California was dedicated to the search for truth and its full exposition," and that the University stood for "freedom of the human mind and spirit." Hence:

> The Regents gladly share with the faculty the responsibility to keep the University free from those who would destroy this freedom. Today this freedom is menaced on a world-wide basis by the Communist Party through its determination by fraud, or otherwise, to establish control by the State over the thoughts and expression of thoughts by the individual. Therefore, the Regents reaffirm their declaration of policy adopted in 1940, that membership in the Communist Party is incompatible with objective teaching and with search for the truth. Pursuant to this policy the Regents direct that no member of the Communist Party shall be employed by the University.[16]

---

[15] University of California, Berkeley, University Archives, "Statement adopted by Regents June 24, 1949." For a timeline of events, see University of California, Berkeley, "Loyalty Oath Controversy: Summary of Loyalty Oath Events." For a bibliography on the controversy, see Benson, *Loyalty Oath Controversy*.

[16] University of California, Berkeley, University Archives, "Statement adopted by Regents June 24, 1949."

Kantorowicz was one of thirty-one University of California faculty members who at that time refused to sign the oath.[17] These faculty members all had their reasons. Leonardo Olschki, a Berkeley colleague, a close friend of Kantorowicz's, with whom he held a steady personal correspondence from 1943 to the early 1960s, when both of them passed away, wrote in a letter to Robert Gordon Sproul, the President of the University of California system:

> Although I am not a member of the Communist party, nor under any oath, or a party of any agreement, or under any commitment that is in conflict with my obligations under my loyalty oath to the United States and the State of California, I am unable to sign the form of oath submitted to me in your letter of August 9, 1949, because, in my search for truth and its full exposition, I cannot recognize any authority other than my own conscience and the elemental principles of personal decency and professional honesty on which reposes the authority of a free scholar and academic teacher.[18]

The Regents reacted with a resolution, dated February 24, 1950:

> Further discussions have now been held, and the Regents have decided that, as trustees for the people of California, they must continue to safeguard the freedom of the University against ruthless, fanatical and subversive minorities in the body politic, such as the Communist Party; that any member of the faculty who is or shall become a member of the Communist Party has violated the terms on which he is employed, and is not entitled to tenure, which involves responsibilities as well as privileges, and shall be dismissed, after the facts have been established by the University administration, which shall consult with the Committee on Privilege and Tenure of the Academic Senate, but only as to the adequacy of the evidence of membership in the Communist Party.[19]

Olschki responded in a letter dated September 6, 1950:

> Gentlemen: I am an old scholar who has never been politically active. Nevertheless I was dismissed by Hitler, in 1933, after twenty-five years of teaching at the University of Heidelberg, and again by Mussolini after six years of activity at the University of Rome. Now, in a free country, a University which proclaims to protect "impartial scholarship" and free pursuit of truth is making a political statement the condition for the continuance of my employment.

---

[17] Gilmore, "Fifty Years After."
[18] Olschki, "Letter to Kantorowicz of 30 September, 1949." The collection contains documentation regarding the Berkeley Oath Controversy, as well as correspondence between Olschki and Kantorowicz. As most of the papers and correspondence of Kantorowicz were destroyed at his death, this collection may well be the largest of the correspondence to and from Kantorowicz that exists.
[19] "Excerpt from Regents' Executive Session Minutes of February 24, 1950," 2.

> After having witnessed in other countries the destructive effect of similar compulsory measures on the character of the teachers, the respect of the students, and the standards of academic institutions, I would consider the acceptance of such condition of employment as a betrayal of professional loyalty and my faith in freedom.[20]

Olschki's stance was that of someone who had just written an extremely influential book, *The Genius of Italy*, and his interpretation of humanistic tradition is based on a lifelong study of the question of state, law, and personhood within the Italian Renaissance.

Having also fled Germany and the Hitler regime, Kantorowicz could have replied in similar fashion. But he was no doubt aware of Maitland's goal, in *The History of English Law* (1895), to "harmonize modern with ancient law" as well as to "bring into agreement the personal with more impersonal concepts of governance."[21] And there was more to this present situation than a contrast-pair of the "natural body" with the "body politic." There was a crucial distinction here between, on the one hand, what one as a faculty member might feel either inclined or disinclined to do, for which one might have good personal reasons, predilections, reservations, or animosities, but for which one could take individual responsibility on the basis of one's own personal courage and career; and on the other, the invisible, untimed, "body" one also possessed as a scholar and teacher, an *Akademiker*, in what was for Kantorowicz the European sense.

But it was also for Kantorowicz an inescapable fact. To reiterate this fact is not to inflate the concept of a scholar-teacher, but to place it in a perspective as an office that was unseen, nevertheless a reality, with the scholar-teacher as a member of a corporate body comprising at once all places and times, much like Cassiodorus' *ecclesia*. The person – the tired, defeated, sometimes bewildered faculty member, lumbering along to senility – was timed, mortal, visible, and subject even to a fear of losing his or her appointment; the other "body" was untimed, beyond time. The faculty member could be coerced, bullied, talked, perhaps, into almost anything, as so many were at German universities during the Nazi era;[22] the office of teaching and research remained intact. Or did it?

In the fall of 1950 Kantorowicz wrote *The Fundamental Issue: Documents and Marginal Notes on the University of California Loyalty Oath*. Though

---

[20] Olschki, "Letter to the University of California Regents of 6 September, 1950."
[21] Maitland, *The History of English Law*, 496; Kantorowicz, *King's Two Bodies*, 5.
[22] Ericksen, *Complicity in the Holocaust*.

it was not distributed at the time, on the advice of the attorney litigating the case, it is in my opinion perhaps the clearest, most forthright paper Kantorowicz produced even with his characteristic mixture of notes, texts, and dates. Throughout the document he explains his refusal to sign the oath, stating for example:

> "If you are not a Communist, why can't you sign the oath?" How often has this question been asked and still is asked? The answer is that from the very beginning it was true that "The issue is not Communism; it is the welfare and dignity of our University" (Alumni Letter, August 17, 1950). The forcibly imposed oath with its economic sanctions and encroachments on tenure, rejected almost unanimously by the Faculties of the University of California, was at first one of the most thoughtless and wanton, later one of the most ruthless attacks on the academic profession at large.[23]
>
> ...
>
> Nothing would have been easier for me than to sign, sit back, tend my garden, books, and manuscripts, and be that "naïve professor" that has been caricatured once more during the oath controversy. However, where a human principle, where Humanitas herself is involved I cannot keep silent. I prefer to fight.[24]
>
> ...
>
> Because I refused to act under duress, work under the threat of supervision by vigilantes, yield to compulsion, intimidation, and economic pressure, or even respond to an alternative comparable to an intellectual and moral hold-up; Because I refused to buy and sell my academic position and scholarly dignity at the price of my conviction and conscience.[25]

Kantorowicz's research into medieval canon law comes to the fore here as well as in the future publication of *The King's Two Bodies,* where he discusses various kinds of oaths, such as those between the king and his subjects. "As a historian who has investigated and traced the histories of quite a number of oaths," Kantorowicz observed that "every oath or oath formula, once introduced or enforced, has the tendency to develop its own autonomous life."[26] To summarize an extensive discussion, there is no guarantee that an oath formula imposed on, or extorted from, the subjects of an all-powerful state will, or must, remain unchanged. On the contrary, the consequences of this proposed oath are unpredictable. The seeming "harmlessness" of an oath is not a protection when such a principle is invoked:

---

[23] Kantorowicz, *The Fundamental Issue*, 1.
[24] Ibid., 2.
[25] Ibid., 33 (Marginal Notes, "Why I did not sign").
[26] Ibid. ("Statement Read Before the Academic Senate, Northern Section, June 14, 1949," §1).

I am not talking about political expediency or academic freedom, nor even about the fact that an oath taken under duress is invalidated the moment it is taken, but wish to emphasize the true and fundamental issue at stake: professional and human dignity.

There are three professions which are entitled to wear a gown: the judge, the priest, the scholar. This garment stands for its bearer's maturity of mind, his independence of judgment, and his direct responsibility to his conscience and to his God. It signifies the inner sovereignty of those three interrelated professions.[27]

This *inner sovereignty* of the scholar constituted the untimed, ultrapersonal side of the faculty, in turn the reason for his or her membership in the corporate body of the university, and the reason why he or she was understood to be not simply an employee of the State of California, similar to the gardeners who tended the campus and the cleaning crew. Rather than the professors serving at the whim of the Regents, as the actors and clowns of the Regents' state, the faculty together with the students were thought to constitute the university. They themselves were the institution, the corporate body – the other body – as the thirteenth century had it, "*universitas magistrorum et scholarium*," "The Body Corporate of Masters and Students."[28] Kantorowicz understood the professors of a university as the institution itself, the body corporate. "One can envisage a university without a single gardener or janitor, without a single secretary, and even – a bewitching mirage – without a single Regent. The constant and essence of a university is always the body of teachers and students."[29] Therefore Kantorowicz believed that "For the same reason the professors have certain vested rights in the institution which they both serve and constitute."[30] In other words, they are not "employees" of the Board of Regents, and the Regents are neither shareholders nor paid directors.

Hence, a professor's job is relatively indefinite, that is, not subject to time constraints or bureaucratic function:

> Whether it takes him two days to prepare a single lecture, or two hours, or two minutes or less, is left to him. Whether he revises his lectures by integrating his own research work and that of others, or simply rehashes some textbook, is left to him. Whether he devotes much or little of time

---

[27] Ibid. ("Statement Read Before the Academic Senate, Northern Section, June 14, 1949," §5). Emphasis mine.
[28] Ibid. ("Marginal Notes," §2).
[29] Ibid.
[30] Ibid.

> and care to the M.A. and Ph.D. theses of his pupils, is his own business. It is left to him whether he indulges in research work from which his classes would profit and his university would reap fame.... In short, it is entirely up to him how much of his life, of his private life, he is willing to dedicate to the University to which he belongs and which he, too, constitutes. The exact amount of time he invests is bound by no regulations. It is purely a matter of Passion, of Love, and of Conscience.... [Y]ou can buy labor, but you cannot buy Passion and Love nor the scholarly Conscience.[31]

He adds:

> It is through his conscience that he acquires vested rights in his office. By this conscience, which is inseparable from his genuine duties as member of the academic body corporate.... Trade and profession are not identical. A profession, as the word itself would suggest, is based upon conscience, and not upon working hours as in the case of modern trades, or on Time in general.[32]

The office of the professor, then, is beyond time and measure, as with the office of the king, above and beyond the ordinary constraints and boundaries of a life lived. In other words, the sovereignty of the "office" of a university professor is evidenced by his or her ability to make a decision within an exceptional – and ultimately extremely serious – situation.

Those dissenting University of California faculty members were all subsequently and unceremoniously fired or resigned. Some of them were rehired; some sued the University of California for back-pay and the benefits they had been denied. The case is well known, an admonition to us all. Kantorowicz eventually left Berkeley for the Institute for Advanced Study, Princeton, where he worked over and published *The King's Two Bodies*.[33] But at the same time, Kantorowicz wrote two pivotal and closely related essays that informed one another. One, *The Fundamental Issue*, concerned the political and moral state of the university of the present. The other concerned the sovereignty and authority of the reigning monarch within the English fifteenth and sixteenth centuries.[34] Both essays concerned making decisions. Both essays were anchored in the past, not only in Augustine and Cassiodorus, but also more recently the 1920s in France and in Germany. In other words, the historical situation and documentation served as a laboratory for the present, as Marc Bloch had pointed

---

[31] Ibid. Emphasis mine.
[32] Ibid. Emphasis mine.
[33] See Lerner, *Ernst Kantorowicz*, 333.
[34] Kantorowicz, "*Pro patria mori* in Medieval Political Thought."

out in 1924.³⁵ Secondly, the issue of the king's two bodies continues to be relevant within the academic profession as to how scholar-teachers regard their work and vocations. We have observed this relevance in Kantorowicz's impassioned plea for the corporate body of the university composed of faculty and students – not primarily a business venture with top-down management of career administrators – as well as the conscience that is required of each member of this body in order to make a considered decision in exceptional situations.³⁶

Political Theology

The Berkeley episode and Kantorowicz's concurrent study and writing project, *The King's Two Bodies*, merged in the book's subtitle: *A Study in Medieval Political Theology*. The subtitle also draws on Kantorowicz's acquaintance, even engagement, with the influential concept of "political theology" developed by Carl Schmitt in his 1922 publication, *Politische Theologie (Political Theology)*.³⁷ Schmitt developed and expanded his interpretation of this concept, especially of the concept of the "political," throughout his career, until his death at ninety-seven in 1985. Pithy captions are hard to come by, and "political theology" was simple, succinct, and provocative. It was attention-getting when it appeared in the early 1920s, harboring fundamental, even quintessential, issues that persisted many decades later in Kantorowicz's work, but without the conceptual foundation that gave coherence to the concept in Schmitt's publication.

Neither the "political" nor what, specifically, is conceptualized as the "theological" is convincingly clarified in *The King's Two Bodies*. For Schmitt, the nature and source of sovereignty is based, most importantly, on the will, capacity, and authority to decide in the *exceptional* case, the "Ausnahme,"³⁸ or even "the emergency." Routine and customary statutes, or the everyday managing of legal practice could be done more or less by

---

[35] Marc Bloch, *Les rois thaumaturges*.
[36] See Jordan, "Introduction."
[37] See Kahn, "Political Theology."
[38] Schmitt, *Political Theology*, 16–35; see Strong, "Foreword," xi–xvi, in which the translational difficulty of "Ausnahme," as well as what constitutes a genuine "decision" is discussed. That Schmitt had not received attention in the United States during the postwar period is due, in part, to the fact that an English translation, by George Schwab (who conferred personally with Schmitt) was completed only in the year of Schmitt's death, 1985.

remote control, even to "transcend the personal sphere" in bureaucracy.[39] At this point, the personhood of the sovereign emerges in an exceptional situation that requires "decisionism" and breaks the normal routine. In addition, the specifically *sovereign* nature of the one who rules is gauged by the will, opportunity, capacity, and authority to make the decision appropriate specifically to that situational instance. The "theology" embedded in this discussion comes from Thomas Hobbes's (1588–1679) *Leviathan* (1651), as Carl Schmitt explains, and this is the foundational argument that gives political theology both political and theological status – the "bread" or structural scaffold that the Oxford medieval historian Beryl Smalley (1905–1984) thought was missing from Kantorowicz's book.[40] As with Hobbes's "miracle" in which God interrupts the normal and predictable, or customary, continuity of natural laws, with a dispositive "event" or "emergency," so the "sovereign," by virtue of his authority, alters the normal, conventional, course of action that would be expected by legal convention, and on that account would otherwise arouse no particular interest. The legal apparatus would simply function normally and predictably without the intervention of a "sovereign." This "decision" then defines both the "political" as well as the "exceptional," referring to a specific divine agency in the world, performing a miraculous intervention, that could be regarded as a "theological" interruption of what would normally otherwise have taken place through natural processes.

Between Schmitt and Kantorowicz, the mental process, authority, and capacity of a jurist and political philosopher contrasts with that of a historian, collecting references as documentary evidence from manuscripts and archived collected papers for a topic or set of topics already in place, or even completely familiar at the time.[41] What is important here is Schmitt's sheer tenacity for dealing over many decades with the two concepts of the "political" and the "theological" and their conjunction.[42] Schmitt's concept of political theology was familiar enough by the time Kantorowicz was working on his study.[43] And many scholars have pointed out the similarities

[39] Strong, "Foreword," xxiii.
[40] Smalley, "Review Article," 32 and 34.
[41] This is one of the reasons for the success of Kantorowicz's work, namely the familiarity of the topics, emerging as they did in the 1920s, such as the ritual of anointing in Marc Bloch, *Le roi thaumaturges*.
[42] Lerner, *Ernst Kantorowicz*, 347, appears to waver in his opinion, first, acknowledging Kantorowicz's debt to Schmitt and stating that work on *The King's Two Bodies* certainly began in the early 1930s when Kantorowicz was in contact with the Frankfurt intellectual milieu, although later dismissing this notion altogether. See also Leyser, "Introduction," xiii.
[43] Leyser, "Introduction," xiii, suggests that *The King's Two Bodies* was conceived and even partially written in the 1930s before Kantorowicz left Germany. See also Lerner, "Kantorowicz and Continuity," 106–10.

between Kantorowicz's political theology and Schmitt's.[44] In the opening paragraphs of his preface to *The King's Two Bodies,* Kantorowicz located the book's origins in a conversation with Max Radin (1880–1950) in 1945, in Berkeley, far away from his German past.[45] It was only later, he explains, that the book turned into a study of political theology, "which had not at all been the original intention."[46] Nevertheless, Kantorowicz would have had to have been completely insensitive to his intellectual surroundings, as well as important publications in the German language, if he had not been strongly influenced by the emergence, publication, and continuing discussion of Schmitt's *Political Theology*. Although the circle of poet Stefan George (1868–1933) is given more credit for influencing Kantorowicz's developing ideas,[47] Kantorowicz was certainly within the Frankfurt aegis. In fact, his years in Germany until his emigration in 1938 coincided with, and were in many ways parallel to, the intellectual trajectory of Schmitt. Political theology, as a notion and phrase productive for both Schmitt and Kantorowicz, did not suddenly appear from nowhere.[48]

Carl Schmitt was one of the most influential political theorists of the twentieth century.[49] In contrast to Kantorowicz's massive, often rambling volume, Schmitt's seminal book, *Political Theology*, is concise and focused.[50] One is never left in doubt as to his focus. The issue is "sovereignty," which is neither given to, nor taken up, by just any contender, but rather relies upon an ability to, and authority behind, making decisions. "Decisionism," then, as it came to be known, was based on an exceptional situation, the "*Ausnahme*," or extraordinary circumstance, the "event"

---

[44] Davis, "Sense of an Epoch," p. 65, n. 19, suggests a resonance, for example, between Kantorowicz's concept of the king's two bodies and Schmitt's "discussion of the priesthood being made into an office."
[45] Leyser, "Introduction," xiii.
[46] Kantorowicz, *King's Two Bodies*, "Preface," viii.
[47] Leyser, "Introduction," x.
[48] Kantorowicz, "Mysteries of State," had a particular idea of how the term "political theology" was popularized: "Under the impact of those exchanges between canon and civilian glossators and commentators – all but non-existent in the earlier Middle Ages – something came into being which then was called 'Mysteries of State,' and which today in a more generalizing sense is often termed 'political theology'" (67). Kantorowicz adds the footnote: "The expression, much discussed in Germany in the early 1930s, has become more popular in this country, unless I am mistaken, through a study by George LaPiana [*sic*];" he means George La Piana (1879–1971) and his "Theology of History."
[49] Schmitt's influence since the 1920s has not abated. But Lerner, *Ernst Kantorowicz*, 347, treats Schmitt superficially; he bases Kantorowicz's freedom from any influence of German-language intellectual life both previous to his emigration and thereafter on a conversation at a dinner party, Autumn, 1949, at which Kantorowicz "insisted on his ability to write history free of the influences of his own time."
[50] Schmitt, *Der Nomos der Erde*, 5, stated that an author was not always responsible – nor could he be held responsible – for the use and interpretation of what he had written.

that rose out of, but was not contained within, ordinary legal practice, an everyday application of convention, or what could be seen as "common law." It is the nature of this event – the totally exceptional situation – that constitutes for Schmitt, on the one hand, the "political" in that it dealt directly with persons, personal circumstances, the application of decisions to specific personal situations rather than a mechanistic bureaucracy operating primarily by remote control, and on the other hand, the "theological," since the *Ausnahme* could be viewed as a kind of "miracle," an interruption by the will of God into the ordinary, everyday, working of "natural" laws. This argumentation, concise as it was, had Hobbes's *Leviathan* to its credit, as Schmitt also points out.[51]

For Schmitt, "the political" was not a field of economic competition or debate adversaries (*Diskussionsgegner*) or private antipathy; rather it was the field of *kämpfende Gesamtheit*, entity opposed to entity; *hostis* not *inimicus*, for the German did not have a word, according to Schmitt, that could distinguish between private and political forms of enmity.[52] Schmitt argued that "all law is 'situational law'."[53] The reality of human life was that the unpredictable case in which sovereignty must be exercised was the crux of the matter. Life could never be contained within, or reduced to, a set of rules: "The exception is more interesting than the rule. The rule proves nothing; the exception proves everything: It confirms not only the rule but also its existence, which derives only from the exception."[54] It is also in the suspension of predictable law that the "theological" breaks into the "political."

I contend that neither the "political" nor the "theological" was grounded or carefully worked out by Kantorowicz, rather, owing to Schmitt's immense influence, political theology was already familiar as a discussion topic in the 1930s. Search for it as one might, the phrase for Kantorowicz lacks the foundational underpinning and the logical argumentation given it – and revised more or less constantly through his long lifetime – by Carl Schmitt. An exemplification of the corporate versus the personal as well as Schmitt's more powerful idea of the nature of the sovereign as able to make and implement the "exceptional event" through "decisionism,"

---

[51] Schmitt, *Political Theology*, 33, "We can perhaps distinguish two types of juristic scientific thought according to whether an awareness of the normative character of the legal decision is or is not present. The classical representative of the decisionist type (if I may be permitted to coin this word) is Thomas Hobbes" (referring to *Leviathan*, cap. 26).
[52] Strong, "Foreword," xvi; Schmitt, *Der Begriff des Politischen*, 9–10; *The Concept of the Political*, 28.
[53] Schmitt, *Political Theology*, 13.
[54] Ibid., 15.

could not have become more relevant to Kantorowicz during the Berkeley Oath Controversy. His reaction was in part founded upon his understanding of the unification of the corporate and the private individual. In the laboratory of the past Kantorowicz had tested a hypothesis that informed his attitude to and practice in the present.

Conclusions

Even more so than his close friend Olschki, Kantorowicz reacted to the life-changing "exceptional event" of the Berkeley loyalty oath by drawing on the learning he had brought together for his project, *The King's Two Bodies*. But his project itself was thoroughly "medieval" in its compositional methodology in that it was a composite from many sources: the influences of his young adulthood in the 1920s and concept behind Schmitt's political theology and the exceptional experience of the Berkeley case. He gathered the tremendous amount of documentary evidence, particularly from England, during his Berkeley and Princeton years, sometimes drawn from elsewhere, from Schmitt's political theology or Maitland's essays. However, as with medieval composition, the connections between the parts constitute the evidence of mastery. One struggles to describe such a compositional process with contemporary language, loaded as it is with negative connotations: words such as "borrow," "appropriate," "influence," "parody" are used with a suspicion of usurpation, even plagiarism, and certainly a lack of "originality." Medieval authors regarded what was "there" as present for the taking, to be used to the fullest extent and with the degree of mastery to which one had access by talent, training, capacity, and perseverance.[55]

Further, Kantorowicz and Olschki made the same decision in the same unprecedented "exceptional event." Both refused to sign the oath; both lost their positions at the University of California, Berkeley. But the two scholar-teachers made the decision for different reasons, based upon the work that they had been doing for their entire adult lives, as well as the inner dialogue that had gone on for decades regarding this work. In other words, not only did they themselves affect the outcome of their mental labor, but they were also shaped and transformed by it. In the extant correspondence between Kantorowicz and Olschki, their intellectual life as well as their relationships to their professions as scholar-teachers appears

---

[55] See, for example, Constable, "Forgery and Plagiarism"; Hathaway, "*Compilatio*."

to have shaped and arbitrated their common decision to dissent. In this notable, exceptional, instance, not only does one *fashion* one's scholarly work, but one is also, perhaps on the deepest level and most importantly, *fashioned* by one's ideas, the working out of one's mental life, and their articulation.

This foundational concept of decision-based sovereignty was available to Kantorowicz, as readers such as Alain Boureau and Conrad Leyser have noticed.[56] Nevertheless, a disjointedness or unstable structural underpinning was sensed, I believe, by many reviewers, and may have been partly responsible for Kantorowicz's delayed acceptance by the German-speaking scholarly community of his generation. Kantorowicz's work was only decades after his death translated into German for the following reasons: first, perhaps foremost, a good deal of the documentation and quotations used to demonstrate the concept of the king's two bodies is based on a relatively small number of English sources mostly from the sixteenth century, collected together and published in the early twentieth century. The *Problemstellung* therefore was not shored up by a medieval intellectual context, even if the notion of sacral kingship is important for the study of the Middle Ages as many have pointed out. Carl Schmitt's training was juridical; Kantorowicz had a derivative relationship to law, as he himself also acknowledged in his book's introduction. Finally, Carl Schmitt was to hone, refine, reinterpret, and reevaluate his concept of political theology throughout his life; but he was also to test his conclusions in perhaps the most brutal of political environments, and having remained a member of the Nazi party from 1933 to 1945 often "found himself on the losing side of several controversies."[57]

Moreover, Schmitt's notion of sovereignty as the ability, will, and authority to make a decision – particularly decisions exercised in exceptional situations – permeated Kantorowicz's dialogue with the Berkeley affair. These issues of sovereignty, "decisionism," and exception have continued to propel dialogue, as well as dispute, with the two intellectuals, Ernst Kantorowicz and Carl Schmitt today. The phrase "political theology"

---

[56] Leyser, "Introduction," specifically states that "*The King's Two Bodies*, sketched as early as 1935, is in tense dialogue with Schmitt, as its subtitle, *A Study in Medieval Political Theology*, effectively announces. The Book is also, and by the same token, a shadow play about political culture in the modern age" (xv). Boureau, *Histoires d'un historien*, notes that "A reference to Schmitt's work thus seems indisputable. And thus the biographer begins to doubt: did Kantorowicz, despite exile, despite his experiences over the oath of loyalty at Berkeley, remain fundamentally an admirer of the strong state?" (105).

[57] Strong, "Foreword," viii.

maintains persuasive power and in its succinctness is easily appropriated. The motivational, conceptual, energy also anchored within a firm, mature, argumentation, was one reason for Schmitt's lasting influence on German intellectual life throughout his career.[58] Schmitt also continued to provide coherence and stimulus to a wide nexus of prominent German thinkers and writers, emanating from Bonn, Frankfurt, and Berlin: Erik Peterson (1890–1960), Kantorowicz, Walter Benjamin (1892–1940).[59]

Kantorowicz's intellectual resonance was quite different. He drew on ideas from Maitland to Marc Bloch to Cassiodorus, and brought them to an American audience in the emerging discipline of medieval studies in North America. His career was further propelled by American sympathy for his decision to leave Nazi Germany and by the almost cultish fascination of his students.[60] In a sense, Kantorowicz's achievement was quintessentially American: advertisement was at least one reason for the book's fame, and Kantorowicz well knew the value of the short, pithy, provocative, phrase in his subtitle. Lives of the mind within turbulent times: both of these intellectual leaders have left a continuing legacy. Just as Jean-François Kervégan has asked "Que faire de Carl Schmitt?" so we might likewise ask, "What to do with Ernst Kantorowicz?"[61] It is evidence for the continuing energy of their contributions that these questions are still relevant – ever more so, in fact – today.

---

[58] As an example of the staying power, see Kahn, *The Future of Illusion*, in which she notes "a powerful resurgence of interest in the problem of Political Theology, understood as the theological legitimation as religious dimension of political authority," which is related to an "upsurge of religion or religious dimension of secular modernity" (1).

[59] See Geréby, "Carl Schmitt and Erik Peterson."

[60] On the perception of Kantorowicz's politics, see the Introduction in this volume, Perry and Saltzman.

[61] Kervégan, *Que faire de Carl Schmitt?*

CHAPTER 4

Hannah Arendt's Middle Ages for the Left

R. D. Perry

This is a conversation we have had before, unfortunately: the appropriation of medieval history and symbols by the alt-right, neo-Nazis, and white supremacists – whatever you want to call them, it amounts to the same thing – is a supposedly legitimating rhetorical strategy they learned from the original Nazis.[1] Then as now, medievalists fought back against what is often the mischaracterization and misunderstanding that accompanies that appropriation.[2] And because a wider range of intellectuals in those years had seriously studied the Middle Ages, the medievalists were joined by a variety of important figures in fighting against a Nazi medievalism.[3] Indeed, returning to the study of the Middle Ages in order to dispel Nazi myths about it, some of these thinkers even found important intellectual inspiration to address not only the problem of fascism and totalitarianism, but also many of the wider issues of modernity. In the 1930s, Ernst Bloch (1885–1977) critiqued the Nazis' use of the medieval period – specifically their attempt to justify their imperial drive and supposedly utopian aspirations – by explaining just how different the medieval

---

[1] The Nazi appropriation of the medieval past was a complex operation, multifaceted and persistent. On Hitler's infamous attendance of the Oberammergau medieval Passion Play and the wider political and social paroxysms caused by the rise of Nazism, see Waddy, *Oberammergau in the Nazi Era*. As Ernst Bloch makes clear, the German appropriation was deeply interested in medieval politics. Many recent discussions of the issue are concerned with the relationship between Nazi Germany and the Catholic Church (see Steigmann-Gall, *The Holy Reich*) as well as the Nazi appropriation of medieval anti-Jewish hatred (Nirenberg, *Communities of Violence*, troubles any easy association between the two). See generally, the *postmedieval* special issue on "The Holocaust and the Middle Ages" and the introduction by Johnson and Caputo, "The Middle Ages and the Holocaust."
[2] Further work remains, but for a tour of responses to the rising political threat in the decade prior to the outbreak of the war, see Wallace, "Medieval Studies in Troubled Times."
[3] The range of thinkers who studied the Middle Ages, even if they were not themselves self-identified "medievalists," is clear from the figures covered in volumes such as this one; see also the thinkers discussed in Holsinger, *The Premodern Condition*; and in Cole and Smith, eds., *The Legitimacy of the Middle Ages*.

concept of empire and the medieval utopian imagination were.[4] Bloch would remain interested in the Middle Ages, even citing medieval thought as an important forerunner for his own philosophical endeavors, including his own unique take on materialism, in his work from 1952, *Avicenna and the Aristotelian Left*, itself an emulation of medieval form: a commentary on Avicenna's commentary on Aristotle.[5]

Hannah Arendt's (1906–1975) engagement with the Middle Ages is even more profound than Bloch's, and more long-standing. Her doctoral dissertation, *Der Liebesbegriff bei Augustin* (1929; published in English as *Love in Saint Augustine*, hereafter *Love*), was written under the direction of Karl Jaspers (1883–1969) and explored the political connotations of St Augustine of Hippo's (354–430) concept of *caritas*.[6] At the other end of her career, in "Willing" – the second volume of her last work, *The Life of the Mind* (1978; hereafter *Life*) – Arendt returns to Augustine as "the first philosopher of the will" (2.84).[7] What is more, her discussion of medieval thinkers is not limited to Augustine, although he remains a key figure for her: in *Life* alone, Arendt discusses Thomas Aquinas (1225–1274) and John Duns Scotus (1266–1308) at length, as a way of following through on insights she first gleans in Augustine, and in the introduction to *Life* she reflects on medieval conceptions of the *vita activa* and *vita contemplativa*.[8] What these discussions of medieval thinkers show is that Arendt's interest in the Middle Ages extends beyond merely correcting Nazi misappropriations, although she does that too. Arendt uses medieval thought in an attempt to solve some of the most profound problems with modernity: its focus on the individual at the expense of the community and its seemingly contradictory skepticism about the efficacy of individual agency to change history. This essay will detail Arendt's use of the Middle Ages in her response to these two problems, and as such it will be divided into two related parts: the first political and the second phenomenological.

Early in her career, Arendt marshals the Middle Ages primarily as a political antidote to modernity's reliance on the individual. Her thinking at this

---

[4] Ernst Bloch, *Heritage of Our Times*, esp. 117–37 ("On the Original History of the Third Reich"), which includes a discussion of Charlemagne and the Victorines as an attack on Nazi appropriation of the Middle Ages.
[5] Ernst Bloch, *Avicenna and the Aristotelian Left*.
[6] Arendt, *Love and Saint Augustine* (hereafter, parenthetically cited).
[7] Arendt, *The Life of the Mind* (hereafter, parenthetically cited by volume and page number).
[8] Arendt, *Life*, 1.6. She confesses that if she had got her way, her book *The Human Condition* would have been titled *Vita Activa*.

stage largely conflated medieval philosophy with Augustine – a tendency shared by other midcentury intellectuals, even those who would be classified as professional medievalists – and her search in Augustine for political alternatives to modernity is evident throughout her dissertation.[9] The political use of Augustine continues, though, into *The Origins of Totalitarianism* (1951; hereafter *Origins*). At two key points in that work, at moments where the analysis seems the bleakest, Arendt offers up hope by turning to an Augustinian political model. Augustine, in *Origins*, serves as a foil for Thomas Hobbes (1588–1679), whom Arendt identifies as the "the only great philosopher to whom the bourgeoisie can rightly and exclusively lay claim, even if his principles were not recognized by the bourgeois class for a long time," largely because Hobbes is "the only great thinker who ever attempted to derive public good from private interests" (139).[10] The exclusive ownership of Hobbes by the bourgeoisie – and through them, modernity's liberal and then neoliberal order – recalls the way that Arendt discusses Augustine, whom she tends to call the "first Christian philosopher and, one is tempted to add [and she normally does], the only philosopher the Romans ever had" (*Life*, 2.84). But this exclusive group ownership signals fundamental opposition between these two philosophers: to Hobbes's emphasis on private interest, Augustine offers love of one's neighbor; to Hobbes's social contract, which is meant to end something, the war of all against all, Augustine emphasizes the capacity for people to begin something new.

But the political includes the personal,[11] even if it does not solely rely on individual interests, and so, in the later part of Arendt's career, she delineates the phenomenological modes in which individuals interact with the world and are therefore able to create the political realm.[12] She begins this exploration in *The Human Condition* (1958), which focuses

---

[9] The reference here is to D. W. Robertson, Jr., and can be seen most clearly in such work as his *Preface to Chaucer*. For a discussion of the importance and method of Robertson, see Justice, "Who Stole Robertson?"

[10] Arendt, *The Origins of Totalitarianism* (hereafter, parenthetically cited).

[11] On the way that Arendt continually blends her life experience with her thought, as well as the way that biography remains an important form for Arendt throughout her career, see Kristeva, *Hannah Arendt*.

[12] As Deborah Nelson has it, "the foundation of individual conscience and political common ground, Arendt's notion of thinking seems to require suffering the painfulness of reality without consolation, compensation, or communion with others"; *Though Enough*, 49. For my part, I will focus on that capacity that allows thinking to become political, that is, the will. For Nelson, Arendt's emphasis on thinking about the painful aspects of experience is part and parcel of Arendt's advice that one must "face up" to reality, advice that aligns her thought with Simone Weil's; see Nelson, *Though Enough*, 48, and for Nelson's discussion of Weil, 15–44. On Weil, see also Chapter 10 in this volume, Kelner, "Medieval Mysticism and the Making of Simone Weil."

more or less on bodily activities: labor, work, and action, the last of which is the key to politics. Her deepest engagement with the Middle Ages in this period, though, comes in *Life*, her last work and one she left unfinished at her death, which explores the activities of thinking, willing, and would have dealt with judging should she have lived to complete it.[13] In that work, Augustine and Duns Scotus are both essential to her understanding of the Will,[14] the human capacity to begin something new and the activity most closely tied to the experience of freedom, and therefore foundational for political action. Whereas Arendt believes that modern thinkers – and here Friedrich Nietzsche's (1844–1900) concept of "eternal return" and Martin Heidegger's (1889–1976) "will-to-not-will" are exemplary for her – denigrate the efficacy of the Will, understanding mankind to be at the mercy of forces outside itself, Augustine and especially Duns Scotus take seriously our capacity to start a series of events, to begin things, what Arendt calls elsewhere in her work the power of natality.[15] This capacity leaves one free to act in a world that is largely contingent, a terrifying thought for many philosophers, but important to the creation of effective political action.

As her career progresses, then, Arendt turns to the Middle Ages not only for a better model of political potential than she finds in modernity, but also to help her understand the way in which human beings interact with the world that makes political community possible. Just as the Nazis had turned to the medieval period in an attempt to justify their rule, Arendt turns to medieval thinkers in an attempt to solve those aspects of modernity that gave us Nazism in the first place. This is not to say, though, that Arendt provides a definitive guide for countering Nazi polemic, even if *thinking* as such is always a good first step.[16] As Arendt would be one of the first to note, hate is sempiternal and must be opposed when and where it arises, and the historical conditions that it addresses will also determine the conditions with which one must meet it. Neither would Arendt herself be a guide to the present moment that one can use uncritically; her own

---

[13] Arendt, *Lectures on Kant's Political Philosophy*.
[14] Throughout, when discussing the human capacity, I will capitalize it as "Will," in order to emphasize it as an abstract quality, as opposed to the actual action, or verb.
[15] Arendt, *The Human Condition*, 9. In this section, my focus will primarily be on Duns Scotus; for a more expansive discussion of the importance of Augustine for Arendt's notion of the Will, see Scanlon, "Arendt's Augustine."
[16] The controversies surrounding Arendt's engagement with the Eichmann trial are suggestive that many found her diagnosis and prescriptions for the Nazi problem wanting in different ways. Many of the critiques come down to the issue of tone and her use of irony in that work and elsewhere. See Nelson, *Tough Enough*, 45–71.

misunderstandings of American and European race relations – despite her acute analysis of anti-Semitism and the preponderance of racism under the Enlightenment – produces what Fred Moten calls "an antiblackness that infuses and animates Arendt's work," and which means that her guidance must be altered to address the contemporary situation.[17] Even so, Arendt still allows us to see one important way in which the Middle Ages can be used to counter the narratives of resurgent fascism: not just by claiming that the Middle Ages are like us, as is often the case at present, but also by celebrating their difference, not in the way the alt-right might claim them, but in a way that uses them to critique modernity and illuminate the possibility of a different world.

Augustine's Politics in the *Origins of Totalitarianism*

How do you solve a problem like Hobbes? This is clearly not the central question of Arendt's *Origins*, which strives to explain what went wrong in the twentieth century. But Arendt does argue that the rise of totalitarianism can be explained largely by two attendant historical conditions from the nineteenth century: the birth of anti-Semitism and imperialism. She claims that "imperialism must be the first stage in political rule of the bourgeoisie" and that this "political emancipation of the bourgeoisie" is underwritten philosophically by Hobbes (138). However, the sickness that the bourgeois philosophy of Hobbes supported in the twentieth century does in fact have an antidote: Augustine. At the end of the final two sections of *Origins*, Arendt follows a procedure typical in her thought, by looking backward into history in order to think forward into the future.[18] In both instances she turns to the thought of Augustine to suggest a political alternative to the one that the twentieth century has produced. While neither thinker is discussed for long in *Origins* – Augustine only receives these two brief mentions and the sustained discussion of Hobbes occupies fewer than five pages, while the Dreyfus affair is discussed over thirty pages – that should not come as any surprise, given the work's interest in economic, historical, and political matters as opposed to philosophical

---

[17] Moten, *The Universal Machine*, 66; see also his broader discussion of Arendt, 65–139, discussed further at the end of the essay.

[18] The very title of her *Between Past and Future* implies such a methodology, and she explicitly talks about such a process being "the path paved by thinking" (13). She returns the phenomenological importance of this characterization of thinking in the first volume of *Life*. Mittleman, *Hope in a Democratic Age*, sees this methodology in Arendt as the "end to any notion of history as progress" (190).

ones. Nevertheless, Augustine and Hobbes provide Arendt with theoretical poles between which she can situate her analysis of the historical and other conditions that led to the rise of totalitarianism; these thinkers provide her with a philosophical foundation for the political and social beliefs that allowed things to get so bad in the first place and, alternately, for a model of political and social life that might provide us with some sort of hope for the future. To understand the antinomy between these thinkers, it is important to first see just what Arendt finds so troubling in Hobbes, and then to articulate what Arendt mostly leaves implicit, that is how she imagines that Augustine might provide answers to the perplexities of political being that Hobbes raises. If Hobbes is one of the founders of modern liberalism and neoliberalism, a system that generates supposedly universal rights from individual interests, then Augustine provides a different model of universalism, one that takes a community of individuals, replete with a variety of differences, as its starting point.[19]

The most obvious way in which Hobbes could be considered a founder of liberalism, and the basic premise that Arendt finds so disturbing in him, is that Hobbes establishes a political system based on individual interests.[20] In this, she is actually in agreement with Leo Strauss (1899–1973), who writes: "the right to a securing of life pure and simple – and this right sums up Hobbes's natural right – has fully the character of an inalienable human right, that is, of an individual's *claim* that takes precedence over the state and determines its purpose and its limits."[21] While Arendt would not agree with Strauss to the extent that he is articulating a problem with liberalism's reliance on rights as such, she would certainly share his distrust, although for different reasons, about "natural" human rights.[22] She would also share his assessment of Hobbes's interest in the individual. In fact, Arendt sees this interest as unique to Hobbes, who "exposed the only political theory according to which the state is based not on some kind of constituting law – whether divine law, the law of nature, or the law of social contract – which

---

[19] See, for instance, Strauss, "Notes on Carl Schmitt," who claims Hobbes as "the founder of liberalism" (107), drawn out of Carl Schmitt's discussion in *The Concept of the Political*. Schmitt and Strauss, of course, provide one, deeply conservative, critique of liberalism and Hobbes's role in it. For a more liberal and feminist critique, see the overview in Wendy Brown, *Undoing the Demos*, esp. 102–4, who takes the critique further and in a more leftist and Marxian direction.
[20] I should be clear that Hobbes's thought – and then later Augustine's and Duns Scotus's work – itself is not my concern in this essay, which is interested in what Arendt claims him to believe, rather than what he actually believes.
[21] Strauss, "Notes on Carl Schmitt," 107.
[22] See her discussion in *Origins*, "The Decline of the Nation-State and the End of the Rights of Man," 267–302.

determines the rights and wrongs of the individual's interest with respect to public affairs, but on the individual interests themselves" (*Origins*, 139). Hobbes, in Arendt's mind, cares only about individual interests. For him, she claims, those interests both undergird the social world and are constitutive of that world. Out of Hobbes's philosophy, Arendt fears, we can never produce a community, only a group of atomized individuals striving for their own isolated and isolating interests.

After all, for Arendt, the structural reliance on the individual in Hobbes means the individual's interests will always be isolating because it is ultimately always an interest in the individual accumulation of power. The way she makes this association is complex:

> Power, according to Hobbes, is the accumulated control that permits the individual to fix prices and regulate supply and demand in such a way that they contribute to his own advantage. The individual will consider his advantage in complete isolation, from the view of the absolute minority, so to speak; he will then realize that he can pursue and achieve his interest only with the help of some kind of majority. Therefore, if man is driven by nothing but his individual interests, desire for power must be the fundamental passion of man. It regulates the relations between individual and society, and all other ambitions as well, for riches, knowledge, and honor follow from it. (*Origins*, 139).

The Hobbesian individual only thinks of his own specific interests (Strauss reduces the possible interests down to just the interest in self-preservation, but such a reduction is not necessary for this critique to stand). That individual then realizes that he needs a broader group to help achieve his interests, otherwise they might oppose him or take what he wants. In aligning himself with the larger group, the Hobbesian man augments his own power, and indeed he must continue to do so in order to ensure that his desires are not frustrated by the group itself or another individual. In the material world of capitalism, the man achieves this by accumulation, fixing prices, and controlling supply and demand, but these are only the specific manifestations of the general interest in increasing his own power. Increasing the individual's power, then, becomes the only way in which the Hobbesian man can relate to society. Society is devalued to only a means for an individual's ends, which are always his own power over that society.

The introduction of means and ends to this discussion of power leads to the imperialist impulse. Arendt cautions that "since power is essentially only a means to an end a community based solely on power must decay in the calm of order and stability; its complete security reveals that it is built on sand" (*Origins*, 142). This community must then expand: "only by acquiring more power can it guarantee the status quo; only by constantly extending its authority and only through the process of power accumulation can it remain stable" (*Origins*, 142). Externally this means continual imperial expansion; internally this is "the 'condition of perpetual war' of all against all" (*Origins*, 142). The affinity between Arendt's thought at this point and a Marxist critique of capitalism is easy to see. Domestically, she gives us the political version of the Marxist "class war," and internationally, one can see the political expansionism that is the counterpart for capital's need to find new markets and new labor to support it, a theory of globalization most robustly articulated in work on "uneven development."[23] Arendt brackets the economic in order to talk about the political in isolation, but the applicability of the point to both spheres is clear. In both cases, the problem is that Carl Schmitt's political distinction between friend and enemy begins to determine every single relationship, resulting in a situation in which one is a friend, really, only to oneself, and an enemy to everyone else.[24] This situation is the logical end of Hobbes's vision of society: man must continue to live in isolation, even within a community, because he can only focus on his own interests, and if he wishes to increase his own power he must make all other members of his society into enemies to be oppressed. A bleak picture, to say the least.

Out of Augustine, though, Arendt finds hope. At different points in *Origins*, Arendt articulates as bleak a view of the world as anything that Hobbes produces, fittingly because it is his thought that underwrites both the liberal and neoliberal forces shaping the world. At the end of the section on totalitarianism, Arendt finds herself describing the twentieth century in the same atomized way that Hobbes thought was the human condition in general. She writes that "what prepares men for totalitarian domination in the non-totalitarian world is the fact that loneliness ... has become an everyday experience of the evergrowing masses of our century" (*Origins*, 478). And she warns that "organized loneliness is considerably more dangerous than the unorganized impotence of all those who are ruled by the tyrannical and arbitrary will of a single man," specifying that "its danger is that it threatens to ravage the world as we know it – a world which everywhere seems to have come to an end – before a new beginning rising from this end has had time to assert itself" (*Origins*, 478).

---

[23] See, for instance, Harvey, *The Spaces of Global Capitalism*.
[24] Schmitt, *The Concept of the Political*, 26.

Augustine helps her articulate the importance of beginnings, and she gives him almost the last word of the book:

> But there remains also the truth that every end in history necessarily contains a new beginning; this beginning is the promise, the only "message" which the end can ever produce. Beginning, before it becomes a historical event, is the supreme capacity of man; politically, it is identical with man's freedom. *Initium ut esset homo creatus est*—"that a beginning be made man was created" said Augustine. This beginning is guaranteed by each new birth; it is indeed every man.[25] (*Origins*, 478–79)

The isolation and loneliness engendered by Hobbes's view of man can only lead to ends, and taken to its extreme point will lead to the end that is totalitarian domination.[26] Arendt uses Augustine to show that as long as man enters into the world, he has the potential to change it, and he can counteract the oppressive rule of totalitarianism. But in order to do that, man must be politically free. This freedom cannot be identical with Hobbes's notion of freedom to pursue one's interests; that is the version of freedom that led to the world being full of enemies in the first place. Arendt's freedom must be one that is expressed in man's belonging to a society – and so in stark opposition to the loneliness she describes – and one that consists of being nurtured by that society.

Augustine allows Arendt to articulate society as the nurturer of man. At the end of her discussion of the stateless, displaced persons that were produced both before and after World War II, Arendt describes the horror of the public sphere when confronted by such persons. These individuals appear on the world stage as representatives of the "merely given," what Giorgio Agamben will call – following Arendt – "bare life."[27] They have no political belonging or economic means; they are totally and absolutely private persons: "this whole sphere of the merely given, relegated to private life in civilized society, is a permanent threat to the public sphere, because the public sphere is as consistently based on the law of equality as the private sphere is based on the law of universal difference and differentiation" (*Origins*, 301). This differentiation is the Other as such, and one tendency that politics has when confronted with alterity is to destroy it: "the 'alien' is a

---

[25] The citation in Arendt's text is slightly off: the quote is not derived from Augustine's *City of God*, book 12, chapter 20 – as the footnote on these pages says – but from the very end of book 12, chapter 21 (pages 108–9).

[26] In this opinion, she is not far removed from what Theodor Adorno and Max Horkheimer articulate in a theoretical register, whereas here Arendt is giving us a historical analysis. See their *The Dialectic of Enlightenment*.

[27] Agamben, *Homo Sacer*.

frightening symbol of the fact of difference as such, of individuality as such, and indicates those realms in which man cannot change and cannot act and in which, therefore, he has a distinct tendency to destroy" (*Origins*, 301). But Arendt uses Augustine again to articulate an alternative to this tendency:

> This mere existence, that is, all that which is mysteriously given to us by birth and which includes the shape of our bodies and the talents of our minds, can be adequately dealt with only by the unpredictable hazards of friendship and sympathy, or by the great and incalculable grace of love, which says with Augustine, "*Volo ut sis* (I want you to be)," without being able to give any particular reason for such supreme and unsurpassable affirmation.[28] (*Origins*, 301)

Such a relation is emphatically without any notion of Hobbesian interest. But it is a kind of foundation for human being-together, for the creation of a community.[29]

Arendt specifies that the Augustinian version of community, which is an alternative to the kind of community laid out by Hobbes, is built upon notions such as "friendship," "sympathy," or "love."[30] We now tend to view those kinds of relationships as being typical of the private sphere, and Arendt's suggestion that "mere existence" is relegated to the private sphere seems to confirm this categorization. However, in her dissertation, Arendt instead argues that these notions, especially the notion of "love," are public virtues for Augustine; they are in fact how one should build a body politic. In her fullest articulation of what Augustinian community looks like, Arendt writes:

> True fellowship rests on the fact of the common faith. Therefore, by observation we can define the society of believers by two distinguishing marks. First, since the society of believers is established by what in principle is not mundane, it is a community with others grounded not in a pre-existing reality in the world, but in a specific possibility. Second, because this possibility is the most radical of all possibilities available to

---

[28] This quotation is not actually Augustine but Martin Heidegger, who attributed it to Arendt in a love letter to Arendt; for more on the relationship between Arendt and Heidegger around Augustine, see Thomson, "Thinking Love." Miles, "Volo ut Sis," argues that Arendt here takes Augustine's notion of love too far. Again, the fact that Arendt ascribes the thought to Augustine is more important for the argument here than the accuracy of the sentiment to his thought. For a broader discussion of Arendt and Heidegger, see Nixon, *Hannah Arendt and the Politics of Friendship*, 61–84.

[29] For a variety of discussions about Augustine's political philosophy that often take it in a different direction than Arendt, see the essays in Dougherty, ed., *Augustine's Political Thought*.

[30] On the importance of friendship in Arendt's thought and life, see Nixon, *Hannah Arendt and the Politics of Friendship*.

> human existence, the community of faith that is realized in loving each other calls for and demands a total response from each person. In contrast to all worldly communities, which always isolate only one definition of being in regard to which the community is the community, the community of faith demands the whole man, and God also demands him. (*Love*, 98–99)

The "specific possibility" is that Christ was born and died and then came back, all for this love of the world, and that the community will be granted eternal life because they believe in that event. More importantly for my purposes here, though, the kind of community they form is not based on one attribute. In contrast to theories of the nineteenth-century nation-state, this community is based around something other than the fact that they are all Germans, for instance, or that they are different from people who are, say, French, owing to the fact of birth and inheritance supposedly (though not in actuality) going back to time immemorial. In its most abstract form, this single-trait notion of community-formation finds expression in Schmitt's friend and enemy distinction. Augustine's community subsumes such a distinction. Whether or not it is wise to live one's life as if one had no enemies is not what is at stake here. What is important is that this community is one that is formed without any kind of foundational and seemingly inherited differentiation, but based on an extension of welcome to potentially anyone who shares a belief; it attempts to be a true universalism.[31] What is more, by demanding the participation and acceptance of the "whole man" by such a community, it also obviates any internal differentiation. The specific qualities of individuals that make for differences within a community – class, race, gender, and so on – likewise become things indifferent, mattering no more than the external differences that the community overcomes by welcoming new members seamlessly into itself.

One can see how this society without differentiation might be an issue, however: was it not precisely such a society that totalitarianism tried to achieve? What is the difference? It seems that in Arendt, as in Augustine, the difference comes from knowing one's place in the universe. In cautioning against the subsuming of the private life by the public, she warns us that "wherever public life and its law of equality are completely victorious, wherever a civilization succeeds in eliminating or reducing to a minimum the dark background of difference, it will end in complete petrifaction and be

---

[31] In this, Arendt's discussion of Augustine here prefigures Alain Badiou's discussion of St Paul. See Badiou, *Saint Paul*.

punished, so to speak, for having forgotten that man is only the master, not the creator of the world" (*Origins*, 302). So the Augustinian society would need to maintain difference, but without distinction and without enemies. What Arendt means in reminding us that man is "not the creator of the world" is that he has no authority to decide whether or not an entire type of people are allowed to inhabit it; we cannot, she thinks, turn difference as such into an enemy to be hunted down and eliminated.[32] In her dissertation, Arendt specifies that Augustine's community of faith is built of two shared likenesses, two foundational universal claims that allow for a complete incorporation into the body politic. The first is that they are created by God, and the second is that all of mankind is descended from a common source; in Augustine's mind, Adam. Both premises are necessary, it seems, for this Augustinian community to prevent itself from being a totalitarian one. All humanity is equal because it all comes from a common source, because it is potentially able to participate in its community, even though its members are individually distinct. "The other person is our neighbor as a member of the human race," Arendt writes, "and in this capacity, too, is singled out with the explicitness that results from the realized isolation of the individual" (*Love*, 114). We fight Hobbes's individual isolation and loneliness, Arendt thinks, by being what Augustine wants us to be: a good neighbor.[33]

Neighborliness, then, takes the place of Hobbes's individual interest in Augustine's vision of community, and it is out of neighborliness that Arendt would have us build a different and better world.[34] Rather than individual interests expressed in opposition to each other, and always finally after an accrual of political and social power to the individual at the expense of everyone else, Arendt would have us love our neighbors as

---

[32] We should keep in mind that it was that assumption, that Nazism "had the right to determine who should or should not inhabit the world," which justified killing Adolf Eichmann for Arendt; see *Eichmann in Jerusalem*, 279.

[33] Here too Arendt appears to be running ahead of the crowd by articulating in 1929 a political concept that would garner such great interest later on; see Žižek, Santner, and Reinhard, *The Neighbor*.

[34] One might recall here that the love of the neighbor has also had some very famous skeptics. Sigmund Freud expresses concerns about it in *Civilization and Its Discontents*, 65–67. Arendt, in turn, expressed her own skepticism about psychoanalysis, again using Augustine: "psychology, depth psychology or psychoanalysis, discovers no more than the ever-changing moods, the ups and downs of our psychic life, and its results and discoveries are neither particularly appealing nor very meaningful in themselves. 'Individual psychology,' on the other hand, the prerogative of fiction, the novel and the drama, can never be a science; as science it is a contradiction in terms. When modern science finally began to illuminate the Biblical 'darkness of the human heart' – of which Augustine said '*Latet cor bonum, latet cor malum, abyssus est in corde bono et in corde malo*' ('Hidden is the good heart, hidden is the evil heart, an abyss is in the good heart and in the evil heart') – it turned out to be 'a motley-colored and painful storehouse and treasure of evils', as Democritus already suspected"; Arendt, *Life*, 1.34–35.

different as they are to us, because those differences amount to nothing compared with our shared capacity to agree to form a community, to exist as human beings together, for "whole men" to express for one another "the great and incalculable grace of love" (*Origins*, 301). And one important thing these human beings share, and the quality that allows them to make such a different and welcoming form of community in the first place, is the power of natality, the capacity to begin something new. This quality, too, Arendt derives from Augustine, who is for her the first philosopher to take that aspect of our humanity seriously, but not the last. Augustine bequeathed to the philosophers of the Middle Ages, especially, a sense of the human Will as our faculty for beginning things anew, that is, as the faculty that corresponds to the political experience of freedom. But Augustine himself is not the philosopher who most thoroughly explores the connection between the Will as the capacity to start something new, human freedom as the expression of that capacity, and love as the fulfillment of it. Instead, Arendt turns to John Duns Scotus for these articulations, and it is to her discussion of Duns Scotus that I now turn in order to show how the creation of a neighborly community is possible in the first place, and indeed what aspect of the human mind allows us to be a good neighbor.

Duns Scotus's Ontology of the Will in the *Life of the Mind*

In moving from the exploration of human communities to the articulation of human capacities one follows the trajectory of Arendt's career as she moves from the political theory of *Love* and *Origins* to the phenomenology of *The Human Condition* and *Life*. But even in *Life*, her last work, the concerns of *Origins* are not ever that far removed from her mind. Arendt explains that her "immediate impulse" for writing *Life* "came from … attending the Eichmann trial in Jerusalem," where she noticed that Eichmann's evil rested in his "thoughtlessness" (*Life*, 1.3–4). When confronted with what he had done and what he was a part of, Eichmann fell back on commonplaces about what makes a good German and on the slogans of the Nazi regime; he was, in other words, unable to think critically about his own life and actions or imagine the thoughts of others, and as such embodied Arendt's controversial phrase, "the banality of evil."[35]

---

[35] This situation was discussed in the reporting on the trial that Arendt did for the *New Yorker*, collected in an expanded version (which also touches on some of the controversy) in Arendt, *Eichmann in Jerusalem*. Nelson argues that, for Arendt, thoughtlessness is "not generated by feeling, much less overwhelming feeling, but by the avoidance of painful feelings (guilt, remorse, discomfort, confusion);" see Nelson, *Tough Enough*, 69.

This experience led Arendt to question whether there was something in the universal human capacity for thinking itself that stands in the way of a person becoming someone like Eichmann. These considerations opened up into a tripartite division of human cognitive faculties – echoing the division of human agency into labor, work, and action in *The Human Condition* – resulting in *Life*'s attempt to account for thinking, willing, and judging, the last of which Arendt did not finish before she died. What Arendt found was that *thinking* had less to tell her about overt political action – although it could still mitigate against totalitarianism, for instance, or prevent someone from becoming like Eichmann – as that capacity was more appropriate for the realm of philosophical contemplation. Instead, political action was more obviously at home in *judging*, even though she was not able to fully articulate that connection.[36] But *willing* also provided some insight into political agency, especially into the phenomenology of freedom that subtends such actions. If *Life* is meant to address Eichmann's failings, one's ability to act otherwise lies just as much in the Will as it does in thought. Moreover, that consideration of the Will returns Arendt to her early writings on Augustine, leading her further into the Middle Ages, and opening up there, especially in the figure of Duns Scotus, an antidote to the pessimism that modern philosophy expresses in regards to the human ability to shape the forces of history and one's political future.[37] To understand the importance of the Will in producing political action that can result in the formation of a political community – like the community of good neighbors discussed earlier – one must first understand what Arendt means by the Will and how both Augustine and Duns Scotus theorize it.

For Arendt, simply put, the Will is "an organ for the future and identical with the power of beginning something new" (*Life*, 2.29). The Will is the mental faculty that allows us to alter the world around us. Through the Will, we begin an action, whose effects will be felt immediately in the present and which will resonate into the future. From this definition, a few aspects of the Will follow. As the Will begins something new whose impact is felt in the present and in the future, it is not simply following the necessary pressures put on it by the past. That is, the Will is inextricably

---

[36] What survives of that discussion is covered in Arendt, *Lectures on Kant's Political Philosophy*. The great "tell" about the placement of these lectures in Arendt's thought is that they focus on Kant's *Critique of the Power of Judgment*.
[37] For Arendt, the philosophy of G. W. F. Hegel offers an exception to that pessimism, but Nietzsche and Heidegger's rejection of Hegel's solution ensures that the pessimistic understanding remains the predominant one; see *Life*, 2.39–51.

bound to contingency, something that has caused many philosophers – obsessed as they are with necessity – to denigrate it. Nevertheless, Arendt is adamant that "there can hardly be anything more contingent than willed acts, which – on the assumption of free will – could all be defined as acts about which I know that I could as well have left them undone." And of course, the Will for Arendt is without doubt a free Will, for she immediately clarifies that "a will that is not free is a contradiction in terms" (*Life*, 2.14). Like its association to contingency, then, the Will is condemned by philosophers for its connection to freedom, "willing, it appears, is characterized by an infinitely greater freedom than thinking," and while philosophers enjoy the freedom thinking provides, they allow thinking to be guided by reason or memory's guise of necessity (*Life*, 2.26). The Will is the mind's capacity to commit free acts in a contingent world that will shape the future.

Much of Arendt's understanding of the Will goes back to Augustine. And for Augustine the Will is split, always involved in a contest "between *velle* and *nolle*, between willing and nilling … *Nolle* is no less actively transitive than *velle*, no less a faculty of the will: if I will what I do not desire, I nill my desires; and in the same way, I can nill what reason tells me is right" (*Life*, 2.89). For Augustine, and for Arendt, the Will is always divided into willing and nilling, which clash with one another, and this internal conflict between willing and nilling is one of the reasons that the willed act is always contingent, that it can always be left undone; nilling, after all, sometimes wins out. This divided will, though, becomes something of a problem for Augustine. As Arendt points out, "within the framework of the *Confessions*, no solution to the riddle of this 'monstrous' faculty is given; how the Will, divided against itself, finally reaches the moment when it becomes entire remains a mystery" (*Life*, 2.96). In Arendt's language – deeply imbued with Augustine as it is – the Will is in need of redemption, and that redemption comes not through another mental act or the negation of willing, but through its fulfillment. Succinctly, Arendt explains that "the will's redemption cannot be mental and does not come by divine intervention either; redemption comes from the act which … interrupts the conflict between *velle* and *nolle*. And the price of the redemption is … freedom" (*Life*, 2.101). That is, we solve the conflict between willing and nilling by acting or failing to act, by affirming either our will or our nill, and because the willed act can just as easily be nilled, we are free to do either one or the other. One should quickly point out, though, that this is not the same as negating the Will, or Heidegger's "will-not-to-will," and Arendt notes precisely that "the Will is redeemed by ceasing to will and starting to act, and the cessation cannot originate in the act of the will-not-to-will because this would be but another volition" (*Life*, 2.102). Ceasing the conflict between willing and nilling in a free act, though, comes at a cost, as Augustine well knew. But Augustine was not the philosopher most accepting of that cost; that would be Duns Scotus, who fully understood that the cost of our freedom is a world of contingency.

In order to understand Duns Scotus's particular notion about the relationship of freedom and contingency, one needs to understands a couple of distinctions that Arendt finds in his work. First, there is a distinction between the individual's freedom and the freedom of the Will. As Duns Scotus makes clear, the fulfillment of the Will in the act does not mean that the individual is radically free, only that their Will is. The individual, in fact, loses their freedom in the act, as indeed "man's normal way of escaping from his freedom is simply to *act* on the propositions of the will" (*Life*, 2.141). One cannot will a thing not-to-have-been-done after one has done it. Surprisingly, though, this is a cause for celebration in Duns Scotus:

> the human will is indetermined, open to contraries, and hence broken only so long as its sole activity consists in forming volitions; the moment it stops willing and starts to act on one of the will's propositions, it loses its freedom—and man, the possessor of the willing ego, is as happy of the loss as Buridan's ass was happy to resolve the problem of choosing between two bundles of hay by following his instinct: stop choosing and start eating. (*Life*, 2.141)

The reason one remains happy is that the Will retains its freedom; one can act again. In fact, there is nothing external that limits the freedom of the Will, only an internal boundary set by one's abilities, what Arendt following Duns Scotus identifies via a second distinction: an "I-can" within the "I-will": "there is an I-can inherent in every I-will, and this I-can sets limitation on the I-will that are not outside the willing ego itself" (*Life*, 2.142). One cannot will oneself to fly, because there is no recognition of ability that attends that willing, no "I-can" inherent in that "I-will" – such a desire for flight would be the activity of a different mental faculty, probably the imagination. The important point here is that activity ends willing, but only as an expression of the freedom of the act of willing itself – a fulfillment of the "I-can" in the "I-will" – and not as a result of some outside determinate.

For Duns Scotus it is crucial that the Will remain free from any outer proscription, bound only by its own capacities because it is mankind's capacity to will, not his intellect or reason, that constitutes his likeness to God. It is only the Will that understands creation *ex nihilo*, that sees that

God created the world, but that He could have just as simply not have created it. Duns Scotus, according to Arendt, "does not deny that two successive volitions are necessary to will and nill the same object; but he does maintain that the willing ego in performing one of them is aware of being free to perform its contrary also" (*Life*, 2.130). This recognition of course lies behind man's happiness – like Buridan's ass – to give up his freedom by ceasing to will and starting to act, and this knowledge on the part of the Will is "an important testimony to human freedom, to the mind's ability to avoid all coercive determination from the outside" (*Life*, 2.131). We are as gods not in our knowledge of good and evil, but in our free will: "God's creature is distinguished by the mental capacity to affirm or negate freely, uncoerced by either desire of reasoning" (*Life*, 2.135). This view of the Will is more radical than Augustine's, for whom desire is coercive, and it is more radical than that of Thomas Aquinas, who understands reason to be the sovereign faculty of the mind.

Duns Scotus's emphatic association of the freedom of the Will with God's freedom has an important metaphysical consequence, one that radically distinguishes him from most other philosophers in that he is willing to believe that the world is contingent and that contingency, moreover, is something to be valued. As Arendt puts it, Duns Scotus's unique position in the history of philosophy is that he understands "contingency as the price to be paid for freedom" (*Life*, 2.134). And this contingency is empirically obvious, as Arendt repeatedly notes, for Duns Scotus offers a simple thought experiment: "those who deny that some being is contingent should be exposed to torments until they concede that it is possible for them not to be tormented" (*Life*, 2.31; 2.134).[38] While Duns Scotus rejects the notion that the Will can be determined by something outside itself, which would limit its freedom, he also recognizes that the Will is not omnipotent, even in cases that should be within its abilities. Someone bound in torment might will it otherwise, but there is no guarantee that they will be able to effect that change in their condition. In order to make sense of a contingent world that is nevertheless a product of historical circumstances – of the Will willing things in the past – he settles on an idea of "partial causes," revealing the extent to which causation is contingent: "it is precisely the causative element in human affairs that condemns them to contingency and unpredictability" (*Life*, 2.138). Arendt illustrates this point with the following example:

---

[38] His position might not be unique, or, at least, it is not without some foundation: James J. Walsh points out that this "proof" of contingency is in part derived from Avicenna's commentary on Aristotle's *Metaphysics*; see Hyman and Walsh, *Philosophy in the Middle Ages*, 592.

> We need only to think of the libraries that have been produced to explain the necessity of the outbreaks of the last two wars, each theory picking out a different single cause – when in truth nothing seems more plausible than that it was a coincidence of causes, perhaps finally set in motion by one more additional one, that 'contingently caused' the two conflagrations. (*Life*, 2.138)

In short, for Duns Scotus, the Will is free and the world is contingent, even though the accretion of willed acts forms a set of partial causes that pragmatically inform the abilities of the individual in any given circumstance, as well as increase the contingency and unpredictability of the world because one can never know with certainty what conflagration that combination of partial causes might produce.

All of which is to say that, out of the philosophers, it is Duns Scotus who most clearly provides hope for Arendt's vision of political change. While that vision might be inspired by Augustine, and might be suffused with his language, it is Duns Scotus that affirms that the world is contingent, that it could be different than what it is, that such a change can be brought about by the coordination of partial causes produced ultimately by individual acts of free will. What is more, some of the same language from Augustine that inspired Arendt also inspired Duns Scotus, and that is the language of love, which brings us back to the vision of political community in *Origins*: "in Augustine, as well as later in Duns Scotus, the solution of the Will's inner conflict comes about through a transformation of the Will itself, its transformation into *Love*" (*Life*, 2.102).[39]

As a way into what Duns Scotus defines as love, it is helpful to understand his thoughts on the afterlife, which "cannot possibly consist in rest and contemplation" (*Life*, 2.144). Because our Will is what makes us like God, it cannot be quieted in contemplation, so it must be fulfilled in some other manner. What that looks like for Duns Scotus is an ongoing affirmation of the Will and the world, the Will's unceasing commitment to stay in heaven, because "what the Will in a state of blessedness, that is, in an after-life, no longer needs or is no longer capable of is *rejection* and hatred, but this does not mean that man in a state of blessedness has lost the faculty of saying 'yes'" (*Life*, 2.144). As Arendt explains – in Latin familiar form *Origins*, where it is attributed to Augustine – that unconditional acceptance is called "Love" by Duns Scotus: "*Amo: volu*

---

[39] For a different discussion of this notion of love as an important part of Arendt's political understanding, despite herself in his view, see Martel, "Amo, Volo ut Sis."

ut sis" (*Life*, 2.144).⁴⁰ As opposed to Augustine, Duns Scotus makes it clear that this is not the cessation of the Will:

> Transformed into love, the restlessness of the will is stilled but not extinguished; love's abiding power is felt not as the arrest of motion—as the end of the fury of war is felt as the quiet of peace—but as the serenity of a self-contained, self-fulfilling, everlasting movement. Here are not the quiet and delight that follow upon a perfect operation, but the stillness of an act resting in its end. (*Life*, 2.145)

Far from Heidegger's "will-to-not-will," love for Duns Scotus is the "will-to-will-*this*," an ongoing engagement and affirmation that the world (or at least Heaven) and the Will are in continual approval of one another. To put that back into the political terms that Duns Scotus makes possible for Arendt, once the contingent world has been changed by acts of the free Will, one must continue to want that world, to hold up the existence and flourishing of others in it. The neighborly love that she first posited in *Love* and imagines as an alternative for our world in *Origins* is shown in the discussion of Duns Scotus in *Life* to be a world that continually affirms the place of others in it, and that is shaped in such a way that it is a place in which you and others continuously want to dwell.

A Middle Ages for the Left

A world of neighborly love, the continual affirmation with which the world greets us and others and with which those others and ourselves greet the world, made possible by the fact that the contingent world can change by means of free acts of the Will. Such, abstractly put, is the world Arendt uses the Middle Ages to envision, a corrective both to modernity's Hobbesian promotion of individual interests – the dead end of which is totalitarianism – and to modernity's Heideggerian skepticism of the individual's capacity to will the world different than what it is. What that world practically looks like is a different question altogether, and perhaps one that it is unfair to ask of Arendt. Such pragmatic concerns, after all, are the purview of political policy, not political philosophy. Arendt has given us the theoretical goals that should guide those policy decisions: isn't that enough? And, in any case, wouldn't her recommendations – because she did, after all, deal with pragmatic concerns from time to time, and was an advocate for specific sorts of institutional

---

⁴⁰ Again, this is not Duns Scotus, but Heidegger. See the discussion at n. 22.

formations and policy position – for addressing the problems she saw in her world be outdated now that we are occupying a very different historical moment?

But rather than dismissing Arendt as obsolete, we might instead recognize that our different historical condition frees us to take up her theoretical outlines without worrying about the bygone responses she had to concrete historical problems. That is not to say that Arendt's particular beliefs cannot continue to inspire us: Judith Butler has drawn productively on her writings on Israel to discuss its relationship to Palestine both in terms of a critique of Zionism and on the matter of cohabitation between the Palestinian and Jewish peoples, and Seyla Benhabib has used Arendt's "right to have rights" in framing the contemporary refugee crisis.[41] But in other respects, abstracting Arendt from her historical moment is a boon, because it is her engagement with other concrete historical problems closer to home that we often find most wanting now. I am referring to her writings on American race relations, most notoriously her "Reflections on Little Rock" (1959), which defends the rights of parents who do not want their children to attend an integrated school, this despite Arendt's insistence that "as a Jew I take my sympathy for the cause of the Negroes [sic] as for all oppressed and underprivileged peoples for granted and should appreciate it if the reader did likewise."[42] One should not dismiss the wrongheadedness of Arendt's comments simply because, as she herself tries to use as a proleptic defense, she is "writing as an outsider."[43] Indeed, such misunderstandings of the political situation in the United States no doubt contribute to Arendt's missed opportunity to engage with other important contemporary thinkers, such as Frantz Fanon (1925–1961), to whom – Fred Moten has written – Arendt "seems unambivalently deaf despite [his works'] resonant relation to the stakes and method of her work."[44] As Moten goes on to show, examining the ways that Arendt misses connection with Fanon, Curtis Mayfield (1942–1999), Antony Braxton (b. 1945), and others, Arendt's work can illuminate disruptive potentials, even if they are nominally "against her will and against her thought."[45]

---

[41] See chapters 5 and 6 in Butler, *Parting Ways*. See chapter 6 in Benhabib, *Exile, Statelessness and Migration*; Benhabib's discussion of Arendt is more expansive than this one intervention, including a sustained discussion of Butler. For a litany of ways in which Arendt's thought applies to our present moment, see Bernstein, *Why Read Hannah Arendt Now*.
[42] Arendt, "Reflections on Little Rock," 46.
[43] Ibid., 46. For a thorough examination of this wrongheadedness, see Burroughs, "Hannah Arendt."
[44] Moten, *The Universal Machine*, 66. On Fanon's own investment in the Middle Ages, see Chapter 1 in this volume, Smith, "Outside History: Fanon's Negative Manicheism."
[45] Moten, *The Universal Machine*, 138.

Following Moten, one can imagine that some of the ways Arendt's vision of neighborly love might be put into practice now would be "against her will and against her thought." One obvious way that governments could embody neighborly love would be through the massive expansion of the social safety net, up to and including universal basic income. For Arendt, this may seem like the political sphere intruding on the economic, but it is not clear that she would altogether object: an universal basic income – to use the language of *The Human Condition* – would meet the needs of laboring, but allow the flourishing of the higher human activities of work and action. Reparations would be another concrete manifestation of Arendtian and Augustinian neighborly love in practice. On the one hand, Arendt's support for returning goods looted by the Nazis to their original Jewish owners or their survivors suggest that she might support reparations, but on the other hand, her broader failings on the question of race and her idealistic characterization of American wealth before the Revolution must give us pause.[46] Regardless of her support for the idea, though, Arendt's distinction between collective responsibility and collective guilt could be a useful bulwark against those who oppose reparations on the grounds that they had no hand in it: the Arendtian point would be "that is true and you are not therefore guilty of the initial dispossession, but you can still be responsible for its redress."[47] In these and similar ways, we can imagine how Arendt's work might inspire a present movement to make neighborly love a political reality.

But Arendt's engagement with the Middle Ages has one further thing to show us, not by attending to the specific way her medieval-inspired vision might be put into practice, but by considering the broad methodology that produced such a vision in the first place, and what it might tell us about our own responses to contemporary alt-right appropriations of the Middle Ages. Much of the contemporary response to alt-right appropriations of the Middle Ages, whether explicitly or implicitly, takes what one might think of as – recalling the beginning of this essay – the Blochian approach

---

[46] "What were absent from the American scene were misery and want rather than poverty," although elsewhere she does note with astonishment that "the absence of the social question from the American scene was, after all, quite deceptive, and that abject and degrading misery was present everywhere in the form of slavery and Negro labor." Both sentiments are from Arendt, *On Revolution*, 58 and 60. On the question of returning Jewish cultural goods, see Arendt, "The Aftermath of Nazi Rule."

[47] The distinction is articulated, among other places, in Arendt, "Organized Guilt and Universal Responsibility." For a discussion of the prevalence – and the inadequacy – of individuals who deny that they hand in oppression and so have no responsibility for reparations, see Coates, "The Case for Reparations."

to the problem. That is, it meets the claim head on, corrects the misunderstanding, and explains the Middle Ages as something more in line with a progressive vision of modernity. One might think of Geraldine Heng and Matthew X. Vernon's important work, which shows how the alt-right vision of a racially white and pure Middle Ages is nonsense, and that the medieval response to its own multicultural society can offer us insight into the birth of race-based thinking (Heng) as well as visions of racial coexistence that can serve as models for African-American thinkers in the earlier part of the twentieth century (Vernon).[48] This is indispensable work that proceeds from one major assumption, that the Middle Ages are similar to our own moment, as indeed they are, in a host of ways covered by Heng and Vernon, among others.

Arendt takes a different tact than Bloch's or these contemporary medievalists. As I have shown, she attends to the alterity of the Middle Ages and finds its difference from our own moment useful.[49] Augustine and Duns Scotus are important to Arendt's thought precisely because they are not Hobbes or Heidegger, even as we might use them – and Arendt herself – in ways that none of these thinkers could foresee and towards ends with which they may not even agree: Augustine's writings on heretics suggest that he may not have been as wholly open to the idea of neighborly love as Arendt finds in his work, and, as I have just suggested, we can take Arendt's ideas beyond what she herself may have supported. In any event, the Middle Ages, Arendt makes us realize, can serve as a storehouse of alternatives to the problems of modernity, and so we do well to recognize that the medieval world is not our own, and we might even find hope in that fact. By this method, Arendt resembles no one so much as her old friend Walter Benjamin, who reminds us to look to the past for those moments that one might "seize hold of a memory as it flashes up at a moment of danger," and so too create a solidarity with the past as it teaches us how we might alter the present.[50] Such was Arendt's approach to the Middle Ages, and it is one that might still benefit us today.

---

[48] Heng, *The Invention of Race*; Vernon, *The Black Middle Ages*.
[49] This is not to say that scholars such as Heng or Vernon do not attend to this alterity; both are careful to point out salient differences between the Middle Ages and the contemporary as they arise in their arguments.
[50] Benjamin, "Theses on the Philosophy of History," 255.

PART II
Arts

CHAPTER 5

Curtius and Jung
Commonplaces, Archetypes, and Literature's Collective Unconscious

Emily V. Thornbury

Ernst Robert Curtius's (1886–1956) immense, expansive masterwork, *European Literature and the Latin Middle Ages* (1953; hereafter *ELLMA*), belongs to a curious subset of the literature of World War II: synthetic works of comparative literary criticism.[1] *Mimesis: The Representation of Reality in Western Literature* (1946), which Erich Auerbach (1892–1957) wrote while in exile in Istanbul, is perhaps the best-known instance of the genre. In his final paragraph, Auerbach presents his work as, ultimately, reparative: "I hope that my study will reach its readers – both my friends of former years, if they are still alive, as well as all the others for whom it was intended. And may it contribute to bringing together again those whose love for our western history has serenely persevered."[2] In *Theory of Literature*, the Czech émigré René Wellek (1903–1995) praised *Mimesis* – and *ELLMA* – as restorers of a scholarly tradition that "ignore the established nationalisms and convincingly demonstrate the unity of Western civilization," and went on to a general programmatic statement: "literature is one, as art and humanity are one; and in this conception lies the future of historical literary studies."[3]

---

[1] References are to Curtius, *European Literature and the Latin Middle Ages*. While I mainly quote only the English for the sake of brevity, I have compared the German whenever Curtius's precise wording is in question. On the Bollingen Series, see pp. 144–45 of this essay.

[2] Auerbach, *Mimesis*, 557. Auerbach's reflection on the formal effects of his working circumstances in the final paragraphs of his Epilogue is fascinatingly ambivalent: "International communications were impeded; I had to dispense with almost all periodicals, with almost all the more recent investigations," but concluding that "On the other hand it is quite possible that the book owes its existence to just this lack of a rich and specialized library. If it had been possible for me to acquaint myself with all the work that has been done on so many subjects, I might never have reached the point of writing" (557).

[3] Wellek and Warren, *Theory of Literature*, 50. In the introduction to the first edition, Wellek was specified as the primary author of chapter 5, the source of this quote. *Theory of Literature* was first published in 1949, and contained the assertion of literature's unity; the reference to Auerbach and Curtius was added in the second edition of 1956. "Western civilization" is itself a limiting concept that has produced a great deal of violence from Curtius's time to now; for more on this issue, see Chapter 2 in this volume, Saltzman, "Hermeneutics and the Medieval Horizon."

While comparative literature was from its inception as a discipline prone to millenarian yearnings, and other fields – most notably art history – also saw a midcentury turn to vast works of synthesis, it is nonetheless striking that so many literary scholars spent the 1940s proving that a common European civilization did – despite all contrary evidence – exist.[4]

To us in retrospect, it is perhaps not surprising that the horror of the war and the subsequent partition of Europe should have dealt a peculiar kind of blow to scholars of comparative European literature; nor that those scholars should react by reasserting the fundamental unity of European culture – poignantly insufficient though such a response might seem. What sets *ELLMA*, as Curtius's vision of this unity, apart from the works of his contemporaries is not his book's range or depth, but the psychological foundations on which it is built. Following what amounted to a conversion experience in the late 1930s, Curtius embraced Carl Jung's (1875–1961) idea of the collective unconscious in his own life. In his work, he went on to elaborate Jung's theory in a profoundly novel way, proposing that literature itself behaved as – indeed, in some sense, *was* – the stratified, partly shared unconscious that Jung proposed for individuals. Through its transformation of the ancient conception of the literary topos, its historicized rejection of historical causality, and its curious structure, *ELLMA* reenvisioned the Latin Middle Ages as the collective unconscious of modern European literature, and in so doing imagined a continent whose unity could never be truly undone.

Curtius's personal background undoubtedly shaped his rejection of rigid national or linguistic divides. He was born in Alsace, at that point German territory, and educated in the largely French-speaking city of Strasbourg.[5] His father held an official appointment as director of the Lutheran church in Strasbourg from 1903 to 1914, when he resigned rather than carry out the official order to end the use of French in local religious services.[6] Curtius's early research centered on French literature: as he described it in his foreword to the English translation of *ELLMA*, "after the war of 1914–18, I saw it as my task to make modern France understood in Germany" through his studies of a number of French authors; he represented his subsequent work as expanding outward to English, Spanish, and Italian.[7]

---

[4] On the unifying hopes of prewar scholars, see Bassnett, *Comparative Literature*, 3–4. The work of Ernst Gombrich (1909–2001), who left Austria for England in 1936, provides an art historical counterpart to the literary scholars discussed here.
[5] Evans, "Ernst Robert Curtius," 85–145, at 89–90, 92.
[6] Ibid., 91.
[7] *ELLMA*, vii.

He was quick to recognize the Nazi Party's threat to these ideals, and in 1932 published *Deutscher Geist in Gefahr* (*The German Spirit in Peril*), an anti-nationalist polemic arguing for a renewed humanist commitment in education and cultural life.[8] This accomplished little other than to bring him to attention as a suspicious character when the party assumed power the next year; while Curtius was allowed to remain in his teaching post in Bonn, he was reportedly monitored.[9] Instead of leaving Germany, however, Curtius turned to his work with a new sense of mission, and a new strategy. The result, published in 1948, was *ELLMA*.[10] In the preface to the English translation – which is more explicit about his programmatic intentions than the German – he states "that my book is not the product of purely scholarly interests, that it grew out of a concern for the preservation of Western culture.... It attempts to illuminate the unity of that tradition in space and time by the application of new methods."[11]

ELLMA is a vast and complex work, the result of many influences and astonishingly wide-ranging reading.[12] In his first chapter, Curtius himself highlights the work of Arnold Toynbee (1889–1975) and Henri Bergson (1859–1941) as particularly crucial to his narrative of the organic development of medieval European culture. But in the preface to the English translation, he also notes that "In my book there will also be found things which I could not have seen without C. G. Jung."[13] Indeed, Curtius himself connected the genesis of *ELLMA* to his encounter with Jungian psychology: in a letter to Jean de Menasce (1902–1973) dated December 22, 1945, Curtius wrote:

> My book will be called: "The Latin and Romance Middle Ages: Studies in the Literary Tradition of Europe." In the foreword, I explain the course of my development, which led me from the study of Romance to that of Latin. From the time of my earliest study, in 1912, Rome had become *the* city of my soul.... In 1932, through deep disturbances in my psyche, I was put into a condition of alternating productive excitement and severe depression. I wrote "Deutscher Geist in Gefahr," then broke down, and had to consult Jung in Zürich. It was a profound crisis, in which I later recognized the

---

[8] Curtius, *Deutscher Geist in Gefahr*.
[9] Lausberg, *Ernst Robert Curtius (1886–1956)*, 96, 113–14.
[10] Curtius, *Europäische Literatur und lateinisches Mittelalter*.
[11] *ELLMA*, viii.
[12] Curtius's career has inspired a significant amount of scholarship: in addition to the biographical works and individual articles cited in this essay, see especially the collections Lange, ed., *"In Ihnen begegnet sich das Abendland;"* Paccagnella and Gregori, eds., *Ernst Robert Curtius e l'identità culturale dell'Europa*; and Baeumer, ed., *Toposforschung*. Peter Godman's afterword, in the most recent printing of *ELLMA*, presents an accessible overview of much of this work.
[13] *ELLMA*, ix.

unconscious anticipation of the horror that began in 1933. Yet out of the crisis came the cure. A psychic compulsion turned me to the study of medieval Latin literature. I held two major lectures on it. Psychically, it signified the polarization toward *Roma aeterna*. She acted in me as an archetype in the Jungian sense, i.e. simultaneously as a symbol freighted with manifold significance and energy. It was as if a bolt had been drawn back, a door broken through. I could choose the beloved and holy Rome as the guiding star of my research and thought. Or, better: it chose me, the German Roman. The road to Rome must lead through the Middle Ages, which for me now also signified an archaic layer of my consciousness.[14]

In this account, whatever clinical benefit Curtius may have gained from Jung's treatment seems to have been overshadowed by the transformative effect of Jung's theories. Indeed, Curtius describes his discovery of the archetype of *Roma aeterna* within himself in terms that closely track William James's definition of religious conversion: a life-altering reorientation of his spiritual energies, and a new sense of his true nature and purpose, which, C. Stephen Jaeger argues, took on a messianic cast.[15] Yet just as striking as Curtius's absorption of Jungian psychology is his creative expansion of it. He does not describe himself as having encountered his anima, although his language is reminiscent of the way Jung speaks of this core archetype.[16] Instead, his true identity as a "Deutschrömer" is revealed

---

[14] From Lange, "'Permets-moi de recourir une fois de plus à ta science': Ernst Robert Curtius und Jean de Menasce," in *In Ihnen begegnet sich das Abendland*, 199–216 at 210–11. ("Mein Buch soll heissen: 'Lateinisches und romanisches Mittelalter. Untersuchungen zur literarischen Tradition Europas'. Im Vorwort erkläre ich die Wege meiner Entwicklung, die mich von der Romanistik zur Latinistik führten. Rom war seit meinem ersten Besuch, 1912, *die* Stadt meiner Seele geworden.... 1932 wurde ich durch tiefe Erschütterungen meiner Psyche in einen Zustand von alternirenden produktiver Spannung und schwerer Depression versetzt. Ich schreib 'Deutscher Geist in Gefahr', brach dann zusammen, mußte Jung in Zürich consultieren. Es war eine schwere Krise, in der ich später die unbewußte Anticipation des Grauens erkannte, das 1933 begann. Aus der Krise kam aber auch Heilung. Einem psychischen Zwang folgend warf ich mich auf das Studium der mittellat. Literatur. Ich hielt zwei große Vorlesungen darüber. Es bedeutete psychisch die Polarisirung um die Roma aeterna. Sie wirkte in mir als Archetyp im Jungschen Sinne und d. h. zugleich als ein mit vielfältiger Bedeutung und Energie geladenes Symbol. Es war als wäre eine Riegel gesprengt, ein Tor durchgebrochen. Ich konnte das geliebte und heilige Rom als Leitstern meines Forschens und Sinnens wählen. Besser gesagt: es wählte mich, den Deutschrömer. Der Weg nach Rom mußte durch das Mittelalter führen, das für mich nun zugleich eine archaische Schicht meines Bewußtseins bedeutete"); translation mine (with deepest gratitude to Prof. C. Stephen Jaeger for directing me to this passage). Elio De Angelis points out that Curtius does not acknowledge the Fascist connotations that "Eternal Rome" would have held at this date: De Angelis, "Sognando Gli Archetipi," 551–72 at 569.

[15] James, *The Varieties of Religious Experience*, 192–93, though all of Lectures VI–X bear on Curtius's account; Jaeger, "Ernst Robert Curtius," 367–80.

[16] For Jung, the anima represents a man's life-principle, which is gendered feminine to counterbalance his outward-facing, masculine persona (women, conversely, relate to a masculine-gendered animus). While a failed or mistaken relation to the anima was fraught with destructive potential,

by Eternal Rome herself, who appears simultaneously as a goddess, symbol, actually existing place, and – crucially – manifested in "eine archaische Schicht meines Bewußtseins" ("an archaic layer of my consciousness"). Unlike the anima, *Roma aeterna* offered a plausible subject for lectures in the philology department at Bonn; but it is nonetheless also an element of Curtius's own psyche. In *ELLMA*, he set out to prove that this medieval Latin stratum was not his alone, but the shared heritage of Western Europeans.

In so doing, Curtius once again built on major principles of Jungian psychology, while also significantly altering them. He incorporated three aspects of Jung's thought into *ELLMA*'s foundations: the idea of the stratified collective unconscious; archetypes, which Curtius argues manifest in literature as "commonplaces" or topoi; and a rejection of causality as the only way of understanding significant historical connections. This final aspect is the one that Curtius's contemporaries (and many later readers) found most difficult to accept. It is, however, not merely a curious side effect of Curtius's use of Jung's thought, but, as we shall see, an organic part of the project represented by *ELLMA*.

The idea that the human psyche is built up of layers, some of which are shared by others, is one of the most characteristic features of Jung's psychology. He often described his understanding of the unconscious as catalyzed by a dream he had in 1909:

> This was the dream. I was in a house I did not know, which had two stories. It was "my house." I found myself in the upper story, where there was a kind of salon furnished with fine old pieces in rococo style. On the walls hung a number of precious old paintings. I wondered that this should be my house, and thought, "Not bad." But then it occurred to me that I did not know what the lower floor looked like. Descending the stairs, I reached the ground floor. There everything was much older, and I realized that this part of the house must date from the fifteenth or sixteenth century. The furnishings were medieval; the floors were of red brick. Everywhere it was rather dark. I went from one room to another, thinking, "Now I really must explore the whole house." I came upon a heavy door, and opened it. Beyond it, I discovered a stone stairway that led down into the cellar. Descending again, I found myself in a beautifully vaulted room which looked exceedingly ancient. Examining the walls, I discovered layers of brick among the

---

this archetype "can appear also as an angel of light, a psychopomp who points the way to the highest meaning," and the encounter "with the anima is the 'master-piece'" in the individual's psychic development: Jung, "Archetypes of the Collective Unconscious," in *Archetypes*, 3–41 at 29. The anima/animus complex is ubiquitous in Jung's writings, but a useful overview can be derived from this essay and Jung, "Anima and Animus," in *Two Essays*, 188–211.

ordinary stone blocks, and chips of brick in the mortar. As soon as I saw this I knew that the walls dated from Roman times. My interest was by now intense. I looked more closely at the floor. It was of stone slabs, and in one of these I discovered a ring. When I pulled it, the stone slab lifted, and again I saw a stairway of narrow stone steps leading down into the depths. These, too, I descended, and entered a low cave cut into the rock. Thick dust lay on the floor, and in the dust were scattered bones and broken pottery, like remains of a primitive culture. I discovered two human skulls, obviously very old and half disintegrated. Then I awoke.[17]

Much of Jung's interest was focused on that "low cave," the base layer, which he conceived as a symbol of the true collective unconscious: a stratum of energies and affinities that was common to all humanity. But the construction and decoration of the dream-house above it indicates a significant corollary. For Jung, all shared experiences remained sedimented within the unconscious. But because not all groups shared the same experiences, the "upper floors" of the unconscious varied: thus Jung's dream-house, with its characteristically European styles built upon Roman cellars, reflects his Swiss nationality. Jung's embrace of the nation as his primary unit of group affinity entailed a series of moral and intellectual problems, as Andrew Samuels has shown; of these problems, the characterization of Jews as essentially nationless and thus psychologically distinct from their fellow-citizens is perhaps the worst.[18] Besides providing a point of intersection between his psychological theory and Nazi ideology, though, Jung's focus on national distinctiveness posed a challenge for Curtius's project, predicated as it was on an idea of Europe as a cultural unity that transcended differences of language or nation. Curtius's solution was simple but radical: he presented education, not heredity or a mystical connection to the land, as the process that laid down the bedrock of affinity.

Quite logically, then, "Literature and Education" is the departure-point from which Curtius begins to connect "European Literature" with "The Latin Middle Ages" (respectively the third, first, and second chapters of *ELLMA*). Across his discussion, he retains the spatial metaphor that structured Jung's conception of the psyche. While phrases such as his description of medieval grammar as "the foundation for everything else" might have been conventional, others suggest conscious use of a

---

[17] From Jung, *Memories, Dreams, Reflections*, 158–59. Jung frequently recounted this dream, with slight variations; see, for example, the 1925 seminar published as *Analytical Psychology* and Jung's contribution to the popular volume on his work, *Man and His Symbols*.
[18] Samuels, "National Psychology, National Socialism, and Analytical Psychology," 3–28.

structuring metaphor.[19] Rhetoric, writes Curtius, "takes us deeper into the world of medieval culture than does grammar";[20] and as his discussion of the subject reaches its goal, he continues:

> Antique rhetoric is a forbidding subject.... And if rhetoric itself impresses modern man as a grotesque bogey—how dare one try to interest him in *topics*, a subject which even the "literary specialist" hardly knows by name because he deliberately shuns the cellars—and foundations!—of European literature? Anxiously indeed must the author ask himself:
>
> *Nunc quid ago et dubiam trepidus quo dirigo proram?*
> (What do I? Where fearful do I steer my doubtful boat?)
>
> "Textbooks," says Goethe, "should be attractive; they will be so only if they present the brightest and most approachable side of learning and science." Let us try to present topics approachably if not brightly. Things human and divine lie hidden even there.[21]

The reference to "cellars and foundations" closely parallels the description of Jung's dream-house, likewise built on Roman foundations. The shared metaphor here is a curiously literal one: in the sentence following this passage, Curtius calls topics a "stockroom." These are cellars, in other words, in which things can be stored; and which are haunted by their own animating spirits.[22] The description of rhetorical topics as troubling, supernatural – yet intimately present – entities aligns them also with Jung's account of the unassimilated anima, which – like other subconscious drives – had a habit of manifesting itself as a powerful, often destructive supernatural entity that took shape in individuals' dreams in the form of various archetypes.[23]

Archetypes are the most explicitly acknowledged point of contact between Jung's theory of psychology and Curtius's of literature: it is worth, therefore, reflecting on their function as well as their various forms. Archetypes, in Jung's view, are instinctive, inborn patterns that provide people with the human terms they need in order to process the world: hence their recurrence in myths, as well as dreams and fantasies.[24] They are not, he emphasizes, ideas in themselves, but rather potential structures in

---

[19] *ELLMA*, 43.
[20] Ibid., 62.
[21] Ibid., 79. The verse is from the exordium to Book II of Paulinus of Périgeaux's *Vita S. Martini*.
[22] Curtius's phrase is "fratzenhaftes Gespenst" (Curtius, *Europäische Literatur*, 87): while Trask's translation "grotesque bogey" well captures the deceptive connotations of *Gespenst*, it diminishes the ghostly implications.
[23] Jung, "Archetypes of the Collective Unconscious," 24–32.
[24] Jung, "Concerning the Archetypes, with Special Reference to the Anima Concept," in *Archetypes*, 54–72 at 66–67 (but also *passim* in his work).

which content repeatedly tends to take shape: an archetype "might perhaps be compared to the axial system of a crystal, which, as it were, preforms the crystalline structure in the mother liquid, although it has no material existence of its own."[25] The archetypes themselves are biological phenomena, then, though their particular manifestations and the meanings attached to them are culturally, and individually, specific.

In his discussion of topoi, Curtius directly invokes Jung's conception of the archetypes, in ways that echo Jung's language. As forms that give imagistic shape to ideas, the archetypes readily lend themselves to analogy with the rhetorical structures that give ideas a linguistic shape. Curtius makes this likeness explicit in his discussion of the purpose of literary forms, describing them as "configurations and systems of configurations in which the incorporeal things of the mind can manifest themselves," and invoking Jung's metaphor of the lattice of a crystal.[26] In commenting on the reappearance of the Late Antique "rejuvenated old woman" image in Honoré de Balzac (1799–1850), he writes: "This is only comprehensible by the fact that [the image] is rooted in the deeper strata of the soul. It belongs to the stock of archaic proto-images in the collective unconscious;" and in his discussion of twelfth-century imagery of a feminine aspect of the divine, he quotes Jung's description of the anima.[27] It would seem, then, that Curtius was quarrying the topoi of Classical and medieval rhetoric and verse for examples of Jungian archetypes, much as Jung himself did (in, for instance, citing the eponymous *She* of H. Rider Haggard's [1856–1926] novel [1886] as an anima-figure).[28] But while Curtius's description of the commonplaces closely parallels Jung's account of the archetypes, the similarities themselves pinpoint some essential differences. This becomes clearest, perhaps, in Curtius's section on "Historical Topics":

> But in all poetical topoi the style of expression is historically determined. Now there are also topoi which are wanting throughout Antiquity down to the Augustan Age. They appear at the beginning of late Antiquity and then are suddenly everywhere. To this class belong the "aged boy" and "youthful old woman," which we shall analyze. They have a twofold interest. First, as regards literary biology, we can observe in them the *genesis of new topoi*.

---

[25] Jung, "Psychological Aspects of the Mother Archetype," in *Archetypes*, 75–110 at 79.
[26] *ELLMA*, 390.
[27] Ibid., 105, 122–23. On 104, Curtius notes that Claudian (*c.* 370-*c.* 404) and Prudentius (348–*c.* 413) apply this trope to the goddess Roma. The Jung essay quoted is "Concerning the Archetypes."
[28] For example, Jung, "Archetypes of the Collective Unconscious," 28, 30, and Jung, "Concerning the Archetypes," 71.

Thus our knowledge of the genetics of the formal elements of literature is widened. Secondly, these topoi are indications of a changed psychological state; indications which are comprehensible in no other way. Thus our understanding of the psychological history of the West is deepened, and we approach spheres that the psychology of C. G. Jung has explored.[29]

In two ways, the commonplaces here function precisely as do the archetypes. First, they emanate directly from a deeper stratum than the conscious – and thus provide a diagnostic index to the state of that deeper level. Because of this subterranean connection, particular instances are not connected by the usual channels of direct influence, but are "suddenly everywhere" (rather than gradually disseminated from author to author). This latter, ahistorical quality we shall turn to presently. Before that, however, I should like to point out an aspect of this passage that appears to be Jungian, but is not: the "literary biology" of which the commonplaces are a part. Where Jung intends the biological aspect of the archetypes quite literally – as inborn, heritable mental qualities analogous to animals' instincts – Curtius's biology here is closer to – though not precisely – a metaphor. In this passage, literature is revealed to be an organic system, complete with heritable traits subject to genetic mutation, and existing in a kind of symbiotic relationship with human communities.

As Elio De Angelis has pointed out, the idea that large groups of people generate an emergent psychology that is subject to analysis, as if the group were itself a human entity, was widespread in the late nineteenth and early twentieth centuries.[30] Curtius seems to take this for granted: the "changed psychological state" that produced these new topoi is attributed to Late Antiquity as a whole, rather than to any individual. But he first specifies that the commonplaces are features of literature, elements of its biology: it would thus seem that mass psychology is, as it were, the mutagen that changes literary form, but not the form's actual matrix. Literature, for Curtius, is thus not coextensive with the mass-psychology of an age, although both literature and Zeitgeist can interact and influence one another. One reason they can do so is that they bear analogous forms: the stratified shape of the Jungian psyche. The precise likeness Curtius draws between the *functions* of literary commonplaces and the psychological archetypes serves as a demonstration of this deep similarity between the shape of literature and that of the human mind.

---

[29] *ELLMA*, 82.
[30] De Angelis, "Sognando gli archetipi," 554–56.

The ahistorical connections Curtius draws between the appearances of various topoi are thus crucial to his argument: by removing the explanatory mechanism of normal, direct literary influence, he leaves the subterranean operations of tradition – the literary collective unconscious – as the only possible source of the topoi.[31] So, for instance, Curtius devotes a section to the problems with source-hunting in Dante (*c.* 1265–1321), attacking the attribution of the "boat of the mind" image to Cassian's (*c.* 360-*c.* 435) *Collationes* (*c.* 420) or to Propertius (*c.* 50 BCE-*c.* 15 BCE). While the works of these earlier authors indeed contain the topos, he writes, editors of Dante mislead readers

> into assuming that these nautical metaphors could not be derived from any other source... No, it is not a crime—unless one makes Dante a reader of Propertius. For by doing that one distorts historical perspective. One turns Dante into a humanistic lover of Roman elegy, detaches him from the poetic and rhetorical tradition of the Latin Middle Ages.[32]

With a remarkable rhetorical twist, Curtius here makes standard literary history, through which influences are traced from book to book, unhistorical. In his account, a true "historical perspective" recognizes medieval authors' connection to a tradition that makes direct influence unnecessary.

This is a literary analogue of Jungian comparative mythography, which seeks out similarities in imagery between mythic traditions that could have had no direct contact, and explains them as archetypal patterns emerging from the human collective unconscious.[33] Jung extended this idea of acausal connection to the events of ordinary life as well, developing a theory of "synchronicity" – meaningful consilience between apparently chance events – that entails the human psyche's ability to influence the physical world.[34] While Curtius is unconcerned with synchronicity as such, he does share Jung's interest in an alternative to history as unbroken chronological succession. Literature, he argues, uniquely offers readers unmediated access both to the past of the dead author, and to the timeless present of the still-living book:

---

[31] Emrich, "Topik und Topoi," 210–51.
[32] *ELLMA*, 129–30.
[33] The essays cited here from vol. 9 of Jung's collected works provide many examples of this tendency, but the best-known such work is probably Campbell, *The Hero with a Thousand Faces*.
[34] This is outlined most clearly in Jung, *Synchronicity*.

> For literature, all the past is present, or can become so. Homer [*fl.* 750 BCE] is brought to us anew in a new translation, and Rudolf Alexander Schröder's [1878–1962] Homer is different from Voss's [1751–1826]. I can take up Homer or Plato [*c.* 427 BCE–*c.* 347 BCE] at any hour, I "have" him then, and have him wholly.... With the literature of all times and peoples I can have a direct, intimate, and engrossing vital relationship.... Here we have a truly ontological relationship and real participation in an intellectual entity.... The "timeless present" which is an essential characteristic of literature means that the literature of the past can always be active in that of the present.[35]

The contention that all literature inhabits a kind of Platonic realm of ideas, simultaneously present and accessible to readers of all eras, removes it beyond normal historiographical categories of period and place, together with all their messy specificities and social entailments. Such a view of literature is doubly incompatible with historicist scholarship (and particularly with Marxian readings), both because it rejects the idea that literary works themselves are inseparably enmeshed with the material world of their creation, and because it rejects the idea that the reader – and thus also the critic – must be also so enmeshed. In place of the entanglements and contingencies of history, Curtius offers an encounter with literature that is intensely personal and creative. The examples he cites following the quotation above include the Homeric inspirations of both Virgil (70 BCE–19 BCE) and James Joyce (1882–1941), as well as T. S. Eliot (1888–1965) and other modern authors: but this passage is ultimately about the creation of *ELLMA* itself, which is designed as just such a generative encounter with the living and fully present past.

ELLMA's form both embodies this encounter and prepares the reader to apprehend it, as Curtius explains in his "Epilogue." Describing his text, he writes that "The arrangement of the presentation and the succession of the chapters are such as to result in a step-by-step progress and a spiral ascent."[36] The book, in other words, was written in the likeness of the mountain of Purgatory in Dante's *Divina Commedia* (1320) – the text that forms the subject of its final chapter or, one might say, its summit.

---

[35] *ELLMA*, 14–15. In this passage, Curtius is drawing a contrast between literature, which he sees as unbounded by place and time, and the visual arts, which he regards as fundamentally bounded and irreplicable (i.e., a book makes a work wholly accessible to whomever reads it, in a way that a photograph of a building or painting does not).
[36] Ibid., 381.

In Curtius's account, the *Commedia* represents the qualities he earlier attributed to Literature in the abstract: "Dante's poem moves wholly in the transcendent. But it is everywhere penetrated by the breath of history, by the passion of the present. Timelessness and temporality are not only confronted and related, they are also merged."[37] What Jungian psychology contributed to his admiration for the poet was a way of describing Dante's accomplishment, an alertness to the functional power of archetypes, and, in the mountain of Purgatory, a powerfully multivalent and useful spatial metaphor. In his discussion of Beatrice, for instance, Curtius argues against the prevalent theory that she was a historical figure, the daughter of a Florentine banker. Instead, he interprets her as "a myth created by Dante … the beatifying female power," using language extremely similar to Jung's description of the anima.[38] In Curtius's view, it would seem that an ability to consciously and effectively deploy archetypal figures within his poetry was one of Dante's particular achievements.

Curtius's account of Dante's Virgil, in particular, reveals both the Jungian substructure of his reading and the full implications of the particular development they have received in the course of *ELLMA*. In the *Commedia*, Virgil "is the mouthpiece of the temporal and the eternal Rome whose name can be symbolically applied to Paradise (*Purg.*, XXXII, 102). At the same time he is adept and mouthpiece of the otherworld."[39] This observation is particularly striking in light of Curtius's own transformative encounter with the archetype of *Roma aeterna*. But Virgil is not simply a vatic, quasi-priestly figure; he is also, above all, a master of Latin rhetoric and poetry.[40] Through him, it would seem, the subterranean elements of medieval literature are permitted to speak and interact directly with the consciousness of the present within the visionary world of the *Commedia*, instructing and guiding the poet. In Jungian terms, Virgil's mediation has allowed Dante to assimilate his unconscious: an unconscious which, in Curtius's model of European literature, equates to Latinity. Virgil's – and, thus, Dante's – ability to give voice to literature's archetypal powers flows directly from this source, just as *ELLMA* itself began with medieval rhetoric and its roots in classical literature. The assimilation of the unconscious, including the coming to terms with one's anima, were for Jung indispensable – yet difficult

---

[37] Ibid., 366.
[38] Ibid., 377–78; on the Jungian anima, see n. 16.
[39] Ibid., 358–59 (the embedded reference is his).
[40] Ibid., 356–57.

and rarely achieved – precursors to a person's full realization as an individual.[41] Curtius's account of Dante is cast in this Jungian language of self-achievement: the *Commedia* "is the projection of Dante's personality... on the total literary tradition.... Goal and accomplishment of the whole: perfect superposition of Dante's within upon the cosmic without, and mutual interpenetration of the two; congruence of soul and world."[42] This psychic unification, however, Curtius attributes not to divine inspiration, but to a mastery of poetic tradition and form, guided by the figure of Virgil and embodied in *terza rima*. In Dante's *Commedia*, the divide between literature's psyche and the human collapse, and give birth to a profound vision of cosmic order.

One can hear an echo of the account of Curtius's own project that he gave to de Menasce when he states of Dante: "The world was out of joint. Upon Dante fell the immense task of setting it right."[43] The point here is not that Curtius considered himself a second Dante, but that in Dante he perceived the author who most perfectly unified literature's conscious and unconscious layers, and as such provided an ideal model for his own work. In conceiving *ELLMA*'s structure as like that of the mountain of Purgatory – a spiral ascent from a broad base to a pinnacle – he drew on the *Commedia*'s power while working toward an articulation of that power's precise nature. But he also chose to emulate the part of Dante's otherworldly terrain that was most like Jung's idea of the psyche, with differentiated layers piled upon a vast shared base. In this way, Curtius used the intersection of literary and psychological forms to articulate "a new perception of the inner connections of European literature."[44]

Curtius's encounter with Jung's theories proved to be remarkably fruitful, then. The psychologist's concept of a universal human nature offered what Curtius seems to have taken as factual grounding for a common substrate that transcended, and eluded, the bounds of ordinary history. But Jung's thought also furnished a conceptual model that Curtius extrapolated beyond the bounds of the individual human, or even the nation. Conceiving of *literature* itself as possessing a stratified psyche, Curtius spent much of *ELLMA* exploring one of its lower layers – not the deep caves common to all people, but the cellars of Roman brick shared by those of Latin Europe. Jung's insistence that the archetypes, which emerged from and gave access to these lower layers, were *formal* features provided Curtius with a point of

---

[41] This process is most clearly laid out in Jung, "The Relations Between the Ego and the Unconscious," in *Two Essays*, 121–241.
[42] *ELLMA*, 379.
[43] Ibid., 366.
[44] Ibid., 381.

convergence between psychological and literary analysis, as he argued for the revelatory potential of formal devices in medieval Latin. But where Jung saw the human psyche as inborn, a biological inheritance, Curtius's vast and subterranean literary organism was one that any person could partake of – and join – by education, and above all by reading. In so doing, one could transcend the limits of nation, circumstance, and self – and, through a new creation, enlarge all three. As Dante envisioned himself meeting Virgil and following him to Paradise, an encounter with *literature* provided unmediated access to the past, and an unending source of inspiration. But, just as the long and difficult process of assimilating one's own subconscious was an unavoidable preliminary to becoming a fully realized individual, assimilation of the Latin heritage – the unconscious of European literature – was the only way to understand the continent's true and indissoluble cultural unity, and to create new literature out of the old. To this heritage, *ELLMA* proposed itself as guide.

It would seem particularly fitting, then, that the English translation of Curtius's apocalypse should have been published through the Bollingen Series. Controlled by the Bollingen Foundation between 1943 and 1969 and now distributed by Princeton University Press, the series was funded by Paul Mellon (1907–1999) – son of Andrew W. Mellon (1855–1937) and heir to his vast fortune – and his wife Mary (1904–1946), who was a devoted Jungian and the primary impetus behind the series.[45] Named for Jung's country house (which the Mellons visited), the series was intended to promote Jung's own writings for American readers, and to publish scholarship on world art, literature, and religion that in a broad way supported Jung's theory of humanity's common archetypal inheritance. The collected works of Carl Jung, in English translation, occupied many of the early numbers of the series. Partly through the nebulous bonds of various Mellon family initiatives, the Bollingen Foundation had connections with Princeton's Institute for Advanced Study, where Curtius was a visiting fellow in 1949.[46] During this time, Curtius, according to William McGuire, offered *ELLMA* to the Bollingen Series to publish in English translation.[47] While the contents and structure of the new edition were unaltered, the new foreword that Curtius contributed to this translation underlined his debt to Jung; it also emphasized, in a way the German foreword did not, Curtius's

---

[45] Information about the series is derived partly from the website of Princeton University Press (https://press.princeton.edu/catalogs/series/title/bollingen-series-general.html) but primarily from McGuire, *Bollingen*.
[46] This visit did not go as well as one might expect: see Jaeger, "Medievalist's Contempt," 378.
[47] McGuire, *Bollingen*, 192–93.

personal trajectory and the fundamentally reparative, extra-scholarly purpose of the book.[48] The foreword serves not only as an apologia for the book itself, but also for its inclusion in the Bollingen Series: which is to say, its connection to Jungian thought.

As we have seen, this connection far transcends the overlap between Jung's archetypes and Curtius's topoi; the structures of Jungian thought really are fundamental to *ELLMA*. The consequences of this for modern scholars will require continued thought. In short: to use *ELLMA*, must one also accept its premises – including the stratified collective unconscious, and the idea of acausal connection?

Some scholars have indeed suggested that the problems with Curtius's work are fundamental and, perhaps, fatal. Hans Ulrich Gumbrecht, for instance, has argued that the way Curtius conceives of literature's exemption from historical time inevitably produces a hopelessly static, conservative mode of criticism, while Edward Said (1935–2003) pointed out the logical flaw – and narrowing, exclusionary consequences – of collapsing the distinction between European literature and literature *tout court*.[49] More recently, Jaeger has also attacked *ELLMA*'s effect on medieval scholarship, particularly highlighting the book's messianic strain and the problems inherent in regarding medieval literature as a safe form of occupational therapy.[50] Earlier critics also questioned *ELLMA*'s insistence on medieval Latin as primarily a vessel for tradition, rather than a varied set of creative innovations on that tradition: this was, for instance one of the primary objections in Leo Spitzer's (1887–1960) review of the first edition.[51] Such criticism stems ultimately from rejection of *ELLMA*'s conceptual core: the idea that medieval Latin is important primarily as the collective unconscious of the vernacular literatures of Europe.[52]

Readers in such a situation might very reasonably respond either by repudiating Curtius's work altogether, or by drawing piecemeal upon its wealth of philological information while ignoring its overall argument. Given *ELLMA*'s vast scope – including its "Excursions," it runs to nearly 600 pages in paperback – the latter has probably been de facto adopted as the prevalent strategy, even by those who never realized it had

---

[48] *ELLMA*, vii–x.
[49] Gumbrecht, "Zeitlosigkeit, die durchscheint in der Zeit," 49–71; Said, *Culture and Imperialism*, 44–45.
[50] Jaeger, "Medievalist's Contempt."
[51] Spitzer, "Review of Ernst Robert Curtius, *Europäische Literatur und lateinisches Mittelalter*," 425–31.
[52] Of course, some readers also simply hated the idea of using psychoanalytic thought in a work of literary scholarship: see Kristeller, "Review of Ernst Robert Curtius, *Europäische Literatur und lateinisches Mittelalter*," 205–8.

argumentative premises to object to. But using bits of *ELLMA* without engaging the whole does not really evade the problem: it is impossible to understand why Curtius placed such stress on the topoi, for instance, without recognizing the structural role they played in mediating between literature's conscious and unconscious layers, as he conceived them.

Ultimately, *ELLMA* forces us to engage with the problem of scholarship as a form of art. It is, without a doubt, a work of awe-inspiring learning, premised on a mastery of literature in seven languages that few have ever achieved. And along every step of its spiral ascent, this learning is deployed according to a deeply personal, yet totalizing, conception of culture and the human mind – one that many, perhaps most, modern scholars would not accept as true.

And yet I do not think that *ELLMA* ought to be consigned to the hell of books that neither instruct nor delight. While much of the information in it can now be found elsewhere – often, because so many people have read and benefited from Curtius's book – the acuity of its author's insights into literature still speak for themselves in elegant and memorable prose. But more than that, *ELLMA* offers poignant testimony to unbroken faith in literature's power, in a generation that had all reason to discard that faith. It is remarkable that Curtius, like Auerbach, Wellek, Spitzer, and others who became scholars of comparative literature between the wars of the twentieth century, should continue to devote their lives to projects that they believed could erode nations' fanatic beliefs in their own purity and singularity. The immense learning in these books, their breadth of reference and philological precision, represent not an escape from the world and the horrors of war, but an attempt to change that world for the better. For Curtius, the thought of Carl Jung offered not just relief from personal psychological misery, but a path by which an entire continent might achieve its own salvation.

Ambitions of this sort are hard to reconcile with literary scholarship as we understand it. But they allow us to expand the bounds of what we might conceive scholarship to be, while prompting us to delve deeper into the foundations of what we read and which has shaped how we read. What we find there may be far stranger than we dreamed.

CHAPTER 6

Old English at the Midcentury
Poetry, Scholarship, and Fiction in Britain in the 1940s and 1950s

Clare A. Lees

> The latest in elegies, proving beyond all cavil
>
> That typewriters' chatter is more than a match for machine guns'
>
> Alexander Scott, *The Latest in Elegies*

In 1949 Alexander Scott (1920–1989) published his first collection of poetry, *The Latest in Elegies*, prefacing it with this wry epigraph.[1] Writing and warfare, typewriters and machine guns place the collection in the immediate aftermath of World War II, while its assertion of the power of poetry echoes W. H. Auden's (1907–1973) *In Memory of W. B. Yeats* (1940).[2] Scott's undergraduate career as a student of English language and literature at the University of Aberdeen had been interrupted by the war. In spite of some early pacifism, he served in the Royal Artillery and the Royal Highlanders, participated in the D-Day landings, was wounded in 1944, and later awarded the Military Cross for his leadership during the battle of Reichswald Forest in 1945. Returning to his studies when war ended, Scott went on to become a poet, playwright, journalist, and university lecturer. He was to be instrumental in developing the first department of Scottish literature at the University of Glasgow in 1971.[3]

Alongside its contemporary war poetry and pastoral elegies, Scott's collection includes versions of two Old English elegies, *Deor* and *The Seafarer*, and the early medieval battle poem *The Battle of Maldon*, adapted into Scots

---

[1] Scott, *The Latest in Elegies*, iii.
[2] For Auden's famous comment about poetry making nothing happen, although it lives on, see *In Memory of W. B. Yeats*, composed in 1939 and published in his collection, *Another Time*, 93–96. For discussion of the relation between poetry and journalism shaped by World War II, see Galvin, *News of War*, esp. 120–61.
[3] Robb, "Scott, Alexander Mackie."

(Scottish English, as it is sometimes known). These latest, most recent elegies draw on Scottish history and culture rather than the English literary history with which the Old English poems are most often associated. *Deor*, with its eponymous and in all probability fictional Old English poet or *scop*, becomes a *Makar's Lament* fit for a Scottish poet, its figures of Germanic myth, Weland and Beadohild, replaced by the Scottish heroes William Wallace (*c.* 1270–1305) and Mary, Queen of Scots (1542–1587).[4] *The Seafarer* becomes a *Seaman's Sang*, and *The Battle of Maldon* is reworked as a *Sang for a Flodden*, which memorializes the sixteenth-century defeat of the Scots by the English at Flodden instead of the tenth-century defeat of the English by the Danes.[5] Old English poetry is here put to Scottish national and cultural use. Indeed, Scott carefully identifies his elegies as "Eftir the West Saxon" and "Frae the West Saxon" (in the case of *Seaman's Sang*), referring to neither "Anglo-Saxon," as this poetic language would usually have been described in this period, or Old English.[6] Scott also eschews the more obvious route of direct translation into Modern English, exemplified by his better-known colleague at Glasgow, Edwin Morgan (1920–2010), in his English "unwritten war poem," *Beowulf*, published in 1952.[7] Like Morgan, first modern Makar of Scotland, Alexander Scott's creative, linguistic, and scholarly investment in reworking early medieval English literature was evident at the midcentury.

The Latest in Elegies is suggestive of the opportunities early medieval English poetry afforded writers and scholars in Britain in the 1940s and 1950s and offers a gateway into the subject of this chapter. Modern writers in this period negotiated the medieval past in their work in different ways. Outright hostility sits alongside an awareness that thinking of the medieval is a necessary component of modern culture. To give a sense of this literary engagement, this chapter offers an account of Old English at the midcentury in relation to four profoundly different writers: Kingsley Amis (1922–1995), Gavin Bone (1907–1942), Bryher (Annie Winifred Ellerman, 1894–1983),

---

[4] Scott, *The Latest in Elegies*, 47–48. For *Deor*, see Bjork, ed. and trans., *Old English Shorter Poems*, 98–101.

[5] Scott, *The Latest in Elegies*, 45–7, 49. For *The Battle of Maldon* and its historical context, see Scragg, ed., *The Battle of Maldon*.

[6] I use "Old English" and "early medieval" to refer to the literature and culture of this period. For the ethnocentric and racial implications of the term "Anglo-Saxon," and their significance for the discipline of Medieval Studies, see the important work of, for example, Dorothy Kim, Adam Miyashiro, Erik Wade, and Mary Rambaran-Olm. Rambaran-Olm, "Misnaming the Medieval," offers a good summary.

[7] Morgan, trans., *Beowulf* (this was first published by Hand and Flower Press, Aldington, Kent in 1952); for discussion, see Chris Jones, "While Crowding Memories Came," 123–44. Morgan was named as Makar in 2004.

and Angus Wilson (1913–1991). The work of these writers and scholars demonstrates that early medieval culture is part of a broader postwar inquiry into society, culture, sexuality, and, as we shall see, race and ethnocentrism. This chapter argues, therefore, that literary practice is a distinctive form of historical thinking and that early medieval culture is an important component of literary creativity and innovation in the 1940s and 1950s.

In 1947, for example, Kingsley Amis, whose career was interrupted by World War II like Scott's, published his first collection of poems. *Bright November* included his first version of "Beowulf," a brief and bitingly comic poem about the long Old English poem with the same title. Unlike Scott's re-versioned Old English poetry, which is relatively unknown to twenty-first-century Anglo-American readers, Amis's "Beowulf," revised and included in anthologies by him up to the 1970s, has been noticed. The 1947 version begins with a quotation from J. R. R. Tolkien (1892–1973) by way of an epigraph: "There is not much poetry in the world like this."[8] Indeed. The epigraph, like the poem it prefaces, is double-edged. By 1947, Tolkien was well established. He had been Rawlinson and Bosworth Professor of Anglo-Saxon at Oxford since 1925, becoming Merton Professor of English Language and Literature in 1945. His essay "*Beowulf:* The Monsters and the Critics" and his first work of fiction, *The Hobbit*, both belong to the 1930s. And while Tolkien continued to explore both fiction and scholarship (most notably with his essay on translating *Beowulf*) during the 1940s, *The Fellowship of the Ring* was to come later, in 1954.[9]

Tolkien clearly influenced the young Amis, who saw in the older scholar – and teacher – an easy target. Amis's first College tutor, Gavin Bone, poet, translator, artist, and early medievalist made less impression on him in these years.[10] Together with his friend and fellow Oxford student and poet Philip Larkin (1922–1985), Amis cultivated an intense animosity towards all things medieval, Old English included, throughout the 1940s and 1950s.[11] This animosity rewarded him in 1953 with his

---

[8] Amis, *Bright November*, 26. The poem was reprinted in *Essays in Criticism*, 85. The epigraph was omitted and the poem significantly revised for *A Case of Samples*, 14. The revised version, later included in Amis, *Collected Poems*, is briefly mentioned by Magennis, *Translating "Beowulf,"* 105. In my view, the 1947 poem is the better poem.
[9] "*Beowulf:* The Monsters and the Critics" (1936) and "On Translating *Beowulf*" (1940) are reprinted in Tolkien, *The Monsters and the Critics*, 5–48 and 49–60.
[10] Bone's career as medieval scholar, poet, and artist at St John's College, Oxford merits further attention. After his premature death, his translations and notes were published as *Anglo-Saxon Poetry* and *Beowulf in Modern Verse*. See, Edwards, "Gavin Bone and his Old English Translations."
[11] Characteristic of Amis's attitude towards *Beowulf* as a student is a comment in a letter to Larkin, April 6, 1946: "I wish the man had burned the manuscript of Barewulf" (the reference is to the fire

best-known comic novel, *Lucky Jim*, dedicated to Larkin. Amis's novel features James (Jim) Dixon, assistant lecturer in medieval history at a provincial university in the Midlands, who escapes the life of a reluctant and luckless academic for London's contemporary scene and love by the novel's end. Two years later, in 1956, another wave of popular enthusiasm greeted the publication of *Anglo-Saxon Attitudes* by Angus Wilson, its title taken from Lewis Carroll's (1832–1898) description of "an Anglo-Saxon Messenger" with his "Anglo-Saxon attitudes," which "he only does … when he is happy."[12] Wilson's novel also features a medieval historian. But unlike Amis's young Jim Dixon with his vague interest in the economy of medieval ships, Wilson's Gerald Middleton, in his late middle age, is an expert in the early Middle Ages whose career – like his marriage – is on the wane.

Wilson's novel turns on the discovery of a pagan icon – a nice case of a misplaced phallic symbol – during an excavation of a fictional seventh-century Christian burial of Bishop Eorpwald at the fictional town of Melpham shortly before World War I. The discovery is eventually revealed to be a playful act of filial deception by Gilbert Stokesay on his professorial father. But *Anglo-Saxon Attitudes* is interested in modern as well as historical acts of fraud, social deception, and self-deceit in a varied cast of characters from all social classes, professions, and sexual orientations. There is some merit in the argument that Wilson's novel, with its insider knowledge of medieval historians and archaeologists, is a response to Amis's comic satire about the attitudes of pre- and post-Second World War university scholars.[13] Certainly, Amis excoriated *Anglo-Saxon Attitudes*, his homophobia fully on view.[14] Both novels might be said to be reactions against the modernism

---

at Ashburnham House in 1731 in which so much of the Cotton Library was lost); Amis, *The Letters of Kingsley Amis*, ed. Leader, 55. By the 1950s, Amis's dislike of medieval literature was reaching a wider audience; see, for example, Amis, "Anglo-Saxon Platitudes." His attitude towards the teaching of Old and Middle English at Oxford remained unchanged throughout his life; see Amis, *Memoirs*, 53.

[12] On Carroll's "Anglo-Saxonism," see Jones, *Fossil Poetry*, 130–35; and Locherbie-Cameron, "Anglo-Saxon Attitudes," 71–82. For a study of Wilson's novel from the perspective of medievalism, see Hahn, "Medievalism," 115–34.

[13] Wilson resigned from the Reading Room of the British Museum in 1955 to write the novel. As Drabble points out in *Angus Wilson*, 198–206, there is some resemblance between Middleton and Sir Thomas Kendrick (1895–1979), Director of the British Museum. Renaissance scholar Frances Yates (1899–1981) of the Warburg Institute and medieval historian Margaret Deansley (1885–1977) of Royal Holloway, University of London, and later Cambridge, are among those linked to the character of Rose Lorimer. See also Hahn, "Medievalism."

[14] Amis's review, "Dodos Less Daring," deemed the novel a failure. His comments on its queer characters, "the expected posse of pansies," is clearly a reference to Wilson as well, whose earlier novel, *Hemlock and After*, was openly queer. Drabble, *Angus Wilson*, 212–13, notes that other reviews were more positive.

associated with prewar Bloomsbury; they offer postwar disenchantment and social realism. Change was in the air. Social issues such as class and institutions such as universities were up for scrutiny.[15] The so-called Angry Young Men were loudly asserting their (straight) masculinity, although queer writers, men and women, were gaining popular traction as well, in spite of the oppressive state laws against male homosexuality.[16] The surprise for twenty-first-century readers, perhaps, is that medieval historians were worth fictional treatment in the postwar period in the first place. But the discovery of the Sutton Hoo ship burial in 1939 and the exposure of Piltdown Man – apparently the evolutionary link between ape and man – as a hoax in 1953 were topics in vogue, and they hover in the background of *Anglo-Saxon Attitudes*.[17]

There was a lot of interest, scholarly and literary, in medieval culture in the postwar period. In the same year that Amis published "Beowulf" (1947), Helen Waddell (1889–1965) published what was to be her last public lecture, *Poetry in the Dark Ages* (the W. P. Ker Memorial Lecture of 1946), after a long career as a popular translator of medieval Latin poetry; she was what would now be called a public medievalist.[18] A year later, in 1948, Bryher published *Beowulf: roman d'une maison de thé dans Londres bombardé*, a novel set in a London tea shop run by two women during the Blitz. Beowulf is the name given to the plaster bulldog who plays a leading role in this delightfully queer novel. The year 1948 also saw the publication of *The Corner that Held Them* by Sylvia Townsend Warner (1893–1978), with its fourteenth-century events set in a twelfth-century convent in Norfolk. As in Rose Macaulay's (1881–1958) *The World My Wilderness* (1950) with its awareness of the long history of London, Bryher and Townsend Warner take up medieval materials in their pursuit of ostensibly modern themes – war and loss, community and isolation.[19]

---

[15] See English, *Comic Transactions*, 128–59.
[16] The term "Angry Young Men" was first used to promote John Osborne's (1929–1994) *Look Back in Anger* at the Royal Court in 1956. It identified a group of writers that included Amis and was also associated with the so-called Movement poets such as Larkin. Drabble, *Angus Wilson*, 219–23, points out Wilson's generous support of Colin Wilson (1931–2013), author of *The Outsider* and another "Angry Young Man" in spite of the widespread misogyny and homophobia of much of the writing of this period. Wilson's own life as a discreetly gay man in a lifelong relationship who came out late in life is well known.
[17] Hahn, "Medievalism," 124–26.
[18] See Lees, "Women Write the Past," 3–22. Waddell is one of the few nonfictional medievalists mentioned in Wilson, *Anglo-Saxon Attitudes*, 21.
[19] See Beckwith, "Preserving, Conserving, Deserving the Past," 205.

Waddell, Bryher, Townsend Warner, and Macaulay, were well-established and much-admired writers by the 1940s and 1950s. Their engagement with medieval literature and culture was not incidental, and it was well informed. Macaulay's postwar inquiry into the history and aesthetics of ruins, *Pleasure of Ruins* (1953), for example, quotes from the Old English poem *The Ruin*, as translated by Edwin Morgan.[20] Macaulay, in short, was sufficiently informed about modern and Old English poetry to read Morgan. Bryher's intense engagement with modernism and women's writing during the interwar years in Paris and subsequently in London during World War II is well known, as is her long-lasting relationship with the poet H. D. (Hilda Doolittle, 1886–1961).[21] Perhaps less account has been taken of her historical fiction. After *Beowulf*, Bryher published historical novels throughout the 1950s and 1960s, beginning with *The Fourteenth of October* (1954), set during the Norman Conquest of 1066.[22]

Amis's career as satirical novelist, poet, literary journalist, and professional agitator on the cultural scene began in the 1940s, as we have seen. He left his post as assistant lecturer in English at the University of Swansea in 1961 (1949–61) to work full time as a writer.[23] Wilson too had begun writing in the late 1940s. He had worked at Bletchley Park in the British Government Code and Cypher School during the war years, like the better-known polymath and gay icon Alan Turing (1912–1954). He retired from his work in the Reading Room of the British Museum in 1955, the year before he published *Anglo-Saxon Attitudes*, and enjoyed a successful career as a writer, patron of literature, and supporter of homosexual rights. In 1962, he joined the University of East Anglia as a part-time senior lecturer, where he cofounded with Malcolm Bradbury (1932–2000) the now famous MA program in Creative Writing.[24] Both Amis and Wilson were knighted for their contributions to literature. Indeed, in their different ways, Amis, Bryher, and Wilson were firm supporters of the arts as well as innovative writers. That their careers were not defined by their interest in the medieval past, but that they use medieval materials in their work is

---

[20] Macaulay, *Pleasure of Ruins*, 10 (the poem was first published in *Horizon*, 1949). Morgan's translations of the Old English elegies and select riddles were included in his *Dies Irae* (1952), to be published the same year as his translation of *Beowulf*, but the press folded and the collection as a whole was only published in the 1990s. See Jones, "While Crowding Memories Came," 123 and n. 3.

[21] See Buchanan, "*Beowulf*, Bryher, and the Blitz," 279–303, for the creative collaboration between Bryher and H. D.

[22] For a brief introduction, see Walwyn and Taylor, "Ellerman, (Annie) Winifred [pseud. Bryher]."

[23] Leader, *The Life of Kingsley Amis*; see also Leader, "Amis, Sir Kingsley William."

[24] Drabble, *Angus Wilson*; see also Bradbury, "Wilson, Sir Angus Frank Johnstone."

precisely my point. Modern British writing has a considerable investment in medieval literature and culture. Tracking this investment across a group of writers and scholars in the postwar period makes sense.[25]

Indeed, the creative legacy of Old English in the mid-twentieth century yields no single overarching narrative nor any individual on whose work such a narrative might hang. Oxford's Tolkien – and Amis's demonization of Tolkien in his "Beowulf" – contrasts with Scott's commitment to Scottish literature at Glasgow. Bryher's *Beowulf* and Wilson's *Anglo-Saxon Attitudes* have dramatically different stories to tell about the literary use of the early English past. Amis's aggressively cisgender masculinity and the casual misogyny of his "lucky" Jim contrasts profoundly with the queer sensibilities of Wilson and Bryher, whose work is interested in offering a more inclusive and complex account of both present and past. To explore Old English at the midcentury, therefore, is to venture well beyond the conventional scope of the disciplines of modernism, early medieval studies, or medievalism.[26] Disciplines are exclusive structures, and this chapter aims to unsettle that exclusivity.[27] In demonstrating how integral to British literary innovation in the immediate postwar period is early medieval culture, this chapter invites further work on other places and periods as well.

It perhaps makes sense that Tolkien has dominated accounts of twentieth-century scholarly and literary engagements with early medieval English literature.[28] Or that the poet best known for his use of Old English poetry – after Ezra Pound (1885–1972) and before Seamus Heaney (1939–2013) – is Edwin Morgan.[29] However, as this overview of poetry, fiction, and public scholarship produced at the midcentury suggests, there is more to be said. This chapter now takes a more detailed look at Amis's "Beowulf" before considering Bryher's *Beowulf* and ending with a reflection on Wilson's *Anglo-Saxon Attitudes*. Amis and Wilson are well

---

[25] Wallace, "Medieval Studies in Troubled Times," is a model for this kind of work.
[26] Carolyn Dinshaw's figure of the "amateur" medievalist goes some way towards the kinds of creative-critical interfaces this material suggests; see Dinshaw, *How Soon Is Now?* and also Lees and Overing, *The Contemporary Medieval in Practice*.
[27] The emphasis on the mid-twentieth century also usefully complements the better-known work on the nineteenth century as the flawed, imperial, and racial origin for the study of Old English literature. See the Introduction in this volume, Perry and Saltzman. See also Kabir, "Analogy in Translation"; Davies, *Visions and Ruins*; and Ellard, *Anglo-Saxon(ist) Pasts*.
[28] The bibliography is extensive: see, for example, Chance, ed., *Tolkien the Medievalist*.
[29] See Jones, *Strange Likeness*. David Jones's (1895–1974) *The Anathemata* (1952) is another important example of midcentury British modernism that draws on early medieval materials (Welsh and English included). See Brooks, *Poet of the Medieval Modern*.

known for their contribution to twentieth-century British literature. A measure of their influence may be had by the fact that their novels have stayed in print since they were first published and attracted television and film versions from the 1950s to the 1990s.[30] Bryher's medieval modernity has enjoyed less sustained attention than her important work in the first half of the twentieth century.[31] But let us turn now to 1947 – to Amis's "Beowulf" and its engagement with the Oxford "language men," as Amis called scholars and writers such as J. R. R. Tolkien and Gavin Bone.[32]

Amis's "Beowulf" and the "Language Men"

> Someone has told us this man was a hero.
> But what have we to learn in following
> His tedious journey to his ancestors
> (An instance of Old English harking-back)?
> –Kingsley Amis, "Beowulf," lines 13–16

Although prefaced by an epigraph from Tolkien ("There is not much poetry in the world like this"), Amis's 1947 version of "Beowulf" delivers itself as a kind of epitaph for the Old English poem and its critics.[33] Its first stanza, for example, finds Beowulf "bored with fighting dragons" and locking down his "wordhoard." In its second, our hero is out of action and out-of-date, his "byrnie" fit now for a "baseball catcher." The third dismisses Beowulf's humanity and his sexuality with it: "Never was human, never lay with women / (Weak conjugation)." And the final stanza, as quoted, targets the Old English poem's valorization of heroic masculinity. The joke is at the expense of Tolkien's "*Beowulf:* The Monsters and the Critics," an essay still at the heart of *Beowulf* criticism in the twenty-first century.[34] Aside from Tolkien, the other scholars name-checked by Amis are Grímur Jónsson Thorkelin (1752–1829), whose transcripts of the Old

---

[30] *Lucky Jim* was adapted by the BBC in 1957, and the *Further Adventures of Lucky Jim* appeared in 1982. *Anglo-Saxon Attitudes* was made into a three-part series in 1992, with the screenplay by Andrew Davies and early appearances by Kate Winslet and Daniel Craig.

[31] Buchanan, "*Beowulf,* Bryher, and the Blitz," 279–303. For a related study of medieval modernity, see Mills, *Derek Jarman's Medieval Modern*.

[32] The phrase is from Amis, "Anglo-Saxon Platitudes."

[33] Amis writes to Larkin on May 18, 1946 about "Bayou Woof," saying: "I enjoyed writing that a good deal. Do you think anybody would mind if I dedicated it to Professor Bollkeen?" (Amis, *The Letters of Kingsley Amis*, 68). The final stanza of the version published in *A Case of Samples*, 18, revises lines 14–15 to "Must we then reproduce his paradigms, / Trace out his rambling regress to his forbears."

[34] Evident from its inclusion in the Norton edition of Heaney, *Beowulf*, 103–30.

English poem represent the beginning of its modern textual history, and Julius Zupitza (1844–1895), who published the first manuscript facsimile of *Beowulf* in 1882.³⁵

Does Amis's "Beowulf" protest too much? The Old English *Beowulf* and its critics are so comically dismissed that Amis's investment in the early medieval poem is all the more transparent. His "Beowulf" does indeed hark back to *Beowulf*. The poem's use of the caesura, perhaps the most distinctive feature of Old English poetry to modern eyes, and its cultivation of quatrains, a modern English verse form that both accommodates and complements the Old English poetic style with its four-stressed syllabic line, are symptomatic of the modern attractions of the older poetry. Alliterative phrases such as the "hope of the heathens" and "hard and hand-locked" are literal translations from the Old English *Beowulf*.³⁶ And the poem's command of philology is firmly on display, with nods to "Thorkelin's transcript B" of *Beowulf*, "Zupitza's reading," and the "Weak conjugation," a reference philologically to the grammar of Old English verbs and, at the same time, an apparent joke about the hero's sexuality. Even Amis's worrying away at heroic masculinity ("never was human, never lay with women") is a homophobic version of Tolkien's homosocial interest in men-as-warriors in "*Beowulf*: The Monsters and the Critics."³⁷

As we have seen, Amis was a student of St John's College, Oxford. Disparaging as he was of Tolkien throughout his life, Amis was to become more complimentary about Gavin Bone, his tutor, who had died of cancer during Amis's first year.³⁸ Bone's two translations, *Anglo-Saxon Poetry* (1943) and *Beowulf in Modern Verse with an Essay and Pictures* (1945), both

---

[35] On Thorkelin, see Fulk, Bjork, and Niles, eds., *Klaeber's Beowulf*, xxvi–vii. See also Zupitza, ed., *Beowulf*.

[36] Fulk, Bjork, and Niles, eds., *Beowulf*, line 179 (a celebrated crux in the poem) and line 322. Compare with Kemble, trans., *A Translation*, 8 and 14. The revised version of Amis's poem draws on the Old English phrase, "Lif is læne," in the second stanza. This is not taken from any Old English work but from Tolkien's "*Beowulf*," 19.

[37] Tolkien's famous essay does not address the women in the poem nor consider the hero's fight with Grendel's mother, which is so central to it. For Amis's poem, compare the 1947 version of the third stanza, "Consider now what this king had not done / Never was human, never lay with women / (Weak conjunction), never saw quite straight / Children of men or the bright bowl of heaven," with the revised version of 1956 and subsequent printings, "Only with Grendel was he man-to-man: / Grendel's dam was his only sort of woman / (Weak Conjugation). After they were gone / How could he stand the bench-din, the yelp-word?" By 1956 Amis was identifying the monstrous elements of the hero, Beowulf, with his opponents, Grendel and Grendel's mother. Both versions, however, imply that men who are not "weak" have sex with women.

[38] Motion, *Philip Larkin*, 41–42, reports that Amis thought Bone "was a very nice, very tolerant man," and detects his influence on Larkin's poetry.

in print long after the 1950s and still widely available in university libraries, were published posthumously by his mother, Gertrude Helena Bone (1876–1962), from work previously printed or in manuscript.[39] Together the anthologies offer evidence of a distinctively modern, if not modernist, critical sensibility that contrasts strikingly with Tolkien's approach to Old English poetry. The influence of Bone on Morgan's translation of *Beowulf*, acknowledged by Morgan himself, has been briefly explored by Chris Jones.[40] But what of his influence on Amis?

Bone's *Anglo-Saxon Poetry* draws on a selection of modern verse forms where Old English poets use alliterative meter. The deployment of stress-based and syllabic meters, rhymed couplets, and quatrains distinguishes Bone's practice from other translations of the period (which are usually in prose or blank verse). Bone's version of *The Wanderer*, for example, makes effective use of rhymed couplets; these are also combined more experimentally with quatrains, verse paragraphs, and long lines in his version of *The Seafarer*.[41] Bone's influence on Amis's *Beowulf* with its four-line stanzas might be detected here, but worth noting too is Bone's positioning of Old English poetry in relation to English poetry after it. In both of these regards – verse form and literary history – Bone's slim anthology is quite different from R. K. Gordon's (1887–1973) prose translations in *Anglo-Saxon Poetry* (first published in 1922), which were firmly aimed at students of Old English and did not have modern poetry in mind. Bone, by contrast, addresses the earliest English literature from the perspective of modern readers. His introduction to *Anglo-Saxon Poetry* includes a reference to Pound. His introduction to *The Seafarer* in this anthology takes on T. S. Eliot.[42] Small wonder Morgan took note. By contrast, no critics or scholars of Old English are identified in Bone's *Anglo-Saxon Poetry* and only Frederick J. Klaeber (1863–1954), celebrated editor of the Old English poem, is cited in *Beowulf in Modern Verse*.[43]

That Bone wanted to engage modern readers in Old English poetry is most evident in *Beowulf in Modern Verse*, with its decisive abbreviation of

---

[39] Gertrude Helena Bone, an artist and writer herself, is identified by her initials in the prefaces to *Anglo-Saxon Poetry*, 6; and *Beowulf in Modern Verse*, vi. The preface to *Beowulf in Modern Verse* also acknowledges the assistance of Kenneth Sisam (1887–1971) in preparing the volume, a distinguished scholar of Old and Middle English himself (see Stray, "Sisam, Kenneth").

[40] Jones, "While Crowding Memories Came," 131–32.

[41] *Anglo-Saxon Poetry*, 68–71 (*The Wanderer*) and 73–77 (*The Seafarer*). Some of the stylistic variation in the collection may be due to the different dates of the translations. *The Seafarer*, for example, appeared in *Medium Ævum* in 1934; see *Anglo-Saxon Poetry*, 26.

[42] *Anglo-Saxon Poetry*, 9–25, 72–73.

[43] *Beowulf in Modern Verse*, 13.

the Old English poem into the hero's three fights with Grendel, Grendel's mother, and the dragon. Characteristic of Bone's approach to translating Old English poetry is his deployment of rhymed quatrains, his willingness to paraphrase and indeed invent on occasion, and his deployment of verse paragraphs of differing length.[44] Syntax and punctuation, particularly dashes, are put to good effect, enabling a rhythmical "pointing" in the modern English that contrasts with the verse syntax and measured half-lines of the Old English poem. And then there are the seven illustrations, which punctuate key moments in the first half of the poem (Beowulf's journey to Denmark is the frontispiece; Grendel's entry into the hall, Heorot, opens the sequence, for example).[45] These are midcentury examples of what was to become a flourishing genre of visualizations of *Beowulf* in the second half of the twentieth century.[46] Like their more recent counterparts, Bone's make limited concession to the antiquity of *Beowulf*. Just as his *Beowulf* is a "modern version," so too are these modern illustrations. The first, "Beowulf's journey", forms the front cover of a collection of essays on *Anglo-Saxon Culture and the Modern Imagination* (2010).[47]

Whether or not Bone's decision to curtail *Beowulf* so radically was influenced by Tolkien (who had described the poem in much the same way in his "*Beowulf*: The Monsters and the Critics"), his overall approach is very different. Tolkien took on the philological establishment and asserted the literary integrity and power of *Beowulf* in his celebrated lecture of 1936, but he had little to say to a more general literary audience. Bone's *Anglo-Saxon Poetry* and *Beowulf in Modern Verse*, however, offered insights into the earliest English poetry for modern writers, translators, and artists. In 1943, C. L. Wrenn (1895–1969), another eminent *Beowulf* scholar, acknowledged Bone as a "young artist-scholar."[48] Bone, in sum, cleared the way for others after him, Edwin Morgan among them, but also Amis. After writing his "Beowulf," Amis would go on to produce his most celebrated novel, *Lucky Jim*, with a medieval scholar at its center: a historian not a philologist.

---

[44] Jones, "While Crowding Memories Came," 131, describes the technique as "interlaced rhyme," but it is used intermittently.
[45] Bone's father, Muirhead Bone (1876–1953), was also a successful artist, one of the first to work as a war artist. Bone's elder brother, Stephen (1904–1958), and mother, Helena, were artists too; see Cooke, "Bone, Sir Muirhead." Cooke is unaware of Gavin Bone's career as poet and scholar.
[46] See, for example, Clarke, "Re-Placing Masculinity."
[47] Bone is credited on the back cover for teaching Amis and Larkin, however; see Clark and Perkins, eds., *Anglo-Saxon Culture*, but there is no account of his work in this collection.
[48] Wrenn, "Review of Bone," 69.

Bryher's *Beowulf*

Meanwhile, back in the 1940s, Bryher was also thinking about *Beowulf*. However, Bryher's *Beowulf* is a more radical and generous comic witness to the creative possibilities of the Old English *Beowulf* than Amis's short poem. Written during the war-years, which Bryher and H. D. spent in Kensington in London, the novel was translated into French by Hélène Malvan (pseudonym of Hélène de Wendel [1903–1986]) and published in Paris in 1948 with a preface by Adrienne Monnier (1892–1955). According to Bryher, the book had found no publisher willing to take it on in England because it dealt so directly with the Blitz.[49] The English version later came out in New York in 1956, dedicated to Sylvia Beach (1887–1962) and in memory of Monnier. Beach and Monnier – partners, owners of the two famous Parisian bookshops *La maison des amis des livres* and Shakespeare and Co., and friends of Bryher and H. D – were central figures in the vibrant and international scene in Paris at the time.[50] Bryher was exiled in London from her Swiss home, and her novel is informed by this international context. But it is firmly set in an English – and, as Bryher tells us, real – tea shop, The Warming Pan, run by two women, Selina Tippett and her partner Angelina Hawkins.[51]

Bryher's *Beowulf* is realistic about the war years, evoking its terrors certainly, though charting more closely the sheer exhaustion of daily life and those unexpected moments of liberation, generosity, and sympathy that punctuate the lives of those connected with The Warming Pan. Austerity, nightly raids, blackouts, and the daily struggle to survive the cold and live out the war (and bake cakes for tea) are the subjects of this *Beowulf*, with its cast of shopowners, office workers, servants, penurious – and grumpy – elderly artists, and middle-class women sticking stubbornly to their customary tea and shopping. The novel is also deft, archly comic, and affectionate about the two devoted women, Selina and Angelina, at its center: the one practical, anxious, a former lady's companion, and the other brisk, determined, self-improving, and radical in her social commitments.

Angelina introduces into this community run by women the large plaster bulldog that gives the novel its title. Bryher had seen one just like it in the rubble of a bombed-out London: not quite a bull in a china shop, then, but close.[52] Too big for the mantelpiece (of course) and placed instead in

---

[49] See Bryher's account of the novel in *The Days of Mars*, 14–15.
[50] See Buchanan, "*Beowulf*, Bryher, and the Blitz."
[51] Bryher, *The Days of Mars*, 11–16.
[52] Ibid., 12–13. Bryher saw the original plaster dog by a pile of rubble in Basil Street, Knightsbridge.

the fireplace, the focus of the room, the dog looks like an extravagance to Selina. But buying it offers an opportunity to purchase, off ration, the powdered eggs that the tea shop needs for their baking. Contrary to Angelina's anticipation of protests from Selina, her name for the bulldog, Beowulf, sticks. This bulldog, the novel asserts, will not be named Winnie after that well-known British bulldog Winston Churchill (1874–1965), who also owned one.[53] Naming the plaster dog Beowulf distances the novel from an uncomplicated patriotism and support for Churchill. Instead, Bryher explores the wide range of attitudes – positive and negative – that Londoners felt toward the war. Put another way, Bryher's *Beowulf* looks the "monster in the face,"[54] just as the early medieval hero, Beowulf, faced his own fights in the Old English poem. The novel is Bryher's account of her London life during the war, inspired by the early medieval war poem *Beowulf*.

So how does *Beowulf*, the Old English poem, inform a novel featuring a plaster bulldog called Beowulf? The French title, with its punning allusion to a *roman-à-clef*, and its dedications to Monnier and Beach, another pair of women like Selina and Angelina, offer one clue. So does the running joke in the novel about women and their dogs: Monnier and Beach were fond of their dogs, as were Bryher and H. D. What those associated with The Warming Pan make of Beowulf the bulldog is an important theme. For Angelina, the bulldog is a "symbol of common sense" and an allusion to an early medieval hero who fought for the people, the "proletariat," against the dragon or the Danes, as she puts it.[55] Angelina too fights for the people, in her case against the twin dragons of bureaucracy and Nazism. To her, however, the plaster dog also looks a bit like Selina, another source of common sense, if an anxious one.[56] To others, the dog is at times frighteningly ugly, a source of antifeminist humor, or camp, or, with the Union Jack tied round its neck, "the tiniest bit vulgar."[57] Yet when the firestorm of the Blitz destroys The Warming Pan, Beowulf survives "still standing" under the mantelpiece.[58] In a remarkable act of creative freedom, Bryher has rewritten the ending of the Old English poem, whose hero dies in his companion's arms, facing his dragon. By contrast, Angelina's plaster dog and Selina's baking ensure the survival of The Warming Pan even after the

---

[53] Bryher, *Beowulf*, 66.
[54] Ibid., 179.
[55] Ibid., 66.
[56] Ibid., 101.
[57] Ibid., 194.
[58] Ibid., 189.

building itself has fallen. Angelina will add wheels and a basket to Beowulf, and hawk the cakes made by Selina with the off-ration egg-powder. "Leave it to me and Beowulf," says Angelina.[59] Hers is a small though heroic act of defiance that condenses the many ways war is survived.

In his reading of Bryher's *Beowulf*, Peter Buchanan takes up the novel through the lens of H. D.'s interest in symbolism and mythic history. For Buchanan, Bryher's *Beowulf* is an act of queer, palimpsestic historiography, offering the opportunity to take a look back at the Old English poem and its women subjects.[60] However, the novel closely identifies Angelina with the early medieval hero, Beowulf. As we have also seen, Bryher's *Beowulf* explores the complexity of war with the early medieval war poem of the same title firmly in mind. Finally, Bryher herself was a dog-lover. Indeed, the original Warming Pan appealed to her because it welcomed dog-lovers and because "I am to those, but only those who know me intimately, Fido."[61] The queer writer and patron of the arts, dog-lover, and doggish Bryher with her clear-eyed understanding of war, are refracted through Angelina and her bulldog, Beowulf.[62]

For Bryher, *Beowulf* is not a novel but a documentary, an "almost literal description" of her first six months in London in 1940, and a charting of her "great friends" and owners of The Warming Pan, Selina and Angelina.[63] Bryher's French subtitle, *roman d'une maison de thé dans Londres bombardé*, is therefore an accurate description of it. The novel is an example of what we would now call creative nonfiction. Between 1940 and 1946, Bryher had also written *The Fourteenth of October*, set in the year of the Norman Conquest (1066). She saw in that earlier invasion and conquest parallels with one that looked at that time to be imminent. Not a graduate herself, Bryher was widely read, learned, intellectually and creatively ambitious. Writing fiction, she described herself in these years as a historian.[64]

Bryher's *Beowulf* is a brilliant redeployment of an early medieval war poem for twentieth-century queer fiction. Bryher herself called it her war novel, and it stands in good company with other novels of this

---

[59] Ibid., 189.
[60] Buchanan, "*Beowulf*, Bryher, and the Blitz."
[61] Bryher, *Days of Mars*, 12. *Days of Mars* also indicates that Bryher's understanding of war in general is informed by her prewar years in Paris and Switzerland in particular.
[62] For the Old English poem's gender politics and animal-human relations, see Pareles, "What the Raven told the Eagle." Bryher, of course, had already implied that Beowulf, both bulldog and early medieval hero, was gender queer.
[63] Bryher, *Days of Mars*, 15, 11.
[64] Ibid., 170.

period by, for example, Sylvia Townsend Warner and Rose Macauley.[65] We can also read Bryher's *Beowulf* as a fine, if unintentional, riposte to Amis's "Beowulf." However often Amis reworked and reprinted it, his "Beowulf" is at base an unreflective product of a young Oxford graduate; Bryher's *Beowulf* is that of an interwar, international, sexually dissident avant-garde.

Anglo-Saxon Attitudes?

Bryher's *Beowulf* did not find an English publisher because, she thought, the English did not want to be reminded about the war, as we have seen. Perhaps that was the case: the two other highly successful midcentury novels inspired by medieval matters discussed in this chapter do not address the war directly either. Amis's *Lucky Jim* (1954) and Wilson's *Anglo-Saxon Attitudes* (1956) are set in the 1950s. Both novels assert a break with the immediate past of the pre- and postwar years, using instead a more remote medieval past to challenge a stultifying present. In *Lucky Jim*, its academic hero as little interested in his subject of medieval history as its author, the break takes the form of a satire about a provincial – redbrick – university and the classbound culture of its little Englanders. London – vibrant, commercial, and forward-looking – is Jim Dixon's escape route. But Gerald Middleton's London in *Anglo-Saxon Attitudes* harbors characters just as petty, hide-bound, narrow-minded, and self-deluded as those in the unidentified university town of *Lucky Jim*. Yet the breadth of characters in *Anglo-Saxon Attitudes* (the novel comes with a list that includes those "already dead before the action of the book") and its historiographical scope (from the seventh century to the twentieth) is far broader than Amis's.[66] Amis's interest in things medieval is characteristically superficial; Wilson's is deeply informed by his time in the British Museum Reading Room and his observations of London medieval historians. *Anglo-Saxon Attitudes* is even more evidently a *roman-à-clef* than Bryher's *Beowulf*, especially to a medievalist. Indeed, one plotline turns on the editorship of the new Medieval History series, which is of great interest to the members of the Historical Association of Medievalists at its annual Stokesay Lecture. Discussion at this lecture of Professor Stokesay's discovery at Melpham on the eve of World War I triggers the plot of the novel.

---

[65] Ibid., 13, 165–69.
[66] Wilson, *Anglo-Saxon Attitudes*, viii.

Anglo-Saxon Attitudes reveals a greater interest in the capacity of its characters to change than *Lucky Jim*. Its break with prewar culture takes the form of a clear-sighted reconciliation and acceptance of what went before. Middleton's interest in history is renewed. He gets to the bottom of the faked seventh-century burial and the collusion of the father, Professor William Stokesay (memorialized in that Lecture, in spite of his pro-German sympathies in the First World War) with the son, Gilbert, responsible for putting the pagan fertility idol in the Christian grave in the first place. Middleton also takes on the editorship of the Medieval History series, reconciles with his former mistress, Dollie Stokesay, Gilbert's widow, and accepts the limitations of his role as a family man. In these ways, the novel excavates the past as a necessary component of self-understanding in the present.

Wilson's humanistic defense of historical research reveals how closely the professional and the personal are intertwined.[67] But the novel is also clear sighted – and often vicious – about the capacity for deceit and self-deception in all the characters who are linked in one way or another with the story of the burial at Melpham; from Middleton's gay son, John Middleton, who has made his name as a media celebrity championing the causes of the underdog at the expense and careers of those middlemen caught up in government bureaucracy to John's sometime lover and Irish petty criminal on the make, Larrie.[68]

Lucky Jim and *Anglo-Saxon Attitudes* are far more interested in men than women. Jim Dixon spends most of *Lucky Jim* trying to extricate himself from an on–off relationship with fellow academic Margaret Peel, who, though depicted as both suicidal and neurotic, sees right through him by the end of the novel. Jim is in pursuit of Christine, beautiful and less poised than she first seems. Gerald Middleton is unhappily married to the cloying, child-like, and cruel Ingeborg. He longs for his former mistress, the blowsy and often drunk Dollie Stokesay, and he is as embarrassed by the extravagant clothes and wayward mythologizing of Rose Lorimer, Senior Lecturer in Medieval History, as Jim Dixon is of Margaret Peel's dress sense. Men come off little better, however. Jim Dixon is weak minded and indecisive, given to complex plotting to evade scrutiny of his own social awkwardness. Gerald Middleton by his mid-sixties has proved

---

[67] See Hahn, "Medievalism."
[68] Drabble, *Angus Wilson*, 205, discusses how Wilson struggled to integrate these different characters and orientations, worrying whether the novel was "too homosexual." Wilson's notes for the novel reveal the compromised life of a gay male writer in this period.

to be a poor father, husband, and demotivated academic, as little given to self-scrutiny as Jim Dixon. Misanthropy is as much on view in these novels as misogyny. The contrast with the woman-centered world of Bryher's *Beowulf* could not be sharper.

The "Anglo-Saxon" attitudes in Wilson's novel come into focus as a satire of 1950s modernity because of the novel's epigraph from Lewis Carroll's *Alice in Wonderland*. Carroll's absurd "Anglo-Saxon Messenger" is given to wiggling his hands in a manner sometimes seen to echo images in the tenth-century Winchester style of manuscript illustration. The characters in *Anglo-Saxon Attitudes* certainly look absurd, often comically so. As Professor Pforzheim muses, "There was nothing, he always believed, Englishmen liked so much as a joke against themselves."[69] Others are joked against too, even more stereotypically. The novel punctures the pretensions of the French and the "histrionic nonsense" of the Germans as much as the reticence and *politesse* of the English.[70]

The use of "Anglo-Saxon" to designate a chronological period of English history is not much on show. Gerald Middleton's interest in Cnut (c. 990–1035) and Edward the Confessor (1003–1066) aside, other scholars in the novel take a broader view of early medieval history. Professor Pforzheim's lecture on "Dark Age and Early Medieval trade" takes in the Chinese Canton, the Iberian Peninsula, the Nile, and the Baltic, for example.[71] It is a midcentury example of what a twenty-first-century medievalist might call world history. There are also few direct references to "Anglo-Saxons" in the novel. The preface, with its fabricated column from *The Times* announcing the preliminary report of Bishop Eorpwald's grave at Melpham near a pagan "Anglo-Saxon" cemetery, is a rare example.[72] Like the Appendix of "Extracts concerning Eorpwald, Bishop of Sedwich and the Melpham Tomb," the preface is a brilliant comic fiction, inventing wholesale its journalistic reportage in the same way as the documents in the appendix invent historical sources and a whole scholarly apparatus of articles, reviews, and popular interpretation.[73] History, these documents say, is made by those in the present. We are the ones with "Anglo-Saxon" attitudes. The joke is on us.

What would modernists and medievalists miss if *Anglo-Saxon Attitudes* were abandoned as a dated, sometimes vicious relic in the form of a satire

---

[69] Wilson, *Anglo-Saxon Attitudes*, 27.
[70] Ibid., 24.
[71] Ibid., 30.
[72] Ibid., ix.
[73] Ibid., 399–412.

on English manners? Quite a lot, I would argue. Wilson's novel reminds us that some in the 1950s saw through the hypocrisies of English social relationships, both personal and professional. University life is a target here, as both *Anglo-Saxon Attitudes* and *Lucky Jim* suggest. Some of the social pretensions pilloried in these novels derive from the specific circumstances of postwar England: classbound, anti-intellectual, sexually conservative, hostile to change and often to Europe as well. That both Wilson and Amis identify these pretensions reveals the force of the critique. Wilson's novel, however, also includes gay men and their relationships. His satire does not target men loving men, but rather the social conventions that so deform their loving. Bryher's *Beowulf*, with its devoted female partners at its heart, again sharpens the contrast. Crucially, *Anglo-Saxon Attitudes* works through the possibility of coming to terms with the past by bringing together Middleton's professional identity as an historian with his identity as an unhappily married man and inept father. The personal is indeed professional. We might take "Anglo-Saxon" to refer to the histories of both the public and personal man, and its "attitudes" to refer to forms of social, sexual, cultural, and ethnonational behaviors, forcefully critiqued.

"Anglo-Saxon" and Empire: One Conclusion and Another Beginning

Bryher wrote *Beowulf* with her typewriter balanced on her lap, she says. On one occasion, she was interrupted by the superintendent of her building armed with a pistol who mistook her noisy typing for a new kind of weapon or signal to the enemy.[74] "Typewriters' chatter" is indeed more than a match for guns, as Alexander Scott's *The Latest in Elegies* reminds us. One conclusion of this chapter is that early medieval English literary culture forms an important source of creative practice and historical thinking evident in poetry as well as novels, writers, and scholars, at the midcentury.

It was during her time in London that Bryher learned of the death of the great cultural theorist Walter Benjamin (1892–1940), one of the many Jewish refugees Bryher had helped in the 1930s.[75] Bryher's *Beowulf* keeps its

---

[74] Bryher, *Days of Mars*, 14.
[75] Ibid., 22–24. For Bryher's support of Jewish refugees, see Zemgulys, "Review of Bryher," 92. The early medievalist scholar, Kenneth Sisam, who had helped to supported the posthumous publication of Bone's writing (see n. 39), also worked to assist Jewish refugee scholars; see Stray, "Sisam, Kenneth."

focus on London, yet Europe and the British Empire are part of its fabric. In the novel, Colonel Ferguson, who has spent most of his life outside Britain, muses whether or not to share his knowledge of the concentration camps.[76] He does not, but his perspective fills out the novel's examination of the general disinterest about what was happening outside London. Ferguson is a figure of empire, who has no place back "home," and a soldier who sees clearly the atrocities of war. A more obvious though minor figure of empire is "Miss Empire," as she is nicknamed, whose friends and relations are scattered across the Commonwealth. Both remind us of the force of imperialism in the novel. And the long reach of the British Empire across the globe in all its offensiveness is even more evident in the character of Horatio Rashleigh, an elderly artist and first voice in the novel, who is haunted by his memory of childhood bullying in a game of "Red Indians," expressed in the characteristically racist language of the times.

The new Elizabethan age of the 1950s, and the Festival of Britain in 1951 in particular, celebrated Britain and its imperial past while looking to a new future in the aftermath of World War II. *Anglo-Saxon Attitudes* has little room for those British subjects of empire born in the Commonwealth; *Lucky Jim* none at all. There is only one Black British character in *Anglo-Saxon Attitudes*, Artie, a West Indian, whose jealousy of his white girlfriend is dismissed in a few lines: "They're as excitable as children, those West Indians."[77] Artie lives in Frank Rammage's lodging house, a home and alternative family for queers, petty criminals, women on the make, and the impoverished. We might argue that the novel's disinterest in World War II closes it off from a wider inquiry into the Commonwealth soldiers who, like the soldiers of African nations, fought in it, although it does find space for passing reference to the camps and the Occupation, but those who lived in the Commonwealth were indeed in the news in the 1950s.

Bryher's *Beowulf* was published the year the HMT *Empire Windrush* docked at Tilbury, carrying British West Indians, citizens of the Commonwealth and the United Kingdom as the British Nationality Act of 1948 was to define them, recruited to help rebuild the country. The *Monte Rosa*, as it was first called, was a German ship captured by the British in 1945 and given the name of an English river, Windrush, first recorded in Old English.[78] The *Monte Rosa* had been used for "Strength through

---

[76] Bryher, *Beowulf*, 196–97.
[77] Wilson, *Anglo-Saxon Attitudes*, 55.
[78] Ekwall, *The Concise Oxford Dictionary of English Place-Names*, 521. Tilbury is also an early medieval crossing on the Thames estuary.

Joy" pleasure cruises in Nazi Germany in the 1930s. One of the uses the Germans found for it during the war was to deport Norwegian Jews.

In 2018, the British Library commemorated the seventieth anniversary of the arrival of the *Empire Windrush* and the Windrush generation with a small exhibition. "Windrush: Songs in a Strange Land" closed on 21 October, two days after the British Library opened its main exhibition of the year, "Anglo-Saxon Kingdoms: Art, Word, War." The significance of these two exhibitions is that both engage with histories of migration: the one very much a live, contemporary political and racial issue; the other apparently historical (although the term, "Anglo-Saxon," has long been freighted with racial implications).[79] The temporal distance between the objects of these two exhibitions, modern and medieval, is bridged by the name of a river, first known in Old English, which was to become centuries later the name of a ship, the *Windrush*. Their connections have yet to be explored, but this chapter's account of Old English literature and "Anglo-Saxon" attitudes in the mid-twentieth century clears a way to begin. As this exploration of the engagement with early medieval culture by midcentury writers and scholars demonstrates, the richer and more complex our knowledge of the past, the more powerful our understanding of the present.

[79] See n. 6.

CHAPTER 7

Erwin Panofsky's Neo-Kantian Humanism and the Purported Relation between Gothic Architecture and Scholasticism

C. Oliver O'Donnell

On December 8, 1948, Erwin Panofsky (1892–1968) presented the Wimmer Memorial Lectures at Saint Vincent College in Latrobe, Pennsylvania on the topic of "Gothic Architecture and Scholasticism."[1] Panofsky had been actively developing his thinking about the connection between these two areas of research since at least 1944,[2] though as Panofsky almost certainly knew, by that point in time the topic itself already had a history in both art historical and philosophical literature. Not only had earlier German art writers such as Gottfried Semper (1803–1879) speculated about a connection between these two prominent chapters in the histories of art and philosophy, but so also had American philosophers such as Charles Sanders Peirce (1839–1914).[3] Perhaps, however, because this specific *geistesgeschichtliche* parallel or analogy – not to mention others like it – had never been fully accepted by art historians, Panofsky did express some hesitation in taking it up, even going so far as to describe his own initial effort as "seemingly insane (*ziemlich wahnsinnig*)."[4] This first reaction would prove partially prescient. When Panofsky published a shortened form of his Wimmer Lectures as a book in 1951, though his arguments were undoubtedly erudite and sophisticated, they also transformed what

---

[1] These lectures were first published as Gothic Architecture and Scholasticism and were republished under the same title with slight corrections in 1957 by Thames and Hudson in London.
[2] For Panofsky's earlier and unexpanded 1944 treatment of the topic, see "Panofsky and Scholasticism," 7. Recent research by Elizabeth Sears shows that Panofsky's book likely had its origins in his unpublished manuscript on "The Gothic Style." For this observation I am indebted to her talk "Panofsky on 'The Gothic Style,'" presented at the Zentralinstitut für Kunstgeschichte on July 3, 2019.
[3] See Semper, *Style in the Technical and Tectonic Arts*; Peirce, "Fraser's *The Works of George Berkeley*," 83ff. The fact that Peirce speculated on this connection does bear on Panofsky's work as it is known that Panofsky was familiar with some of Peirce's writings thanks to his doctoral student Edgar Wind (1900–1971). For a discussion of this connection, see Viola, "Peirce and Iconology."
[4] Erwin Panofsky to Edgar Wind, November 20, 1944, in Wuttke, ed., *Erwin Panofsky Korrespondenz*, vol. 2, 514–15.

previous authors had largely left as a speculative aside into a more serious and thus also more controversial claim.[5] The reviews of the book, in turn, were almost Janus-like. Whereas one reviewer highlighted the book's "magnificent humanistic breadth, illuminating depth, and superb scholarly craftsmanship," another complained of its "monolithic view" that "not only disregards the nuances but also tends to distort the historical development of Gothic architecture."[6]

In this essay I put forward an interpretation of Panofsky's claims about the relationship between Gothic architecture and scholastic philosophy. My goal in doing so is not to adjudicate decisively the validity of Panofsky's arguments but rather to attempt to make some sense, first, of why Panofsky was drawn to the controversial topic and, second, why he failed to resolve the long-standing debates surrounding it. My strategy for pursuing these two goals is to place Panofsky's book within the context of what I see as a long-term, though unevenly pursued, continuity within his thought, specifically his attenuated neo-Kantian leanings.[7] Though Panofsky's neo-Kantian tendencies are often thought to be restricted to the pre-immigration stage of his career, the first half of my essay compares aspects of Panofsky's early theoretical essays to his later programmatic statements about art historical method to show that an important dimension of Panofsky's relationship with Kantian ideas recurred in his later writing as well.[8] To make this argument, I emphasize both Panofsky's recurring citations of Ernst Cassirer's (1874–1945) particular form of neo-Kantianism and the relation of that form of neo-Kantianism to Panofsky's frequent yet ambiguous appeals to the "human," the "humanistic," and "humanity." In so doing, I argue that, like Cassirer's *Philosophy of Symbolic Forms* (1923–29), Panofsky's particular version of "humanistic" art history repeatedly shares basic, though undoubtedly strained, analytic affinities with fundamental assumptions of the particular school of Marburgian neo-Kantianism in which Cassirer was trained: specifically the Marburg school's focus on the

---

[5] Panofsky, *Gothic Architecture and Scholasticism*.
[6] Bober, "Gothic Architecture and Scholasticism," 310; Branner, "Review of *The Church of St. Martin at Angers*," 31.
[7] Elsewhere I have pursued and developed my interpretation of Panofsky's neo-Kantianism in relation to his frequent use of neo-Platonic sources and his disagreement with Edgar Wind over the interpretation of Titian's (c. 1488–1576) *Venus Blindfolding Cupid* (c. 1565). See O'Donnell, "Two Modes of Mid-Century Iconology," 113–36.
[8] For discussions of the divided view of Panofsky's career, see Holly, "Panofsky, Erwin," 437; Moxey, "Perspective, Panofsky, and the Philosophy of History," 777; Elsner and Lorenz, "The Genesis of Iconology," 493–506. Panofsky himself even discusses the changes in his writing in Panofsky, "Three Decades," 321–46.

importance of systematic, holistic, and mathematic descriptions of nature as a secure ground for knowledge of the external world.

Coming from the second, supposedly more common sense or empirical phase of Panofsky's career, *Gothic Architecture and Scholasticism* serves as a fitting test case for my initial claim about a neo-Kantian continuity within Panofsky's thought. Panofsky's insistence that medieval architects shared scholastic habits of mind is an attempt to ground art historical knowledge about Gothic architecture in a mode of thinking – medieval scholasticism – which by its systematic nature can be analogized not only to the abstract systems, patterns, or structures that make up Gothic architecture itself but also to the mathematic and systematic descriptions of nature that were championed by the Marburg school of neo-Kantianism. Panofsky's book, in so directly arguing for the existence and causal influence of a structural isomorphism between the mental and material worlds of medieval culture, was in conflict with the often tacit ideographic nature of most art historical research – a conflict that still haunts the reception of the book today.[9] The eponymous claim of *Gothic Architecture and Scholasticism* as well as the controversy surrounding the book is, therefore, as much about the ongoing debate on the nomological requirements for secure knowledge *tout court* as it is about the specific case of the stylistic origins of Gothic cathedrals.[10] Because of these broader stakes and for better or worse, it should come as no surprise that *Gothic Architecture and Scholasticism* proved to be more influential among scholars who were welcoming of and enchanted by the power of natural scientific reasoning – especially, thanks to Pierre Bourdieu (1930–2002), among sociologists and anthropologists – than among art historians.

Panofsky's Neo-Kantian Humanism

While it is almost a commonplace to note Panofsky's flirtations with neo-Kantian philosophy, what that means for Panofsky specifically and how exactly neo-Kantian premises might have played themselves out in his art

---

[9] Recht, *Believing and Seeing*, esp. 24–27. For one of the most influential descriptions of art history's ideographic nature, see Baxandall, *Patterns of Intention*.

[10] This debate plays itself out in much twentieth-century scholarship, art historical research being no exception. Wilhelm Windelband (1848–1915) is often named as the scholar who first brought the stakes of the distinction between ideographic and nomological research to light. For a contextualization of his work, see Bambach, *Heidegger, Dilthey, and the Crisis of Historicism*. For a classic analytic treatment of some of the implications of Windelband's claims, see Mandelbaum, *The Anatomy of Historical Knowledge*.

historical scholarship is all too often left uninterpreted. Though I am not alone in arguing for a persistence of neo-Kantian premises from Panofsky's early writing in his later work,[11] arguments concerning continuities within Panofsky's thinking more often focus on his defense of a general Hegelian conception of history rather than what I will here be calling a neo-Kantian humanism.[12] In clarifying what I mean by this turn of phrase, in what follows and as already suggested, I start by placing Panofsky's arguments within the much longer academic genealogy of the Marburg school of neo-Kantianism. Despite the fact that Panofsky himself never studied in Marburg, a comparison of Panofsky's and Cassirer's writing shows that like Cassirer, Panofsky repeatedly defended central, though diluted, propositions that are often associated with the Marburg school.

Those propositions are usually and most proximately traced back to Cassirer's *Doktorvater*, Hermann Cohen (1842–1918), who had founded the Marburg school in the 1870s based on an influential interpretation of what was termed the Kantian "fact of science."[13] This interpretation entailed defending the Kantian *a priori* in what is now a fairly standard way: the *a priori* does not shape our experience of the world in conjunction with objects in that world but is actually constitutive of experience or even actively generates it.[14] By making this claim, Cohen shifted the definition of the *a priori* away from Immanuel Kant's (1724–1804) original assertion that space and time in general were *a priori* intuitions of the mind and replaced it with the claim that the mathematic descriptions of space and time used in the natural sciences can be understood as such. Cohen positioned the mathematical systems and laws underlying those descriptions as the formal conditions of the possibility of experience, and in turn defined philosophy as the investigation and identification of these systems. This shift in Kant's original program allowed Cohen to frame the problem of the objectivity of knowledge as a pseudo-problem that was explained away by a more fundamental theory of experience itself.

Integral to Cohen's revision of Kant's model was his discarding of one of the most debated parts of Kant's original argument: that there are "things-in-themselves" that both constitute the external world but which we can never access. By removing "things-in-themselves" from Kant's

---

[11] Cheetham, *Kant, Art, and Art History*, 72–73.
[12] Wood, "Introduction," 21; Holly, "Panofsky, Erwin," 437.
[13] See, for instance, Cohen, *Das Prinzip der Infinitesimal-Methode*, 119–20.
[14] The binding nature of the "fact of science" on philosophy was first stated by Cohen in 1883; see Cohen, *Das Prinzip der Infinitesimal-Methode*, 119–20. See also Cohen and Natorp, "Zur Einführung," i; Natorp, "Kant und die Marburger Schule," 219.

doctrine, Cohen was able to ground science's claim to knowledge purely on mathematic systems and laws because those systems and laws now made experience itself possible.[15] As Michael Friedman has pointed out, this change to Kant's original thesis was necessitated by the earlier development of non-Euclidian geometries such as those put forward by Bernhard Riemann (1826–1866) and Carl Friedrich Gauss (1777–1855), geometries whose very existence and axiomatic coherence meant that the Euclidian system presupposed by Kant's original project could not be a part of any *a priori* synthesis of the mind.[16] Indeed, if space was not necessarily definable by Euclid's (*fl*. 300 BCE) axioms – for instance, if two-dimensional space is curved instead of flat – then Euclidian space could not be part of an *a priori* intuition because then that *a priori* intuition would be both false and an impediment to, rather than an explanatory ground for, our ability to gain knowledge of the external world.

Marburgians seized on this insight and put forward what they termed the genetic (*erzeugende*) conception of knowledge. According to this characteristically Marburgian view, knowledge mutates and develops over time not based on new empirical observations alone but also and much more fundamentally on the underlying mathematic principles and systems that are used to describe those observations.[17] Under this model, the scientific revolutions that took place between Euclid and Riemann or between Isaac Newton (1643–1727) and Albert Einstein (1879–1955) not only advance knowledge but also transform what is observable. Accordingly, rather than see knowledge as something that is established once and for all, the Marburgians defined knowledge as an "infinite task" (*unendliche Aufgabe*).[18]

Much in keeping with this Marburgian project, Cassirer's only partially translated series of books collectively titled *The Problem of Knowledge* (1907; *Das Erkenntnisproblem in der Philosophie und Wissenschaft der neueren Zeit*), which today would be categorized as a contribution to the history and philosophy of science, traces the scientific project of refining mathematic models of nature back to Galileo. Later in his career, however, Cassirer radically broadened the scope of the Marburgian epistemological

---

[15] For Cohen's own initial statement of this idea, see his *Kants Theorie der Erfahrung*, 615.
[16] Friedman, *A Parting of the Ways*. Cassirer's most developed exploration of the implications of non-Euclidian geometries comes in his *Zur Einstein'schen Relativitätstheorie*.
[17] On the ideas that characterized and distinguished the Marburg school of thought, see Krijnen and Noras, eds., *Marburg versus Südwestdeutschland*; see also Friedman, "The Neo-Kantian Background," 25–37.
[18] See, for instance, Rickert, *Der Gegenstand der Erkenntnis*, 139.

project away from the school's traditional focus on scientific knowledge and asked how other forms of thought were possible. In so doing, and as would prove to be essential for Panofsky's very ability to adapt the Marburgian project to his own, Cassirer transformed Cohen's search for the conditions of the possibility of knowledge into a search for the conditions of the possibility of meaning.[19] While some commentators have seen this transformation in Cassirer's career as so extensive as to mean that he abandoned his neo-Kantian training altogether, Cassirer himself saw a continuity between his early books on the history and philosophy of science and his later magnum opus *The Philosophy of Symbolic Forms*, the latter having been written while both Cassirer and Panofsky were close associates of the Warburg Library.[20] Much as in his early work and much as the Marburgian project in general, *The Philosophy of Symbolic Forms* emphasizes the importance of reconstructing man-made systems or structures in order to make its claims – exemplified by the book's treatment of myth, religion, and language as structural entities that undergird the creation of meaning.[21] This focus is, of course, but an echo of the original Marburgian project, but it nevertheless can be understood to follow from Cohen's original interpretation of Kant.

Focusing on this attenuated Marburgian aspect of Cassirer's writing helps make sense of Panofsky's own neo-Kantian leanings, not to mention the much-debated relation between Panofsky's and Cassirer's writing.[22] In this regard, Panofsky writes one especially important passage in his 1924 book, *Idea: A Concept in Art Theory*. That book had been written as a companion volume to a lecture that Cassirer gave at the Warburg Library on Plato's (c. 427 BCE–c. 347 BCE) theory of art, a fact that makes the Marburgian dimension of *Idea* quite fitting. In the concluding pages Panofsky states,

> We believe to have realized that artistic perception is no more faced with a "thing in itself" than is the process of cognition; that on the contrary the

---

[19] For a discussion of the implications of this broadening, see Skidelsky, "The Philosophy of Symbolic Forms."

[20] For Cassirer's acknowledgment that his *Philosophy of Symbolic Forms* exists in the same tradition as his earlier, more clearly Marburgian philosophy of science, see Cassirer, *Philosophy of Symbolic Forms*, vol. 3, xiii–xvii. For a scholar who went so far as to deny Cassirer's late neo-Kantianism, see Krois, *Cassirer*. For the bearing of Cassirer's association with the Warburg on his work, see Wimmer, "The Afterlives of Scholarship," 245–70.

[21] For Cassirer's own statements about the importance of reconstructing these systems, see Cassirer, *Philosophy of Symbolic Forms*, vol. 3, 67; vol. 4, 150.

[22] Some scholars have argued that Panofsky fundamentally misunderstood Cassirer. See, for instance, Alloa, "Could Perspective Ever Be a Symbolic Form?" 51–72.

one as well as the other can be sure of the validity of its judgments precisely because it alone determines the rules of the world (i.e., it has no other objects other than those that are constituted within itself).[23]

Here Panofsky's rejection of the "thing in itself" as well as his claim that the rules of cognition and even the rules of the world itself are dependent on the mind seems to be a clear reference to Cohen's modification of Kant's transcendental method, and suggests that Panofsky conceptualized art as Marburgians conceptualized knowledge, as an "infinite task." At the most basic level, doing so would mean explaining art historical change first and foremost by analyzing fundamental transformations in underlying art historical structures. Moreover, and more radically, taken as a first epistemological principle of art history, the Marburgian genetic conception of knowledge ultimately would imply that studying the changes in underlying art historical structures is more important than studying changes in individual historical documents or artworks because our ability to make sense of the empirically observable changes within individual art objects rests upon our understanding of the structural principles that sustain those observations. Consequently, just as the book from which this citation comes traces the structural or systemic changes in Plato's theory of art from Plato through to Michelangelo (1475–1564) by highlighting the divergences within Platonic and neo-Platonic doctrine and the bearings of those divergences on art theory and practice, so too does his *Perspective as Symbolic Form* trace similar changes by comparing the differences between the dominant optical theories of antiquity and the Italian Renaissance, and the effects of those theories on perspectival systems of depiction.[24]

While this rather extreme position has the ring of the young Panofsky's penchant for philosophical debate, central aspects of it are also present within scholarship from Panofsky's supposedly more empirical and commonsense American phase. In 1953 and in 1960, for instance, Panofsky republished and continued to defend the thesis from his 1924 essay on perspective in his books *Early Netherlandish Painting* and *Renaissance and Renascences*.[25] The most perspicuous and evident recurrence of Panofsky's

---

[23] Panofsky, *Idea*, 126; *Idea*, 70–71: "Wir erkannt zu haben glauben, daß die künstlerische Anschauung ebensowenig einem "Ding an sich" gegenübersteht, als der erkennende Verstand, vielmehr – genau wie jener – der Gültigkeit ihrer Ergebnisse gerade deswegen sicher sein darf, weil sie selbst ihrer Welt die Gesetze bestimmt, d. h. überhaupt keine anderen Gegenstände besitzt als solche, die sich allererst in ihr konstituieren."
[24] Panofsky, *Perspective as Symbolic Form*.
[25] Panofsky, *Early Netherlandish Painting*, esp. chapter 1; Panofsky, *Renaissance and Renascences*, 136–41.

neo-Kantian leanings, however, likely comes in the introduction to his 1939 book *Studies in Iconology*, an introduction that Panofsky republished with minimal changes in 1955. There Panofsky directly appeals to Cassirer's philosophy and states that "in thus conceiving of pure forms, motifs, images, stories and allegories *as manifestations of underlying principles*, we interpret all these elements as what Ernst Cassirer has called 'symbolical' values'."[26] To reinforce this point, later on in the same introduction Panofsky again evokes Cassirer by name and claims that the "ultimate goal" of his method is to reveal these "underlying principles."[27] What these underlying principles actually are in the individual cases he was discussing, however, was difficult for Panofsky to pin down, and he even confesses that he cannot adequately explain them. He admits that he can do no better than to use "the rather discredited term 'synthetic intuition'" to describe the mental faculty necessary to grasp them.[28] Considering the neo-Kantian background of his work, it is important to take Panofsky's apology for the term "intuition" in the context of the controversy surrounding the Kantian *a priori*; as noted earlier, the very notion that there are *a priori* "intuitions" of the mind was what the Marburgian school of neo-Kantianism reworked with their notion of an "infinite task." Much like the Marburgians, Panofsky makes it clear in *Studies in Iconology* that he does not believe that "synthetic intuition" was static and universal – as Kant had – but rather that scholars could change and correct their "synthetic intuition" by way of knowledge of "the manner in which, under varying historical conditions, the *general and essential tendencies of the human mind* were expressed by specific *themes* and *concepts*."[29] However obliquely or even unwittingly, the "general and essential tendencies of the human mind" that Panofsky refers to here evoke the mathematic systems that his Marburgian peers had used to rework and defend the Kantian *a priori*.

If we accept this connection, it also becomes apparent that Panofsky would run into trouble in pinning down the artistic correlates of these mathematic systems; after all, Panofsky's approach here borrows epistemological premises that were originally developed within the philosophy of the natural sciences as a response to the development of non-Euclidian geometries. As mathematic descriptions, the geometries of figures such as Riemann and Gauss are much more clearly systematic, internally

---

[26] Panofsky, *Studies in Iconology*, 8; emphasis mine.
[27] Ibid., 8 and 16.
[28] Ibid., 15.
[29] Ibid., 15–16.

consistent, and axiomatically comprehensive than any of the underlying principles that Panofsky could cite in relation to human behavior or art making. However, despite this major obstacle, and as the earlier quotes suggest, Panofsky still attempted to apply a version of the Marburgian genetic theory of knowledge to art history. The result is that the last level of his iconological system – where he appeals to "synthetic intuition" and "general tendencies of the human mind" – remains unspecified and rather vague. Seemingly because further specificity was not within his powers, Panofsky repeatedly justified this highest level of his iconological method by appealing to the fundamental humanness of it, a fitting, if ambiguous, assertion given the fact that both he and Cassirer spent much of their careers researching the very figures – the humanists of the Italian Renaissance – who did so much to both champion and mystify the term. Much like Cassirer's humanism, however, the neo-Kantian dimension to Panofsky's work assures that his appeals to "the humanistic" clearly go well beyond his own interest in the afterlife of antiquity, a fact that distances Panofsky's humanism from what is perhaps the original definition of the word.

This distance becomes most literal in Panofsky's 1938 essay "The History of Art as a Humanistic Discipline," a text that begins not with a discussion of the early modern "humanists," but rather with a historical anecdote about Immanuel Kant himself.[30] Citing an early biographer, Panofsky recalls how in the last days of Kant's life the frail philosopher was visited by his physician. According to the story, after being greeted by the doctor in his room, Kant stood "trembling with weakness and muttering unintelligible words." Finally, the doctor realized that Kant would not sit down until he had first seated himself. Once the doctor had done so, Kant allowed himself to be helped to his chair and after regaining his strength announced to his guest, "the sense of humanity has not yet left me (*Das Gefühl für Humanität hat mich noch nicht verlassen*)."[31] Much in keeping with my interpretation, Panofsky explains the import of this anecdote rather obliquely in the essay, noting that "humanity" had a deep significance for Kant, one grounded in the tension between man's claims to universal, eternal principles and his confrontation with his utter fragility and mortality. What the anecdote also makes clear, in my view, is that humanity also had a Kantian significance for Panofsky. The anecdote

---

[30] Panofsky, "The History of Art," 1–25.
[31] Wasianski, *Über Immanuel Kant*, reprinted in Kant, *Sein Leben in Darstellungen von Zeitgenossen*, 298; quoted in Panofsky, "The History of Art," 1.

directly ties Panofsky's concept of "humanity" to Kant's by implicitly defining humanity through Kant's own claims about universal and eternal principles – claims, of course, that manifest themselves in Kant's famous assertions concerning *a priori* mental faculties, the very claims that the Marburgians reworked with their focus on systematic yet fallibilistic mathematic descriptions of nature. The implication of this introductory anecdote for Panofsky's "humanistic" art history, therefore, is that art history is not immune to Kant's "humanistic" concerns; that art historical investigation – at least in Panofsky's version of it – is also engaged in a search for the eternal principles that were a cornerstone of Kant's original project.

Gothic Architecture and Scholasticism

In light of my interpretation of what I've called Panofsky's neo-Kantian humanism, it is fitting to begin my analysis of *Gothic Architecture and Scholasticism* by noting Panofsky's own justification for pursuing the book's eponymous analogy. In the book's opening paragraphs Panofsky emphasizes that he is aware of the dangers inherent in his topic but nevertheless pursues it because of what he takes to be an all-important question, one raised by the seemingly simple and banal fact that history is based on periodizations. As Panofsky continues, however unavoidable the divisions of periodization may be, the act of breaking up the otherwise continuous and unordered flow of previous events into independent, ordered units raises the immediate question of the unity of those units. Whereas much history necessarily presupposes the periods upon which it is based for reasons of efficiency, for Panofsky the analogy pursued in *Gothic Architecture and Scholasticism* offers itself up as a possible way to explore and potentially verify the unity of the historical periods that the book interprets.[32] Leaving the validity of such a motivating assumption aside, this idea speaks to Panofsky's fascination with what might also be called the form of history, a fascination that points back to Panofsky's neo-Kantian tendencies; form can well be understood as the very mystery that Kant's *a priori* faculties – and the Marburgian's revision of those faculties – were intended to explain. The Kantian assumption that space and time are *a priori* intuitions of the mind amounts to an explanation of why human experience can be effectively broken down into those categories, categories

---

[32] Panofsky, *Gothic Architecture and Scholasticism*, 1.

whose very coherence is what makes them effective units for describing the "form" of human experience. Indeed, it is well known that the perception of "form" is the very human capacity that Kantians have long used to describe and approach the peculiarities of human experience;[33] this classic Kantian premise only takes on more importance when "form" is historicized as part of an "infinite task" of knowledge, which binds both the historical agent and the historian. Thus it should come as no surprise that Panofsky was motivated by the question of the form of history in the case of *Gothic Architecture and Scholasticism.*

Panofsky pursues this stated goal in that book by attempting to show that certain central premises of scholastic philosophy – the form, we might say, that made scholastic philosophy scholastic – also took hold of the reasoning behind the design process of Gothic architecture. In other words, these same scholastic mental habits lay behind the modus operandi of Gothic architects. In making this claim, Panofsky hoped to move beyond the older and more general assertions concerning parallelisms or analogies between period styles of art and period modes of thinking, claims that nineteenth-century philosophers such as G. W. F. Hegel (1770–1831) and Wilhelm Dilthey (1833–1911) had attempted to establish with mixed results. For instance, whereas Hegel rested content with his identification of the general quality of self-reflexive inwardness (*Innigkeit*) that he found both in the entirety of Christian painting and theology from the early Middle Ages through the Renaissance, Panofsky wanted to be able to point to more specific forms of both intellectual and artistic production in more delimited historical periods so as to be able to identify a true cause and effect relation between the two.[34] Because of this, Panofsky doubly focused his study, first on the specific geographic local of the 100 or so miles around the city of Paris and second on the 140 years between 1130 and 1270. As Panofsky notes – and takes as a primary mandate for his investigation – it is a quite remarkable fact that during this particular time and in this particular place both scholastic philosophy and Gothic architecture assume their most characteristic form.

With this warrant in hand, Panofsky first begins pursuing his thesis by way of the scholastic notion of *manifestatio.* He pithily defines

---

[33] For Cassirer's own defense of this version of the Kantian project, see Cassirer, *The Philosophy of Symbolic Form*, vol. 4, 46. For a contextualization of Cassirer's claim in relation to Kant's project, see Gordon, *Continental Divide*, 73–77.

[34] Panofsky, *Gothic Architecture and Scholasticism*, 20. For Hegel's famous assertions about Christian art and theology and *Innigkeit,* see Hegel, *Philosophie der Kunst oder Ästhetik*, 136–37.

this principle as the goal of "clarification for clarification's sake" and he argues that it takes on its most classic form in the "three requirements" of Thomas Aquinas's (1225–1274) *Summa Theologica* (1265–1273): "(1) totality (sufficient enumeration), (2) arrangement according to a system of homologous parts and parts of parts (sufficient articulation), and (3) distinctness and deductive cogency (sufficient interrelation)."[35] Panofsky claims that these "requirements" could have been absorbed by everyone in the period who went to school and attended sermons, and he identifies several interesting examples that can be understood as their architectural manifestations.[36] First, as for the stated scholastic goal of totality, Panofsky points to the well-known ambition of Gothic cathedrals to embody the totality of Christian knowledge. Thanks in large part to the work of Émile Mâle (1862–1954), such an observation was well established by the time of Panofsky's writing; even those critical of Panofsky's book acknowledged its purchase.[37] As for the second principle of "sufficient articulation," Panofsky notes that Gothic cathedrals are easily seen as ordered by divisions and subdivision of homologous parts: the ubiquitous use of the newly developed rib vault in almost every part of the Gothic cathedral is perhaps the best example. Finally, in terms of the third principle of deductive cogency, Panofsky argues that the interior and exterior of Gothic cathedrals are often "mutually inferable," a point that he states quite boldly by claiming that the "organization of the whole [Gothic architectural] system" can be inferred "from the cross section of one pier."[38] This last point was, it seems, long established in architectural education, even if many found it to be simply unbelievable.[39]

Despite such objections that could already be made to *Gothic Architecture and Scholasticism*, Panofsky continued to pursue the basic argument of the book by way of the additional scholastic principle of *concordantia*, a principle that allowed him to transition away from explaining a hypothetical, synchronic cause behind various characteristic Gothic forms to explaining a hypothetical diachronic cause for the development or evolution of those forms over time. By *concordantia*, Panofsky meant "the

---

[35] Panofsky, *Gothic Architecture and Scholasticism*, 35, 31.
[36] Ibid., 23.
[37] Branner, "Review of *Gothic Architecture and Scholasticism*," 30. For Mâle's classic exploration of this fact, see Mâle, *Religious Art in France*.
[38] Panofsky, *Gothic Architecture and Scholasticism*, 50, 51.
[39] In his letter to Panofsky about his book, Schapiro notes that he was taught this basic idea of "mutual inferability" but never believed it; see Meyer Schapiro to Erwin Panofsky, September 30, 1951, in Wuttke, ed., *Panofsky Korrespondenz*, vol. 3, 191–94.

technique of reconciling the seemingly irreconcilable," and in order to define it further he points again to the *Summa* where Aquinas explicates the notion of *concordantia* with the dialectical process of the *quaestio*, a process that begins with (1) an authoritative statement (*videtur quod*), then proceeds to (2) a contradiction of that statement (*sed contra*), which is resolved by (3) a resolution to the contradiction (*rispondeo dicendum*).[40] In his search for an architectural correlate of this scholastic process of argumentation, Panofsky points to three different aspects of Gothic style: the development of the rose window, the development of the triforium, and the development of the nave piers. Summarized schematically, the rose window in its original form at St Denis (Figure 1) is said to be the negation of the central arched window below it. A resolution of this conflict is then said to be the huge but no longer extant central window of St Nicaise in Reims (Figure 2), a window that contains a full-size rose window inside its pointed-arch frame. Within the development of the Gothic triforium, a similar conflict is said to revolve around the contradiction between designs that emphasize either the horizontal or the vertical qualities of that space, a contradiction that is exemplified for Panofsky by the oppositional qualities of the triforiums of Chartres (Figure 3) and Amiens (Figure 4) and that is supposedly resolved in the triforium of St Denis (Figure 5). Finally, as *piliers cantonnés*, Gothic nave piers and their membrified pilasters are shown to create problems of interrelation. Specifically, according to Panofsky, Gothic architects had to decide between scaling the capitals of the nave piers either in relation to the breath of the pier as a whole or in relation to the breadth of the individual pilasters that composed those piers. This tension was further exacerbated by the additional function of the nave piers as continuations of the ribs of the vaults of the nave ceiling. In the case of this architectural conflict, the piers of the Cologne cathedral (Figure 6) are said to be the *rispondeo dicendum* of the opposition between the piers of Amiens (Figure 7) and St Denis (Figure 8).

With this summary of some of the book's more specific arguments in place, it now becomes possible to better understand how the claims of *Gothic Architecture and Scholasticism* relate to what I have called Panofsky's neo-Kantian humanism. The two major scholastic principles of *manifestatio* and *concordantia* that Panofsky leverages are used as basic structures that undergird Panofsky's ability to make the empirical observations that he does. Without these structural principles, neither the observation that the rib vault is a homologous, modular part of the

---

[40] Panofsky, *Gothic Architecture and Scholasticism*, 67–68.

Figure 1 St Denis, west facade, authoritative statement (*videtur quod*) and contradiction of the authoritative statement (*sed contra*)
Photo: Andrew Tallon. Image courtesy of the Mapping Gothic Project, Media Center for Art History, Department of Art History & Archaeology, © The Trustees of Columbia University.

Figure 2 St Nicaise, Reims, resolution to the contradiction (*rispondeo dicendum*)
Image courtesy of Philadelphia Museum of Art. Purchased with funds contributed by
Lessing J. Rosenwald, 1960, 1960-139-5.

Figure 3 Chartres, triforium, authoritative statement (*videtur quod*)
Photo: Andrew Tallon. Image courtesy of the Mapping Gothic Project, Media Center for Art History, Department of Art History & Archaeology, © The Trustees of Columbia University.

Figure 4 Amiens, triforium, contradiction of the authoritative statement (*sed contra*)
Photo: Andrew Tallon. Image courtesy of the Mapping Gothic Project, Media Center
for Art History, Department of Art History & Archaeology, © The Trustees of Columbia
University.

Figure 5 St Denis, triforium, resolution to the contradiction (*rispondeo dicendum*)
Photo: Andrew Tallon. Image courtesy of the Mapping Gothic Project, Media Center for Art History, Department of Art History & Archaeology, © The Trustees of Columbia University.

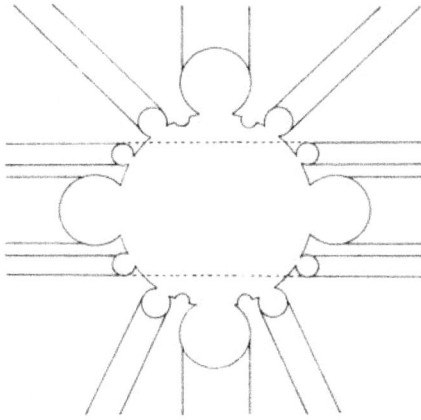

Figure 6 Cologne, pier cross-section, resolution to the contradiction (*rispondeo dicendum*)
Image from Erwin Panofsky, Gothic Architecture and Scholasticism, Meridian, 1957.
With kind permission from Gerda Panofsky.

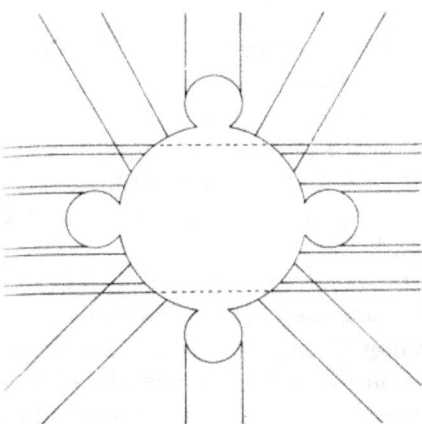

Figure 7 Amiens, pier cross-section, contradiction of the authoritative statement
(*sed contra*)
Image from Erwin Panofsky, Gothic Architecture and Scholasticism, Meridian, 1957.
With kind permission from Gerda Panofsky.

Gothic system nor the observation that the rose window of St Nicaise in Reims is a *rispondeo dicendum* to what came before it, would have been evident. Just as mathematic, systematic descriptions of nature were understood by Marburgians as the conditions of possibility of scientific experience and observation, so too does Panofsky here leverage *manifestatio* and *concordantia* as conditions of possibility of art historical knowledge. In his own terms, *manifestatio* and *concordantia* are the "general and

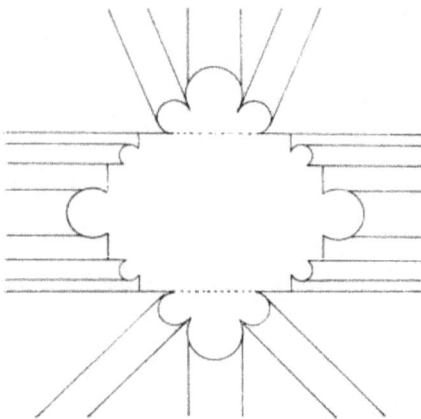

Figure 8 St Denis, pier cross-section, authoritative statement (*videtur quod*)
Image from Erwin Panofsky, Gothic Architecture and Scholasticism, Meridian, 1957.
With kind permission from Gerda Panofsky.

essential tendencies of the human mind" of the period that Panofsky is able to use to correct his own "synthetic intuition" and thus secure his understanding of Gothic architecture. Whatever one thinks of the coherence or danger of such a project, the breadth of characteristic Gothic forms that Panofsky is able to address within the compact narrative he tells as well as the sheer number of examples that he is able to fit into his scheme is undoubtedly impressive.

This strength of the book, of course, can well be understood to be outweighed by other weaknesses, some of which stem most directly from Panofsky's marshalling of empirical facts, others from his sophisticated theoretical assumptions. A good example of the former is presented in the review of the book by Ernst Gall (1888–1958), himself one of the most accomplished historians of Gothic architecture of the period.[41] Gall notes that the climactic document to which Panofsky refers in his text – a drawing of ground plans of two *chevets* by the medieval architect Villard de Honnecourt (*c.* 1200–*c.* 1250) with the conspicuously scholastic phrase "inter se disputando" written on it – is not nearly the smoking gun that Panofsky implies; that inscription was in fact made by a later owner of the manuscript. Though Panofsky does acknowledge this crucial fact in his text, he also downplays it by describing the inscription as only "slightly later" than Villard de Honnecourt's original drawing, the implication

---

[41] Gall, "Review of Erwin Panofsky," 42–49.

being that the inscription could still be from the same period as Villard de Honnecourt's original drawing.⁴² Even if the inscription is from the exact period in question, however, what is more important and seemingly beyond doubt is that the all-important scholastic phrase on the document was not written by Villard de Honnecourt. This fact means that the inscription – no matter how contemporaneous it may be with the original architectural drawing – is not really evidence for scholastic "habits of mind" among Gothic architects, only among the later owners of the manuscript, whoever they might have been. As an empirically based objection to Panofsky's argument, this example makes especially clear that Panofsky's project came with the real risk of historical overstatement, an overstatement that, in this particular instance, understandably seduced Panofsky because it suggested precisely the kind of direct evidence for his book's eponymous analogy that many have doubted.

However penetrating such a criticism may be, and as Meyer Schapiro (1904–1996) indirectly pointed out to Panofsky in private correspondence, a more theoretical and potentially more important objection to *Gothic Architecture and Scholasticism* can also be made.⁴³ Panofsky's argument rests in no small part on the equation of the operational possibility of negation in linguistic representation with the operational possibility of negation in visual representation. The problem with such an equation is that it overlooks what Nelson Goodman (1906–1998) called the unusual density of visual representations, a density that makes visual representations importantly different in kind from their linguistic counterparts.⁴⁴ For instance, at the very heart of the scholastic "habits of mind" upon which Panofsky places so much emphasis, lies the law of the excluded middle: $A \neq \sim A$. Without this law, the dialectical form of scholastic argumentation loses a central tenet of its coherence. But what, we can and should ask, is the visual equivalent of this commonplace law of logic? Any attempt to negate a visual form results in something that is much more polyvalent than a linguistic negation; in the latter, the very functional possibility of the word "not" changes the stakes. Approaching one of Panofsky's own examples as if it were a kind of logical thought experiment helps make this point clear:

---

⁴² Panofsky, *Gothic Architecture and Scholasticism*, 87.
⁴³ Meyer Schapiro to Erwin Panofsky, September 30, 1951, in Wuttke, ed., *Panofsky Korrespondenz*, vol. 3, 191–94. Here Schapiro points out the obscurity of Panofsky's description of Gothic pinnacles and crockets as "a self-analysis and self-explication" of architecture. This point resonates with Schapiro's long struggle with similar arguments; see Schapiro, "Philosophy and Worldview in Painting." For a contextualization of Schapiro's work, see my own *Meyer Schapiro's Critical Debates*.
⁴⁴ Goodman, *Languages of Art*.

if we imagine a hypothetical large square window replacing the large rose window on the west facade of St Denis, it becomes evident that such a window would be as much a "negation" of the arched window below it as the famous rose windows of which Panofsky makes so much. A square, in other words, is no more the negation of an arched form, than is a circle, a pentagon, a line, or simply nothing at all. These objections – not to mention other potential ones – no doubt provide good reasons for why *Gothic Architecture and Scholasticism* was and remains controversial.

In closing, however, it is fitting to note that Panofsky's book was also a powerful source of inspiration, especially for scholars in other fields. For instance, in a prominent essay of 1964, the paleographer Robert Marichal (1904–1999) adapted Panofsky's claims about the pervasive impact of scholastic habits of mind in the Middle Ages to describe and explain the design and organization of European manuscripts produced between the twelfth and fifteenth centuries.[45] Panofsky had hinted that manuscripts from this period also betrayed scholastic tendencies in his own book, and from correspondence we know that Panofsky took Marichal's article as providing important additional proof for his original thesis, not to mention being a powerful repudiation of his critics.[46] Important though Marichal's article was, the real retribution for Panofsky came in 1968, the same year that Panofsky passed away. In that year the then still burgeoning sociologist Pierre Bourdieu translated Panofsky's book into French and wrote a lengthy "Postface" to his translation that defended the import of Panofsky's arguments. Bourdieu had been emboldened by Panofsky's claims about scholastic "mental habits," and in his "Postface" he broadened Panofsky's analogy even further, turning Panofsky's "mental habits" into what would prove to be one of Bourdieu's most influential sociological terms: "habitus." By "habitus" Bourdieu meant "a system of internalized schemes that have the capacity to generate all the thoughts, perceptions, and actions characteristic of a culture."[47] Though *habitus* as a term had a deep and complex history, by Bourdieu's own confession, it was through Panofsky's book that Bourdieu came to develop his especially influential understanding of it. As Bourdieu saw it, the notion of "habitus" challenged a more atomistic, positivistic, and nominalist approach to the study of history and culture by providing a hypothetical

---

[45] Marichal, "L'écriture latine," 199–247.
[46] Erwin Panofsky to Robert Marichal, March 22, 1965, in Wuttke, ed., *Panofsky Korrespondenz*, vol. 5, 639–40.
[47] Bourdieu, "Postface to Erwin Panofsky," 233.

basis for the hold of social regularities – dare one say, social laws – on individual cultural and historical agents. Bourdieu himself reinforced this point in his "Postface" by comparing Panofsky's arguments to those of Noam Chomsky (b. 1928), Émile Benveniste (1902–1976), and Ferdinand de Saussure (1857–1913), scholars whose work had identified other law-like cultural regularities – especially within the domain of language – and whose work is often grouped under the structuralist label. Thus it would seem that what I have here been calling Panofsky's neo-Kantian humanism – though always somewhat veiled within his writings and certainly never entirely accepted within his own discipline – was a kind of Structuralism *avant la lettre*, a label with which Panofsky's work has been saddled before.[48] Fully tracing and substantiating such a comparison, of course, is another paper, though it serves as a fitting, concluding reminder that the long-standing art historical resistance to *Gothic Architecture and Scholasticism* is more limited in its epistemological purchase than the discipline as a whole may still be prone to suppose.[49]

---

[48] Hasenmueller, "Panofsky, Iconography, Semiotics," 289–301.
[49] Art history's resistance to the structuralist project has been noted – and lamented – before. For instance, see Crow, *The Intelligence of Art*. For an example of the unease that art historians have expressed when faced with highly structuralist interpretations, see Elsner, "Review of Whitney Davis," 535–36.

CHAPTER 8

"Are Women Human?"
Authority, Gender, and Dante in Dorothy L. Sayers's Scholarship

Helen Brookman

They do me honour, and therein do well.[1]

Dorothy L. Sayers (1893–1957) first met Dante (*c*.1265–1321) in an air-raid shelter.[2] On the evening of August 11, 1944, in Witham, Essex, the fifty-one-year-old writer, hearing the sirens, took something to read during the long hours waiting for the all-clear: Dante's *Inferno* (1320). She later presented this moment as a pivotal one in her literary career, sparking a deep and intimate connection with Dante and his work that would occupy her for the rest of her life. In the following five days, she raced through the rest of the *Inferno* in the Temple Classics edition, "slipping and scrambling," she writes, "between the original and the crib."[3] She quickly learnt to read the medieval Italian, relying on the Latin she had begun learning with her father as a child, and an Italian grammar. She writes, "I found myself panting along with my tongue hanging out, as though it were a serial thriller, careful not to read the argument of each canto beforehand, lest it should spoil what was coming." This intense immersion quickly became a full-blown "Dante-mania": "I bolted my meals, neglected my sleep, work and correspondence, drove my friends crazy, and paid only a distracted attention to the doodle-bugs which happened to be infesting the neighbourhood at the time, until I had

---

[1] Dante, *Hell: The Divine Comedy*, trans. Sayers, Canto IV, 93. My sincere thanks to the editors for their input and support and to Natalia McCormick for her assistance.
[2] In Barbara Reynolds's estimation, this meeting was "the beginning of a cultural event which was to change awareness of Dante in the English-speaking world" (Sayers, *The Letters of Dorothy L. Sayers, 1944–1950*, ed. Reynolds, vol. 3, 45). This was a highly literary air-raid shelter, the same in which Sayers kept safe from bombs and fires a working archive of manuscripts, hers and those of friends and collaborators, protecting them against the damp at night by putting them "to bed in the bunk with a hot-water bottle" (Moulton, *The Mutual Admiration Society*, 258).
[3] Sayers, *The Letters of Dorothy L. Sayers*, vol. 3, 47.

panted my way through the Three Realms of the dead from top to bottom and from bottom to top."[4]

Sayers had first become immersed in the literature of the Middle Ages as a student; she read medieval and modern languages at Somerville College, Oxford (1912–1915) with Mildred Pope (1872–1956) and then published some medievalist poetry and translations (including her *Tristan in Brittany*, 1929, and a rhyming translation of the *Song of Roland*, 1957).[5] She went on to work in advertising; build a career as a successful detective fiction novelist (as the creator of Lord Peter Wimsey and Harriet Vane); develop a reputation as a lively and provocative essayist and public speaker on numerous subjects, especially Christianity; and find success as a playwright of religious drama for stage and radio. Sayers then negotiated a new role as a translator and interpreter of Dante, giving lectures (in Oxford and Cambridge, and around the world), writing essays on his life and poetry, and publishing her best-selling translation of the *Divine Comedy* for Penguin Classics. Her *Hell* was published in 1949; her *Purgatory* in 1955; and her *Paradise*, completed after her death by her friend and biographer Barbara Reynolds (1914–2015), in 1962. Each was accompanied by an extensive critical apparatus.

With her expert understanding of popular audiences – honed over decades as advertiser and novelist – Sayers's translation sought to "bring Dante home to English-speaking people in all his moods, from the homely and humorous to the terrible and the sublime."[6] She saw her ability to speak to the common reader as a skill she shared with Dante himself. He became, to her, "a living poet, who has something vital to say to them here and now" who could "bridge time and space."[7] She experienced a similar sense of the "complex contemporaneity" to that which Carolyn Dinshaw identifies between Hope Emily Allen (1883–1960) and Margery Kempe (d. after 1438): an "affectionate familiarity … [an] intimacy borne of 'living with' their authors (as Roland Barthes [1915–1980] would say)."[8] Particularly, she positioned him as a poet of enormous relevance for the mid-twentieth century, both timely and timeless. His Europe had, she

---

[4] Sayers, "… And Telling You a Story," 2.
[5] Sayers, *The Letters of Dorothy L. Sayers*, vol. 3, 8: "The skill of translating verse had fascinated her from her school days on… 'It is almost as satisfying as working with one's hands,' she said, and she compared it with laying a mosaic."
[6] Dante, *The Divine Comedy: Hell*, dustjacket.
[7] Letter to Cesare Foligno, July 25, 1952, quoted in Reynolds, *The Passionate Intellect*, 117.
[8] Dinshaw, *How Soon Is Now?*, 119–20. On Barthes, see Chapter 2 in this volume, Saltzman, "Hermeneutics and the Medieval Horizon."

states in the introduction to her *Hell*, "much in common with our own distracted times, and his vivid awareness of the deeps and heights within the soul comes home poignantly to us who have so recently rediscovered the problem of evil."[9] The wartime and postwar context seeps constantly into her engagement with Dante. In her essays and notes to her translations, she frequently brings home the grotesque and poignant aspects of Dante's otherworlds through comparison with modern war. Her initial impressions of Dante's passage through the wall of fire (*Purgatorio*, Canto XXVII) "jotted down hot-and-hot at the first reading" were of Dante, with a "queasy clutch at the pit of the stomach ... powerfully imagin[ing] ... the burnt bodies he has just seen: just the nasty trick a strong visual imagination plays on you in the middle of an air-raid. Some nasty, charred thing that has been lurking at the back of your eyeballs for years comes horribly up at you, and you imagine *hard*."[10] She felt that the experience of the two world wars had brought the modern British imagination closer to Dante's "theology of hell" than any intervening century had: "We have seen in our time the abyss of wickedness yawn open at our feet: school-children have witnessed things which to our Victorian forbears would have seemed quite unthinkable, though they would scarcely have surprised Dante."[11]

Although by this date she was known in some circles for her religious drama and radio plays, Sayers was throughout her career most well known for her detective fiction, as part of the group of "Golden Age" mystery writers, and this was the limiting reputation she sought to escape in recasting herself as a translator of Dante. Popular fiction more broadly, and detective fiction in particular, were genres that allowed significant numbers of women to earn a living as professional writers for the first time in the 1920s and 1930s. Andreas Huyssen describes the "great divide" of modernity, in which middlebrow fiction was disdained as the feminized "other" of high modernism, lacking the "cachet and edginess of high culture" while also "in want of the authenticity of the low."[12] The production of avant-garde modernity (which Sandra M. Gilbert and Susan Gubar have argued was a reaction of "intensified misogyny" against women's entry "into the literary marketplace"), relied, Melissa Schaub argues, on the "explicit othering of textual production deemed to be inferior and

---

[9] Sayers, "Introduction" to Dante, *The Divine Comedy: Hell*, 10.
[10] Sayers, *Introductory Papers on Dante*, 165.
[11] Ibid., 46
[12] Huyssen, *After the Great Divide*, 44; cited and refuted in Schaub, *Middlebrow Feminism*, 2. Also Botshon and Goldsmith, *Middlebrow Moderns*, 3; cited in Schaub, *Middlebrow Feminism*, 11.

feminine," producing, in Huyssen's term, an "anxiety of contamination" of literary by mass culture.[13] More recently, literary critics have sought to rethink this "great divide" and abandon the midcentury prejudices about those popular genres in which Sayers wrote. Schaub argues that the use of everyday contemporary speech in middlebrow fiction (as distinct from the formal experimentalism of the highbrow modernist novel) and its wide and ongoing distribution in print made it the more genuinely influential genre, whereas Crystal Downing explains the way that Sayers "mimics and critiques the discourses that shaped her sensibilities" through a series of "theoretically sophisticated … writing performances."[14] As Mo Moulton has explored, Sayers's belief in enlightening and educating the masses was firmly rooted in her democratic understanding of medieval literary culture, having recognized early on that "even illiterate audiences shaped the development of medieval drama."[15]

Both Sayers's detective fiction and her Penguin translation addressed themselves to that new phenomenon of the early mid-twentieth century: the common reader. She argued that far from being remote and unmodern, Dante's allegory could be more meaningful to the confused postwar souls of the modern common reader, if only they were taught how to interpret it. For her "common" readers, Sayers sought to make Dante engaging, but not easy, balancing readability with scholarly rigor and poetic effect: a process that required her to adopt multiple stances simultaneously – popularizer, scholar, poet. The audacity of Sayers's popularizing mission ruffled feathers in the literary establishment, with some responses being framed in notably gendered terms. Peter Russell (1921–2003), editor of the literary journal *Nine*, published a sneering satirical sonnet "On First Looking into Miss Sayers' Dante," ridiculing her popular intent: Sayers's "rearrangement" had "flung wide" the "minster gates" of Dante's poetry, and he finds himself horrified "To see the madcaps of the motley season / Capering round their Abbot of unreason."[16] To become an interpreter of Dante for modern times, Sayers had to escape the far-reaching shadow of the male literary critical establishment and her reputation as a popular novelist, and negotiate for herself a hybrid intellectual and literary authority as an authoritative translator. Sayers wrote, defensively, to the influential editor of Penguin Classics, E. V. Rieu (1887–1972) in 1949:

---

[13] Gilbert and Gubar, *No Man's Land*, 233; Schaub, *Middlebrow Feminism*, 4; Huyssen, *After the Great Divide*, vii.
[14] Downing, *Writing Performances*, 10.
[15] Moulton, *Mutual Admiration Society*, 7.
[16] Quoted in Reynolds, *The Passionate Intellect*, 119–20.

> [I]t is certainly not good for my reputation, to encourage the idea ... that I am merely a middle-aged sensation novelist amateurishly dabbling in this or that gigantic subject, without training or qualifications. If I have not long been a Dantist, I am at least a Romance linguist and, to some extent, a medievalist. I was a scholar of my college, I am a Master in my University; I took First-class Honours, and was, after all, a scholar and poet before I was anything else."[17]

She engaged in various authorizing maneuvers in an attempt to mitigate the audacity of the female detective novelist stepping into Dante's shoes, positioning herself as a modern writer worthy to take him on (in Stephanie Trigg's term, to "countersign" his work).[18] Moving from an uncertain role in modern literary culture and seeking to establish herself in an even more fiercely governed position as Dantean authority required a challenging reorientation of Sayers's authorial identity. Throughout her transition, she oscillated between poking fun at traditional forms of authority and tentatively beginning to trespass on the same territory. As an independent writer, successful in several fields, she purported to feel no compulsion to abide by the hidebound and dull conventions of contemporary scholarship.

This article will bring Sayers's interpretations of Dante's erotic poetry into conversation with her feminist writings to understand how this midcentury medievalist theorized and remodeled literary and scholarly authority. Reading Sayers's feminist essays "Are Women Human?" (1938) and "The Human-Not-Quite Human" (1941) and drawing on recent feminist work on Sayers as writer, it will trace her performative maneuvers towards her self-authorization. Radically remodeling patriarchal genealogies to create a space for herself as Dante's unlikely modern heir allowed the strong-minded and irreverent author to sidestep the limitations of gendered hierarchies and play with her own relations with genre, reputation, canon, tradition, and temporality.

Are Women Human?

Sayers participated in a characteristically contrarian (and at times contradictory) form of feminism, strongly based in an individualistic sense of fairness and equality of opportunity between the sexes. Although she positioned herself outside and sometimes in opposition to contemporary

---

[17] Sayers, *The Letters of Dorothy L. Sayers*, vol. 3, 457.
[18] Trigg, *Congenial Souls*, 45.

feminist movements, understanding her feminist thought – as a context for her understanding of Dante's own gender politics – is crucial to understanding her engagement with the medieval world. Her readings of Dante, and especially her extensive preoccupation with the poem Sayers calls "The 'Terrible' Ode," Dante's "*Così nel mio parlar voglio esser aspro*" (*c.* 1294) can be observed to circle around questions of the treatment of women and ideas of sexual equality that she theorized at some length across her two feminist essays.

In "Are Women Human?," originally an address to a women's society given in 1938, she begins by explicitly positioning herself against mainstream feminism: "I was not sure I wanted to 'identify myself,' as the phrase goes, with feminism …. [U]nder present conditions, an aggressive feminism might do more harm than good."[19] She had written to her agent in 1936, "I have a foolish complex against allying myself publicly with anything labelled feminist … the more clamour we make about 'the woman's point of view,' the more we rub it into people that the woman's point of view is different, and frankly I do not think that it is."[20] In 1941, she reflected privately that she had been made "lazy and deeply prejudiced by a Tory Church of England upbringing;" she hadn't been "a 'feminist' – I didn't have to be" but rather occupied a "semi-detached position."[21] She rails in a letter to the Bishop of Coventry, written in June 1944, against the unfairness that men were commonly regarded as "complete human beings with certain sexual functions" whereas women were merely "perambulating sex-organs with a distant resemblance to humanity."[22] Men were allowed to occupy the position of universal human, whereas women were always particularized by sex: they are simultaneously "forced to think of themselves in terms of sex" (not a liberating prospect in the absence of class-based analysis), while being "jeered at for not being capable of thought," an impossible position from which to write with any authority.[23] This is a position she expands across the course of the essay, disavowing the often-romanticized essentialism of contemporary feminism that viewed women as having a special sphere of experience or knowledge, to which they could then be limited. It is, she argued,

---

[19] Sayers, "Are Women Human?" 17.
[20] Sayers, *The Letters of Dorothy L. Sayers*, vol. 1, 391.
[21] Ibid., vol. 2, 271–72; cited in Moulton, *Mutual Admiration Society*, 261. Such prejudices can also be seen to emerge in elements of her writings as anti-Semitism, racism, classism, snobbery, and homophobia.
[22] Sayers, *The Letters of Dorothy L. Sayers*, vol. 3, 29.
[23] Ibid., 29; quoted in Downing, *Writing Performances*, 65.

"unreasonable and irritating *all* one's tastes and preferences have to be conditioned by the class to which one belongs."[24] Rather than working with sex- or gender-based class analysis to overturn oppressive or exclusionary structures, she negotiates with the society she finds herself working in, seeing herself as an exceptional woman, who could get ahead if only she were given the same opportunities as a man. "It is stupid," she argues, "to insist that there are as many female musicians and mathematicians as male … the most we can ask is that if a Dame Ethel Smyth [1858–1944] or a Mary Somerville [1780–1872] turns up, she shall be allowed to do her work without having aspersions cast on either her sex or her ability. What we ask is to be human individuals."[25]

In the witty "The Human-Not-Quite-Human," she extends her argument that women are always particularized as female, while men get to be universal. Men and women should be "neighbouring," not "opposite" sexes, as they are both human beings, and more like one another than anything else in the world: "*Vir* is male and *Femina* is female: but *Homo* is male and female … Man is always dealt with as both *Homo* and *Vir*, but Woman only as *Femina*."[26] She muses, wryly,

> Probably no man has ever troubled to imagine how strange his life would appear to himself if it were unrelentingly assessed in terms of his maleness; if everything he wore, said, or did had to be justified by reference to female approval; if he were compelled to regard himself, day in and day out, not as a member of society, but merely (*salva reverentia*) as a virile member of society.[27]

Following a similar line of argument to one Virginia Woolf (1882–1941) makes in *A Room of One's Own* (1929), Sayers notes, "People would write books called, 'History of the Male,' or 'Males of the Bible' or 'The Psychology of the Male,' and he would be regaled daily with headlines, such as 'Gentleman-Doctor's Discovery,' 'Male-Secretary Win Calcutta Sweep,' 'Men-Artists at the Academy'."[28] Women, as they are described and treated in contemporary society, she concludes, "are not human. They lie when they say they have human needs.… They are far above man to

---

[24] Sayers, "Are Women Human?" 20.
[25] Ibid., 29–30. Humble, *The Feminine Middlebrow Novel*, finds such feminism – rooted in "the ability of individual women to transcend their gender, rather than represent it" (209) – endemic to the feminine middlebrow novel as produced by Sayers and her contemporaries this period.
[26] Sayers, "The Human-Not-Quite-Human," 37.
[27] Ibid., 39–40.
[28] Ibid., 40.

inspire him, far beneath him to corrupt him; they have feminine minds and feminine natures, but their mind is not one with their nature like the minds of men; they have no human mind and no human nature."[29]

As Crystal Downing notes, professional females during the 1920s and 1930s often identified themselves as "humanists" rather than feminists, and were invested in a universalizing, gender-neutral category for defining "people now – not men and women."[30] As Schaub argues, "this identification of rationality as human, not male, is a feminist act."[31] Sayers was suspicious of any absolutist or totalizing ideology (particularly socialism, but also fascism) and rejected organized political movements in general.[32] Schaub notes that "it is easy to dismiss Dorothy Sayers and her contemporaries as nothing more than premature postfeminists – or to acclaim them as ahead of their time for the same reason." As Moulton has explored, this position was inherently contradicted by Sayers's own experience, not least the female solidarity she found at Somerville (then a "hotbed of feminism") and particularly among the group mockingly self-titled the "Mutual Admiration Society."[33]

In her personal life and her relationships, Sayers had always moved flexibly between more masculine and more feminine roles. She had a love of cross-dressing as a younger woman, strongly identifying with the Three Musketeers and taking male roles in plays. Downing notes that her presentation of masculinity can be read as gendered performances that deconstruct "hegemonic vocabularies" and question the "scripts" of gendered identity, allowing her to take multiple contrasting positions.[34] Her aim throughout her life was to be able to have the social and financial freedom to write professionally, but also to have a fulfilling personal and sexual life. She followed a career path marked at the period as more traditionally masculine: earning a living in advertising and then as a writer, and then, when she had a child, not taking the direct caring role, but providing financially for the child (and her husband) as a breadwinner and otherwise acting as an absent parent. She wrote in 1925 at the age of thirty-two of her desire to be treated by men as a woman, and not a "literary freak": it was evidently a source of deep frustration that as "universal humans," men could occupy

[29] Ibid., 46.
[30] Downing, *Writing Performances*, 47.
[31] Schaub, *Middlebrow Feminism*, 24.
[32] Ibid., 14.
[33] Moulton, *Mutual Admiration Society*.
[34] Downing, *Writing Performances*, 5.

both literary and sexual selves, without the one risking canceling the other out as it apparently did for her.[35] The problem she was facing was the one that would later be characterized by Luce Irigaray as the lack of a viable subject position for female authority that also allowed for a personal and sexual identity.[36]

"The 'Terrible' Ode"

Sayers had often been complimented for writing men well in her novels, and she attributed this success to the same approach she identified in Dante's treatment of women, but found sadly lacking in most other authors, making them "ordinary human beings."[37] Such an approach allowed for a deep identification with Dante and, in turn, insight into just how much Dante could identify with women. In October 1944, ill in bed and "feverish," Sayers began reading Dante's minor poems: slipping between reading and dozing, and dreaming of "strange, visionary ladies with stony hearts and golden hair."[38] There was one particular ode – one of the *rime petrose*, a group of *canzoni* dedicated to the "Donna Pietra," beginning "*Così nel mio parlar voglio esser aspro*" ["Now in my speech I would be harsh"] – at which she "dug her toes in," returning repeatedly to its interpretation in the following years. The overt eroticism and violent imagery in this poem had long puzzled critics, leading to a tendency in the nineteenth and early twentieth centuries to interpret it allegorically. The poem's speaker, rejected by the object of his love, describes a desired sexual encounter, using imagery of pain as well as pleasure, which has been read as a sign of Dante's own cruel personality. Sayers was particularly incensed by Giovanni Papini's recent *Dante Vivo*, which focused on Dante's "savage fantasy" and "atrocious desires," accusing him, across the course of a chapter entitled "Dante's Cruelty," of sadistic tendencies. Privately in letters and, later, publicly, in her essay "The 'Terrible' Ode," Sayers sought to set the scholarly record straight on "Dante's charge of sadism," even as she admitted that "The book in which this particular piece of nonsense lurks concealed has been published over ten years, and is probably now forgotten."[39] The first sentence of her essay – "Let us amuse ourselves

---

[35] Letter to John Cournos dated August 25, 1925; quoted in Brabazon, *Dorothy L. Sayers*, 73.
[36] Irigaray, *Speculum of the Other Woman*.
[37] Sayers, "Are Women Human?" 34.
[38] Sayers, *The Letters of Dorothy L. Sayers*, vol. 3, 96.
[39] Sayers, "The 'Terrible' Ode," 42.

by demolishing a foolish piece of criticism" – declares her no-nonsense attitude to the kind of "objectionable 'studies' in which the author, having first wrested a poet's text in order to make it bear witness to a psychosis, then invents biographical data to explain it."[40] She affirms:

> [I]t is plainly and simply a poem about going to bed with a girl. In the first part Dante complains bitterly that the girl refuses to go to bed with him; in the second he says what he would do if she consented. It is not perverted or maniac or sadistic at all, nor is it coarse or brutal, though it might be called violent. The worst that can be said of it is that it is rather powerfully aphrodisiac.[41]

She emphasizes that the consent of the woman is not in question: "Nobody ... is going to be raped, even in imagination. Nobody is to suffer anything except the very thing passionately desired."[42] This, she claims, is the key aspect overlooked by male critics: the possibility of female desire. She highlights the line (translated here in her prose), "Alas! why does she not howl for me, as I for her, in the burning cauldron?" arguing that the imagined encounter only takes place under the premise that the Donna Pietra burns with the "same fire as her lover."[43] "It is," she notes wryly, "difficult to help thinking that part of the critics' horror at this poem is due to a secret conviction that women ought not to 'burn in the hot cauldron' and ought not, consequently, to have any standard of bedworthiness in the man."[44] Based on such views of female sexuality, she concludes, "'love-making' is a cruel business, however it is done."[45]

She draws attention again to Dante's emphasis on female pleasure: "'E piacerei le allora' – the pleasure, then, is to be hers as well as his – and indeed, his pleasure is to be to do her pleasure. That is mutuality and the first mark of bedworthiness."[46] The imagery of bears at play are the "very fee-fi-fo-fum of love," (mis)invoking Shakespeare's famous line: "have not these ursine gambollings something of the lover's hug [pinch] 'which hurts and is desired?'"[47] The much-criticized vengeance Dante threatens is a pleasurable game: "He will impose an avid delay upon her passion, and hold

---

[40] Ibid., 42.
[41] Ibid., 44.
[42] Ibid., 46.
[43] Ibid.
[44] Ibid.
[45] Ibid., 47.
[46] Ibid.
[47] Ibid., 48.

her there, panting and frustrate as she now holds him."[48] When he makes his peace with her at the poem's close, he does so, according to Sayers, "by satisfying her passion."[49] The Ode, she declares, is "a celebration of passion fulfilled, remarkable both for its candour and for its recognition of mutuality as the essential condition of pleasure": "It is a poem which says how much Dante suffers because a girl will not have him for her lover, and how much pleasure he could give to both of them if she would."[50]

Performing Gender: Masculinity, Femininity, Androgyny

Sayers's emphatic rereading of this poem indicates its significance as a site of working through an aspect of her feminist thought, playing out ways that men and women could relate to one another as whole selves, without a limiting or reductive outcome for the female participant. In her writings, especially in her correspondence with fellow authors, she often pursued an authorizing strategy of self-masculinization, presenting herself confidently as a "literary bloke" who would "boil the bones of their grandmother to make soup."[51] Consistently, she refers to authors and translators as "he," even when referring to her own work, although she is careful to refer to her readers as "he or she."[52] Such use of androgyny – also notably utilized by Virginia Woolf and many others at the period – can variously be understood as liberating or limiting. While, as the mystery novelist Carolyn Heilbrun (Amanda Cross) (1926–2003) remarked, the use of androgynous characters allowed detective writers to "dabble in a little profound revolutionary thought," it was particularly rejected by gynocentric feminist critics of the 1970s and 1980s as a process of what Judith Fetterley terms "immasculation."[53] Feeling forced to pursue this strategy, the female author acquiesces to patriarchal culture, drowning in alien male identities: "intellectually male, sexually female, one is in effect no one, nowhere, immasculated."[54] She is taught "to identify with a male point of view, and to accept as normal and legitimate a male system of values, one of whose central principles is misogyny."[55] To the gynocritics, such an approach generates androcentric

---

[48] Ibid., 48.
[49] Ibid., 49.
[50] Ibid., 49–50.
[51] Sayers, *The Letters of Dorothy L. Sayers*, vol. 3, 75; quoted in Reynolds, *The Passionate Intellect*, 36.
[52] For example, Sayers, "On Translating the *Divina Commedia*," passim.
[53] Quoted in Schaub, *Middlebrow Feminism*, 22; Fetterley, *The Resisting Reader*, xx.
[54] Fetterley, *The Resisting Reader*, xxii.
[55] Ibid., xx.

interpretative strategies and reinforces the canonization of androcentric texts. The female writer suffers "not simply the powerlessness which derives from not seeing one's experience articulated, clarified, and legitimized in art, but more significantly, the powerlessness which results from the endless division of self against self, the consequence of the invocation to identify as male while being reminded that to be male – to be universal ... – is to be *not female*."[56] The similarity of Fetterley's language to Sayers's is notable: although she does not have the benefit of later generations of feminist work, Sayers understood the importance of challenging the universality of masculinity and articulated powerfully the effect of being constantly marked as excluded from universal humanity. But within the restrictive culture she experienced in the postwar period, she was keen to retain the option to uphold tactically the default masculinity of the author and co-opt his authority in cases where challenging it was not viable. In a "Panegyric" written on her death, C S. Lewis (1898–1963) praised Sayers's "richly feminine qualities – which showed through a port and manner superficially masculine and even gleefully ogreish;" she retained a fluid range of gendered subject positions and chose to move flexibly between them.[57] Schaub has explored how Sayers promoted the notion of the "female gentleman," in which the medievalizing ideal of noble gentlemanliness – not killed by World War I as commonly understood – could be aspired to regardless of one's sex. Sayers, Schaub argues, recasts "the ultimate Victorian hegemonic vocabulary word, 'gentleman', as a gender-neutral signifier" in order to "rewrite the scripts of gender."[58]

Sayers also deployed performative femininity with roles such as "Topsy," whom she borrowed from A. P. Herbert's (1890–1971) "brainy flapper" character who had appeared in *Punch* in the 1920s. Topsy is, in Sayers's words, a "scatter-brained debutante" who made "naïve but often penetrating comments on life and art."[59] She offers "Topsy's Caution to Critics" ("1. Be sparing of the words 'naïve,' 'quaint,' and 'unsophisticated;' the laugh may be on you. 2. The word 'mediaeval' has something to do with dates: it is not necessarily a term of abuse") and frequently conjures the satirical Germanic "Professors Pumpernickel and Cumberthump."[60] She once declared to the novelist and lay-theologian Charles Williams (1886–1945),

---

[56] Ibid., xiii.
[57] C. S. Lewis, "A Panegyric for Dorothy L. Sayers," 95.
[58] Schaub, *Middlebrow Feminism*, 131.
[59] Sayers, *The Letters of Dorothy L. Sayers*, vol. 3, 75.
[60] Ibid., 88; for example, 93, 103.

whose own work and friendship was hugely formative of her engagement with Dante, "I don't care whether Professor Cumberthump has discovered this or not. *I* have discovered it."⁶¹ She wrote later to Lewis (who called her the "best letter writer of her generation") that the appeal was "not because I knew anything about Dante, but precisely because I had come to him knowing absolutely nothing of all the tarara-boom-de-ay of Dantean scholarship, so that my naïve astonishment had (Charles said) a Topsy-like naivety of approach which might be useful to students and young people and others as unsophisticated as myself."⁶² She continues: "He is the only absolutely world's-top-rank writer I have ever been able to come to with an unbiased and unstaled mind … and I prefer to stay that way."⁶³ Williams immediately noted that such a fresh approach would offer an invigorating introduction to Dante for the first-time reader, and proposed that they work together to publish her letters. Having viewed the exchange as an intimate shared joke, Sayers was initially taken aback, but she immediately warmed to the idea of "Topsy's Guide to Dante," as long as she could forget about creating an effective guide for a prospective reader and continue "to write to YOU."⁶⁴ She describes their correspondence as an ideal alternative model of scholarship, egalitarian and non-confrontational: "we will (for once) publish letters that are not exclusively occupied with knocking down each other's theories, converting each other to something, or displaying our own superiority to one another and to the subject!"⁶⁵ In the humorous figure of Topsy, she reclaims and utilizes an unflattering female stereotype, playing up to the role of ditzy novice – untroubled by prior knowledge – with a knowing wit, and thus without actually losing face regarding her relative lack of expertise and authority.

Sayers's mobility between gendered roles, utilization of gender neutrality, and resistance of essentialist difference sits fairly comfortably with aspects of contemporary feminism – certainly more so than with gynocriticism – although not in her individualism and detachment from intersections with other forms of inequality. To her, the "Brain is the great and sole true Androgyne, that can mate indifferently with male and female and beget offspring upon itself."⁶⁶ As she tackled the most established elements of the male canon, Dante's treatment of women, and the sexual politics of "The

---

⁶¹ Ibid., 111.
⁶² Ibid., 148.
⁶³ Ibid., 149.
⁶⁴ Ibid., 79.
⁶⁵ Ibid.
⁶⁶ Sayers, "The Human-Not-Quite-Human," 44.

'Terrible' Ode" in particular, took on a broader signification, providing liberating grounds for her negotiation of literary authority and fashioning of her place in tradition.[67]

"Exchange of Hierarchies": Authority, Tradition, and Gender

The period since World War I had seen several influential contributions around the role of tradition in literary criticism, most notably T. S. Eliot's (1888–1965) "Tradition and the Individual Talent" (1919).[68] With his own fascination with his predecessors and his imagined exchanges with them, Dante was a crucial figure in these twentieth-century efforts to theorize notions of tradition, influence, canon, and hierarchy in relation to the attempts of the modern author to produce original and valuable work. Sayers herself showed a strong interest in these questions, ultimately following Eliot's observation that "no poet, no artist of any art, has his complete meaning alone" to pursue a project in her later life – never completed – with the working title *The Burning Bush*, in which she sought to bring "Dante into relation with other poets," instead of his being always a "lonely monument."[69]

Her writing repeatedly explores various enabling and unconventional models of tradition and authority. In the preface to her *Further Papers on Dante* (1957) she described how:

> Every poet that ever wore the bays is a perpetual competitor in the Olympian games, on an equal footing with his heirs and his ancestors. Poets do not merely pass on the torch in a relay race; they toss the ball to one another, to and fro, across the centuries. Dante would have been different if Virgil [70 BCE–19 BCE] had never been, but if Dante had never been we should know Virgil differently.[70]

Expanding on her theme in an essay on Charles Williams himself as a "Poet's Critic," she criticized Dante scholars for seeing everything as a matter of "sources" and "influences": "they have never been ashamed to acknowledge their debts to one another; neither was such 'borrowing' ever thought dishonourable until we decided to make a fetish out of the word

---

[67] As explored by Barbara Reynolds and Kathleen Verduin, Sayers is often understood to have "fallen in love not only with [Dante's] poetry, but with the man as she imagined he might have been," Reynolds, *The Passionate Intellect*, 220. Verduin, "Sayers, Sex, and Dante."
[68] Eliot, "Tradition and the Individual Talent."
[69] Reynolds, *The Passionate Intellect*, 207.
[70] Sayers, *Further Papers*, v.

'originally'."[71] But she says, drawing on Eliot and endorsing the notion with examples from her detective fiction, in "the tradition – which means the 'handing over' – of the symbols of art, time's arrow flies both ways," which "means in a very real sense poets do sometimes write more greatly than they know; and it also means that every poet's work enriches not only those to whom he transmits the tradition, but also all those from whom he himself derived it."[72] She celebrates Williams as the only critic who, "in discussing Dante's poetic theme and treatment, will readily and as it were casually bring in Shakespeare, Milton, Wordsworth, Coleridge, Bernard Shaw, Coventry Patmore, George Fox, Sir Thomas Browne, Spenser, Keats, Kierkegaard, Raymond Lully and Christopher Marlowe, to exchange ideas with him as though they were all democratic citizens of one and the same poetic Athens."[73] Williams's approach to tradition is clearly an enabling one for Sayers: democratic, inclusive, nonhierarchical, nonlinear, based on a playful reciprocal exchange of ideas across time. The translator does not need to grapple with or overcome the author, but can catch the ball from him and toss it back, in mutual exchange.

This concept of mutual exchange – the doctrine of "continuous exchange of hierarchies" – was crucial to Williams's theology, and, as Barbara Reynolds notes, one of three key ideas Sayers shared with Williams. Sayers explained it thus:

> To Dante, living in an age of fixed hierarchies and penetrated by the doctrines of courtly love—which is the one-sided devotion of a man to a woman—the communication of the glory is always from above downward. Throughout the great ladder of creation, each rank draws up the one below it by the cords of love; every being looks up in love (*eros*) to the one above it and downward in charity (*agape*) to the one below it, so that, as Dante says of the heavenly hierarchy, "*tutti tirati sono e tutti tirano*—all are drawn and draw." To this noble conception, Charles Williams, living in an age which calls itself (for want of a better word) democratic, and one in which the relations between men and women are somewhat differently conceived, brings the further concept of the exchange of hierarchies ... Not wholly abandoning the conception of hierarchy, not wholly accepting an absolutism of equality (a thing difficult enough socially and impossible when it is

---

[71] Sayers, "Charles Williams," 78.
[72] Ibid., 79.
[73] Ibid., 80. The writers Sayers mentions are William Shakespeare (1564–1616), John Milton (1608–1674), William Wordsworth (1770–1850), Samuel Taylor Coleridge (1772–1834), George Bernard Shaw (1856–1950), Coventry Patmore (1823–1896), George Fox (1624–1691), Sir Thomas Browne (1605–1682), Edmund Spenser (c. 1552–1599), John Keats (1795–1821), Søren Kierkegaard (1813–1855), Raymond Llull (c. 1232–c. 1316), and Christopher Marlowe (1564–1593).

> a question of an equality of gifts) the later poet sees a humanity in which the relation of higher to lower is fluid. I am superior to you, it may be, in certain respects – very good; for that "you do me honour, and therein do well;" in other respects, you are superior to me – that too is right and good, and for that "I do you honour and therein do well." ... In this elaborate exchange of hierarchies, moving from man to woman, and from woman back to man, and from the present into the past and back again, we see what one original poetic mind can do with the image implanted in it by another ... [These examples] show how pregnant the images of a great poet are, and how another, inheriting his tradition, may (like the householder in the parable) bring out of his treasure things new and old. For though in a sense the later poet, bringing fresh thought and fresh experience to his task, adds fresh lustre to the original image, which thereafter shines with all the new light he has thrown back upon it, yet in another sense the new images were always latent in the old; so that it is not possible to say that there is nothing in Williams which was not potentially in Dante, and, *a fortiori*, that there is nothing in Dante which is not, actually, in Christ.[74]

As in her feminism, she resists the "absolutism of equality," but wants to see a person recognized as superior as and when they are exceptionally, demonstrably so. Benefiting as she does from many current social structures, she does not want to abandon hierarchy, but to ensure "the relation of higher to lower is fluid," so that authors "draw one another up." This is a collaborative model of mutual improvement that benefits all participants (although it fails to recognize those who have never been able to set foot on the first rung), that has cross-gender exchange at its heart.

Explicitly, this is a model that allows for female authority: Beatrice was the "Image of Woman" "about whose person the Theology of Romantic Love is assembled" but, in Sayers's reading, this is not an image "of femaleness as such": "Williams was the first to insist that the adoration need not be (though in literature it most frequently is) that of a man for a woman. It might be, in the exchange of hierarchies, be that of a woman for a man; if, he would say, Beatrice had written her version of the *Commedia*, Dante himself might have figured in it as the "God-bearing Image."[75] The fluidity of Williams's model of exchange allows Sayers to invert centuries of the male gaze back on the author himself. But this inversion is by definition temporary. As she had written in one of her early letters to Williams, Beatrice's "intolerable ... attitude

---

[74] Sayers, "The Poetry of the Image," 193–97.
[75] Sayers, "Charles Williams," 75–76. She explicitly wrote to him to check this interpretation, as cited in Reynolds, *The Passionate Intellect*, 41, 176.

to Dante when they first meet" – which, she notes, is only the "harshness and humiliation" of the tradition of courtly love – would, if "taken seriously from a human point of view," be "as objectionable as "he for God only, she for God in him" (Milton's line stuck so jaggedly in her throat that she comes back to it time and again).[76] She concludes: "I do not think any human relationship is wholesome if it involves a permanent inferiority or subjection of the one party to the other. An inter-change of hierarchies, yes – but in such a way that nobody is degraded by the mere fact of what he or she is."[77] This dynamic model of exchange, across the boundaries of language, gender, and time, was crucial to unlocking new possibilities for authorial relations.

How transformative Charles Williams's moderate encouragement was to Sayers's interests suggests how significantly her medievalist work might have been enhanced by the broader support of a like-minded intellectual cohort such as the Inklings, who met regularly in Oxford to read and comment on one another's work and shared valuable information and contacts with one another. Owing to J. R. R. Tolkien's (1892–1973) and especially C. S. Lewis's antipathy towards women and particularly to their involvement in academic matters, the Inklings were an avowedly and exclusively male fraternity.[78] Williams, unlike Tolkien or Lewis, had been brought up from a young age in mixed company and was notably more comfortable with female company and exchange – indeed, it was a crucial underpinning of his "theology of romantic love," which turned on a mutuality of desire. The Inklings' ethos was fully out of step with the sense of equality that Sayers sought, and found in Williams. She identified in Milton "a certain discomfort about sex which imparts a discomfort [with women] to me. It is in fact that same trouble I find in Lewis himself." She identifies this as "a real error of taste which ... points to a failure of something more fundamental." Dante, in contrast – and Williams, by association – has an appealing lack of this discomfort: "down at the bottom of him is something that knows where it lives and is not really bothered about 'this woman-business'."[79]

Resistant as she was to being particularized as a female author, there were doubtless common issues that she shared with other women writers. In the lineage of translators of Dante she lacked any female predecessors: although

---

[76] Sayers, *The Letters of Dorothy L. Sayers*, vol. 3, 57.
[77] Ibid., 57.
[78] Fredrick and McBride, *Women among the Inklings*.
[79] Sayers, *The Letters of Dorothy L. Sayers*, vol. 3, 80.

she did not frame her experience in the same way as later generations of feminists, her struggle was, as they identified, not just with the individual forebear but with the whole patrilineal, genealogical tradition, which presented no obvious woman's role through which to relate to the poet. The image of the source poet as father – whether a kindly paternal influence or an inhibiting power the strong poet must prevail over – left little space for the woman writer. This would be laid out in later feminist critiques, such as the gynocritics' engagement with Harold Bloom's (1930–2019) patriarchal model of Freudian agonistic struggle, and particularly Sandra Gilbert and Susan Gubar's "anxiety of authorship" and Annette Kolodny's (1941–2019) "influence of anxiety."[80] In the 1930s and 1940s, Sayers lacked theorized feminist frameworks to authorize her contributions. She consistently refused to speak as a "woman author" because her usual overt strategy was to be included and amplified as an honorary "literary bloke," not excluded and diminished as she anticipated she would be as a woman writer. The one place where she was particularly inhibited in "speaking as a woman" was in her discussions of literary tradition and authority, because to do so without a feminist tradition to draw on would have been to cement her location outside it. But, as her repeated rereading of "The 'Terrible' Ode" reveals, she needed – perhaps mostly for her own mental adjustment as she sought to step into Dante's shoes – other models that allowed for female authorities, which did not constantly remind her that to be the universal author was to be "not female."

The dominant metaphors for literary relations have long been familial, androcentric, and rooted in heteronormative models of sexual reproduction, with writers variously expressing a complex mix of love, sex, and conflict with the source author. One curious paradox of textual transmission – explored in different ways by Eliot, Bloom, Barthes, Gilbert and Gubar, and Eve Kosofsky Sedgwick (1950–2009), among many others – is that it is ostensibly rooted in heteronormative male-female sexual reproduction, but predicated upon male–male bonds. Eliot wrote of "a peculiar personal intimacy … a genuine affair with a real poet"; Bloom later described his defining concept of poetic misprision as "a profound act of reading that is a kind of falling in love with a literary work."[81] The patriarchal model emerged originally from Aristotelian models of sexual reproduction, in which the father's seed is passed onto the son, rather than as a coproduct

---

[80] Gilbert and Gubar, *The Madwoman in the Attic*; Kolodny, "The Influence of Anxiety."
[81] Eliot, "Reflections on Contemporary Poetry," 39; Bloom, *The Anxiety of Influence*, xxiii.

of father and mother, eliding the need for female generativity. Renaissance humanism had inherited the loving encounters of the classical tradition, which in the twentieth century came to be primarily understood as a Freudian struggle for authority.

As one for whom the intellect was androgynously self-generating, Sayers's primary model is not a familial or reproductive imagining, but rather strongly invested in what Stephen Guy-Bray calls the "author as desirable man."[82] Although literary relations were less frequently imagined as cross-sex, there was an established subject position for the female writer as the "daughter" of a textual tradition, and Sayers did in her later years become interested in this relation, most notably in her unfinished historical novel *Dante and his Daughter Bice*.[83] But even here she sees Dante more as lover than as father, her focus on pleasure rather than procreation. The novel is set in fourteenth-century Ravenna, where Dante "looks back over his life and meditates on four women: Beatrice Portinari, the Donna Gentile, the Donna Pietra, and his wife Gemma." On his marriage to Gemma, Sayers speculates on the "simplest of all conjugal remedies": "He knew how to give pleasure with his body – readily, considerately, satisfyingly; and she brought to the game a simple enjoyment, too lazy to be called passion, too cheerfully animal to be called love, too purely physical for it to matter if he bestowed his embraces with his mind elsewhere – and perhaps on somebody else."[84] This notion was so liberating for Sayers because imagining the author as "desirable man" dissolved his "formidable paternity," to use Barthes's phrase.[85] The Father is unimpeachable: the daughter cannot kill him, nor inherit his line; but, as lover, Dante can be "drag[ged] down to one's vile level ... for a change."[86]

Approaching the author as "desirable man" engaging in a fluid, eroticized exchange of hierarchies, with a focus on pleasure rather than procreation, opened up new (heteronormative) possibilities for a woman writer. Sexing him fully as *vir* and not just as universal *homo*, Sayers was no longer alone in being imprisoned by her gender as non-human; sexualizing herself, and placing the focus on the woman's pleasure, she was no longer an asexual "literary freak."[87] As men could, she could be both a writer and an

---

[82] Guy-Bray, *Loving in Verse*, 99; discussing Barthes, *The Pleasure of the Text*.
[83] Explored in the Romantic period, for example, by Newlyn, *Reading, Writing, and Romanticism*.
[84] Reynolds, *The Passionate Intellect*, 205.
[85] Barthes, *The Pleasure of the Text*, 27.
[86] Sayers, *The Letters of Dorothy L. Sayers*, vol. 3, 86.
[87] Ibid., vol. 1, 237.

adult human with desires: she turns the female gaze onto the body of the male author. As in the "Human-Not-Quite-Human," her playful inversion of gendered types reveals the myth of the masculine universal.

Particularly, the charged erotics of "The 'Terrible' Ode," with its opaque, challenging exploration of violence and consent, allowed her to confront the limiting models of literary relations she found herself trapped within, and imagine new configurations. She had no desire to unseat or tear down the male author completely: she was invested in the existing canon and retaining the structures that she – as an "exceptional" heterosexual, socially elite, white, Christian woman – was learning to negotiate. She was attracted to Dante's mastery and did not wish to replace it with a lineage of mothers and daughters. Although there is an erotically charged play of dominance and submissiveness in this theorizing of authorial relations, this is not a permanent subjection based on "the mere fact of what he or she is," but rather a continual and consensual mutual exchange of power.[88] *Her* pleasure, and his eagerness to grant it, is placed repeatedly at the center.

Sexual difference is visible and present in this model – its heteroerotics rely upon it – but as the exchange goes back and forth, and author changes place with author, the categories blur; Sayers wrote that the creative process was about "the realisation of the other in the self."[89] This is particularly true for translation, often considered a feminized practice, in which the female translator cross-dresses in the "mantle" of the canonical male author. Through her challenges to the universality of the male in her feminist essays, her case for the mutuality of pleasure and countersexualization of the male author in her writings on Dante, and her flexible utilization of androgyny and fluidity in her work more broadly, Sayers experimented with redefinitions of gendered authorial relations and enabled her much-desired role as a modern interpreter of Dante.

Conclusion

Recent work in medieval studies – now extended in this essay collection – has developed a new understanding of the ways the medieval shaped the construction of modernity and how the Middle Ages were marginalized by modernity's own self-narratives. But Sayers's example serves to caution us

---

[88] Ibid., vol. 3, 57.
[89] Sayers, "Poetry of the Image," 197; quoted in Downing, *Writing Performances*, 110.

not to reproduce unwittingly modernity's other marginalizations in tracing these narratives: not to continue to exclude the contributions it sought to diminish, nor to uphold unquestioningly the patriarchal intellectual and literary genealogies and traditions it created. She reminds us that we cannot absorb uncritically its valorization of certain work as "influential" or "major," nor attribute to certain figures "importance" or "talent," without recognizing how these judgments emerge from gendered (or racialized, elitist, or ableist) assumptions. Susan Sniader Lanser describes how "discursive authority," a blend of "intellectual credibility, ideological validity, and aesthetic value," is "produced interactively ... with respect to specific receiving communities," most readily attaching itself to "white, educated men of hegemonic ideology," requiring writers who do not possess those characteristics to pursue a "project of self-authorization" via particular textual strategies.[90] In drawing on the work of Amanda Anderson, Lois Cucullu articulates a feminist "anxiety of agency" as distinct from Bloom's masculinist "anxiety of influence," which obeys a "circular logic": "because feminist critics lack long-standing historical referents or antecedents, their claims to agency stand out and appear contrived; and because feminist critical agency seems contrived, so, too, do the historical precedents that feminist critics claim appear overstated."[91] Of all the figures considered in this volume, Sayers probably is least frequently awarded the description "intellectual," even though she spent her life in intellectual circles doing intellectual work, and saw herself as such. Engaging constantly with broad public readerships, and providing them with a vivid and fresh modern Dante, Sayers's work had a significant role in shaping popular understandings of Dante and the medieval world more broadly, and in some sense therefore was more "influential" than otherwise elite or specialist contributions.

Throughout her career, Sayers engaged in repeated reperformances of the authorial self to establish herself in new genres and fields, often making use of a performative "outsider" status to negotiate entry to new domains. She wrote to her agent in 1946, comparing Peter Wimsey, whose name she professed to "loathe and detest," to the "gaily-spotted Leopard" who "continually hindered" Dante in the first canto of the *Inferno*, "skipping around his feet when he wanted to get on."[92] She compared her desire to press on

---

[90] Lanser, *Fictions of Authority*, 6–7.
[91] Cucullu, *Expert Modernists*, 167.
[92] Sayers, *The Letters of Dorothy L. Sayers*, vol. 3, 199.

with translating Dante to the frequent pleas from fans for another novel: "Even if I were not panting to get on, at last, with what I want to do, the job of wrenching my machinery round again to tackle detection would be as slow and laborious as reconverting a factory from war-time to peace-time production." Understanding that her explicit authority claims "stand out and appear contrived" ("I am, to some extent, a medievalist"), her letters and writings reveal the various personas she utilized in "retooling" for her most challenging role as Dante's translator. At the midcentury, women could not in uncomplicated fashion join cozy fraternities or grapple with their forebears; Sayers's erotic readings of Dante, her feminist essays, and her remodelings of literary tradition perform her self-authorized transition from "popular detective writer" to "expert medievalist," and in the process enact a forward-looking feminist enquiry into the functions of gender and power within literary and scholarly authority.

PART III

Epochs

CHAPTER 9

Periodization Trouble
Auerbach, Huizinga, and the Question of Medieval Realism

Jane O. Newman

> Not even the term 'realistic' is unambiguous.
> Erich Auerbach[1]

Periodization Trouble?

The name of the German-Jewish Romanist Erich Auerbach (1892–1957) is not often associated with the kinds of critical positions (past and present) that challenge the "space–time concept" at the heart of debates about periodization, at least when it is understood in the traditional sense.[2] In part, this may be because of the choreography of his most famous book, *Mimesis: The Representation of Reality in Western Literature* (German, 1946; English, 1953). More often than not, its twenty chapters have been taken to record a sequential march through the epochs of European literary history, all lined up in a row, complying obediently with the kinds of period labels that Rita Felski has described as "coffin-like containers."[3]

When they read *Mimesis* as moving inexorably from "Antiquity" and the "Middle Ages" through the "Renaissance" and (French) "Classicism" and then up to European "Naturalism" and nineteenth-century (again, French) "Realism," lay readers and professionals alike seem to accept the story that it follows a predictably progressivist, even teleological, path, its goal allegedly the epoch with which Auerbach shared both his world

---

[1] Auerbach, *Mimesis*, "Epilogue," 556.
[2] See Rowlett, "Ralph Cohen," 129. In the tradition of "modern" U.S. literary criticism, we might set as the bookends of this questioning of periodization on one end the founding of the journal *New Literary History* in 1969, the second issue of which was devoted to a "Symposium on Periods" (1970), and on the other end, Rowlett's retrospective essay of 2019. In his essay, where Rowlett gives a fulsome account of this tradition, Auerbach is not mentioned.
[3] Felski, "Context Stinks!" 577–78; cited in Rowlett, "Ralph Cohen," 132.

and (at least according to him) his method, namely modernity.⁴ Such assumptions have led both those who admire *Mimesis* as a manifestation of the entirety of the European canon from Homer (*fl.* 750 BCE) to Virginia Woolf (1882–1941) and those who would fault it for the very same reason to see the book and its author as reliant upon a discernible structure of period sequence and its assumed corollary, coverage. This is curious, for when they read *Mimesis* in this way, even some of the book's most careful readers seem to overlook not only that it skips over a good number of periods, but also that its author expresses a kind of regret in the "Epilogue" about the ones that are missing.⁵ In the "Introduction" to the posthumously published *Literary Language and its Public in Late Latin Antiquity and in the Middle Ages* (1958), this apparent desire for coverage reappears in his lament about *Mimesis*'s "obvious gaps" that Auerbach claims "the present book" has sought to fill.⁶ If a comprehensive survey organized by periods was what Auerbach was after, *Mimesis* does not seem to have delivered.

But what if Auerbach's several concessions about his failure in *Mimesis* to include all of Western literary history's periods actually indicates his possible hesitations about whether epochal thinking is a useful tool of literary history? And what might such doubts help us understand about the project of *Mimesis* overall? As it turns out, Auerbach was in fact deeply involved in debates that could easily have caused him to question the premises of periodization. One of the most conspicuous of these – and the one that would of course have been of interest to him as a life-long medievalist – was the one about the relation of the Renaissance to the Middle Ages. Already in his *The Renaissance in Historical Thought* (1948),⁷ Wallace K. Ferguson (1902–1983) chronicled the surprising intensity of the early twentieth-century controversy about this relation as it emerged in reaction to Jacob Burckhardt's (1818–1897) famously provocative assertion in his *The Civilization of the Renaissance in Italy* (1860) that a "dark" Middle Ages, hidden behind its "veil" of "faith, illusion, and childish

---

⁴ As Auerbach states in the final chapter of *Mimesis*, where he compares the "technique of modern writers with that of certain modern philologists": "the present book may be cited as an illustration" (548). Unless otherwise stated, citations of *Mimesis* will refer to the 2003 English language edition.
⁵ See Auerbach, *Mimesis*, "Epilogue," 556–57; cf. Marcus, "Erich Auerbach's *Mimesis*," 300, on *Mimesis* as spanning "over two thousand years of literary history, from Homer and the Old Testament to Virginia Woolf and Marcel Proust [1871–1922], with erudite discussions of almost every epoch in between."
⁶ Auerbach, *Literary Language*, 22.
⁷ Ferguson, *The Renaissance in Historical Thought*, 290–385.

prepossession," had ceded pride of place to the glittering Renaissance that signaled the birth of a political and cultural modernity.[8] The immense heat thrown off by these debates can be best explained by noting that they were not just the stuff of intra-academic squabbling at the time. Rather, this was a contest at whose core lay the very question of exactly which modernity the early to mid twentieth century Auerbach and his "bewildered" generation, "shaken" by the multiple "irrationalism[s]" of their times, understood themselves to have inherited from Europe's past.[9] Could this legacy provide them with tools with which to think about how to move beyond their own social, economic, and military woes, or could it not?[10] Both Auerbach's work and the work of his fellow medievalist and near contemporary, the Dutch cultural historian Johan Huizinga (1872–1945), work that Auerbach encountered in different formats at several crucial moments in his career, were deeply marked by these concerns.

In what follows, I investigate several instances of contact between Auerbach's and Huizinga's thought – and, in one case, possibly even between the two men themselves – as a way of explaining the impact that Huizinga's reading of the Francophone culture of late medieval Burgundy in his famous *The Autumn of the Middle Ages* (1919) appears to have had upon Auerbach's version of the Middle Ages-Renaissance periodization debates.[11] This impact is clearly visible in the changes Auerbach makes to his discussion of these same Burgundian texts from his 1921 dissertation on the tradition of the "Renaissance novella" in Italy and France to the primer on Romance philology that he wrote for his university students in Turkey, probably sometime around 1943.[12] Understanding what these changes may have suggested to Auerbach about the frailty of period concepts in general allows us to read not only chapter 10 of *Mimesis*, "Madame du Chastel," where Auerbach discusses these same texts a third time, but also potentially the entire project of *Mimesis* in new ways. When Auerbach cites *Autumn* in chapter 10 and does so in the specific context of

---

[8] Burckhardt, *The Civilization of the Renaissance*, 87.
[9] Ferguson, *The Renaissance in Historical Thought*, 294.
[10] On Burckhardt's own awareness of the parallels between the Renaissance and late nineteenth-century Europe, see Gilbert, *History*. For other early twentieth-century scholars' accounts of the need to understand Europe's past in the midst of its sorry present, see Newman, "The Present Confusion."
[11] Huizinga, *Herbst des Mittelalters*; *Autumn*.
[12] Auerbach, *Zur Technik der Frührenaissancenovelle* (hereafter cited as *Renaissance Novellas*); Auerbach, *Introduction aux Études de Philologie Romane*. *Renaissance Novellas* has not been translated into English. All translations of it and of the *Introduction* volume here are my own. For a full translation of *Introduction*, see Auerbach, *Introduction to Romance Languages and Literature*.

the question of medieval – as opposed to Renaissance – realism, it is clear, in other words, that he *was* involved in an important periodization debate at the time.[13] His position in this debate emerges when he offers an alternative to conventional periodization in the form of a theory of what he calls the "creaturely realism" there for the first time. Auerbach's discussion of this realism and its "origin" in "Christian figuralism" and the "Passion of Christ" in the end complicates the assumption that a clear, progressivist period logic governs the book.[14]

Which Realism?

Auerbach's historical encounter with Huizinga's work on medieval realism may have caused him to have doubts about the periods to which specific texts ought to be assigned. Before turning to the question of the realism of Auerbach's Middle Ages, however, it is important to understand how another period of realism has functioned in receptions of his work to render these doubts difficult to see, namely the realism associated with the nineteenth century. While the subtitle of *Mimesis* makes it quite clear that it is "reality" (*Wirklichkeit*) rather than any particular period of realism in which Auerbach is interested there – indeed, he carefully distinguishes in his 1933 essay, "Romanticism and Realism," for example, between "realistic" representation and the period "we call Realism" (the German here is: "Realistik" and "sog[enannten] [so-called] Realismus")[15] – students of *Mimesis* often mingle the two. Harry E. Shaw and Matthew Beaumont, for example, write that *Mimesis* "is the greatest history of realism we have" and describe Auerbach as realism's "champion."[16] In both cases, the "realism" to which they are referring is the "classical realism"[17] of the nineteenth century as it can be found in the novels of Stendhal (1783–1842), Honoré de Balzac (1799–1850), and Gustave Flaubert (1821–1880), the texts at the center of *Mimesis*, chapter 18, "In the Hôtel de la Mole," the texts so often taken as the yardstick by which Auerbach measures realism writ large.[18] As a result, these texts also come to function as the highpoint of *Mimesis*'s

---

[13] See Auerbach, *Mimesis*, 247–48.
[14] Ibid., 247.
[15] Auerbach, "Romantik und Realismus," 426; "Romanticism and Realism," 144.
[16] Shaw, *Narrating Reality*, 5; Beaumont, "Introduction," 10.
[17] Beaumont, "Introduction," 10.
[18] These are the same texts and times that Roman Jakobson (1896–1982) describes as only one of the five possible ways of parsing what realism is, namely the one that designates realism as a "separate artistic movement" or "current" identified with the "nineteenth century," one that ultimately became

allegedly period-based literary historical account, which is as a result also presumed to be an evolutionary one that tracks with the "growth" of a "multiperspectival, dynamic, and holistic way of representing history and reality" emerging out of and completing the realisms of earlier texts and times, as Edward Said (1935–2003) writes.[19] Somewhat surprisingly, even the more complex and nuanced readings of *Mimesis* that would refigure or resist or even reverse its "historical trajectory" trade (both implicitly and explicitly) in equally as traditional period assumptions about realism and its sequencing.[20]

Auerbach's own diction and explanations of his project undoubtedly play a role in permitting such assumptions. In the same "Epilogue" where he declares his regret for not having written about the "German realism of the seventeenth century," for example, he writes that the novels of Stendhal and Balzac "*completed a development* which had long been in preparation" and also "opened the way for modern realism."[21] Similar claims also appear, albeit in a more guarded fashion, in his essay "Romanticism and Realism" (1933), written almost a decade and a half earlier, in which he refers to the nineteenth century as the "age" of what "we call Realism" as both a period unto itself and as "entirely new and unique" insofar as it provided a kind of benchmark against which even the newer realisms of the "contemporary" twentieth-century novel and cinema were still

---

"identified as the ultimate manifestation of realism in art and was made the standard by which to measure the degree of realism in preceding and succeeding artistic movements." See Jakobson, "On Realism in Art," 39 and 43.

[19] Said, "Introduction," xxvii.

[20] On the "historical trajectory" of *Mimesis*, see Said, "Introduction," xiv. See also, Bahti, "Auerbach's *Mimesis*," 124–45, who describes Auerbach's readings of Dante (c.1265–1321) and Flaubert as "two decisive moments ... in realism's overcoming of the doctrine of the levels of style" that he claims relate to one another less as a matter of temporal sequence than as rhetorically figural "prefiguration" and "fulfillment." White, "Auerbach's Literary History," 124–39, describes *Mimesis* as a "figural" "history of western literature," but uses Hegelian-inflected language to disinter as the book's purpose the tracking of the "ever fuller consciousness of western literature's unique project," which is to "fulfill" its "unique promise of "represent[ing] reality realistically." Porter, "Old Testament Realism," 187–224, argues differently that Auerbach's account of both Dante's and Virginia Woolf's "awareness of history" is based not on unfolding and fulfillment, but, rather, on a productively regressive "return to Old Testament realism." Recognizable period nomenclature and assumptions persist in all of these cases. Bahti describes Auerbach's Dante and Flaubert as belonging to two representative "moments, medieval and modern"; White argues that Auerbach's "figural historicism" is based on a "diachronic 'plot'" between "successive periods of literary history," such as "the Renaissance," "realism," and "modernism"; and Porter tracks Auerbach's commitment to highlighting the afterlives and "continuities" of Old Testament "lessons" into an unglossed "modern and modernist era" of his own "immediate present."

[21] Auerbach, *Mimesis*, 557 and 554, respectively; emphasis mine.

measuring themselves as "developments" that scramble to capture "reality" in new ways.²² In both of these cases, and in others like them, Auerbach thus himself uses conventional period terms and relies on a recognizably evolutionist literary-historical period model. We might therefore pardon some of his later readers for following the master along the "supersessionalist" literary-historical route on which this model relies, which, following the model of the New Testament "fulfilling" the Old Testament, sees a later generation of texts taking over from and replacing an earlier one.²³

And yet, in the "Romanticism and Realism" essay, as in the "Epilogue" and in several chapters in *Mimesis* too, Auerbach clearly demurs, both when he uses this kind of language and when he appears himself to assume period supersessionalism with respect to realism. In the "Epilogue," for example, he writes that the developments in the "serious ... representation" of "reality" in the nineteenth century could "not possibly have been the first of [their] kind;" "before that time, both during the Middle Ages and on through the Renaissance, a serious realism had existed."²⁴ The 1933 essay on "Romanticism and Realism" is blunter. "But did such an endeavor," namely the representation of the "real existential conditions of each and every individual living human being without excluding anything" and anyone, "really have no precedent in earlier times?" Of course it did, he observes, and the essay's final paragraph goes on to stand the directionality of period sequencing on its head. The argument is noteworthy for the position in which Auerbach leaves his reader, and deserves to be cited at length:

> There once was a form of tragic realism ... able to grasp our chaotic world as an authentic reality.... I am referring to the tragic realism of the Middle Ages and to its source in the story of Christ. This form of realism achieved the most radical destruction of the separation of styles since antiquity and brought about the most radical instantiation of tragic realism that has ever been seen. It originated in God's sacrifice of Himself to earthly reality. The reality of our world has changed so significantly that any recourse to this earlier notion would be absurd. But how else could an order and truth of reality even be imaginable if not by seeing God in it?²⁵

---

²² See Auerbach, "Romantik und Realismus," 426; "Romanticism and Realism," 146 and 154–55.
²³ Here I am adapting Kathleen Davis's use of the term "supersession" in describing the "periodizing operation" in her *Periodization and Sovereignty*, 4.
²⁴ See Auerbach, *Mimesis*, "Epilogue," 554. The argument echoes the stuttering argument of *Mimesis*, chapter twelve. "Montaigne [1522–1592] is something new," he declares, but then hesitates: but "[d]o we really think there is no comparable work" of self-examination "from earlier times?" (295). Of course there was, he insists and notes that St Augustine's [354–430] earlier method is "preserved" ("erhalten," *Mimesis* [2001], 286) in that of the later Montaigne (*Mimesis* [2003], 300).
²⁵ Auerbach, "Romanticism and Realism," 145 and 156.

Auerbach's phrasing here suggests that it is "this earlier notion" – the "tragic realism" of the "Middle Ages" and "its source in the story of Christ" – that constitutes the highest form of "tragic realism that has ever been" – higher perhaps even than the tragic realism of nineteenth-century Realism that the essay is about. It will be worth remembering his words here when we turn to *Mimesis*, chapter 10.

Auerbach's observations about the priority of "earlier" versus "later" realisms in publications from 1933 until 1946 suggest that both before his exile and in Turkey he was worried about the assumptions of what he calls the "theory of historical knowledge" as they drive supersessionalist periodization. Much later, in the "Introduction: Purpose and Method" to *Literary Language and its Public in Late Latin Antiquity and the Middle Ages* (on which he was working when he died in his second exile—this time in the US—in 1957), he explicitly eschews the use of "words and phrases" and "categories of classification" such as the period concepts "baroque" or "Romantic" entirely and declares them unhelpful.[26] In what follows, I argue that the "periodization trouble" to which these various doubts and uncertainties attest may have been provoked by Auerbach's several encounters with Huizinga and his thought, and may have been what caused him to try and develop a differently ordered, non-supersessionalist way of reading about the "reality" that "Western literature" represents.

Close Encounters

Little discussed in work either on Huizinga or on Auerbach is the fact that, in January of 1932, the former delivered a lecture in the German university town of Marburg.[27] Serendipitously, Marburg had just three years earlier appointed a new faculty member in the Department of Romance Language, namely Auerbach. The title of Huizinga's talk was "Burgundy: A Crisis in the Relation between Romania and Germania." The famous lecturer was sixty years old (to the novice professor, Auerbach's, forty) at the time and exceedingly well known; the 1924 German translation of his *Autumn of the Middle Ages* (originally 1919), was already in its third edition, and by 1932, the book had already been the subject of countless reviews in the leading German-language journals across the disciplines.[28] It is difficult to imagine in this context that Auerbach would not have attended the lecture,

---

[26] Auerbach, *Literary Language*, 7 and 19.
[27] See Krumm, *Johan Huizinga*, 314.
[28] See Krumm, *Johan Huizinga*, 241–52; Köster, *Johan Huizinga*, 100–1.

doing so not only because of Huizinga's reputation, but also in light of his announced topic, namely Burgundy, which was one with which Auerbach had himself in fact spent considerable time. Indeed, in his 1921 dissertation, *Zur Technik der Frührenaissancenovelle in Italien und Frankreich* (*On the Technique of the Renaissance Novellas of Italy and France*), he had written about many of the very same Franco-Burgundian texts about which Huizinga was to speak and on which he had of course already written in the earlier *Autumn* book. Auerbach would have been all ears.

Huizinga's lecture, which was published one year later in the *Historische Zeitschrift*, is as interesting methodologically as it is for the material on which it focuses.[29] In it, he engages in a blend of what he calls "imaginary" and "hypothetical" (what we might now call counterfactual) history with analyses of a variety of historical artifacts and texts. His tight focus is on the fifteenth-century Burgundian leader Charles the Bold (1433–1477), and the significance for the future of European conflict (even up to the modern day in 1932) of the fact that Charles had failed to make good on his father Philip the Good's (1396–1467) commitment to creating an autonomous Burgundy capable of functioning as a buffer power and state between France and the German Empire (the Romania and Germania of the lecture's title). What might have happened, Huizinga asks, if Charles had acted otherwise at key historical moments, indeed, if the "accidents" of his behavior and actions, and thus the contingencies of history (rather than the "deterministic" economic and political factors) had been different? Might the relations between these two cultures and states have turned out to be more harmonious in the end? The question was not a casual one at the time, coming as it did on the heels of more than a half-century of French–German conflict, leading up to and including World War I (1914–1918), in which Auerbach, among others, had served.

There are of course no real answers to such hypotheticals, Huizinga admits, just a recognition of the terrible future impact of Charles's – and thus Burgundy's – failure to have been able to keep the balance of power between the French and the Germans in place at the time. More interesting for him than these political questions are the cultural ones, questions that it is in fact more plausible to address, given that sources do exist for answering them. Prominent among them – and at the heart of the rest of the talk – is the one that emerges from what Wessel Krul describes as Burgundy's "modern" "early capitalist economy," which was one of the reasons for its

[29] Huizinga, "Burgund," 3–20.

and Charles the Bold's incredible power and wealth at the time; the main question is, namely, how was it possible for Charles to have acted as he did, in an archaically knightly, even "medieval way," as more of a "chivalric" warrior-hero whose "adventure[s]" were "sanctioned by religious vows," than as the modern head of state that he could and even should have been – and that Europe had desperately needed, both at the time and since?[30] The rest of the lecture addresses the "culture" – music, art, architecture, and painting – of the Franco-Burgundian period in an attempt to answer this question, turning, for example, to the texts of the period by which Charles would have been surrounded, including the fourteenth-century Francophone chronicles written in Burgundy by authors such as Georges Chastellain (c. 1415–1475), Jean Froissart (1337–1405), and Jacques du Clerq (1420–1501), in order to learn from them what Charles could have understood and would have promoted as a leader's proper profile. What Huizinga finds in these texts are descriptions of what he calls a "fantastic Middle Ages," based on "illusions of inherited forms" that included "archaizing" celebrations of the Order of the Golden Fleece and of the Crusades and of Burgundy as the chivalric protector of Christianity too, alongside other forms of equally as outdated, highly stylized, and overly "ornamental" art. Huizinga argues that this kind of textual–cultural environment goes a long way towards explaining the kinds of values that could have motivated Charles to engage in the brash but ultimately unproductive military adventures that eventually cost Burgundy its future statehood and him his young life.

Regardless of what we might or might not accept today about his readings of the geopolitical pressures Huizinga claims shaped both the politics and the culture of fifteenth-century Burgundy, what is clear in this 1932 lecture is that he saw evidence, especially in the narrative sources of the time, of what in the earlier *Autumn* book he had already characterized as the "tremendous self-deception"[31] that would have allowed, even encouraged, Charles to pursue what were ultimately the anachronistic medieval "heroic dream[s]" that he describes in *Autumn*'s third chapter, which is so entitled. In the lecture, Huizinga reports that the political manipulations and messages that these "illusions" were meant to send were in fact already the object of criticism at the time, and that other cultural artifacts of the period – including sculpture by Claus Sluter (c. 1340–c. 1406) and

---

[30] On Huizinga's lecture, see Krul, "In the Mirror of van Eyck," 355–56.
[31] Huizinga, *Autumn*, 85.

paintings by Jan van Eyck (*c.* 1390–1441), on the one hand, and additional texts by, among others, Antoine de le Sale (1386–1426), on the other – reflected "melancholically," as he writes, the "gloom"-filled atmosphere (*Stimmung*) of an age that had understood the untimeliness of the court's actions well.[32] For anyone in the room that day in Marburg who had read Huizinga's *Autumn* – which again had by that time already been available in German for eight years in three editions, and contains the names of the artists and writers he discusses in the lecture as well as Huizinga's argument about the contradictions and "tensions" of the late Middle Ages in Burgundy, whereby "colorful beauty" and highly "formalized behavior" could exist side by side with a clear "despairing of the world" – all of this would have been familiar, since it is the same material that *Autumn* covers and the same argument it makes.[33] Hearing the great Dutch scholar discuss texts by some of the very same authors about whom he had written in his dissertation a decade before, Auerbach in particular might have been motivated to go out and reread *Autumn* – or perhaps read it for the first time (discussed later in this section) – with special interest, since it would have been obvious to him that Huizinga's account of these texts differed markedly from his own.

Before turning to Auerbach's treatment of Franco-Burgundian texts in his 1921 dissertation (*Renaissance Novellas*) – the very title of which already makes it clear how his initial reading of them as belonging to the Renaissance had differed from Huizinga's description of them as medieval – it is important to note the greater political and historiographic context within which Huizinga's position on late medieval Burgundy, both in *Autumn* and then in the 1932 lecture, found a place. This context was part and parcel of the periodization debates that Huizinga argues had been ignited in the Netherlands in particular by the reception there of Burckhardt's claims in his *The Civilization of the Renaissance in Italy* about the dawning of the new "modern" age of both individualism and realism in fifteenth century Italy – and by extension in northern Europe too – as that which defined the Renaissance as categorically different than the pre-modern Middle Ages.

Wessel Krul describes how Huizinga, in his late autobiographical statement, "My Path to History" (1943), soundly critiques the nationalism of the way that Burckhardt's thesis had been received during the early years

---

[32] Huizinga, "Burgund," 20 and 25–26.
[33] Huizinga, *Autumn*, 207 and 53.

of the twentieth century by the Dutch, when scholars sought to assimilate what was thought of as the cultural capital of Burckhardt's Renaissance to their own nations north of the Alps.[34] Numerous art exhibits and well-known scholars, such as Henri Pirenne (1862–1935), sought to demonstrate that, as in Italy, so too in Belgium, a fifteenth-century "Renaissance" had established the conditions of possibility for a future of "modern" national glory. Huizinga profoundly disagreed with such claims, based on his assessment of Burckhardt's assessment of the Italian evidence and also because he had found during his own trips to Florence grounds for believing that even Italy's "Renaissance" had been a much more mixed, even continuous medieval–Renaissance affair. He also explicitly resisted seeking justification for "present-day political ideals by reference to" a clearly stylized Belgian-Burgundian past, writing in a 1911 lecture entitled "On the Origins of Our National Consciousness," for example, that it was anachronistic to locate modern "national feelings" or state-identified loyalties, identities, and cultural traditions in these earlier periods; rather, structures of social and political organization in fifteenth-century Burgundy much more resembled "archaic" and what Huizinga called "primitive" forms of life and thought.[35] Finally, what Krul calls the "extraordinary realism" for which the so-called "Flemish School" of art was traditionally famous, while indeed realistic, ought not to be considered evidence of anything resembling either Italian Renaissance realism or a Renaissance in the North.[36] Rather, Huizinga claimed, this realism was a specifically local – and residually medieval – Burgundian attempt to negotiate the strains of living in a time of great political upheaval and unrest. Remember Charles the Bold's escapades.

Huizinga held lectures and wrote a series of articles in the years leading up to and including World War I about what he considered to be the pronounced medievalism of the fifteenth century in the North, articles that were thus clearly preliminary studies for *Autumn*. The year after *Autumn* appeared, he went on to publish a magisterial – and exceedingly witty – account of the battles over periodization raging among his peers in an essay entitled, "The Problem of the Renaissance" (1920), in which a fictional interlocutor pleads with a fellow scholar (obviously channeling Huizinga) not to "deprive us of the Renaissance! We cannot do without

---

[34] See Krul, "In the Mirror of van Eyck," 357–69; Huizinga, "My Path to History."
[35] Cited in Krul, "In the Mirror of van Eyck," 367–68.
[36] Ibid., 365.

it."³⁷ "The Problem of the Renaissance" was followed by "Renaissance and Realism," a lecture Huizinga held, also in 1920, both in London and in four German-speaking university towns (it was only published almost a decade later in Dutch), in which the realism of the Renaissance, as Burckhardt had defined it, is differentiated from medieval Burgundian realism in no uncertain terms.³⁸ As it turns out, both of these essays also appeared in German (in several editions) in prominent venues between 1928 and 1930, almost the very same years in which the second and third editions of the German *Autumn – Herbst des Mittelalters* – also appeared (1928 and 1931).

In "The Problem of the Renaissance," Huizinga floats the possibility that it might in fact be "better to stop using the term Renaissance altogether for the time being." Or, if we do continue to use it, he suggests that it must be acknowledged that "the spirit of the Renaissance is … much less modern than one is constantly inclined to believe;" indeed, it is actually "medieval," he thinks.³⁹ In "Renaissance and Realism," he narrows the focus, suggesting that, while an explicitly non-Burckhardtian realism may in fact have been important to the Middle Ages, it had "nothing to do with the Renaissance." Associating the images and the texts of the Burgundians in particular with the Renaissance is only possible by "distorting the concept hopelessly."⁴⁰ Auerbach could have turned to these texts and their arguments about the relation between the Middle Ages and the Renaissance – and about realism – for clarification after he heard Huizinga speak in Marburg. Again, he would have had ample access to them in German translation at the time. And he would have had good cause to do so, given his own interests.

That is, just a little over a decade *before* Huizinga held his talk in Marburg, Auerbach had handed in his second dissertation to the faculty of Romance Languages at the northern German university of Greifswald (his first dissertation, on the concept of "co-perpetratorship," had been delivered to the Law faculty in Heidelberg in 1913).⁴¹ The thesis would soon thereafter be published. And in it, Auerbach examines

---

³⁷ Huizinga, "The Problem of the Renaissance," 244. For the German text, see Huizinga, "Das Problem der Renaissance."
³⁸ Huizinga, "Renaissance and Realism."
³⁹ Huizinga, "The Problem of the Renaissance," 267, 217, and 282.
⁴⁰ Huizinga, "Renaissance and Realism," 295–97. According to Hugenholtz, "The Fame of a Masterwork," 92–95, *Autumn* was in fact received rather "coolly" in the Netherlands and in Belgium (and in Belgium in fact almost not at all) for its at-the-time unpopular assessment of the art and culture of fifteenth-century Burgundy as *not* a sign of a northern Renaissance.
⁴¹ See Auerbach, *Die Teilnahme*.

several of the very Franco-Burgundian chronicle texts on which Huizinga had commented in *Autumn* and went on to revisit in the "Burgundy"-lecture, among them, texts by Chastellain, Froissart, and Antoine de la Sale (*c.* 1385–*c.* 1461). As the title of his thesis makes clear, Auerbach's project was, among other things, to demonstrate that the novella texts from fifteenth-century Burgundy, identified here as the products of France, were what he calls a "new creation of the Renaissance (*eine Neuschöpfung der Renaissance*)," clear evidence, that is, of a positively Burckhardtian age of worldly individualism that signaled that the Middle Ages were at an end.[42] While the "realism" of these "French" texts differs from that of their Italian models (most prominently Giovanni Boccaccio [1313–1375]) in their domesticity and increased misogyny, Auerbach explains, both traditions were clearly "Renaissance" ones, as he notes over and over again.[43] In light of such claims, it does not seem surprising that when we turn to what appears to be the fulsome bibliography the aspiring academic provides at the start of his thesis, we find no indication that in 1921 Auerbach had read either Huizinga's *Autumn* of 1919 (although he could have, although only if he had read Dutch) or knew about the two Renaissance essays, all of which considered the Burgundians medieval.

However, by the time Auerbach set about the task of writing the literary historical part three of his *Introduction to the Study of Romance Philology*, which appears to have been written and made available to his Turkish students for the first time in Istanbul in 1943, where he had been teaching since 1936 after fleeing Hitler's Germany along with several hundred other German-Jewish scholars,[44] it is clear that he had changed his mind about the texts he discussed in the dissertation. Part three of the *Introduction* is divided into three clearly period-based chapters: "The Middle Ages," "The Renaissance," and "Modern Times." Here, the Francophone Burgundian texts – including Froissart and Eustache Deschamps (1346–*c.* 1407) – that had been cast as the proof of the "Renaissance" of "French" literature in the 1921 dissertation are discussed exclusively in the section of chapter 1 (on the Middle Ages) entitled "The Decline." The section title – "Le déclin" – is an obvious echo of the title of *Autumn* in its 1932 French-language translation, *Le déclin du moyen âge*, and *Autumn* is in fact the only secondary text Auerbach cites in this section, describing it as "Huizinga's magisterial book on the decline of the Middle Ages (*le livre magistral de Huizinga sur*

---

[42] Auerbach, *Renaissance Novellas*, 1–3 and 11.
[43] Ibid., 15 and 27. For Auerbach's use of the term "Renaissance" in this context, see 29, 35, 38, etc.
[44] Konuk, *East West Mimesis*.

*le déclin du moyen âge)."*⁴⁵ An earlier reference describes Huizinga as "a successor (*un successeur*)" to Jacob Burckhardt, and as "comparable" to him in method and "spirit (*esprit*)," signaling that Auerbach was now explicitly weighing in on the periodization debates.⁴⁶ The details of the "decline" section of the *Introduction* make it clear that it was now an *Autumn*-al Middle Ages to which the students were being introduced. Auerbach in fact uses a string of only lightly edited quotes from Huizinga's book, including a discussion of "the antithetical themes (*les themes antithetiques*)" and of the period's "extreme realism (*réalisme extreme*)" to describe the Burgundian texts.⁴⁷ The switch in period assignment is unmistakable. By 1943, the very texts that provided evidence of an upbeat Renaissance in the dissertation of 1921 belong entirely to a "declining" Middle Ages, exactly as that period had been described in the lecture by Huizinga that Auerbach may have heard, as well as in *Autumn*, which he finally appears to have read.

We may justifiably speculate that it may have been after he heard Huizinga's Marburg lecture in 1932 – and was perhaps just a little embarrassed that he got the Franco-Burgundian texts so entirely wrong, at least according to the senior scholar's reading – that he began to revise his Burckhardtian account in the company of Huizinga's work, which he appears to have purchased fairly quickly and taken with him when he left Marburg for Istanbul. At least this is the impression left by the list of books that Auerbach's widow, Marie Auerbach (1892–1978), made of his personal library in Connecticut after Auerbach died in 1957. At the time of his death, Auerbach owned eight texts by Huizinga, all of them published between 1924 and 1936, including the 1933 publication of the "Burgundy"-lecture and the 1924 German-language *Autumn*.⁴⁸ Reading *Autumn* soon after he heard Huizinga speak in Marburg, Auerbach would have been provoked to reconsider his approach to the Burgundian texts and their period affiliation in significant ways. We see the fruits of such reading in the *Introduction* of 1943.

And yet, in light of the ease with which Auerbach appears to have reassigned the Burgundian texts from one period to another, which he clearly did, we may wonder – as he may have wondered too – just how securely

---

⁴⁵ Auerbach, *Introduction*, 118–20.
⁴⁶ Ibid., 31.
⁴⁷ Ibid., 119.
⁴⁸ See Harry Ransom Center, "Erich Auerbach Collection" (Catalogue list), 38. Auerbach did travel back to Germany after he emigrated to the United States in 1947, and so it is possible that he could have purchased these volumes in used book stores during his visits.

are texts actually anchored in their home cultures and the periods they are conventionally assigned to represent? Teaching European literature in Turkey might have given him additional reasons for rethinking the period conventions of the literary history that had become more or less naturalized in Europe, but that his Turkish students had to be "introduced" to, or taught, before they could be questioned. The university primer does seem to respect a more or less standard sequencing of the periods of the Western tradition, carved up into neat and period-identified bundles of time (albeit with the Burgundian texts switching periods, as noted earlier). But by the time Auerbach comes to write the chapter of *Mimesis* in which he discusses this same Burgundian tradition once again, namely chapter 10, he appears to have come to a somewhat different understanding of the nature of medieval realism in particular, and to have begun to feel his way forward in the direction of a way around – or beyond – traditional periodization schemes.

"Medieval" Realism in Huizinga and Auerbach

I have argued that in his *Introduction to the Study of Romance Philology* from about 1943, Auerbach channels Huizinga's thesis about the waning Middle Ages when he recasts the argument of his dissertation about the Burgundian sources as Renaissance ones now as evidence of the medieval period's "decline." We may nevertheless wonder about the staying power of even this second, new version of the Burgundians, and about what appears to be the (substantially revised) clarity of the period to which they are said to belong, especially in light of the way Auerbach analyzes some of these same sources in *Mimesis*. The timing of when Auerbach might have planned and written this third version is complicated and worth dwelling upon because of several factors that may have influenced its composition.

In chapter 10, Auerbach makes specific reference to Huizinga when he turns yet again to the case of Burgundy, represented in this case by the *Réconfort de Madame de Fresne* (c. 1457) by Antoine de la Sale. In the original German of this chapter, Auerbach refers to Huizinga's work as a "study of this epoch," namely the Middle Ages, that we have had for "twenty years (*zwanzig Jahre*)."[49] Even though he famously leads in the published

---

[49] See Auerbach, *Mimesis* (2001), 236. The English translation of *Mimesis* changes the timeframe to "thirty years" (*Mimesis* [2003], 247), since it appeared nearly ten years after *Mimesis* was originally published in German in 1946.

version of *Mimesis* with the note that the book was "written between May, 1942, and April, 1945," the dates of the remark about Huizinga's book in the chapter itself suggest that Auerbach's discussion of the *Réconfort* in particular was composed in approximately 1939, twenty years after *Autumn* had first appeared, in other words. This was not so very long after Auerbach had arrived in Istanbul and began teaching his classes there, but also not so very long after he had finished one of the last essays he wrote before fleeing Germany, "On the Serious Imitation of the Everyday" (1937), where his explicit question is one of periodization, namely how we might understand nineteenth-century French realism as differing "fundamentally from imitative (*nachahmende*)" "works of early times."[50] In the "Epilogue" to *Mimesis*, Auerbach refers both to this essay and to the earlier "Romanticism and Realism" essay of 1933 (discussed earlier) as the product of reflections about "the principles of modern realism" that had occurred to him, as a trained medievalist and, most recently, the author of a book on Dante, in the course of his new teaching assignments in Marburg's Department of Romance Languages, presumably courses that included the French nineteenth century.[51] "Romanticism and Realism" itself, of course, appeared just one year after Auerbach would have heard Huizinga speak.

Auerbach's next new teaching assignments in Istanbul may have recalled the questions he posed in these essays to him as he pondered which version of Huizinga's thesis about the Burgundian texts to adopt in *Mimesis*, chapter 10, now understood to have been written in 1939, as perhaps one of the next installments in his several confrontations with periodization. The chapter ends by proposing a theory of "creaturely realism" whose premises differ in significant ways from the periodization regime that governs the 1943 primer.[52] In order to understand "creaturely realism" as a response to the challenges of periodization represented by the various realisms – medieval, Renaissance, and nineteenth-century French – jostling for position in his mind, it is helpful, first, to review some of the claims of Huizinga's *Autumn* about realism and then to see how Auerbach handles them in his reading of de la Sale.

---

[50] Auerbach, "Über die ernste Nachahmung des Alltäglichen," 442 (my translation).
[51] Auerbach, *Mimesis*, "Epilogue," 571.
[52] We might speculate that the differences could be explained by the fact that its "intended" readers were not that volume's student audience, but rather the "readers" (many of them his "friends of former years," in Marburg, we can assume) that Auerbach has *Mimesis* so famously and so poignantly seeking in the "Epilogue" at the very end of the book (557), the friends with whom he would have been debating what medieval and modern realisms had to do with one another just before he had to flee.

Huizinga's *Autumn* is often misunderstood because of its author's forceful rhetoric and emotional claims about the extremes of the Middle Ages, as well as by dint of his incredible attention to detail, both of which make it difficult to dig his thesis out from under what seem to be merely mountains of descriptions of his understanding of "wie es eigentlich gewesen," "how it really was," during the Middle Ages, as Leopold von Ranke (1795–1886) would have said. The shape of this in fact quite un-Rankean thesis, as it structures both the individual chapters and the text overall, is difficult to track as a result. Both Huizinga's argument and the choreography of the book in which he presents it may in fact be best understood as articulating how the antinomies of cultural production functioned during the Middle Ages and, more specifically, how Burgundian culture was responding to the contingencies of its time as the period began to lean toward its end. It is in this context that, as Huizinga argues repeatedly, the magnificent achievements of the period's art, including its "realism," may be best understood as indicating not renewal, but, rather, decline, as old norms continued to be invoked to divert attention from the fact that times had changed in ways that Burgundy's political leadership neither understood nor controlled.

This argument is not always easy to discern. The surface clutter of the text in chapter 1, "The Passionate Intensity of Life," for example, is the result of Huizinga's focus there on the "glittering," but inevitably also cruel aspects and "brutal barbarism" of public life; his cascading examples of itinerant preachers and princely entry processions, of bells, executions, and tears, and of pride and greed all issue in Huizinga's emotional declarations about the "fervent pathos" and "general insecurity" of medieval life.[53] Chapter 5, "The Vision of Death," famously teems with images of rotting corpses, "gruesome skeletons," and ghastly "image[s] of decay" in a similar way.[54] Seeing these as so many responses to the darkness of an unstable world, Huizinga then turns to the period's other reactions, its striking interest, that is, in the "fairy tale"-like and "fantastic" accounts that are the stuff of the chronicles about the "life of the princes," on the one hand, and what many think was the calm and Renaissance-like "sunlight of the century of the Van Eycks," on the other.[55] That such a fraught age "craves" a "more beautiful life" (chapter 2), either via asceticism (Huizinga repeatedly refers

---

[53] Huizinga, *Autumn*, 25, 9, and 27.
[54] Ibid., 172 and 165.
[55] Ibid., 9–11 and 24.

to the practices of the *devotio moderna,* for example),⁵⁶ or, earlier and more expansively described, in its craving for a "land of dreams," "illusion[s]," and "old fantastic ideals," makes perfect sense.⁵⁷ Court etiquette, highly codified and ritualized rituals around childbirth and mourning, archaic courtly and chivalric ideals of combat, and elaborate scenarios of devotion and heroic love are all nothing other than artificial means and "forms" of life invented to stem the tide of "violence and passion" and permanence of the "crass, hard, and cruel" "reality" of the time.⁵⁸

The consequences of Huizinga's arguments here for rattling at the foundations of periodization logic are several. Although he is not as explicit in *Autumn* in his critique of how period labels can be manipulated as he is in the essays on the Renaissance discussed earlier, Huizinga does state repeatedly that this ideological, but perhaps also existentially necessary deployment of culture occurs in all "primitive" cultures, including, he notes, "in our [own] time."⁵⁹ Even though the culture of the late Middle Ages is historically specific and arose out of particular "intellectual and emotional conditions" and needs of their day, in other words, it may best be assessed in "ethnological" terms.⁶⁰ As further examples, Huizinga adduces the mishaps, failures, and tragedies of mounting expeditions against the Turks based on an outdated chivalric code and the catastrophe of invoking chivalric honor "in the midst of real war."⁶¹ The *Annales* School historians, Marc Bloch (1886–1944) and Lucien Febvre (1878–1956), who reviewed *Autumn* in 1928 and called it an "original and suggestive book," were thus correct to see in it an exploration of the complexities of a particular period's "historical psychology." But the book was also a study of how culture works to manage the anxieties and tensions of everyday life. Another contemporary reviewer, the German Heinrich Günter (1870–1951), teased out the period-confounding lesson that both Huizinga's position and Bloch's and Febvre's readings imply in greater detail. In his 1926 review of the German translation of *Autumn* in the *Historisches Jahrbuch der Görresgesellschaft,* Günter writes that the "tension which the book discusses ... is not medieval but

---

⁵⁶ Ibid., 205 and 221–22.
⁵⁷ Ibid., 37–38 and 41. That Huizinga references Burckhardt's "Renaissance man" in this context (43) suggests either that the Renaissance was already in evidence in the Middle Ages or that the Middle Ages persisted into the Renaissance; in both cases, Huizinga writes, "the line between the Middle Ages and the Renaissance is too sharply drawn" (39; cf. 74).
⁵⁸ Ibid., 50 and 85.
⁵⁹ Ibid., 42, 53, 56, and 91.
⁶⁰ Ibid., 130 and 137.
⁶¹ Ibid., 105–6 and 111.

universally human, and indeed modern too."[62] It's a conclusion to which Auerbach also appears to have come.

In Huizinga's argument, realism provides an excellent example of how culture in general as well as Burgundian culture in particular worked. He locates one of the important forms of this kind of "historical psychology" in the illusionism, which he calls the "conscientious realism," of the paintings of the van Eyck brothers, which he discusses at length in chapters 12 and 13, "Art in Life" and "Image and Word."[63] These were precisely the kinds of cultural artifacts that had so often been received as a sign that the grand realism of the Renaissance, with its (alleged) focus on the individual, had had a northern life too. For Huizinga, however, they were actually the most artificial, "contrived," and "genuinely medieval" expressions of realism of all, their "naturalism" only an illusion of "peace and serenity." Represented "pedantically" and "down to the most minute detail" and "delighting in the surface appearance of things," their devotion to a "fabulous perfection" and "absolute truthfulness to nature" functioned precisely to divert viewers, through their "colorful forms," from the unsettling realities of their time. Although less well known, their "literary equivalents," the chronicles whose "realism" Huizinga treats with equal care in chapter 13, were produced in exactly this same context and capture its insecurities and horrors with much the same attention to what Huizinga calls "unbridled elaboration" and detail.[64] In the face of the "permanent pressure from injustice and violence … under which the century lived," "life had to be ennobled through [the] beauty" of what were often "genuine works of art," to be sure, but works that were commissioned by the very same people who also sponsored gargantuan festivals and ostentatious entertainments full of anachronistic codes.[65] In both cases, leaders used both artifice and art to distract themselves and their subjects from the recognition that their behavior no longer lined up with their world. In *Autumn*, Huizinga thus draws back the curtain on the ways that these texts, like the "realistic" paintings and altarpieces of the van Eycks, are "entirely medieval," both the artists and the writers entirely embedded in

---

[62] Bloch, Febvre, and Günter are cited in Hugenholtz, "The Fame of a Masterwork," 101–2. Hugenholtz cites Günter as "Hans," but the original *Jahrbuch* clarifies that his name was "Heinrich" and that he was the editor of volume 46 in which his commentary on Huizinga appears.
[63] For "conscientious realism," see Huizinga, *Autumn*, 329. The brothers van Eyck are Jan (c.1390–1441) and Hubert (c.1385–1426).
[64] Huizinga, *Autumn*, 294 and 319–47.
[65] Ibid., 103 and 306–7.

and dependent on the largesse of their "princely sponsors." "Art served," he bluntly observes, as the culture that sponsored it stumbled to its end.[66] No Renaissance rebirth here. Rather, only "barbarian splendor" as evidence that what was in fact the "medieval spirit" was "in its last gasps."[67]

In light of the compelling account that Huizinga gives of the way this "splendor" functioned within a dying Middle Ages and given the incredible details that crowd the pages of his book, especially in *Autumn*, chapter 13, which reads the very same narrative sources about which Auerbach wrote in his dissertation on the Renaissance with an almost Auerbachian care, it is no wonder that in *Mimesis*, chapter 10, Auerbach returns to a text that he had already discussed in the dissertation on the Renaissance novellas, namely Antoine de la Sale's fifteenth-century *Réconfort de Madame de Fresne*. He now reads it, however, at least initially, as *medieval*. (In *Autumn*, Huizinga discusses de la Sale, but mentions this particular text only in passing.)[68] The tale is one of astonishing brutality in its details; the sacrifice of a young son by his father and above all by his mother for the sake of the father's honor is described in horrific detail – including the pleas of the child as he is led to his death, straining against the chains that bind him, "bruis[ing] his legs" and cutting down "to the bone."[69] The impression the text makes, Auerbach now writes, is "incomparably ... medieval and unmodern," especially in the "elaborate solemnity" and "pompous," yet also "pedantic" "ceremony" of its "style."[70] It is a "class language," he claims, that is "un-humanistic" – which is Auerbach's way of saying the text's style is not (or no longer) of the "Renaissance" – and thus entirely proper to the culture out of which it emerged and which it depicts, the very late medieval culture of pointless, yet "ostentatious" "knightly ceremony" that Huizinga describes.[71] In the chapter, Auerbach briskly rehearses Huizinga's argument about the anachronism of such behavior in times of "impending change," but without citing him, leading us to assume that he (that is, Auerbach) will dismiss de la Sale's text – and the other Franco-Burgundian ones he discusses in the chapter – precisely as class-bound illusions along Huizinga's lines that have nothing to do with the "everyday" realities of their times.[72]

---

[66] Ibid., 319 and 310–11.
[67] Ibid., 383.
[68] Ibid., 171.
[69] Auerbach, *Mimesis*, 239–40. See also de la Sale, *Sa vie et ses ouvrages*.
[70] Auerbach, *Mimesis*, 241
[71] Ibid., 242, 244, 247.
[72] Ibid., 244, 250.

What he does, however, is precisely the opposite. Indeed, he veers immediately what appears to be way off course, pointing out that he is in fact profoundly moved by de la Sale's account, in awe of how it "represents a truly tragic occurrence of the highest dignity ... with great warmth and simplicity of feeling."[73] The text depicts a "piece of practical, graspable reality," namely the wife's desperate "trial," her struggle, that is, to negotiate between her son and his father.[74] It is a piece of the "everyday" "tragedy" of a family presented with "a simple beauty and grandeur," Auerbach claims, in the midst of this socially most highly overdetermined of ceremonial texts.[75] Initially puzzled by this combination and its power, Auerbach sets out to examine its source, which he soon identifies in clarifying fashion as the eruption of an astonishing "measure of unconcealed *creatural realism*" (my emphasis) out of an "event" so marked by "heraldic ostentation."[76] This was, of course, precisely the kind of counterintuitive combination to which Huizinga had himself drawn attention in the culture of this period. It is thus not surprising to discover that Auerbach cites *Autumn* directly here. And yet, although it may describe pretty well precisely what Huizinga thought he was referring to in his description of rotting corpses and decay, the term "creatural," yoked together with "realism" here for the first time in the chapter – and in *Mimesis* overall – is not one Huizinga uses. What does Auerbach mean by what he himself describes as this "new term," which he emphasizes he is using here for the first time, and what does his deployment of it have to do with the fact that, following Huizinga, he has now (in a text he apparently wrote before the 1943 primer) so easily translated the formerly Renaissance de la Sale into his medieval twin?[77]

Auerbach glosses the term "creaturely" in *Mimesis*, chapter 10, by referring to the realm of the "suffering creature" as associated specifically with the Passion of Christ, the realm of the human body, that is, into which divinity descended in the case of Jesus of Nazareth, representing the highest moment of both tragedy and glory in that case, but in general signifying the weight of mortality that ensnares all of humanity equally and at all times.[78] Auerbach claims – and goes on to explore at some length – that it is this, the logic of the Incarnation made secular, that characterizes

---

[73] Ibid., 244.
[74] Ibid., 245.
[75] Ibid., 246.
[76] Ibid., 247.
[77] Ibid., 249.
[78] Ibid., 247.

the "creatural realism" of the other fifteenth-century texts he discusses – including "Froissart, Chastellain, etc."[79] They thus continue the tradition of what he calls "Christian anthropology," a tradition that, with its emphasis on "man's subjection" – like Christ's – to "suffering," throbs at the heart of their texts and of de la Sale's too.[80] The "radically creatural picture of man" – here, of the mutilated son, who, for all his privilege as a member of the upper classes, is revealed in the end to share with all of humanity the transitoriness of the "flesh" – is central to the texts of the period that espouse a "radical theory of the equality of all men" when they represent "average everyday life [also among the middling bourgeois classes] … often with gripping power," in ways that Auerbach somewhat surprisingly suggests are among the "antecedents of modern realism."[81] The observation is crucial to his argument in the chapter and perhaps in *Mimesis* overall. In the medieval texts, husbands and wives are "fettered to" each other as we observe them in the midst of their struggles to survive both one another and life, facing the daily "immediacy of human existence," he writes, as the realities of that existence bind all of humanity together in the "common creatural conditions of life" he identifies at the end of the chapter as one of "contingency."[82] The condition of contingency afflicts not just God's human creatures during the medieval period, as it were, but, rather, all of humanity – regardless, that is, of the incidental differences that time, and thus periods, create.

In *Mimesis*, the texts assigned first to the Renaissance and then to the Middle Ages are thus said to capture the more or less timeless condition of facing the "sensory, almost physical, horror" of "life's transitoriness" which defines the "common creatural conditions of life," "*la condition de l'homme*."[83] The yoking together of medieval and "modern" realism here suggests that this "condition" and the "creaturely realism" of texts that represent it cannot be confined to or within the period to which they may appear to have belonged. Franco-Burgundian "realism" may have been "narrow and medieval," but the "creaturely realism" Auerbach now sees in its texts is not.[84] The impact that this argument has on his evolving position on the specific period rubrics with which he had been wrestling

---

[79] Ibid., 248.
[80] Ibid., 249.
[81] Ibid., 249–50, 256.
[82] Ibid., 257, 260.
[83] Ibid., 259, 257.
[84] Ibid., 261.

in his serial readings of the Burgundian tradition, namely the medieval and Renaissance ones, becomes clear in what is nearly the very last breath of the chapter, when he writes that the "creatural realism of the Middle Ages" was in fact "passed on to the sixteenth century" and thus continued to animate the best parts of "the Renaissance" (before moving on, we can conclude, to "modern realism" in turn).[85] What becomes of period designations when we discover, as we do in claims such as these, that Burgundian realism, visible in the artifacts of the late Middle Ages, was itself not one, but, rather, plural to the core, overwrought, yet humanely moving, and, perhaps more importantly, a sign of both the last gasps of a desperate culture and of a new, "modern" age all in one? Auerbach's answer seems to be that such labels fall away in the face of the divine time of God's Creation that he describes in a text written about the same time, namely his famous "*Figura*" essay (1938). For God, there is no "*differentia temporis.*" His is an indifferent time, we might say, that knows no "temporal differences (*kein Unterschied der Zeiten*)." The "reality (*Wirklichkeit*)" his "creatures" face unites us all.[86]

The untiming, or release, from the confines of period of the kind of realism in which Auerbach appears to be interested here – a release that Auerbach had in fact himself already anticipated when he so handily converted Renaissance texts into medieval ones – meant that it could circulate freely into places it might not have been expected to be. This kind of deperiodization may have been what allowed him to consider experimenting with an entirely differently timed and scaled literary-historical narrative and frame, one that tracked neither with the emergence nor with the decline of a Burckthardtian-Renaissance realism – or of a Huizingian-medieval realism, for that matter – but, rather, with the realism that Auerbach was attempting to define in *Mimesis*, chapter 10. In the 1954 "Epilegomena to *Mimesis*," Auerbach describes the project of *Mimesis* as it was originally intended, as a study of another, probably related, kind of realism, namely

---

[85] Ibid., 261.
[86] For the original German, see, Auerbach, "*Figura*," 71 and 81; for the English, see Auerbach, "*Figura*," 88 and 101. I discussed the usurpation of periodization by figuration in "Figural Passion," a talk held at the Renaissance Society of America conference, 2016. Even though he completed and published "*Figura*" only after arriving in Istanbul, Auerbach began thinking and talking about it with colleagues already in Marburg, as detailed in the essay's first footnote, with its reference to his conversation with a Marburg colleague, the classicist Paul Friedländer (1882–1968). Friedländer taught in Marburg until 1932, and then in Halle, but was dismissed by the Nazis in 1935 and detained in a concentration camp until 1939. He was then released, thanks to the efforts of his Marburg colleagues, and escaped to the United States.

"existential realism."[87] This description picks up a term that he had already used quite a bit earlier to describe his project in the 1937 essay, "On the Serious Imitation of Everyday Life."[88] In the "Epilegomena," Auerbach is responding to critics of his book – some prominent medievalists among them – explaining what *Mimesis* was actually about. But he alludes to this idea even earlier in *Mimesis* itself, in chapter 12, which is tellingly entitled "L'humaine condition." The very creatureliness that he had examined for long stretches of chapter 10 is the focus of his reading of texts by Montaigne here, texts that he understands in terms of "certain modern philosophical methods," perhaps like Existentialism, which he does not himself name, but the "informed reader will supply these technical terms."[89]

The existential moment, "situation," or event can of course occur at any moment in time, in any epoch, and in any place. Like "creaturely realism," then, "existential realism" knows no period limits. Reaching to these kinds of frames for understanding not only Burgundian realism and Montaigne, but also Émile Zola (1840–1902) and Flaubert and Woolf, suggests that Auerbach may have understood the difficulty of working within what were inevitably always already reductive period terms, difficulties made manifest to him in his reception of Huizinga's thought. That he appears to have been trying to develop a way of moving beyond them in the project that became *Mimesis* was already clear to René Wellek (1903–1995) in his 1954 review of the English translation of the book, where Wellek describes what *Mimesis* is *not*, namely "a general history of occidental realism" or even about a "specific movement," such as "modern literary realism." Rather, it is a "short history of the human condition."[90] For all his peevishness throughout this review, Wellek seems to have got Auerbach right in this regard.

---

[87] Auerbach, "Epilegomena to *Mimesis*," 560–61.
[88] Auerbach, "Über die ernste Nachahmung," 448.
[89] Auerbach, *Mimesis*, 299. For Auerbach's exposure during his Marburg years to the thought of the "modern philosophical methods" of prominent Christian Existentialists in particular, including his friend and colleague, the Lutheran theologian, Rudolf Bultmann (1884–1976), see Newman, "The Gospel According to Auerbach."
[90] Wellek, "Auerbach's Special Realism," 301 and 299.

CHAPTER 10

Medieval Mysticism and the Making of Simone Weil

Anna Kelner

Simone Weil (1909–1943) often appears as something like a Christian mystic or saint in accounts of her life and writing. T. S. Eliot (1888–1965), in his preface to *L'enracinement* (French, 1949; *The Need for Roots*, 1953), a collection of some of her political writings, famously asserted that "she had a kind of genius akin to that of the saints."[1] A 1977 review of the English translation of Weil's first full-length biography in the *New York Review of Books* draws a more specific comparison between Weil and medieval and early modern holy women, declaring that she "can be placed with Teresa of Avila [1515–1582] and with the two Catherines, of Genoa [1447–1510] and of Siena [1347–1380]."[2] The historian Caroline Walker Bynum portrays her similarly in the 1987 book, *Holy Feast and Holy Fast: The Religious Significance of Food to Medieval Women*.[3] In the epilogue, Bynum describes a number of modern women who undertook ascetic practices like those of medieval holy women, and Weil – who was born in 1909 in Paris and died in 1943 in Ashford, England, likely from complications surrounding tuberculosis – is one of them.[4] In Bynum's account, she was a "philosopher and mystic" who "undertook fatal self-starvation in an effort to identify with the poor and oppressed of the world."[5] Weil's asceticism and attestations to mystical experiences, in this view, make her like the medieval women who took on similar acts of willed suffering.[6]

Weil has another major likeness to the medieval women mystics. The vision of her as a mystic is the effect of a careful framing of her life and

---

[1] Eliot, "Preface," in Weil, *The Need for Roots*, vi.
[2] Cameron, "Life and Death of Simone Weil," 7. On the reception of Weil, see Nelson, *Tough Enough*, 15–20.
[3] Bynum, *Holy Feast and Holy Fast*, 8.
[4] For more on Weil's death, see the reports recorded in Weil's first biography, Cabaud, *Simone Weil*, 346–51.
[5] Bynum, *Holy Feast and Holy Fast*, 297.
[6] On Weil and suffering, see Nelson, *Tough Enough*, 20–24.

work, both by the editors of Weil's works and by Weil herself. Though scholars have often observed parallels between Weil and the medieval mystics, the ways in which Weil and her early editors effected this parallel have not been thoroughly explored.[7] This essay argues that Weil and her editors fashioned her as a modern iteration of the medieval mystics, replicating a key feature of the archive of medieval women's mystical writing: the construction of medieval women's textual afterlives by male clerics. As Bynum points out, "most of the information on late medieval women comes from male biographers and chroniclers."[8] Men associated with the Catholic Church have likewise played a major role in narrating Weil's life and in editing the version of her writings that have reached the widest public audiences. Almost all of Weil's writing was published posthumously.[9] Weil charged Joseph-Marie Perrin (1905–2002), a Dominican friar, and Gustave Thibon (1903–2001), a Catholic philosopher, with publishing the first two volumes of her writings. Thibon edited the 1947 collection *La pesanteur et la grâce* (translated into English as *Gravity and Grace* in 1952) by gathering excerpts from Weil's unpublished notebooks.[10] Weil entrusted the volume that would eventually be published in 1950 as *Attente de Dieu* (translated into English as *Waiting for God* in 1951) – a collection of her letters and essays dating from as early as 1937 – to Perrin in 1942.[11] These men penned what Thibon, in the 1952 volume he and Perrin wrote about their relationship with Weil, called her "hagiography."[12]

This essay shows that Weil and her editors constructed her as a Christian mystic – drawing both on contemporary discussions of the topic and on the archive of medieval mysticism for points of comparison – in a distinctly modern sense of the term, as it was coming to be understood in twentieth-century France. They did so to make sense of her vexed relationship with the Catholic Church. Weil was born into a non-practicing

---

[7] For a recent account of Weil's relationship to medieval mysticism, see Nava, *Mystical and Prophetic Thought*, esp. 22–29, 53, and 69. For an account of Weil's relationship to medieval mysticism in the context of French feminist philosophy, see Pinnock, "Mystical Selfhood and Women's Agency." For an older account from the first phase of Weil scholarship, see Davy, *The Mysticism of Simone Weil*, esp. 38–43.

[8] Bynum, *Holy Feast and Holy Fast*, 28. For a more extended account of the discrepancies between male-authored hagiographies and women's accounts of their own experiences in the *vitae* of the thirteenth-century beguines, see Hollywood, "The Religiosity of the *Mulieres Sanctae*," in *The Soul as Virgin Wife*, 26–56.

[9] For Weil's publication history, see Moulakis, *Simone Weil and the Politics of Self-Denial*, 14–15.

[10] Thibon, "Introduction," in Weil, *Gravity and Grace*, xl; *La pesanteur et la grâce*, xxxiii.

[11] Fiedler, "Introduction," in Weil, *Waiting for God*, 11.

[12] Perrin and Thibon, *Simone Weil as We Knew Her*, 5; *Simone Weil telle que nous l'avons connue*, 11.

Jewish family and was not baptized.[13] She expressed skepticism about the value of institutional religion and about proofs of the existence of God.[14] In the "Spiritual Autobiography," one of the letters collected in *Waiting for God*, Weil legitimates her refusal of baptism, expressing her determination to remain "at the intersection of Christianity and everything that is not Christianity."[15] To understand how Weil's editors made sense of her vexed relationship with the Church, we must first consider what Weil and her editors mean when they call her a "mystic." This essay first shows how thinkers defined the term in twentieth-century France. That context will make clear how Weil and her editors fashion her as a mystic as that category found definition in midcentury, transforming her image much as the editors of the medieval mystics did in transmitting their works into modernity.

***

In the first half of the twentieth century in France, philosophers, psychologists, theologians, and scholars sought to redefine mysticism's meaning. Although scholars often draw on "mysticism" to describe medieval visionary writing, the application is anachronistic; the terms "mystic" and "mysticism" were not coined until the eighteenth century.[16] Many of the most prominent French thinkers represent their discussions as significant departures from those of the preceding centuries, during which time mysticism came to be associated with mental illness, and the perils of the kinds of spiritual passivity condemned as quietism.[17] In the 1932 book, *Les deux sources de la morale et de la religion* (*The Two Sources of Morality and Religion*), for instance, the philosopher Henri Bergson (1859–1941), an influential figure in these discussions, expresses astonishment that mystics "ever could have been classed with the mentally diseased."[18] Bergson found

---

[13] For more on Weil and Judaism, see Mandel, "Simone Weil." For Weil's refusal of baptism, see Cabaud, *Simone Weil*, 339; Fiori, *Simone Weil*, 317. There is one disputed report that Weil's friend Simone Dietz baptized her at the end of her life; see Allen and Springsted, "The Baptism of Simone Weil."
[14] On Weil's religious thought, see Rozelle-Stone and Stone, "Atheism and Mysticism," in *Simone Weil and Theology*, 9–30.
[15] Weil, "Spiritual Autobiography," in *Waiting for God*, 76; *Attente de Dieu*, 44.
[16] For this claim as it relates to the canon of Middle English "mystical" writing, see Watson, "The Middle English Mystics," 544.
[17] See Nelstrop, "Acting and Enacting," 1.
[18] Bergson, "Dynamic Religion," in *The Two Sources of Morality and Religion*, 217; *Les deux sources de la morale et de la religion*, 243.

worth in the mystic's attestations to kinds of inner experience that had been badly misinterpreted in preceding centuries.

These thinkers used the term "mystic" to describe a religious figure who attested to personal, immediate encounters with the divine.[19] Weil cites one book in her 1942 New York notebook – the 1900 *Essai sur le mysticisme spéculatif en allemagne au quatorizième siècle* (*Essay on Speculative Mysticism in Germany in the Fourteenth Century*), by Henri Delacroix (1873–1937), a professor of psychology at the Sorbonne – that portrays the mystic along these lines. As Delacroix shows with reference to the works of Meister Eckhart (*c.* 1260–*c.* 1328) and other fourteenth-century German mystics, mystical theology describes "the connection of the soul to God."[20] Mystical encounter is interior, for the mystic "finds universal life at the base of himself."[21] Bergson offers a similar account. "The ultimate end of mysticism is the establishment of a contact," Bergson writes, "with the creative effort which life itself manifests. This effort is of God, if it is not God himself."[22]

Mystical experience finds definition over and against institutional religion and doctrine. Bergson understands mysticism as an iteration of the "vital impetus" of what he terms "dynamic religion," in contrast with the myths and social organizations of "static religion."[23] In Delacroix's account, the inner life of the mystic emerges when doctrine falls away. Eckhart exemplifies "speculative mysticism," which, broadly put, has a dialectical relationship with philosophy; in Eckhart's case, with medieval scholastic philosophy. In the "great clarity which inner life takes," the mystic surpasses the dogma of scholastic philosophy.[24] There is a paradox inherent to these accounts of mysticism. It is a highly personal experience of God, and yet these encounters also share similarities across religious cultures. Bergson accordingly discovers evidence of mysticism in traditions ranging from those of ancient Greece and Egypt, to Buddhism and Hinduism.[25]

---

[19] For useful overviews of the conversations surrounding mysticism among French intellectuals, including Delacroix and Bergson, during the early twentieth century, see Pattison and Kirkpatrick, "Blondel to Bergson," in *The Mystical Sources of Existentialist Thought*, 71–97; Conway, "With Mind and Heart."

[20] Delacroix, *Essai sur le mysticisme spéculatif*, 10. The English translations from the *Essai* are my own.

[21] Delacroix, *Essai sur le mysticisme spéculatif*, 13.

[22] Bergson, "Dynamic Religion," in *The Two Sources of Morality and Religion*, 209; *Les deux sources de la morale et de la religion*, 235.

[23] Bergson, "Dynamic Religion," in *The Two Sources of Morality and Religion*, 202; *Les deux sources de la morale et de la religion*, 227.

[24] Delacroix, *Essai sur le mysticisme spéculatif*, 13.

[25] Bergson, "Dynamic Religion," in *The Two Sources of Morality and Religion*, 206–07, and 211–12; *Les deux sources de la morale et de la religion*, 232–33 and 237–38.

In the *Études*, Delacroix characterizes the "mystical type" in psychological terms, as it exists among mystics "separated by time, space, and historical milieu," while acknowledging that he cannot fully account for variations among these traditions.[26] Mysticism involves the apprehension of a divine presence that, in its most basic features, transcends the particularities of religious cultures, existing outside historical time.

Weil and her editors enter into these conversations by framing her as a mystic. In the introduction to *Gravity and Grace*, Thibon writes that Weil "was infinitely more advanced than I am in the experimental knowledge (*connaissance expérimentale*) of supernatural truths, but outwardly she always remained on the borders of the Church and was never baptized."[27] Thibon draws on a phrase, "experimental knowledge," used by a thinker he cites elsewhere in the introduction: the Catholic philosopher Jacques Maritain (1882–1973).[28] He was one of the major figures in the twentieth-century intellectual movement that called itself "Thomism," made up of French philosophers and theologians aiming to revitalize scholastic philosophy, especially the works of Thomas Aquinas (1225–1274), and who also added to the volumes on mysticism and its history.[29] Maritain discusses mysticism in his 1932 book, *Distinguer pour unir, ou les degrés du savoir* (*Distinguish to Unite, or The Degrees of Knowledge*), an account of Thomistic epistemology. In Maritain's terms, the kind of divine knowledge acquired by the mystic is "an experimental knowledge (*connaissance expérimentale*) of the deep things of God;" the soul goes through "a series of states and transformations until within the very depths of itself it feels the touch of divinity and 'experiences the life of God.'"[30] In drawing on Maritain's phrase, Thibon suggests that Weil's mystical encounters constitute a form of experience that stands apart from her vexed relationship with the Church.

Maritain, like many of his contemporaries, understands mystical experience as a direct encounter with the divine, but he draws mystical experience into much closer relation with formal theology. Mystical

---

[26] Delacroix, *Études d'histoire et de psychologie du mysticisme*, v.
[27] Thibon, "Introduction," in *Gravity and Grace*, xxxi; *La pesanteur et la grâce*, xxiv.
[28] Thibon, "Introduction," in *Gravity and Grace*, xxxiii; *La pesanteur et la grâce*, xxvi. Weil corresponded with Maritain; see Pétrement, *Simone Weil*, 474–76.
[29] For more on Thomism, see Chenaux, "Le retour à la scolastique," in *Entre Maurras et Maritain*. On Maritain and Thomism, see Amato, "Maturity and Prophecy," in *Mounier and Maritain*, 55–71.
[30] Maritain, "Mystical Experience and Philosophy," in *Distinguish to Unite*, 263–64; *Distinguer pour unir*, 489–90. For a Thomistic account of Maritain and mysticism, see Delfino, "Mystical Theology in Aquinas and Maritain."

theology involves a kind of divine knowledge that is affective in character; during mystical encounter, "the soul is inwardly turned, turned back, converted and ordered" to the presence of God "as to an object of loving knowledge."[31] Maritain compares this kind of knowledge with those in the two other branches of divine wisdom: metaphysics and speculative theology. Metaphysics, classed with philosophy and natural theology, conveys knowledge of God by reason; speculative theology develops according to reason but is rooted in faith, drawing its truths directly from a divine source.[32] The experimental knowledge in mystical encounter occurs above reason, but sustains a relation to the two other branches.[33] Maritain establishes this understanding of mysticism by using theological methodology, setting it apart from that articulated, for instance, by Bergson, who taught Maritain at the Collège de France in 1903–1904.[34] Maritain criticizes Bergson for using the tools of philosophy to study mysticism, rather than the "information of theology, to whose scientific competency that object belongs."[35] Bergson comes in for critique alongside "psychologists and sociologists," as well as "philosophers and metaphysicians," who erroneously apply their own methodologies to mystical texts.[36]

Thibon, following Maritain's logic, frames Weil as a mystic who embodies the truths of Christian teachings. Scholars often distinguish between Weil's early period as a student, agnostic, and radical leftist – she studied philosophy at the Lycée Henri-IV under Émile Auguste Chartier (1868–1951), known as Alain, before attending the École Normale Supérieure and teaching at secondary schools – and her later religious phase.[37] In Thibon's account, though, the affinity that Weil found with Christianity at the end of her life seems to permeate it from the start. Near the beginning of the introduction, he describes the conditions of their meeting during the summer of 1941, which Weil spent working on Thibon's farm, at Perrin's advice: "she was just then beginning to open with all her soul to Christianity, a limpid

---

[31] Maritain, "Mystical Experience and Philosophy," in *Distinguish to Unite*, 274; *Distinguer pour unir*, 510.
[32] Maritain, "Mystical Experience and Philosophy," in *Distinguish to Unite*, 264–65; *Distinguer pour unir*, 491–93.
[33] Maritain, "Mystical Experience and Philosophy," in *Distinguish to Unite*, 265; *Distinguer pour unir*, 494.
[34] For more on Maritain's relationship to Bergson, see Amato, "The Education of Jacques Maritain," in *Mounier and Maritain,* esp. 40–47.
[35] Maritain, "Mystical Experience and Philosophy," in *Distinguish to Unite*, 307, n. 96; *Distinguer pour unir*, 570, n. 1.
[36] Maritain, "Mystical Experience and Philosophy," in *Distinguish to Unite*, 306; *Distinguer pour unir*, 569.
[37] See, for instance, Nava, *Mystical and Prophetic Thought*, 7; Meaney, *Simone Weil's Apologetic Use of Literature*, 191.

mysticism emanated from her." Though "delicate and ill," Weil worked assiduously and barely ate; she resembled "certain medieval saints" in her "asceticism."[38] In the biographical account that follows, Weil's earlier years appear as preceding stages in her hagiography. In her youth, Weil "fought in the ranks of the extreme left," often taking her political commitments into the realm of lived experience.[39] To understand the suffering of the working classes firsthand, she went to work at a Renault car factory; she volunteered during the Spanish Civil War, and was involved in the Resistance movement. Thibon portrays her death in 1943 as an intensification of earlier instances of politically motivated asceticism. According to him, she insisted on eating no more than the rations permitted to the French in wartime. Forced to enter the hospital, Weil "suffered acutely on account of any special comforts" given to her, much as she had once refused food on Thibon's farm. Her death emerges as the inevitable conclusion to these acts of saintly abnegation: a mystical apotheosis. "I have no details of her end," Thibon writes, instead offering a quote from Weil on the "death agony" as the "supreme dark night," a figure that she repeatedly uses for mystical union.[40] In presenting this quotation as the conclusion to Weil's life, Thibon assimilates its many contradictions into the image of the Christian mystic.

Thibon accordingly presents *Gravity and Grace* as a mystical text: a veritable, and verified, testimony to Weil's encounters with God. "The texts are bare and simple like the inner experience that they express. No padding is interposed between the life and the word," he maintains.[41] Thibon, like many of his contemporaries, understands mysticism as a kind of "inner experience."[42] He frames the volume as the unmediated instantiation of Weil's encounters with God. But Thibon, in making this claim, also faces a challenge common in the study of mystical writing both medieval and modern: if mysticism involves an inner contact with God, how is it possible to verify that encounter, and the teachings conveyed in it?[43] The

---

[38] Thibon, "Introduction," in *Gravity and Grace*, ix; *La pesanteur et la grâce*, iii.
[39] Thibon, "Introduction," in *Gravity and Grace*, xvi; *La pesanteur et la grâce*, x.
[40] Thibon, "Introduction," in *Gravity and Grace*, xviii; *La pesanteur et la grâce*, xii. For Weil's use of the phrase "dark night," see the fragments that Thibon collected under the heading "To Accept the Void," in *Gravity and Grace*, 11 and 15; *La pesanteur et la grâce*, 13 and 18.
[41] Thibon, "Introduction," in *Gravity and Grace*, xix; *La pesanteur et la grâce*, xii.
[42] Thibon's characterization of mysticism resonates with that of Georges Bataille (1897–1962) in his 1943 book *L'expérience intérieure* (*Inner Experience*), as well as that of Maritain. See Irwin, *Saints of the Impossible*, xi–xxviii, on Weil's relationship to Bataille. See also Hollywood, "Bataille and Mysticism."
[43] For a study of a prominent method used in the later part of the Middle Ages to verify women's mystical writing, see Caciola, *Discerning Spirits*.

philosopher William James (1842–1910) – another major thinker on mysticism in the early twentieth century, and one who was in close dialogue with Bergson – makes reference to the "problem of truth" in his discussion of mysticism in his 1902 book *The Varieties of Religious Experience*. "Do mystical states establish the truth of those theological affections in which the saintly life has its root?" he asks.[44] Thibon anticipates similar questions surrounding the truth value of Weil's writings. "Even if I had not known Simone Weil personally, her style alone would in my opinion guarantee the authenticity of her testimony," he concludes.[45] Thibon gestures to two criteria – the simplicity of Weil's style, as accentuated by the aphoristic fragments he has culled from her notebooks, and his personal friendship with her – to substantiate Weil's account. Thibon's editorial authority, as evinced by his privileged access to Weil's writings and her life, legitimates Weil as a Christian mystic, a category that could make sense of the aspects of her biography and writings that might challenge that categorization.

Thibon's authority, though, is far from absolute, but rather is entangled with Weil's own. Thibon makes clear that Weil selected him as her editor by carefully accounting for the transmission of *Gravity and Grace*. Thibon compiled the volume from excerpts from Weil's notebooks, which he received in May 1942 when Weil, fleeing the Vichy regime with her parents, was leaving France for New York. At the railway station, Thibon says, she handed him "a portfolio crammed with papers" consisting of a "dozen thick exercise books."[46] Thibon describes Weil's influence on their subsequent publication history: she wrote twice to Thibon, giving him permission to read the notebooks, and eventually to edit and publish them.[47] The volume results from the exchange of textual authority between the mystic and her editor. Thibon's authority, indeed, is contingent on the near-conflation of his identity with that of Weil. Thibon includes selections from one of Weil's letters to him, in which she asks him to edit her work, in the *Gravity and Grace* introduction. As Thibon records it, Weil writes of her ideas: "I should be very happy for them to find a lodging beneath your pen, whilst changing their form so as to reflect your likeness." Weil asks Thibon to reformulate her image in his own: into that of a Catholic. In subjecting her writings to Thibon's pen, Weil authenticates her writings

---

[44] James, *The Varieties of Religious Experience*, 453. For more on the relationship between James and Bergson, see Loerzer, "William James," 73–77.
[45] Thibon, "Introduction," in *Gravity and Grace*, xix; *La pesanteur et la grâce*, xii–xiii.
[46] Thibon, "Introduction," in *Gravity and Grace*, xii–xiii; *La pesanteur et la grâce*, vi.
[47] Thibon, "Introduction," in *Gravity and Grace*, xii–xv; *La pesanteur et la grâce*, vi–ix.

as Christian teachings, in spite of their apparent deviations from official doctrine. "I have a feeling that my own fortunes will never be good in the world," Weil writes in the same letter, in exile in Oran.[48] Weil was still considered a Jew under the Vichy Regime's Statut des Juifs of October 1940. Selecting Thibon as editor offered Weil a way to link herself and her works with the name of a reputable Catholic philosopher, substantiating her authority as a Christian mystic.

Though neither Weil nor Thibon acknowledge it, this relationship rehearses a central trope in medieval women's mystical texts. As Lynn Staley has argued, most of these medieval works participate in "a tradition whereby the female text – whether that text was written word or the life of a holy woman – was mediated and thus verified by a male author or scribe." A male scribe could function as a "theological censor," as in the case of the fifteenth-century Middle English translation of Marguerite Porete's (c. 1250–1310) *Mirror of Simple Souls* (c. 1300).[49] But Staley shows that many of these works were produced through a more complex textual entanglement between the female mystic and her male scribe. The writings of Hildegard of Bingen (1098–1179), for instance, figure one of her scribes as her partner in transmission of divine teachings, and even as subservient to her.[50] Weil and her male editors framed her as a Christian mystic through a similar kind of textual collaboration. In so doing, they drew her into relation with the medieval female mystics in ways that they do not acknowledge.

***

Medieval women mystics often constructed themselves in the accounts of their lives and visions, as Staley has shown with regard to the fifteenth-century English laywoman and mystic, Margery Kempe (c. 1373–c. 1438).[51] Weil engaged in a similar process of mystical self-fashioning.[52] *Gravity and Grace* shows how Thibon reshaped Weil's work at her insistence, but *Waiting for God*, which Weil compiled for Perrin in 1942, shows how Weil framed herself as a mystic with Thibon as her intended audience. Weil relates most of her mystical experiences, which took place from 1935 to 1941, in a letter ("Spiritual Autobiography") that she wrote to Perrin from Marseilles around May 15, 1942. As in their other letters collected in

---

[48] Thibon, "Introduction," in *Gravity and Grace*, xiv; *La pesanteur et la grâce*, vii.
[49] Staley, "The Trope of the Scribe," 827.
[50] Ibid., 823.
[51] Staley, "Authorship and Authority," in *Margery Kempe's Dissenting Fictions*, 1–38.
[52] For an account of Weil's practices of self-stylization in the construction of sacred biography, see Irwin, *Saints of the Impossible*, esp. xvi–xviii.

Waiting for God, Weil and Perrin were discussing her possible baptism. Turning to address Perrin directly, she writes, "in making the problem of baptism a practical problem for me, you have forced me to face the whole question of the faith, dogma, and the sacraments."[53] Baptism, for Weil, is emblematic of the rituals and doctrines of the institutional Church. To legitimate her refusal of the sacrament, Weil draws on the idea of the mystic being formulated at the time: a figure who can derive religious authority outside of religious institutions.

Weil frames mystical experience as an alternative source of divine authority. Like many of her contemporaries and near-contemporaries, she understood mysticism to involve direct encounters with the divine: "real contact, person to person, here below, between a human being and God," she writes.[54] In comparing divine contact to that shared between humans, Weil elevates the importance of personal testimony in mystical experience. Weil's direct experience of God legitimates her refusal of baptism. "I have never once had, even for a moment, the feeling that God wants me to be in the Church," she says to Perrin.[55] Weil describes her position outside the Church as resulting from a kind of mystical experience, a "feeling" of what God wants for her. It is produced by the force that Weil terms the "Christian inspiration." As she says to Perrin, "you neither brought me the Christian inspiration nor did you bring me to Christ," because by the time she met him, "it had been done without the intervention of any human being."[56] Formal baptism is unnecessary, since Weil has experienced continuous contact with Christianity since birth.

For Weil, mysticism entails an experiential contact with the divine that becomes more valuable when it occurs without external mediation, be it from the ecclesiastical institution or textual sources. She writes that "God in his mercy had prevented me from reading the mystics" before her encounters with the divine, "so that it should be evident to me that I had not invented this absolutely unexpected contact."[57] Scholars such as Alexander Nava recapitulate the distinction that Weil draws between mystical experience and knowledge of mystical texts. The significance Weil found in mysticism, he writes, "went much deeper than her reading and knowledge of the classic Christian mystics. It is with mystical epiphanies

---

[53] Weil, "Spiritual Autobiography," in *Waiting for God*, 73; *Attente de Dieu*, 42.
[54] Weil, "Spiritual Autobiography," in *Waiting for God*, 66; *Attente de Dieu*, 38.
[55] Weil, "Spiritual Autobiography," in *Waiting for God*, 74; *Attente de Dieu*, 43.
[56] Weil, "Spiritual Autobiography," in *Waiting for God*, 61–62; *Attente de Dieu*, 32.
[57] Weil, "Spiritual Autobiography," in *Waiting for God*, 69; *Attente de Dieu*, 38.

in her own life that we witness her emergence as a Christian mystical figure."[58] Nava, however, takes Weil's distinction at face value, ignoring how Weil interprets her mystical experiences as she recounts them. Perhaps Weil did experience direct, unmediated contacts with the divine. Her knowledge of Christian mysticism, however, deeply informs her narration of these experiences.

Weil's recounting of her mystical experiences to Perrin is retrospective, occurring as much as seven years after the event. She had, in fact, read widely in the mystical tradition by the time she wrote to him in 1942. The reading lists in one of her notebooks from 1942, written during her exile in New York, include a number of medieval mystics and their works, such as Bonaventure (1221–1274), the thirteenth-century Minister General of the Franciscan Order; Jan van Ruusbroec (c. 1293–1381), the fourteenth-century Flemish priest; Meister Eckhart, the Dominican preacher who was condemned for heresy in 1329, shortly after his death in about 1328; and the early fourteenth-century *Le miroir des âmes simples* (*The Mirror of Simple Souls*) by the beguine Marguerite Porete, a work that Weil would have known from Clare Kirchberger's (c. 1894–c. 1958) 1927 modern English translation, the only edition available at the time.[59] In her notebooks, Weil often mentions other medieval and early modern mystics and visionaries such as Joan of Arc (c. 1414–1431), who "makes war because inspired by God,"[60] and St John of the Cross (1542–1591), the sixteenth-century Carmelite friar and priest, who calls "faith a night."[61] As Weil narrates her mystical experiences, she draws on a number of theological concepts – in particular, what she terms "affliction" – that she developed in full with reference to the works of the medieval mystics. Weil formulates her own theology to interpret her mystical experiences, with Perrin in mind as her intended audience.

Weil relates two of her mystical experiences to affliction, which she understands as a kind of pain that makes human beings like Christ.[62] Weil develops her thinking on affliction most fully in the essay "The

---

[58] Nava, *Mystical and Prophetic Thought*, 23.
[59] Weil, "New York Notebook, 1942," in *First and Last Notebooks*, 78–79 and 205; "Cahier XII," in *Cahiers*, vol. 6, no. 3, 393.
[60] Weil, *The Notebooks*, vol. 1, 25; "Cahier III," in *Cahiers*, vol. 6, no. 1, 296.
[61] Weil, *The Notebooks*, vol. 1, 238; "Cahier VI," in *Cahiers*, vol. 6, no. 2, 338.
[62] For more on Weil's concept of affliction, see Vetö, "Suffering and Affliction," in *The Religious Metaphysics of Simone Weil*, 70–88. Moore, *Sacred Dread*, 2, situates Weil's concept of affliction in relation to conversations surrounding Catholic themes of mortality and suffering in her extended intellectual circles.

Love of God and Affliction," in *Waiting for God*, as if offering readers a fuller explanation for ideas referenced only briefly in her letter. "Christ was afflicted,"[63] she writes, and "extreme affliction, which means physical pain, distress of soul, and social degradation, all at the same time, is a nail whose point is applied at the very center of the soul."[64] Christ's crucifixion is the model for affliction: it makes God's love for humankind manifest, but takes shape through the absence of God. "Affliction makes God appear to be absent for a time," Weil writes, and "during this absence there is nothing to love."[65] Humans, though, must continue to love God despite his apparent absence, or it becomes final. When love persists through periods of divine absence, human beings take on a likeness to Christ. Affliction thus provides a means for human beings to become Christ-like through a triply physical, social, and spiritual form of pain.

Affliction also involves a form of self-annihilation, a crucial part of mystical union for Weil. In one of her 1942 notebooks, Weil describes two ways of annihilating the self, from within and without. Affliction can effect "the destruction of the 'I' from without," representing the "plenitude of the Cross," in the soul that has already "completely destroyed the 'I' in himself."[66] Weil situates this process of self-negation as distinctly mystical in character, developing it with reference to several works of the medieval mystics in her late notebooks. Weil cites Meister Eckhart in another 1942 notebook as she reflects on the imperviousness of the part of the soul that is "situated in the other world" to affliction. She writes, "affliction has no power over it – for perhaps, as Meister Eckhart says, it is uncreated."[67] Eckhart discusses the uncreated part of the soul in, for instance, Sermon 48, where he describes "the man who has annihilated himself in himself and in God and in all created things," and who has "taken possession of the lowest place," so that "God must pour the whole of himself into this man."[68] This form of annihilation enables the meeting of God and humankind in the part of the soul closest to creation. Eckhart, though, also mentions "a light that is created and not capable of creation and that

---

[63] Weil, "The Love of God and Affliction," in *Waiting for God*, 125; *Attente de Dieu*, 88.
[64] Weil, "The Love of God and Affliction," in *Waiting for God*, 134–35; *Attente de Dieu*, 97.
[65] Weil, "The Love of God and Affliction," in *Waiting for God*, 120–21; *Attente de Dieu*, 84.
[66] Weil, *The Notebooks*, vol. 2, 342; "Cahier VII" in *Cahiers*, vol. 6, no. 2, 467.
[67] Weil, "New York Notebook, 1942," in *First and Last Notebooks*, 136; "Cahier XIV" in *Cahiers*, vol. 6, no. 4, 179.
[68] Meister Eckhart, "Sermon 48," 197; "Predigt 48," 712, lines 20–23. On Eckhart and modern philosophy, see Dubilet, *The Self-Emptying Subject*.

is in the soul."⁶⁹ Weil seems to have identified this light as the uncreated part of the soul. With the reference to Eckhart, Weil gestures to the part of the soul that remains coterminous with God even after the destruction of the ego.

Weil turns to *The Mirror of Simple Souls* to further develop her thinking on self-annihilation in affliction. Among several direct references to the *Mirror* in her 1943 notebook, written during her time in London, Weil cites "*Mirror of Simple Souls*, ix, 18," commenting: "*exhaust* the human faculties (will, intelligence, etc.) so as to pass over to the transcendent."⁷⁰ In this section of Kirchberger's edition, Porete describes how self-annihilation gives way to indwelling in God. The "all-naked, naughted, or clarified souls" have left behind lower levels of approach to the divine, and "the soul is abandoned in God for him, in himself, of himself."⁷¹ The souls approach God through the process of negation, and God – whom "they may not know nor love nor adore" – is likewise figured as a kind of nothingness: as that which is beyond the reach of human intelligence and love.⁷² With these references to the medieval mystical tradition, Weil demonstrates how negating the self in affliction can inform the apprehension of God.

The theology of affliction takes on narrative form in Weil's account of her mystical experiences. The first of these experiences occurred on a trip to a fishing village in Portugal after Weil's year in the Renault factory in 1935. Weil draws on the framework of affliction to describe her time there: "As I worked in the factory," Weil writes, "the affliction of others entered into my flesh and my soul."⁷³ There are multiple temporal levels to Weil's account of her experience. Weil depicts her past self as a kind of persona, in the process of formulating the theological concepts upon which Weil, as the present narrator of these events, draws to describe past events. Through affliction, Weil becomes conjoined with the factory workers, whom she describes as an "anonymous mass." Weil surpasses the limitations of the self – a crucial aspect of affliction, and of mystical union – and becomes part of the collective.⁷⁴ Affliction confers "the mark of a slave" on Weil,

---

⁶⁹ Meister Eckhart, "Sermon 48," 198; "Predigt 48," 713, lines 1–2.
⁷⁰ Weil, "London Notebook, 1943," in *First and Last Notebooks*, 361; "Carnet de Londres," in *Cahiers*, vol. 6, no. 4, 391.
⁷¹ Porete, *The Mirror of Simple Souls*, cap. 18, 207.
⁷² Ibid. 208.
⁷³ Weil, "Spiritual Autobiography," in *Waiting for God*, 66; *Attente de Dieu*, 36.
⁷⁴ For more on the intersection between Weil's mysticism and Marxism, see Nava, *Mystical and Prophetic Thought*, esp. 29–44.

allowing her to take on the experience of the working classes, despite her economic privilege and elite educational background. As Weil presents it, her encounter with God in the Portuguese village at once emerges from this lived experience of affliction, and crystallizes it as such. Weil's persona recognizes the essentially Christian character of affliction as she watches a procession of the fishermen's wives, "carrying candles and singing what must certainly be very ancient hymns of a heart-rending sadness."[75] In witnessing this performance, undertaken by the wives of the working classes, Weil says, "the conviction was suddenly borne in upon me that Christianity is pre-eminently the religion of slaves." Weil recognizes that her experience in the factory, in making her like the working classes, has also made her like Christ.

The function of affliction to make human beings like Christ becomes even more apparent in Weil's description of her third mystical experience, which occurred in 1938, at Solesmes, France. Striking parallels emerge with her earlier experience in the Portuguese village. As Weil's mystical persona attended church services from Palm Sunday to Easter Tuesday, she was struck by "splitting headaches," but was still able to "find a pure and perfect joy in the unimaginable beauty of the chanting and the words."[76] Much as Weil recognized the connection between Christ's affliction and her own as she listens to "ancient hymns" in the village, so does she gain "a better understanding of the possibility of loving divine love in the midst of affliction" upon hearing the liturgy. During these services, Weil says, "the thought of the Passion of Christ entered into my being once and for all." As Weil receives divine teachings into her suffering body, she makes the Passion incarnate, surpassing the limitations of the self. Weil develops the concept of affliction to relate her own experience to that of Christ, giving her an immediate spiritual authority that bypasses the institutions and sacraments of the Church. She thus constructs her resemblance to Eckhart and Porete, the medieval mystics whose work she uses to develop the concept of affliction.

In response to Perrin's exhortation towards formal baptism, Weil narrates a series of mystical experiences that, in turn, substantiate an alternative vision of Christianity. Catholicism's true meaning is borne out in the etymological sense of the term: its universality.[77] Christianity

---

[75] Weil, "Spiritual Autobiography," in *Waiting for God*, 67; *Attente de Dieu*, 36–37.
[76] Weil, "Spiritual Autobiography," in *Waiting for God*, 68; *Attente de Dieu*, 37.
[77] For more on Weil's syncretism, or her belief that evidence of Christianity could be discovered in non-Christian traditions, see Kennedy, "Simone Weil," 210–15. For a critique of Weil's universalizing vision of Christianity, see Levinas, *Difficult Freedom*, 134.

is "catholic by right but not in fact," Weil writes later in the "Spiritual Autobiography."[78] The Church erroneously excludes many things that "God loves": the list includes "the immense stretches of past centuries," "all the countries inhabited by colored races," "all secular life in the white peoples' countries," and "all the traditions banned as heretical, those of the Manicheans and Albigenses for instance."[79] This Christianity seems to exist almost everywhere but in the institutional Church. Weil fashions herself as a mystic who can represent this form of Christianity, testifying to messages from God that authenticate it as divine in origin.

***

What happens to Weil, as her image finds reflection in Thibon's own in *Gravity and Grace*, and as she narrates her encounters with God to Perrin in *Waiting for God*? Weil emerges as a mystic as the term was coming to be understood in the first half of the twentieth century in France: a figure attesting to a direct experience of God outside the flow of historical time, in tension with institutional religion and doctrine. The textual exchange between Weil and her editors shapes her as such. Their dialogue, though, also belies the differences in how they interpreted Weil's position in relation to the Church. Thibon and Perrin present Weil's antagonism towards the Church as a deviation from her true accord with its teachings. Weil on the other hand, emphasizes her anti-institutional stance as a crucial component of what makes her a mystic.

For Weil, mystical speech conveys divine truths that may radically conflict with the teachings of the institutional Church. She describes the transmission of mystical experience through speech acts in the "Spiritual Autobiography," writing that "when genuine friends of God – such as was Eckhart to my way of thinking – repeat words they have heard in secret amidst the silence of the union of love, and these words are in disagreement with the teachings of the Church, it is simply that the language of the marketplace is not that of the nuptial chamber."[80] Weil would have known Eckhart as a condemned heretic from Delacroix's *Mysticisme spéculatif*, and from Kirchberger's introduction to her edition of the *Mirror*.[81] Indeed, Eckhart's notion of the uncreated part of the soul, on which Weil

---

[78] Weil, "Spiritual Autobiography," in *Waiting for God*, 75; *Attente de Dieu*, 43.
[79] Weil, "Spiritual Autobiography," in *Waiting for God*, 75; *Attente de Dieu*, 43–44.
[80] Weil, "Spiritual Autobiography," in *Waiting for God*, 79; *Attente de Dieu*, 47.
[81] Kirchberger, "Introduction," in Porete, *The Mirror of Simple Souls*, xxx; Delacroix, *Essai sur le mysticisme spéculatif*, 3.

draws in developing her thinking on affliction, was one of the aspects of his thought condemned in the "In agro dominico" papal bull on March 27, 1329.[82] In handing her works over to her would-be hagiographers, Weil ensured that the aspects of her thought that align her with those outside the Church would be minimized. Weil thus takes her place in the historical tradition of holy women she was *made* to inherit.

[82] For this portion of the Latin bull, see Denifle, "Acten zum Processe Meister Eckeharts," 639. For the English translation, see Colledge and McGinn, trans., "The Bull 'In agro dominico' (March 27, 1329)," in *Meister Eckhart*, 80.

CHAPTER 11

Hermeneutics and the Medieval Horizon
Zumthor, Jauss, Barthes, and Gadamer

Benjamin A. Saltzman

In 1980, Paul Zumthor (1915–1995) published *Parler du moyen age* (*Speaking of the Middle Ages*), an elegant little book on the state of the discipline and the task of the medievalist, tracing a history of medieval studies from its prewar associations with romanticism and positivism up to Zumthor's own view from the horizon of the late 1970s. Through this retrospective, Zumthor in part recounts the transformation of the field by medievalists such as Erich Auerbach (1892–1957), Ernst Robert Curtius (1886–1956), and Leo Spitzer (1887–1960), but also positions himself as a kind of bridge between that generation of medievalists whose most influential works came out in the years immediately following World War II and the work of medievalists today, with the rise of post-structuralism, for instance, breaking in between. One of the central concerns of the book is precisely this movement between eras, not only between postwar medievalism and its romantic heritage, but also between the present moment of a reader and the objects of the past being read.[1]

Such concerns with interpretation across historical distance have a long and crucial history in the field of hermeneutics, which reached a peak between the 1960s and 1980s in the hands of German thinkers such as the philosopher Hans-Georg Gadamer (1900–2002) and the literary theorist Hans Robert Jauss (1921–1997) and French thinkers such as Paul Ricoeur (1913–2005) and Roland Barthes (1915–1980). Following Zumthor's lead, therefore, this chapter will look backwards, performing a genealogy of philosophical and literary hermeneutics that traces Zumthor's engagement with this tradition (particularly on the German side) and attending to the place of the medieval within it.

---

[1] See Chapter 5 in this volume, Thornbury, "Curtius and Jung," on Curtius's navigation of a similar question about the relation between a reader's present and literature's past: "Literature, he argues, uniquely offers readers unmediated access both to the past of the dead author, and to the timeless present of the still-living book" (140).

The story begins at the end. It begins with Zumthor's characterization of the way the once romantic impulse in medieval studies sought to fill in the gaps of history:

> The temptation to which many medievalists succumbed, and still succumb (including Curtius, around 1950, on another level), was to dissimulate the gaps, not in their documentation, but in that mantle full of holes, history itself; to take some plaster kneaded with their ideology and patch those fissures: those ruptures potentially threatening to their own (good) conscience.[2]

Zumthor's language is striking not only for its beautiful metaphor (the plaster of ideology), but also for the appositive description of those holes that such plaster served to fill (*"ces fissures: ces ruptures"*). These *fissures* and *ruptures*, split apart here by a colon, are clearly symptomatic of Zumthor's intellectual environment and the post-structuralism of the late 1970s, but they nonetheless define Zumthor's understanding of hermeneutics, especially when applied to medieval texts.

As Zumthor explains towards the end of *Parler du moyen age*, "our task (who can seriously doubt it today?) is to grasp the places of rupture, the points of breakdown: our own fragmentation, brought about by reading."[3] Rather than patching, then, medievalists should seize the ruptures in the mantle of history which frustrated earlier generations. By taking up those ruptures ourselves, such reading entails "our own fragmentation." And such fragmentation is evident even in the way Zumthor interrupts the syntactic flow of the sentence, counterintuitively positing the unanimity of "our task" with his little aside ("who can seriously doubt it today?"), which avows agreement about the state of the field in 1980s in order to acknowledge a gap between the contemporary moment of the field and the preterit moment of the text.

This distance between present and past is a problem central to Zumthor's thinking. It is a distance, in his view, that should be embraced rather than patched up with either the plaster of ideology or what he elsewhere calls "naive historicism" on the one hand or "blind modernism" on the other.[4] In other words, interpretation requires an awareness of our own historicity. This philosophical position has a long history and intersects with a number of other hermeneutic theories that were taking shape around the 1970s,

---

[2] Zumthor, *Speaking of the Middle Ages* (hereafter *SMA*), 43; *Parler du moyen age* (hereafter *PMA*), 51.
[3] *SMA*, 83 (modified); *PMA*, 92.
[4] Zumthor, "Comments on H. R. Jauss's Article," 370–71.

theories and debates that certainly influenced Zumthor's approach. I'd like to trace a few of these theories through two of Zumthor's contemporaries: Jauss and Gadamer. Setting aside the precise intellectual nature of these connections for the time being, it is worth briefly plotting out the contours of their relationships, which were at times direct; at other times, elusive.

Zumthor, Jauss, Gadamer: Some Contours

In 1970, just as Zumthor was finishing his *Essai de poetique medievale* (which would appear in 1972), he first came to encounter Jauss's more theoretical writings (such as his *Literaturgeschichte als Provokation*, published first in 1967 and then again in 1970). In his preface to the 1992 English translation of the *Essai*, Zumthor retrospectively credits these theoretical writings by Jauss with helping him to clarify his views on "the very complex epistemological phenomena arising from the confrontation of the Self and the Other, of myself with the object of my study, of identity and otherness."[5] Before that, Zumthor was only familiar by his own admission with Jauss's work on medieval texts such as the *Roman de Reynard* (*c.* 1175).

By the late 1970s, Zumthor began responding to Jauss more directly; they both published articles in a 1977 issue of the journal *Poetique* where, for instance, Zumthor is quick to cite Jauss in the second paragraph of his article.[6] And in 1979, both were featured in the *New Literary History* special issue on "Medieval Literature and Contemporary Theory." In the issue, the first chapter of Jauss's *Alterität und Modernität der mittelalterlichen Literatur* is translated as "The Alterity and Modernity of Medieval Literature," which engages critically with Zumthor's *Essai* and in turn receives a formal response from Zumthor himself.[7]

Behind much of Jauss's and Zumthor's views on literary interpretation lies Gadamer's work on philosophical hermeneutics, particularly his seminal 1960 book *Wahrheit und Methode* (translated into English as *Truth and Method* in 1975 and into French in 1976). Jauss would first come under Gadamer's influence while spending six years after World War II at Heidelberg, where he completed his doctorate and his *Habilitationsschrift*. Gadamer's work would become foundational for Jauss's thinking, as in the

---

[5] Zumthor, *Toward a Medieval Poetics*, xii.
[6] Zumthor, "Médiéviste ou pas"; Jauss, "Littérature médiévale et expérience esthétique."
[7] Jauss, *Alterität und Modernität*; "The Alterity and Modernity of Medieval Literature"; and Zumthor, "Comments on H. R. Jauss's Article," 367–76. Zumthor also contributed his own essay to the issue, "From Hi(story) to Poem, or the Paths of Pun."

preface to *Ästhetische Erfahrung und literarische Hermeneutik*, where he notes that "Gadamer's theory of hermeneutic experience, its historical unfolding in the history of humanistic guiding concepts, his principle of seeing in historical impact the access to all historical understanding, and the clarification of the controllable process of the 'fusion of horizons' (*Einheit von Verstehen*) are the indisputable methodological presuppositions without which my undertaking would have been unthinkable."[8] But Gadamer's influence on Zumthor, who rarely makes direct reference to him, is far more opaque.

Back in 1963, three years after the publication of Gadamer's *Wahrheit und Methode*, Jauss (along with colleagues such as Wolfgang Iser [1926–2007]) established a research group at the University of Constance called *Poetik und Hermeneutik*, where they began conducting research on the aesthetics of reception (or *Rezeptionsästhetik*), a variety of which would become known in America as reader response theory. In 1967, Jauss gave the research group's inaugural lecture *Literaturgeschichte als Provokation der Literaturwissenschaft* ("Literary History as a Challenge to Literary Theory"), which was in part an outgrowth of Gadamer's thinking, yet departed from it in several deliberate ways. It is this theoretical work (republished in 1970) that begins to enter Zumthor's radar just as he is finishing his *Essai* in the late 1970s.

What connects these three thinkers over the course of the 1970s is a concern for the way hermeneutics must mediate the distance between subject and object, between the reader and the text, between the present and the past, between the self and the other. By 1980, Zumthor will reassess these ideas in *Parler du moyen age*, where his engagement with Jauss subtly reorients his approach to the interpretation of medieval texts. One can discern three interrelated themes that underlie this engagement:

> *Pleasure*: That the reader, particularly the reader of medieval texts, should take pleasure in his encounter with his object of study—my pronoun is deliberate because, as we will see, Zumthor is certainly thinking of a masculine reader.
>
> *Dialogue*: That the encounter with the object of study in all its alterity should be in the form of a dialogue between self and other.
>
> *Horizons*: That this dialogue traverses the historical distance in the form of a horizon.

Sometimes, these ideas directly intersect with one another, as when Zumthor posits:

---

[8] Jauss, *Aesthetic Experience and Literary Hermeneutics*, xxxvi; *Ästhetische Erfahrung und literarische Hermeneutik*, 26.

The text exists only inasmuch as it is read. To know it, is to read it; and reading is a practice, realizing the union of our thought with this thing it accepts, perhaps provisionally, as real. Thus, reading is, at least potentially, a *dialogue*; but in it two agents confront one another: I am in some way produced by this text, and in the same moment, as a reader, I construct it. A relationship of active solidarity rather than a mirror-effect; a solidarity promised rather than given, *pleasurably* felt (*savoureusement ressentie*) at the end of the long preparatory work required by *the traversing of two historical distances* (*le double franchissement de la distance historique*), going and coming back.[9]

There are other moments in the book where Zumthor explains each of these terms on their own more vividly, but here we see the basic connections between them: reading a text involves a dialogue with the Other that is the pleasurable outcome of traversing historical distance. I'd like to suggest that each of these themes – pleasure, dialogue, and horizons – has for Zumthor some basis in Jauss's writings, particularly those where Jauss differentiates his position on aesthetic and literary hermeneutics from Gadamer's philosophical hermeneutics.

Pleasure

"The only thing that justifies the effort of our reading," according to Zumthor, "is the pleasure (*le plaisir*) it gives us .... The pleasure of being confronted with historical knowledge, in an apparent mutual refusal – a tension and, once again, a rupture between two different ends which, however, could never be separated without ruining the whole enterprise."[10] On the final page of his book, these comments seem like a diminutive justification for reading, but Zumthor is really evoking a more profound relationship between reader and text in the capacity for the text to shape the reader and vice versa.

This profound and pleasurable relationship is at its core one of somatic eroticism, as Zumthor explains a few pages earlier:

> It is through erudition that the discovery of otherness must pass. And from otherness comes the pleasure; there is pleasure only in the Other, a concrete, historical Other. Pleasure carries a trace of history: if my object is a loved woman, history is there in the very fact that she exists, hic et nunc. If the object is a medieval text, I must come to know its body.[11]

---

[9] *SMA*, 66 (emphasis added); *PMA*, 74.
[10] *SMA*, 93; *PMA*, 103.
[11] *SMA*, 81; *PMA*, 90.

While Zumthor may draw this corporal epistemology at least in part from his personal experiences of love, he also seems to draw it from the medieval experience of reading itself, which by his logic was a distinctly bodily act of textual reception. As he explains at the beginning of *Parler du moyen age*,

> [W]e speak well only about things we know concern us personally, about things we love, perhaps. Every relationship we maintain with a text involves some latent eroticism. Only this dynamism puts the critical reader in a situation comparable to that of the medieval reader or listener, whose whole body, not only his visual and auditory faculties, was engaged in the reception of the text.[12]

Zumthor's subtle nod to Jauss is apparent in his concern with the reception of the text, but the nod is also initiated more directly two paragraphs earlier as Zumthor recounts Jauss's historiography of scholarship on the genre of the epic, framed as it is by the ideological preoccupations of historians, whether the psychoanalyst Alfred Adler (1870–1937) or Ernst Robert Curtius or Jacques Le Goff (1924–2014).[13] For Zumthor, then, Jauss's mode of historiography specifically demonstrates how in "speaking of the Middle Ages" one can only do so from "what happens to be my place in the sun: a place circumscribed as much by the intellectual demands of the day as by the sociohistoric conditions that engender them."[14] The very title of Zumthor's little book is thus framed by what Jauss had already shown to be true in the previous century of medieval scholarship. And just as Jauss traced those intellectual demands in the scholars of medieval epic, Zumthor acknowledges them not only in himself (on behalf of all scholars of the Middle Ages), but also in the medieval audience first engaged in the reception of a given medieval text; both engaged with their bodies, the one in latent ideological eroticism, the other in overt and complete corporal absorption.

What Zumthor does not make apparent in this passage about the latent erotic pleasure of reading, however, is that as he was developing these ideas in the years before publishing *Parler du moyen age*, he was

---

[12] *SMA*, 22; *PMA*, 29. Though Zumthor attributes it largely to the medieval reader, this kind of embodied reading – or somatic aesthetic response – arose as a theory with particular force during the Victorian period and was especially influential (as a methodology to be resisted) during the rise of New Criticism; see Morgan, *The Outward Mind*, 242–54. It has also reemerged in the critical attention to the materiality of texts: for an introduction, see Bill Brown, "Textual Materialism;" for a critique, see Altieri, "The Sensuous Dimension of Literary Experience."

[13] For his thoughts on Adler, for example, see Jauss, "Paradigmenwechsel in der Rezeption mittelalterlicher Epik," in *Alterität und Modernität der mittelalterlichen Literatur*, 359–66. *SMA*, 21; *PMA*, 28.

[14] *SMA*, 21; *PMA*, 28.

doing so even more directly in response to Jauss than we might suppose from his footnotes. In 1978, Zumthor began composing his commentary on Jauss's article for *New Literary History*, and in his response he notes that aesthetic pleasure had been a critical concept for Jauss's recent work, not just in his "Alterität und Modernität der mittelalterlichen Literatur" (translated in the 1979 *New Literary History* issue), but also in his major study, *Ästhetische Erfahrung und literarische Hermeneutik* (1977), where Jauss traces aesthetic pleasure back to Aristotle's *Poetics* and argues that "aesthetic enjoyment always occurs in the dialectal relationships of self-enjoyment in the enjoyment of something other (*Selbstgenuss im Fremdgenuss*)."[15]

While responding to Jauss's discussion of pleasure with general agreement, however, Zumthor offers the following critique:

> Some critics affirm that all relationships that we maintain with a text (or with a work of art) involve a latent eroticism. In a less metaphorical manner, I would say that the foundation of all true reading resides in the feeling of being personally affected by the text. The critic, if he meets this condition, places himself in what was the situation of a medieval reader or listener whose very body ... was involved in the reception of the text in a much more complete way than by the visual or auditory functions alone.[16]

These words should sound familiar, for Zumthor repeats them almost verbatim two years later in *Parler du moyen age*, where this bodily connection joins modern and medieval readers in their complete reception of a text. But an important transformation takes place in the intervening year. In 1978, Zumthor tried to distinguish Jauss's too generalizing erotic pleasure from his more nuanced and metaphorical idea of personal affection, but by 1980 he would altogether conflate this distinction, embracing what he had dismissed in Jauss to conclude that, in fact, "every relationship we maintain with a text involves some latent eroticism."[17]

We might expect that when Zumthor is thinking about the nature of pleasure, particularly the pleasure of reading, he more than likely is thinking in dialogue with French critics such as Roland Barthes, whose *Le plaisir*

---

[15] Jauss, *Aesthetic Experience and Literary Hermeneutics*, 32; *Ästhetische Erfahrung und literarische Hermeneutik*, 84.

[16] Zumthor, "Comments on H. R. Jauss's Article," 369; Dr. Sapir, Zumthor's translator, kindly responded to my request for the original French of Zumthor's commentary that served as the basis for the *New Literary History* translation, but unfortunately no longer had access to it. It is hard to know, therefore, the precise degree to which these correspondences are verbatim, even though they are notably close.

[17] *SMA*, 22; *PMA*, 29.

du texte was published a few years earlier in 1973.[18] Zumthor satisfies that expectation, even giving some credit directly to Barthes at the end of *Parler du moyen age*. While reflecting on pleasure as the "only thing that justifies the effort of our reading," he pauses to consider his terminology, recalling that "Philippe Verdier [1912–1993] used to tell me that Focillon, in his courses at the Collège de France, spoke about *happiness* (*bonheur*). I prefer *pleasure* (*plaisir*), maybe because of Barthes, and because of the connotations that enrich the word."[19] The choice Zumthor gives himself is between two French influences: the favored one comes from his friend Barthes; the other comes from a rumor passed down from Verdier through the halls of the Collège de France and the lectures by the historian of medieval art, Henri Focillon (1881–1943). In directing our attention to Verdier, Focillon, and Barthes, Zumthor passes over any indebtedness to Jauss, even though it is in response to Jauss's essay that he seems most directly to formulate – or at least put to paper – his views on the pleasure of reading medieval texts.

But Barthes and Jauss ultimately differ in their approaches to the "rehabilitation of aesthetic pleasure." Jauss, for instance, readily notes the nearly simultaneous, though independent publication of his *Kleine Apologie der ästhetischen Erfahrung* (1972) and Barthes's *Le plaisir du texte* (1973), but critiques the way Barthes "slips into the circle of negativity and affirmation" (that is, of an inauthentic affirmative pleasure or *plaisir* and the authentic negative aesthetic bliss or *jouissance*, a French counterpart to Theodor Adorno's [1903–1969] negative aesthetics), and by doing so he "generally denies any dialogue between reader and text, and thus brackets the macrostructure of the communicative reading situation so that '*lecture*' reduces itself to the perception of microstructures, all that is left to the reader is a passive, purely receptive role, and his imagining, testing, and meaning-creating activity never figures as a source of pleasure."[20] Jauss's attention to the importance of active dialogue between reader and text as

---

[18] On Barthes's absorption of "premodern critical practices" (especially the medieval exegetical framework of the four senses of scripture elucidated by Henri de Lubac), see Holsinger, *Premodern Condition*, 152–94. Perhaps Zumthor could have also been thinking about Jacques Lacan's (1901–1981) Seminar on *jouissance* (given in 1972–1973 and published in French in 1975). Or perhaps his interest in pleasure could have been influenced by, as Andrew Cole suggested to me, Alexandre Kojève's (1902–1968) reading of desire in G. W. F. Hegel's (1770–1831) master–slave dialectic. Or perhaps, as Zumthor elsewhere describes a kind of face-to-face encounter with the Otherness of medieval texts, he also could have been influenced by Emmanuel Levinas (1906–1995); see Cole and Smith, "Outside Modernity," in *The Legitimacy of the Middle Ages*, 17–18.

[19] *SMA*, 93; *PMA*, 103.

[20] Jauss, *Aesthetic Experience and Literary Hermeneutics*, 29; *Ästhetische Erfahrung und literarische Hermeneutik*, 81. On Jauss's response to Adorno's "Negative Aesthetic," see Johnson, "An Aesthetics of Negativity."

a source of aesthetic pleasure plays out to a greater degree in Zumthor's thinking than the negative aesthetic bliss emphasized by Barthes, even though it is to Barthes that Zumthor seems to give credit for inspiring his views on the pleasure of the text.

Dialogue

For Zumthor, however, the erotic pleasure of reading really manifests, as we have seen, in the form of a dialogue in which "two agents confront one another."[21] This pleasurable dialogic exchange between reader and text reflects, on the one hand, a medieval conception of interpretation, such as we find in Gregory the Great (c. 540–604):

> We see the faces of strangers and know nothing of their hearts, but if we connect to them with intimate speech (*familiari ... locutione*), though habitual conversation (*colloquii*) we also discover their thoughts. So when we find only the surface story in Scripture, we see nothing but the face; but if we connect to it with habitual practice, we can penetrate its mind as if in intimate conversation (*mentem quasi ex collocutionis familiaritate penetramus*).[22]

On the other hand, it obviously draws on that fundamental philosophical tool that we encounter from Plato (c. 427 BCE–c. 347 BCE) to G. W. F. Hegel: dialectic.[23] And with a third hand, it would also reflect a particularly Jaussian conception of understanding, which I'd like to consider here.

When he refers to dialogue, Zumthor mentions neither Gregory, nor Plato or Hegel, and he hardly mentions Jauss, for that matter. But instead, in at least one instance, he claims to be thinking of "that dialogic critical discourse of which Roland Barthes spoke, one that grasps the points of rupture and identifies the place where the real breaks forth."[24] Zumthor goes on to explain that "Whatever I write about this old text that I love is only a provisional transition between me and it, that Other definitively absent from our community, except in my discourse.... Making explicit my own rapport with the past, this discourse sets the scene for the Other in our present: it does not recreate what is dead."[25] So dialogue, for Zumthor,

---

[21] *SMA*, 66; *PMA*, 74 ("deux instances y sont confrontées").
[22] Gregory the Great, *Moralia in Iob*, vol. 143, lib. IV, praef., p. 158, lines 19–24.
[23] On the Hegelian indebtedness to premodern dialectic (though distinct from dialogue, per se), see Cole, *The Birth of Theory*.
[24] *SMA*, 89; *PMA*, 99.
[25] Ibid.

arises in the scholar's engagement with a text, an always present and personal form of discourse that transports or translates the past into the singular orbit of the reader. But this transportation necessarily retains (indeed produces) rupture; the past always remains dead, even as the discursive desire of the reader transports it through the present into its future.

Despite Zumthor's open preference for Barthian rhetoric of "rupture," his dialogic framework is just as, if not more, indebted to Jauss's central critique of Gadamer. This indebtedness can be seen, for example, in the way Zumthor's notion of dialogue shares what Jauss later calls "dialogic reciprocity," the idea that my dialogue with a text does not merely illuminate the text, but also illuminates me to myself; that we do not merely reach back to a text, but that the text reaches out to us; that I, in other words, am not only communicating with the text, but also developing self-awareness or self-reflection in the process.[26] This self-reflection is pivotal to Zumthor's unique futurity, which was already taking shape in his *Essai* and according to which the Middle Ages projects itself into the future and medieval texts project themselves towards future readers; as Andrew Cole and D. Vance Smith explain, for Zumthor this "self-recognition, then, transpires not only between the present and the past, between medievalist and medieval remainders, but also between the Middle Ages and the future that lies ahead of it."[27]

But at the same time, if we allow for the possibility that Zumthor's notion of "self-recognition" passed through Jauss's concept of "dialogic reciprocity," then it also, by extension, drew upon the notion of self-understanding so central to Gadamer's hermeneutics ("it is true in every case that a person who understands, understands himself, projecting himself upon his possibilities").[28] And Gadamer, in turn, was responding to the Hegelian idea of experience as a dialectical process that produces self-consciousness (when this dialectic is applied to history it fails to "do justice to hermeneutical consciousness" because "experience itself can never be science" in the Hegelian sense); he was also, of course, thinking of the "existential futurality" of

---

[26] Jauss, "Horizon Structure and Dialogicity," 205; and "Einleitung," in *Ästhetische Erfahrung und literarische Hermeneutik*, 657–703, at 669 ("dialogische Reziprozität"). This chapter, which is perhaps Jauss's most direct and explicit engagement with Gadamer and the hermeneutic concepts of horizon and dialogue, was published as the introduction to the second and expanded edition of *Ästhetische Erfahrung und literarische Hermeneutik* in 1982, but the ideas were already evident in his thinking much earlier; by the late 1970s, Vance, "A Coda," could claim that "Jauss is perfectly at ease with a long-standing paradox of hermeneutic theory which makes of 'understanding' at once a process of communication with voices of the past and a process of self-awareness" (378).

[27] Cole and Smith, "Outside Modernity," 19.

[28] Gadamer, *Truth and Method*, 261; *Wahrheit und Methode*, 246.

dasein in Martin Heidegger's (1889–1976) conception of historical knowledge.[29] We can see this notion of reciprocity drawn from Gadamer not only in Jauss's theory of reception, but also in his critique of Adorno's negative aesthetics, for according to Jauss literature not only reflects social reality, but also has the potential to shape it, particularly over time.[30]

Like Jauss, Zumthor also credits the past with being able to influence the present, as we see in his notion of aesthetic pleasure, for our pleasure in reading a medieval text comes from that text exerting its force upon us and our self-consciousness. This force arises, in part, from the text's alterity and distance as well as the reader's corresponding willingness to be surprised. Jauss thus speaks of the "surprise of *alterity*" (*Befremdung der Alterität*) – a phrase that he claims to take from the debates around Zumthor's *Essai* – and he understands the "characteristic hermeneutic problem posed by medieval literature" to be "the double structure of a discourse which not only appears to us as evidence of a distant, historically absent past in all its surprising 'otherness,' but also is an aesthetic object which, thanks to its linguistic form, is directed toward another, understanding consciousness – and which therefore also allows for communication with a later, no longer contemporary addressee."[31]

It is on this point – the force of reciprocal dialogue – that Zumthor addresses Jauss directly and in agreement: "From the point of view of our own historicity, one can maintain with Jauss that the masterpiece manifests itself in the perspective of the past, in the guise of an unexpected and admirable change in the horizon of consideration (*l'horizon considéré*)."[32] As the perspectives of the present and the past come into contact with one another, the anticipation of the encounter (anticipation that perhaps takes the form of desire) is disrupted through some surprise or change that alters the reader's view along the way. The reader must be willing to be surprised.

By allowing for hermeneutic surprise, both Zumthor and Jauss are responding to Gadamer's slightly different position. Gadamer too viewed dialectical hermeneutics in terms of the reciprocity of conversation,[33] and

---

[29] Gadamer, *Truth and Method*, 362–64 and 261; *Wahrheit und Methode*, 338 and 247; see also Gadamer, "On the Problem of Self-Understanding," esp. 49–50 (essay first published in 1962).
[30] Jauss, *Ästhetische Erfahrung und literarische Hermeneutik*, 37–46; republished in *Ästhetische Erfahrung und literarische Hermeneutik*, 2nd ed., 44–71; *Aesthetic Experience and Literary Hermeneutics*, 13–21.
[31] Jauss, "The Alterity and Modernity of Medieval Literature," 182 and 187; Jauss, *Alterität und Modernität der mittelalterlichen Literatur*, 10 and 14. Note that Jauss's word *Befremdung* also primarily implies a kind of disconcertment or alienation, a connection to alterity lost in the English translation to "surprise."
[32] *SMA*, 44; *PMA*, 52.
[33] Gadamer, *Truth and Method*, 385; *Wahrheit und Methode*, 359.

thus linked "the understanding of a text and the understanding that occurs in conversation;" and he envisioned dialogue as a necessarily passive enterprise, for we "say that we 'conduct' a conversation, but the more genuine a conversation is, the less its conduct lies within the will of either partner. Thus, a genuine conversation is never the one that we wanted to conduct. Rather, it is generally more correct to say that we fall into conversation (*in ein Gespräch verwickeln*)."[34] Central to the dialogic form of interpretation, for Gadamer as with Jauss, is an exchange of question and answer – and this exchange, for Gadamer, is likewise passive in the subject's experience of the unexpected: "we have experiences when we are shocked by things that do not accord with our expectations. Thus questioning too is more a passion than an action. A question presses itself on us; we can no longer avoid it and persist in our accustomed opinion."[35]

However, even if Jauss allows for surprise (what he terms *Befremdung*, implying a passive encounter with the Other), he formulates hermeneutic dialogue as a distinctly more active dialectic of questioning and answering in contrast with Gadamer's notion of passive conversation. Put in different terms, whereas Gadamer views the goal of dialogic understanding to be a *fusion of horizons* in which "understanding is to be thought of less as a subjective act than as participating in an event of tradition, a process of transmission in which past and present are constantly mediated,"[36] Jauss rather views it as a *differentiation of horizons*.[37] For Jauss, this process of dialogue thus involves an active acknowledgment of difference between self and other, which enables both surprise and the enjoyment of self in the other. It is Jauss's active and affirmative differentiation of horizons that transforms Gadamer's horizonal negative hermeneutics into something that Zumthor can take up for himself as a process no longer of Gadamerian fusion, but rather of fragmentation and rupture.

Horizons

The first chapter of Zumthor's *Parler du moyen age* is entitled "Tour d'horizon," the significance of which – belied by its ordinary rendering in English as "An Overview" – subtly announces one of the central

---

[34] Gadamer, *Truth and Method*, 401; *Wahrheit und Methode*, 361.
[35] Gadamer, *Truth and Method*, 375; *Wahrheit und Methode*, 348.
[36] Gadamer, *Truth and Method*, 302; *Wahrheit und Methode*, 274–75.
[37] This distinction is well recognized; see Rush, *The Reception of Doctrine*, 101–5.

Hermeneutics and the Medieval Horizon 267

intellectual investments of the book: the horizon as a metaphor for historical distance, across which hermeneutic dialogue must traverse. Here is how Zumthor characterizes and animates the "extreme ends" of this historical distance:

> On the one hand, the singer Taillefer [*fl.* 1066] or the romancer Chrétien de Troyes [*fl.* 1160–1191]; on the other, you and me. Further: on the one hand, the way in which the *Chanson de Roland* [*c.* 1040–*c.* 1116] was received by the warriors at Hastings (a dubious anecdote, but never mind that for now), or *Le Chevalier au lion* [*c.* 1180] by the lords and ladies gathered before the lectern of a reader; on the other hand, my reading and the one to which, as mediator, I invite you. Between these extremes, the text: historicized as words pronounced in the eleventh or twelfth century; yet, as a formal composition, in a way transhistorical—perceptible at once, then, in a chronological verticality *and* in a transcultural horizontality.[38]

For Zumthor this chain of historical distance does not merely link two extreme points, but is also composed of infinite points of dialogue in between – both vertical and horizonal, temporal and cultural. As it moves along, this dialogue calls up a deep theoretical tradition that has sought to account for the ways interpretation and historical understanding move "between these extremes." As such, Zumthor's claim must be understood in terms of that theoretical tradition.

In Zumthor's articulation of historical understanding, Jauss again appears to be one of his primary, though quiet, interlocutors. To explain this problem, Jauss had formulated his own notion of a "horizon of expectation" (of which Zumthor was aware even as he wrote the *Essai*), which he conceived in response to Edmund Hussurl's (1859–1938) important phenomenological concept of the "horizon of experience" and also, as we might expect, in dialogue with Gadamer's horizon of understanding.[39] So when Zumthor reflects upon hermeneutic horizons, he is engaging not just with Jauss, but also with Gadamer, and by extension Heidegger and Hussurl, among others.[40] In Gadamer's view, for example,

> The horizon is, rather, something into which we move and that moves with us. Horizons change for a person who is moving. Thus the horizon of the past, out of which all human life lives and which exists in the form of tradition, is always in motion…. When our historical consciousness transposes

---

[38] *SMA*, 25; *PMA*, 32–33.
[39] Zumthor references Jauss's "horizon of expectation" only once in *Toward a Medieval Poetics*, 16.
[40] However, it is surprising that Gadamer himself should hardly engage with Husserl; see Vessey, "Who Was Gadamer's Husserl?"

itself into the historical horizons, this does not entail passing into alien worlds unconnected in any way with our own; instead, they together constitute the one great horizon that moves from within.[41]

This concept of a singular, yet movable horizon eventually makes its way into the transhistorical nature of Zumthor's "text," perceptible all "at once" ("à la fois"), connected and reaching out to the modern reader, whose readership in turn transforms the text. Yet the two theories are nevertheless radically different, not just because of the incompatibility of Zumthor's poststructuralism with Gadamer's hermeneutics, but more specifically because Zumthor associated Gadamer with the persistence of a "heavy and complex romantic heritage," seeing "in the German hermeneutic, under Gadamer's influence," the preservation of romanticism's "most fertile elements," which continue "to engender lively continuations."[42]

Those "lively continuations" that Zumthor has in mind are probably related to Jauss. For in response to Gadamer's *fusion of horizons*, Jauss insisted instead upon a *differentiation of horizons* that acknowledges the reader's own horizon of *expectations* as it confronts the Other's horizon of *experience*. Reflecting back on his thinking in a 1983 reply to Paul de Man (1919–1983), Jauss thus explains that "as a result of my critique of Gadamer's fusion of horizons I have developed a more sophisticated conception of the process of *active* historical understanding – that of a differentiation of horizons."[43] This more sophisticated departure from Gadamer really became crystallized in the early 1980s in his introduction to the second volume of *Ästhetische Erfahrung und literarische Hermeneutik*, where Jauss asserts, for example, that "literary understanding first becomes dialogic when the alterity of the text is sought out and acknowledged before the horizon of one's own expectations – with the result that instead of attempting a naive fusion of horizons (*naive Horizontverschmelzung vorgenommen*), one's own expectation will be corrected and expanded through the experience of the other."[44] This lively continuation of Gadamer's thinking advanced by

---

[41] Gadamer, *Truth and Method*, 315; *Wahrheit und Methode*, 288. Putting it another way, Gadamer explains that "The horizon is the range of vision that includes everything that can be seen from a particular vantage point.... Since [Friedrich] Nietzsche [1844–1900] and Husserl, the word has been used in philosophy to characterize the way in which thought is tied to its finite determinacy" (313).

[42] *SMA*, 45; *PMA*, 53.

[43] Jauss, "Response to Paul de Man," in Waters and Godzich, eds. and trans., *Reading de Man Reading*, 203 (emphasis added). Jauss wrote the response as a letter to de Man shortly after his death in 1983, belatedly in gratitude for and in dialogue with de Man's introduction to the English translation of *Toward an Aesthetic of Reception* (published a year earlier in 1982).

[44] Jauss, "Horizon Structure and Dialogicity," 207–8; "Horizontstruktur und Dialogizitat," in *Ästhetische Erfahrung und literarische Hermeneutik*, 671. The second volume of *Ästhetische Erfahrung*

Jauss opened up the possibility for Zumthor to think through historical distance in a particular way – combining both the fusion and differentiation of horizons into a single mode of historical understanding.

Despite their different philosophical approaches and their "different intellectual backgrounds" (as Zumthor put it),[45] there was nevertheless mutual influence between Jauss and Zumthor, and this influence was largely engendered by the fact that they shared in the study of the Middle Ages. For both thinkers, there was something about the medieval period uniquely suited to the theories of interpretation that they were each advancing. Of course, Gadamer too made use of medieval thinkers such as Augustine (354–430), Nicholas of Cusa (1401–1464), and especially Thomas Aquinas (1225–1274) to arrive at his argument for the linguistic universality of hermeneutics; the influence of the medieval in his work is worthy of its own attention.[46] But what Zumthor and Jauss allow us to see is not just the usefulness of medieval philosophy and exegetical theory as a foundation for modern philosophical and hermeneutical ideas, but also and more importantly, the way that the Middle Ages – its temporality, its texts, its art, its readers, then and now – invite and challenge hermeneutic understanding *in practice*. For Gadamer, "temporal distance" is the "positive and productive condition enabling understanding. It is not a yawning abyss, but is filled with the continuity of custom and tradition."[47] For Jauss and Zumthor, the medial temporality of the Middle Ages opens up a space in which such paradoxical continuity and distance actually play out. The Middle Ages at once incline themselves towards this kind of Gadamerian continuity of custom and tradition, and yet at the same time their alterity invites differentiation and rupture.

This paradox was one of the central themes of Jauss's important essay in *New Literary History* on "The Alterity and Modernity of the Middle Ages," and it resonates with Zumthor's concern in *Parler du moyen age* about "the chronological distance that separates the medievalist from his object."[48] To demonstrate the uniqueness of this distance, Zumthor claims that "the otherness of the Middle Ages ... is more relative than that of the primitive world or, for Westerners, that of ancient China. Our Middle

---

und literarische Hermeneutik was published in the same year (1982) as the English translation of his *Toward an Aesthetic of Reception*, with its introduction by de Man.
[45] Zumthor, "Comments on H. R. Jauss's Article," 367.
[46] Vessey, "Gadamer, Augustine, Aquinas, and Hermeneutic Universality"; Arthos, "The Word Is not Reflexive."
[47] Gadamer, *Truth and Method*, 308; *Wahrheit und Methode*, 281.
[48] *SMA*, 28; *PMA*, 35.

Ages include a past that is both close and distant, foreign and familiar.... The Middle Ages belong to our history: belong to us, in a very special way, because biologically and culturally we are their direct descendants."[49] This argument is deeply problematic in its eurocentrism, not only for the way it ignores the actual diversity of the Middle Ages (what, for example, has now come to be known as the Global Middle Ages), but also for the way it assumes a masculine European "us" to whom these Middle Ages belong as a cultural and even biological inheritance, thus foreclosing the perspectives of non-European medievalists and precluding scholarly diversity. That is the nature of hermeneutic horizons, for they depend on the perspective of the individual in relation to some distant alterity (though not so distant as to remove sight of it altogether), often reaffirming and solidifying the one perspective over the other. But horizons are also fragmentary.

Zumthor's remarks on the unique and relative alterity of the Middle Ages occur at several critical moments in *Parler du moyen age*, but they are also found verbatim in his earlier comments on Jauss's essay in the journal *New Literary History*.[50] As we have seen, these are not the only instances in which Zumthor's ideas in *Parler du moyen age* took prior form in direct response to Jauss. But in this case, Zumthor formulates his argument about historical alterity by differentiating it from Jauss's notion of a medieval world-model (*Weltmodell*), a term that encompasses for Jauss both the medieval view of the world and "the model character of medieval texts" as the basis for a theory of literature.[51] Zumthor, of course, had already begun to formulate a theory of the model in his *Essai* as a way of thinking through poetic genres,[52] but when responding to Jauss's *Weltmodell* in 1979 and when he theorizes the concept more fully in *Parler du moyen age*, he sees models as methodological frames that guide and constrain scholarly research so that we can "discover the other in our pleasure."[53] Models are the means, rather than the end of scholarly activity. But while models suggest coherence, for Zumthor they also already contain the possibility of rupture. He writes in the *Essai*, for example:

> What we are presented with is not so much a system (*système*) as a set (*ensemble*); this may indeed be relatively coherent, but it is constantly producing shifts, partial modifications, *ruptures*, and occasional mutations. If

---

[49] *SMA*, 28 and 67–68; *PMA*, 36.
[50] Zumthor, "Comments on H. R. Jauss's Article," 370 and 369.
[51] Jauss, "The Alterity and Modernity of Medieval Literature," 191 and 182; Jauss, *Alterität und Modernität der mittelalterlichen Literatur*, 18 and 10. See *SMA*, 76.
[52] For example, Zumthor, *Toward a Medieval Poetics*, 106–16.
[53] *SMA*, 68; *PMA*, 76 ("découvrir l'autre dans le plaisir").

we take our starting point in the texts, we are apt to observe manifest or latent changes in them.... In order to account for this phenomenon it is possible to construct a systematic model for each text or group of texts, but this will not account for changes in the model itself.[54]

The horizon as one kind of model is thus subject to these constant shifts and, indeed, ruptures.

But what exactly does this horizonal rupture look like? In recent years, we have seen something like it, for instance, in Kathleen Biddick's unfusing of the past, present, and future through what she characterizes as a process of mourning, or in Carolyn Dinshaw's exposition of the asynchronicity of the medieval now.[55] But already in 1972, even before getting his hands on Jauss's more theoretical writings, Zumthor was setting the stage for this intellectual move with his now famous concept of *mouvance* – that is, the way medieval texts (contrary to the impression given by *stemmata codicum* that neatly outline relationships between different versions of the same text) are fundamentally variable and unstable, from scribe to scribe, manuscript to manuscript.[56] Almost a decade later, in *Parler du moyen age*, Zumthor would retrospectively reflect on the significance of this idea, explaining that *mouvance* "constitutes the key" to the hermeneutic problems at hand:

> [T]he manner in which medieval texts confronted the "horizon of expectations" of people in their own time? ... The recipient of the text has a role inscribed in the text: reception and interpretation, concretization and reelaboration cannot be dissociated—still less in oral performance than in written transmission. The text aims to intoxicate (*intoxiquer*) the one who receives it, even when it has to invent him (*il se l'invente*).[57]

In light of *mouvance*, medieval texts do not merely constitute a horizon of *experience* (on which the reader projects her expectations), but also constitute their own horizon of *expectations* that reaches out towards the reader, producing a constant state of perspectival movement. Unlike the passive horizon of experience, the role of expectations in both Zumthor and Jauss thus entails the subject's projection of a model onto the past and the past's projection of a model onto the future: this projection of expectation always allows for the possibility of surprise and rupture. *Mouvance*, then, is one aspect of the radical gap between past and present, between author and

---

[54] Zumthor, *Toward a Medieval Poetics*, 35 (emphasis added); *Essai de poétique médiévale*, 58.
[55] Biddick, *The Shock of Medievalism*, esp. 9–12; Dinshaw, *How Soon Is Now?*
[56] For a brilliant take on the concept of *mouvance*, see Chaganti, "Choreographing *Mouvance*."
[57] SMA, 61; PMA, 69.

reader, which manifests in the medieval text itself.[58] And this radical gap is only further fragmented by the move from orality to textuality, from intimate gestures to a mediated document, moves that take place within a medieval subject's own horizon of expectations. *Mouvance* exemplifies Zumthor's rupture of horizons even before he conceptualizes it precisely as such.

Zumthor started to formulate these ideas in the *Essai*, but once he began engaging more closely with his fellow medievalist, Hans-Robert Jauss, they took shape as a more cohesive and sophisticated theory of literary interpretation. It was Jauss, for instance, who actually critiqued Zumthor's *Essai* for fusing the medieval and modern to too great a degree: "If Zumthor had given this different status of the text as a nonwork its due, then his interpretations would have had the benefit of the hermeneutic difference, interpretations which in their present form still lack a dimension of significance, given his unreflected symbiosis of medieval and modern 'poeticity'."[59] If Gadamer envisioned hermeneutic dialogue as a fusion of horizons and Jauss envisioned it rather as a differentiation of horizons, then Zumthor's eventual adoption of a more radical rupturing of horizons seems in part to respond to Jauss's critique, even if it does so within the framework of poststructuralism.

Through the particular phenomenon of textual instability inherent to medieval texts – *mouvance* – the Middle Ages provide a unique opportunity for such a rupture; in part this uniqueness relates to Jauss's treatment of the alterity of medieval *experience* in terms of a world model as a source of aesthetic pleasure; but for Zumthor, it also entails a slippage of horizons at both ends, where the medieval text is also undergoing a kind of rupture, a separation of textual manifestations from the bodily immediacy of oral poetics. To circle back to where we began, Jauss finds hermeneutic pleasure in the alterity of the medieval as a singular model, while Zumthor finds it in "our own fragmentation, brought about by reading."[60]

---

[58] See *SMA*, 85; *PMA*, 94.
[59] Jauss, "The Alterity and Modernity of Medieval Literature," 195; Jauss, *Alterität und Modernität der mittelalterlichen Literatur*, 22–23.
[60] *SMA*, 83; *PMA*, 92.

Afterword

Martin Jay

Hazarding an "Afterword" to the remarkable essays collected in this volume is no easy task, as "afterness" haunts the "Middle Ages" from its inception. The name attached to the epoch could never have been a self-designation, but only coined by those who celebrated its passing and wanted to give it a proper burial.[1] It was understood, in fact, by some as little more than a hiatus between two eras of grandeur. It also came to serve as the "other" of modernity, which was thought to have fully surpassed it. In reaction, its defenders argued it was the enduring, if hidden kernel of a self-proclaimed "*Neuzeit*" that was not really as new as it thought. But whatever meaning it carried, a distinct era called "the Middle Ages" was a posthumous product, as Fredric Jameson once noted in his own Afterword to an earlier collection of essays on this subject, of the "Imaginary" of a later period.[2]

"Afterness" is, to be sure, always a highly fraught category, implying a following that departs from and is yet indebted to what came before.[3]

---

[1] Sometimes it is dubiously attributed to Petrarch (1304–1374), who did speak of the "dark ages." But the earliest noted use of the Latin phrase *medium aevum* seems to have been 1469. The English term, "Middle Ages," became current only in the early seventeenth century, the adjective "medieval" only in the nineteenth. The importance of the modern insistence on an epochal divide is stressed by Hans Blumenberg (1920–1996) in the passage from *The Legitimacy of the Modern Age*, 116, cited in the Introduction to this volume by Perry and Saltzman. Champions of modernity defined themselves explicitly in opposition to what they claimed to have left behind. It is important to note that Blumenberg criticized not only the reductive secularization argument of Karl Löwith (1897–1973) and Carl Schmitt (1888–1985), which stressed substantive continuity, but also the contrary claim that modernity was entirely self-created *ex nihilo*. His point was that the questions addressed in early periods persisted, but that modernity sought new answers. It was thus a "second overcoming of Gnosticism" (126), after the failure of the first in the early Middle Ages, and "reoccupied" (e.g., 224) positions left vacant rather than creating them from scratch.

[2] Jameson, "Afterword," 243. The Imaginary of medieval Christians may have drawn on the belief that they were living between the Incarnation and the Parousia, the First and Second Comings of Christ, but insofar as the second bracket was still open, it did not support the sense of afterness informing the modern identification of the Middle Ages.

[3] See Richter, *Afterness*.

Rather than observing a straightforward, linear succession, what happens "later" may well contain echoes and repetitions that betoken the uncanny return of something familiar from what happened "earlier." The unidirectionality of time can turn out to be less inexorable than it seems at first glance, the succession of discrete and incommensurable historical "periods" can falter, and the prohibition on anachronism can weaken. Any strict opposition between radical epochal rupture, on one hand, and the stubborn continuity of substance across period thresholds, on the other, can come to seem inadequately simplistic. What purports to be a postmortem autopsy turns out instead to be a vivisection.

Our increasing recognition of this complexity draws on the interpretative lessons of the past century. Sigmund Freud's (1856–1939) *Nachträglichkeit* and *Unheimliche,* Jacques Lacan's (1901–1981) *après-coup,* and Jacques Derrida's (1930–2004) *hantologie* have sensitized us to the revenants and specters that bedevil our understanding – perhaps even our "experience" – of the past. But there have also been more practical reminders of the dangers in naïve linearity. As the now rapidly receding moment of what was once called "postmodernism" revealed,[4] when we hastily assume that an era or historical period has definitely ended, we can be mocked by the interruption of what can be called "preposterous" chronicity. The word is apt, for as Patricia Parker reminds us in her study of William Shakespeare's (1564–1616) "Preposterous Events," it "comes from *posterus* ('after' or 'behind') and *prae* ('in front' or 'before') and connotes a reversal of 'post' for 'pre,' back for front, second for first, sequel for beginning."[5] So no one writing from the apparent vantage point of a Minerva's owl flying at dusk – not only after an historical period seems over, but, more modestly, at the end of a volume of essays – can really be confident that his inner clock has got the time of day right.

Rather than dwelling on the abstract paradoxes of "afterness" as such, however, I want to turn to the specific challenge of considering their

---

[4] We are still untangling the lessons of the "postmodernist" moment. On the one hand, the label was introduced to signal a recognition that classical modernity (however that was understood) had ended, but that a new era with its own independent designation had not yet arrived. But then ironically, it too was shown to be only a passing fad, perhaps just a fold in a "modernity" that hadn't really ended. It left us with the odd alternative of calling our own moment "post-postmodernist" or trying to repress the episode entirely.

[5] Parker, "Preposterous Events," 186. It was not by chance that the pushback against the denigration of the Middle Ages by triumphalist modernists picked up momentum during the years when postmodernism was in vogue. Not only did it challenge naïve historicist notions of linear temporality, but also repositioned the "modern" period as itself "in the middle" of other epochs. Now that postmodernism as a concept has lost its momentum, however, the uncompleted project of modernity, to cite Jürgen Habermas's (b. 1929) familiar phrase, has once again opened its concluding bracket.

implications for the essays in this volume. Composing an "Afterword" to them may have an added dose of preposterousness because the essays themselves are already exercises in self-reflective "afterness," which call into question the forward momentum of naïve chronology. That is, they are contemporary ruminations on previous attempts at posterior reflection conducted by mid-twentieth-century scholars offering fresh assessments of the Middle Ages. Often seeking to rescue forgotten wisdom or modes of human interaction as an antidote to the crisis of Western modernity brought about – or hastened – by the world wars, those scholars were looking, we might say, to recover and apply old answers to new questions. The essays in this collection are second-order evaluations of the results of their efforts from the later perspective of our own time. As a result, any Afterword to such a collection may seem merely like a phase in a *mise en abyme* of reflexivity about the temporal instabilities of "afterness," a kind of metareflection on what came before.

The metaphor of a *mise en abyme* may, however, too neatly suggest an orderly enfolding of temporal moments depicted in a spatial frame. The historical moment in which this Afterword is being composed is arguably an even more radical and violent scrambling of the preposterous challenge to the before/after temporality of premodernity and modernity than any we have experienced before. For in the plague year of 2020, we have suddenly found ourselves closer than the mid-twentieth-century protagonists of these essays to repeating one of the most traumatic episodes in medieval history. The "Black Death" that decimated Europe in the mid-fourteenth century has returned in ways that shatter whatever remained of the complacent belief that modernity produced a radical and irreversible break with the past. We have been made acutely aware of the precarity of modern life and our vulnerability to forces that we complacently assumed were mastered by scientific progress and cultural enlightenment. As was the case in the fourteenth century, the shock produced by the random cruelty of nature has let loose cultural demons that were once thought under control. The late medieval period suffered demographic decline, economic depression, religious turmoil, political destabilization, and even climate change – the Little Ice Age, which led to widespread famine – which may well find their echo in the years ahead.

There is therefore little chance of nostalgia today for the return of this moment in late medieval history or even of finding inspiration in the ways it handled the crisis. In contrast, the mid-twentieth-century reflections on the period discussed in this volume by and large still sought to recover the untapped resources of the Middle Ages for a potentially recuperative – or at least clear-sighted – alternative to the alleged pathologies of modernity itself. And the essays written about them for this volume, mostly composed, as they were, just before the pandemic abruptly changed everything, could more easily empathize with that redemptive perspective in a way an "Afterword" written only a short time later cannot.

Let me now engage with the specific essays assembled in our collection, while performatively enacting a preposterous temporality by ignoring their order in its table of contents. I want to begin with Jane O. Newman's exploration of Erich Auerbach's (1892–1957) debts to Johann Huizinga (1872–1945), whose classic study of *The Autumn of the Middle Ages* focused on what was assumed to be the terminal "crisis" of the era, because it illustrates many of the challenges presented to conventional chronology suggested earlier. Huizinga's skepticism about supersessionist replacement and his distrust of traditional periodization led him to question the alleged rupture in Western history that Jacob Burckhardt (1818–1897) had made famous as the Renaissance.[6] Newman reads Auerbach's celebrated argument in *Mimesis* that the origins of literary realism lie in Christian figuralism as itself indebted to Huizinga's resistance to the idea of cultural progress. She argues that Auerbach shared Huizinga's belief in the universal, existential implications of the "creaturely realism" of human suffering. In so arguing, Auerbach and Huizinga represent for Newman one strategy for pushing back against the putative epochal change that sets apart the Middle Ages from the period that succeeded it, whether called the Renaissance, Early Modernity, or Modernity *tout court*. Rather than simply reversing the typical positive evaluation of the epochal change, they drew on a perennial notion of the human condition, one that transcends periods and is most baldly manifest in moments of crisis. Here both conventional diachronic unidirectionality and the reverse temporality of preposterous chronicity are replaced by an atemporal synchronicity in which what endures – the perennial suffering that defines our existentialist reality – is more important than what changes.

A similar alternative is evident in Emily V. Thornbury's analysis of Ernst Robert Curtius (1886–1956), along with Auerbach one of the esteemed

---

[6] It is curious to see Burckhardt positioned as a champion of historical progress, because of his positing of the Renaissance as epochal shift. He is normally seen as the exception to the dominant historicist tendencies of his era, the Swiss resister to the German triumphalist narrative of his day, symbolized by his refusal to take up Leopold van Ranke's (1795–1886) chair in Berlin. In addition, his most notable book, *The Civilization of the Renaissance in Italy*, was written less as a diachronic narrative than as a synchronic presentation of characteristics of the epoch as a whole. Like his great friend Friedrich Nietzsche (1844–1900), he was highly ambivalent about the virtues of modernity.

pioneers of comparative literature. While Auerbach, under the influence of Huizinga, focused on the late Middle Ages as the moment when the human condition was most powerfully revealed, Curtius sought his model in an earlier time. He celebrated the prenationalist unity of the "Latin Middle Ages" – his own coinage – rooted in Roman universalism and still powerful in the time of Charlemagne (768–814). Thornbury foregrounds the ahistorical impulse in Curtius's reading of literary *topoi*, which can be found as early as Aristotle's (384–322 BCE) *Rhetoric*, were ubiquitous in the literature of the High Middle Ages, and remained potent even in the modern era (Curtius was a champion of T. S. Eliot [1888–1965] and James Joyce [1882–1941] in his own time).

Curtius's hostility to historicist contextualization – he also polemicized against Karl Mannheim's (1893–1947) sociology of knowledge – and belief in perennial forms places him in a lineage that goes as far back as Johann Wolfgang von Goethe's (1749–1832) natural *Urformen* and the nineteenth-century zoologist Richard Semon's (1859–1918) mnemic traces or engrams, organic memories of acquired characteristics. Closer to his own moment, it put him in the company as well of the art historian Aby Warburg (1866–1929), whose "pathos formulas" were emotionally laden visual tropes transcending time and place. But, according to Thornbury, his most explicit inspiration came from the archetypes of Carl Jung (1875–1961), whose "analytic psychology" he had therapeutically experienced on a personal level.

The racist and anti-Semitic elements in Jung's psychology have often been decried, as has his curator's attitude towards culture as "a vast museum" with no impediment to the "transfer of symbolic artifacts from one museum to another."[7] Thornbury does acknowledge in passing the tension between his bias for the "Aryan" collective unconscious and Curtius's cosmopolitan anti-nationalism,[8] but there is another inconsistency that is also worth foregrounding. Whereas Jung's archetypes were

---

[7] Rieff, *The Triumph of the Therapeutic*, 133. Philip Rieff (1922–2006), like many other detractors of Jung, was a partisan of Freud, but the problematic aspects of Jung's theories are evident without favoring alternative psychoanalytic theories; see, for example, Wolin, *The Seduction of Unreason*, chapter 2.

[8] Curtius, to be sure, was capable of defending Germany, at least an ideal version of it, against what he assumed were its detractors, as evidenced by the ugly attack he made in 1949 on Karl Jaspers's (1883–1969) critique of the cult of Goethe and the question of German war guilt. See his "Goethe oder Jaspers," which was a reply to Jaspers' "Unsere Zukunft und Goethe." For contemporary accounts of the controversy, see Milch, "Goethe, Curtius, Jaspers"; and Spitzer, "Zum Goethekult." Werner Milch (1903–1950) tried to provide an even-handed account, but Leo Spitzer (1887–1960) was very critical of Curtius. Goethe functioned as a model of the "other Germany" for many after the war, for example, the historian Friedrich Meinecke (1862–1954), in *Die deutsche Katastrophe*. But his political legacy remains controversial. See, for example, W. Daniel Wilson, *Das Goethe-Tabu*.

alleged to be hardwired in the collective unconscious, and thus archaic in the sense of deriving from mythic origins, the topoi in which Curtius was interested were generated, both in formal rhetoric and poetry, during a specific period in human history, that of the Golden Age of Latin culture, from Cicero (106 BCE–43 BCE) to the death of Augustus (63 BCE–14 CE). Arthur R. Evans, Jr. paraphrases Curtius's position in the following way: "the medieval interpretation of history is governed by the concept of *renovatio*, the *translatio imperii*: that is, the contemporary moment is conceived of as a renewal of the old and derives its validity through its approximation to a period of time in the past (Roman antiquity loosely and vaguely understood) considered as an absolute norm."[9]

Thus, *pace* Thornbury's emphasis on Curtius's fascination for Jung's eternal archetypes, he was also exploring a medieval version of the problem of "afterness," in which pagan antecedents haunted the culture of Christendom.[10] The celebration of *Roma aeterna* can, after all, valorize Rome as much as it does eternity. One recent commentator has even gone so far as to say that Curtius harbored "contempt for the Middle Ages" because of his exaggerated admiration for its classical roots.[11] I cannot judge this charge, but what does seem clear is that Curtius helps us understand that any radical distinction between the Middle Ages as a period of immanent cultural consolidation in which the past no longer haunted the present and allegedly eternal forms prevailed, on the one hand, and the Renaissance as a period of dissatisfaction where renewal was sought through returning to the classical past, on the other, will have to be qualified. Modernity may be said to have begun when Petrarch discovered Cicero's letters or Poggio Bracciolini (1380–1459) came upon Lucretius's (fl. first century BCE) *De rerum natura*,[12] but the impulse to recover forgotten or neglected classical wisdom had, in fact, never entirely disappeared.

---

[9] Evans, "Ernst Robert Curtius," 114.
[10] It is important to note that the term "pagan" refers not only to the philosophical and literary residues of high culture, but also to the ubiquitous persistence of popular customs and beliefs that made Christianization of the population an uneven and imperfect project. For a discussion of this issue, see van Engen, "The Christian Middle Ages as an Historiographical Problem."
[11] Jaeger, "Ernst Robert Curtius."
[12] Such attempts to fix a specific date or event as the symbolic turning of the historical page always have to be taken with a grain of salt, as it is inevitable that they will highlight only some of the distinctions that have been invoked to separate epochs. Virginia Woolf's (1882–1941) famous, tongue-in-cheek claim in her essay on "Mr. Bennett and Mrs. Brown," that "on or about December, 1910, human character changed" (*Collected Essays*, 1.320), gently mocks the attempt to describe such shifts with any precision.

The search for universal forms that transcend historical contexts also animated the efforts of Erwin Panofsky (1892–1968) to locate in Gothic cathedrals the same theologically inspired principles that informed the Scholastic philosophy of the High Middle Ages. C. Oliver O'Donnell argues that the ultimate source of Panofsky's universalist assumptions was the enduring influence of the Marburg School neo-Kantianism he had absorbed at an early stage of his career and shared with his philosopher friend Ernst Cassirer (1874–1945). In contrast to the gentile Curtius who could find his universal forms in Jungian archetypes, Panofsky and Cassirer were liberal Jews whose pre-exilic collaboration has allowed the historian Emily Levine to group them along with Aby Warburg into a distinct "Hamburg School."[13] Also unlike Curtius, his humanism is drawn less from an exaggerated respect for the world of antiquity than from the Enlightenment principles articulated by Immanuel Kant (1724–1804) and neo-Kantians such as Hermann Cohen (1842–1918).[14]

O'Donnell's stress on the neo-Kantian underpinnings of Panofsky's holistic interpretation of the relationship between architecture and theology helpfully moves us past earlier interpretations, such as that of Ernst Gombrich (1909–2001), who claimed Panofsky was a latter-day Hegelian who believed in the unity of a *Volksgeist*.[15] While Marburg neo-Kantianism abolished the unknowable noumena that Kant had posited as ontological obstacles to full cognitive adequacy between mind and matter, it nonetheless stressed the role of our *a priori* transcendental cognitive faculty in constituting the world of experience. Cassirer, whose interest was more in historical than natural scientific knowledge, shared the neo-Kantian rejection of ontological substances in the name of functions, such as symbolic forms that provide our lives with meaning.[16] The lineage O'Donnell draws

---

[13] Levine, *Dreamland of Humanists*. The complicated role, if any, played by their Jewish backgrounds in the work of distinguished scholars of the Middle Ages such as Panofsky, Auerbach, Kantorowicz, Spitzer, Marc Bloch (1886–1944), Fritz Saxl (1890–1948), Richard Krautheimer (1897–1994), Meyer Schapiro (1904–1996), and Norman Cantor (1929–2004), not to mention converts to Christianity such as Gustave Cohen (1879–1958) and Simone Weil (1909–1943), would be worth exploring. Among the obvious issues would be its effect on their reading of the implications of Christian supersessionist theology, which invites consideration in terms of the question of "afterness." For an attempt to address this issue in the case of one such scholar, see Porter, "Erich Auerbach and the Judaizing of Philology." Jane O. Newman provides another perspective in stressing the importance of Christian existentialism in Auerbach's early formation; see her "The Gospel according to Auerbach."

[14] A more extensive analysis would also have to address Panofsky's complicated debt to Alois Riegl (1858–1905), whose idea of *Kunstwollen* has also been understood as having neo-Kantian roots; see Efal, "Reality as the Cause of Art."

[15] Gombrich, "I Think Art Historians Are the Spokesman of Our Civilization."

[16] For a detailed account of Cassirer's debts to Cohen and the Marburg Neo-Kantians, see Luft, "Philosophical Historiography in Marburg Neo-Kantianism."

from Panofsky's neo-Kantian humanism to later sociologists of culture like Pierre Bourdieu (1930–2002) is thus plausible.[17]

But too narrowly focusing on the transcendental humanism of the neo-Kantian tradition may prevent us from appreciating one of the intrinsic tensions emerging from Panofsky's attempt to find homologous principles shared by Gothic cathedrals and Scholastic theology. The tension can be more easily appreciated if we recall the common ambition of Panofsky's *Gothic Architecture and Scholasticism* and Otto von Simson's (1912–1993) contemporaneous *The Gothic Cathedral* to reveal the mutual entanglement of theological texts and sacred architecture.[18] Both works sought to replace a purely aesthetic or formal analysis of Gothic cathedrals with a symbolic one, in which spirituality was carved into stone. In so doing, they had to acknowledge the crucial role of the substantive metaphysics that culminated in Scholasticism, which was theocentric rather than anthropocentric. Panofsky noted that Abbot Suger (1081–1151) had been influenced by the "light metaphysics" of Pseudo-Dionysius the Areopagite, the sixth-century neo-Platonist mystic, which led to the prominence of large stained glass windows in the Abbey Church of Saint-Denis.[19] Otto von Simson (1912–1993) acknowledged Panofsky's argument about Suger, but went further in arguing that the Gothic cathedral sought to imitate the ontological harmonies of the cosmos manifest in geometry and music, which were a legacy of Platonic idealism and Pythagorean mathematics. They were already influential a century before Thomas Aquinas (1225–1274) in the School of Chartres, whose master Thierry (d. *c*. 1150) saw God as drawing on geometry to create a cosmos from chaos.

In other words, Panofsky's neo-Kantian humanism may have led him to appreciate the formal systematicity common to both the architecture and theology, but it was less of a help when it came to making sense of the substantive, ontological premises underlying Scholastic metaphysics. As von Simson pointed out, the cathedrals of the High Middle Ages were built without any dependence on the principles of perspectival space until

[17] What makes it even more persuasive is that Panofsky developed his ideas in dialogue with an earlier sociologist of culture, Karl Mannheim (1893–1947), before both were forced into exile by the Nazis; see Hart, "Erwin Panofsky and Karl Mannheim."

[18] The first edition of von Simson's *The Gothic Cathedral* was published in 1956, a year before Panofsky's book and half a decade after Hans Sedlmayr's (1896–1984) *Die Entstehung der Kathedrale* (1950) and Günter Bandmann's (1917–1975) *Mittelalterliche Architektur als Bedeutungsträger* (1951). These works all shared the ambitious agenda of reading the Gothic cathedral as a kind of *Gesamtkunstwerk* in the context of a larger religious cosmology.

[19] For a critical assessment of his case, see Kidson, "Panofsky, Suger and St Denis."

the end of the fourteenth century.[20] That is, they were not built for a privileged subjective viewer, transcendental or empirical, at the apex of a visual pyramid, but in accord with eternal harmonies that were assumed to exist in a divinely created cosmos independent of a human point of view.

Whether or not all of these interpretations are fully persuasive,[21] introducing them in response to O'Donnell's suggestive essay allows us to appreciate more clearly the ambivalent status of "afterness" in both the Middle Ages and the work of mid-twentieth-century scholars of its legacy. While Panofsky's neo-Kantian humanism may suggest that he eschewed the earlier humanists' excessive veneration for classical antiquity, his quest for a unifying principle in the culture that produced both Suger and Aquinas meant he had to acknowledge the metaphysical legacy of pre-Christian paganism. Von Simson reinforces this conclusion by stressing the vital importance of Platonic and neo-Platonic influences on medieval culture. Once again, what came before haunts what seems to succeed it.

Another variant on the theme of uncanny doubling is played out in Nancy van Deusen's essay on "Ernst Kantorowicz, Carl Schmitt, and the University of California Regents." There is, to be sure, little evidence of any significant pagan origin of the topos of the "king's two bodies,"[22] although it has been argued, albeit controversially, that some anticipations can be found in the idea of kingship that began with the House of David in the Hebrew Bible. Instead, the larger issue, encapsulated in the subtitle of Kantorowicz's (1895–1963) book, is the role of "political theology," the alleged transfer from religion to politics of a concept of rulership and sovereignty. The Christian model of divinity in which immortal God becomes incarnated in the creaturely figure of mortal Jesus, and then paralleled in the miracle of transubstantiation in the Eucharist, not only legitimized the Church, understood since the time of Cassiodorus (c. 490–c. 585), as a corporate body transcending its current instantiation. It also subtended a model of kingship that distinguishes between the eternal institution – the ruler's *corpus mysticum* – and its ephemeral, contingent embodiment in the fallible human temporarily holding the office.

---

[20] von Simson, "The Gothic Cathedral: Design and Meaning," 173.
[21] For a critique, see Crossley, "Medieval Architecture and Meaning."
[22] Kantorowicz, "*Deus per naturam, Deus per gratiam,*" claims that "It is true that the contrast of *physis* and *mimesis*, which in the last analysis is Platonic, was adapted by the Pythagoreans to political theory as a means of harmonizing the state with the cosmos, of attuning men to the king, and the king to God, and thereby also of exalting the king and making him for cosmic reasons as similar as possible to the godhead" (274), but then adds that "the difference between *mimesis* of pagan thought and *gratia* of Christian thought remains nevertheless considerable" (276).

Political theology in general and Kantorowicz's argument in particular have stimulated intense and heated debates well beyond the boundaries of medieval studies.[23] Van Deusen prudently focuses only on two issues: his relationship with Carl Schmitt and his reliance on the "king's two bodies" argument to justify refusing to sign a loyalty oath during his tenure at the University of California, Berkeley. Both raise important questions about the issue of "afterness" and the direction of time's arrow. Both assume the alleged persistence of the Middle Ages in the present and indeed the enduring priority of certain of its deepest beliefs.

Schmitt was one of the major proponents of what has come to be called the "secularization thesis," in which modern concepts such as progress were covertly indebted to Christian theological antecedents. Its intention, as Blumenberg pointed out, was to undermine the immanent "legitimacy" of the Modern Age by seeing it as inherently derivative and tacitly parasitic on what it had claimed to surpass.[24] Authority deemed "legitimate" founded legality, Schmitt argued, rather than the rule of law having priority over the legislator. Legitimate authority was ultimately expressed in the idea of sovereignty. Whether embodied in a concrete figure – the absolute state – or the abstraction of a popular will, sovereignty, according to Schmitt, signified the power to decide in a state of emergency when the established legal order was in crisis. Ultimately, that power derived, at least through metaphoric transference, from an omnipotent God's ability to suspend even the natural order He has created and perform miracles.

This is not the first time that Schmitt's alleged influence on Kantorowicz has been the object of critical scrutiny,[25] as it has been arguable that the latter was loath to acknowledge the actual role of the former because of the Nazi "crown jurist's" tainted political associations. Despite the apparent tension between Kantorowicz's stress on the dual nature of monarchical bodies, at once eternal and ephemeral, and Schmitt's insistence on the singularity of sovereign power, the former's invocation of "political theology" does suggest a possible filiation. However one judges their complicated relationship, the question raised by van Deusen is still worth pondering:

---

[23] In addition to the literature cited in van Deusen's notes, see Davis, Milbank and Žižek, eds. *Theology and the Political*; and de Vries and Sullivan, eds. *Political Theologies*.

[24] See Blumenberg, *The Legitimacy of the Modern Age*. For one account of the convoluted intellectual interaction of Kantorowicz, Blumenberg, and Schmitt, see Haverkamp, *Shakespearean Genealogies of Power*, chapter 4.

[25] See, for example, Davis, *Periodization and Sovereignty*; Herrero, "On Political Theology"; and "Acclamations." See also Whalen, "Political Theology."

does the political theological claim that the secularized, modern notion of rulership that was derived from a medieval theological notion of God tacitly inform the argument of *The King's Two Bodies*? One way to address this question is by focusing on the idea of divinity underlying their analyses. Putting aside the issue of possible reciprocity in the original relationship between politics and theology – did the idea of God's powers mirror that of a king, rather than vice versa?[26] – what needs to be clarified is the assumed nature of the God who allegedly foreshadowed that of a modern sovereign ruler.

One of Schmitt's most persistent critics was the theologian and church historian Erik Peterson (1890–1960), who claimed that the Christian God understood as a trinity, firmly established in the sixth century when the Athanasian creed triumphed over Arianism, was an implausible candidate for the model of a singular ruler, whose unconstrained will was the source of sovereign decisions.[27] Schmitt and his supporters struggled to find answers to this challenge, and they often got lost in the weeds of obscure theological debates doing so. There is, however, another objection that may be even more difficult to resolve. Schmitt's notion of a singular, omnipotent divinity and by extension a political sovereign was based on a late medieval notion of a God whose omnipotent will was powerful enough to override any constraints, including those of the logical natural order he had Himself created (the order, we have noted, whose cosmic harmonies scholars such as Panofsky and von Simson saw manifest in the geometric regularities of Gothic cathedrals). Its origins, as Blumenberg and others have pointed out, lay in the nominalist revolution against Scholastic ontological realism launched by the Franciscan William of Ockham in the fourteenth century.[28] By challenging the real status of universals, the nominalists elevated a God whose will was unconstrained by rules or institutions or indeed even His "prior" decisions.[29] Rather than a finite, ordered cosmos, such as the one whose regularities were, according to Panofsky and von Simson, mirrored in church architecture, the way was open for belief in an infinite

---

[26] For an argument that monotheism itself was initially a reflection of Egyptian monarchic absolutism, see Assmann, *Herrschaft und Heil*.
[27] See Geréby, "Political Theology versus Theological Politics."
[28] Blumenberg, *The Legitimacy of the Modern Age*, 160, locates a turning point in the condemnation of high Scholasticism in 1277 by Étienne Tempier (1210–1279), the Bishop of Paris, only three years after the death of Aquinas. For other accounts of the importance of nominalism, see Gillespie, *The Theological Origins of Modernity*; and Blanton, "Medieval Currencies."
[29] The notion of a "prior" decision is complicated because it assumes that God is beholden to linear temporality rather than being somehow eternal and omnitemporal. I will leave the reconciliation of this contradiction to theologians.

universe ruled – if that's the right verb – by contingency.³⁰ And when the image of God as a providential meddler in human affairs was supplanted by that of a distant and indifferent *Deus absconditus*, it was possible for human self-assertion to grow and the transference of sovereignty to mundane authorities to take place. The discussions of Shakespeare's *Richard II* and Dante (1265–1321) at the end of *The King's Two Bodies* may be read as acknowledging this transformation.³¹

Regardless of how one interprets the secularization thesis or the implications of political theology, a great deal depends on which version of God – resolutely monotheistic or Trinitarian, rationally bound or exercising an omnipotent will, serenely eternal or interrupting the flow of time – is taken as normative. It might even be possible, as shown by Georges Bataille's (1897–1962) derivation of sovereignty from a heterogeneous rather than homogeneous definition of the sacred, to come to totally different conclusions about the decisionist power of a strong, indivisible subject.³² The resulting ambiguity about the nature of divinity is manifest, I would argue, in Kantorowicz's often-remarked evocation of the university's corporate identity in his refusal to sign the Berkeley loyalty oath in the early 1950s. Van Deusen cites Kantorowicz's claim that the "inner sovereignty" of the faculty meant he was a member of an enduring corporate body – on the model of the king's *corpus mysticum* – rather than a mere state employee, and thus not bound by the rules laid down by the Regents of the University.

Kantorowicz's resistance to signing the oath may have been laudable and his reputation as an elitist reactionary justly tempered by his courageous act, but his rationale shows how easily the legacy of the king's two bodies argument, filtered through Schmitt's political theology or not, could be creatively, but imprecisely, applied. By locating sovereignty not in the unconstrained decision of a legitimate ruler who constitutes the laws, but rather in an inner *corpus mysticum* that can only resist the laws made somewhere else, it turns an all-powerful will into little more than a symbolic won't. And by identifying the king's "first body," which channels the immortal, divine spirit of the incarnated, creaturely Christ, with

---

[30] The classic account of the change remains Koyré, *From the Closed World to the Infinite Universe*.
[31] See Kahn, "Political Theology and Fiction," who argues that there is a humanist implication in the idea of making and unmaking symbolic forms; and Santner, *The Royal Remains*, who responds that the "underside of fantasy" undercuts conscious human intention.
[32] For a discussion, see Jay, "The Reassertion of Sovereignty in a Time of Crisis." Here the model for sovereignty is not so much a theological notion of an omnipotent divinity as the experience of religious effervescence, which Emile Durkheim (1858–1917) had assigned to elementary forms of religion.

an impersonal institution without a unified subjective consciousness, it merely displaces the question of who has the legitimate right to represent the corporate institution as a whole.³³ In other words, if the "inner sovereignty" of the faculty as a kind of *corpus mysticum* has not coalesced into a single voice when its empirical members disagree (as they did when some signed the oath and others refused), Kantorowicz was stretching the logic of his argument to arrogate to himself the representative role of the corporation as a whole.³⁴ Or perhaps he was just concocting what one commentator has called a "mythistory" recycling his earlier notion of a "secret Germany," worshipped when he was a devotee of the Stefan George (1868–1933) circle, and attributed back to a no less fantasized image of a politically untouched medieval university that had never really existed.³⁵

Much more can be said about the complex legacy of *The King's Two Bodies* and its various manifestations in the modern, supposedly secular world. In terms of the theme of "afterness," there is also a great deal that might be conjectured. Let me make only one point about the directionality of time's arrow. Schmitt's political theological assertion that originally theological content was transferred in diluted form into secular politics can be challenged by Peterson's historical argument that the original Trinitarian content was ill-suited to a strongly unitary notion of sovereignty. But it also can be accused of reading back into the Middle Ages that very notion, which Schmitt saw emerging in secular terms with modern theorists such as Thomas Hobbes (1588–1679) and Juan Donoso Cortés (1809–1853). Consonant with his disdain for liberal regimes based on deliberative rationality and market relations, it fit well the non-normative, decisionist dictatorships of the twentieth century Schmitt so admired.

Despite Schmitt's claim that popular sovereignty was merely another version of the same pattern, with the "people" or the "nation" substituted for the king (or the dictator), Claude Lefort (1924–2010), the eminent twentieth-century French political theorist, has argued that attempts to fill the empty space left behind by the dethroned monarchs of the *ancien régime* actually lead only to totalitarianism. Democracies, in contrast, comprise individuals who have been "decorporealized" and who resist

---

[33] For a discussion of the tensions between Kantorowicz's horizontal stress on corporate solidarity, derived from the Pauline idea of the body of the faithful, and Schmitt's vertical emphasis on personalist sovereignty, see Rust, "Political Theologies of the *Corpus Mysticum*."

[34] For an analysis of the way in which metonymic displacements often allow *soi-disant* representatives of a collectivity to assume the role of spokesperson, see Pels, *The Intellectual Stranger*, chapter 7.

[35] Wimmer, "Kantorowicz's Oaths."

filling the empty space left behind by a discredited political theology with a strong unitary political sovereign.[36] They get into trouble when they attempt to move from a symbolic to a literal embodiment of sovereignty, leading to a forced homogenization of the healthy pluralism of modern politics. In the latter, the *corpus mysticum* is not incarnated in a literal body, but instead "excarnated"[37] in permanent dispersion. It would perhaps be worth pondering the implications of this argument for a fresh reading of medieval politics, at least before a strong notion of sovereignty in Schmitt's sense was in place. That is, the question has to be asked: did Schmitt project back a version of political decisionism that characterized totalitarian rather than democratic versions of modern politics into the Middle Ages, supporting it by a tendentious identification of the medieval version of divinity with the unconstrained voluntarism of the nominalist God rather than the rationalism of his Scholastic predecessor?

If the political theological reading of the Middle Ages, exemplified by Schmitt and to some extent by Kantorowicz, has opened up possibilities for a right-wing, sometimes even racist appropriation of its alleged legacy,[38] R. D. Perry wants to salvage a more progressive alternative by turning to Hannah Arendt (1906–1975). Arendt is in some ways an unlikely choice, as the political theological residues in her theorizing can be compared in certain respects with those of Schmitt.[39] They shared, for example, a belief in the importance of will, which Perry locates in particular in Arendt's last work on *The Life of the Mind*. Drawing on Augustine (354–430) and Duns Scotus (*c.* 1266–1308), she affirmed the world of radical contingency ushered in to medieval thought by nominalist anti-realism.[40] It is, Perry argues, related to her belief in the importance of natality, the birth of new humans who can change the world they enter through free action.

---

[36] Lefort, *The Political Forms of Modern Society*, chapter 9.
[37] Although this term is actually not Lefort's, but Michel Foucault's (1926–1984; *Discipline and Punish*, 208), it captures the gist of his argument.
[38] For an account of the right-wing appropriation of "the Middle Ages," see Kaufman and Sturtevant, *The Devil's Historians*.
[39] See, for example, Moyn, "Hannah Arendt on the Secular," in which he writes: "her focus on sovereign *will* as the key site of continuity between Christianity and modernity is an exact replica of Schmitt's earlier claims" (83).
[40] Arendt affirmed the link between theological voluntarism, an ontology of radical contingency, and the possibility of human self-assertion that was noted by Blumenberg. Scotus, it might be noted, was not as radically nominalist as Ockham, but he contributed to the transition from a God beholden to reason to one whose will was omnipotent. Human will was not as powerful, but it was still the ground of human freedom. On other issues, Arendt and Blumenberg did not always agree. See the discussions in Brient, "Hans Blumenberg and Hannah Arendt"; Bajohr, "The Unity of the World," Jay, "Against Rigor"; and Paulina, "The Reinforcement of Political Myth?"

The most compelling motivation for making that change, Perry argues, can be found in Arendt's thoughts on the political importance of love, which she investigated in her first book on Augustine and counterposed to the selfish individualism that marked modern philosophy ever since Hobbes. Love transforms the will without extirpating it, especially when it is channeled into the neighborly love that sustains communities. It even provides an inspiration, Perry concludes, for repairing damaged human relations, including between the races, an area where Arendt, alas, was not always as progressive as we might want her to have been.

In this view, Arendt's critique of modern politics, both the disintegrative liberalism based on an abstract notion of self-interested individuals and a totalitarian alternative grounded in excessive integration, can be traced to her recovery of medieval ideals. Can, however, a politics based on the exercise of will and the community-building of love suffice to support a progressive politics in the current world? Over her career, Arendt, in fact, was inconsistent in her estimation of the political implications of love.[41] She may have valued it highly while writing her dissertation on Augustine, and also celebrated it in the passionate letters she exchanged with her married lover Martin Heidegger (1889–1976) during the same period,[42] but was not always so sure about its political efficacy. In *The Human Condition*, she was to charge that "love, by its very nature, is unworldly, and it is for this reason rather than its rarity that it is not only apolitical but antipolitical, perhaps the most powerful of all antipolitical human forces."[43] When she was accused by Gershom Scholem (1897–1982) during the Eichmann Affair of lacking *Ahavath Yisrael* (love for the Jewish people), she famously replied, "I have never in my life 'loved' any people or collective – neither the German people, nor the French, nor the American, nor the working class or anything of that sort. I indeed love 'only' my friends and the only kind of love I know of and believe in is the love of persons."[44] And in a 1962 letter to James Baldwin (1924–1987), she wrote:

> What frightened me in your essay was the gospel of love which you begin to preach at the end. In politics, love is a stranger, and when it intrudes upon it nothing is being achieved except hypocrisy.... Hatred and love belong

---

[41] For one discussion, see Chiba, "Hannah Arendt on Love and the Political."
[42] Arendt and Heidegger, *Letters*.
[43] Arendt, *The Human Condition*, 242.
[44] Arendt, *The Portable Hannah Arendt*, 392.

together, and they are both destructive; you can afford them only in the private and, as a people, only so long as you are not free.[45]

Arendt did, however, posit a more general "amor mundi" or love of the world, and it is here that Perry's argument becomes persuasive. Distinguishing between the love of lovers, which "by reason of its passion, destroys the in-between which relates us to and separates us from others,"[46] and the love of friends, which maintains them, she argued for a politics that combined respect for otherness without any desire for fusion, thus avoiding the homogenizing pressure that engenders totalitarianism.[47] The answer to the self-absorbed individualism of a Hobbes was thus not communitarian solidarity, but the building of a shared world of institutions and practices that respected the space between and yet connected the participants who entered it.

If Arendt's notion of a politics drawing on the power of love was nuanced in this way, so too was her argument for the freedom associated with the exercise of will. Natality may mean bringing something fresh into the world, but it is not a function of the will of the newborn. That is, we are all passive benefactors of the acts, intentional or not, of others, dependent not only on our progenitors for our existence, but also dependent on them for years of nurturance. Translated into political terms, this means that any fantasy of absolute self-assertion or decisionist founding comes up against our debts to a past we cannot entirely escape. In *On Revolution*, Arendt, in fact, celebrated the American Revolution's (1775–1783) recessive narrative of legitimation in a series of prior acts, such as the Mayflower Compact (1620), as superior to the French Revolution's (1789–1799) attempt to wipe the slate clean and found a new order *ex nihilo*. Love of the world thus involves acknowledging the abiding residues of what preceded us, not just honoring what we are capable of creating ourselves. Once again, the assumption of a straightforward linear narrative – whether political theology's declension story of delegitimizing secularization or a progressive tale of radical self-assertion in a context of absolute contingency – falters.

---

[45] Arendt, "The Meaning of Love in Politics." This letter from Arendt to Baldwin has spawned a literature of its own; for example, Sean Butorac, "Hannah Arendt, James Baldwin and the Politics of Love"; Caver, "A Different Price for the Ticket."

[46] Arendt, *The Human Condition*, 242.

[47] In extolling the virtues of friendship, Arendt echoed a variety of German thinkers of her period, including Siegfried Kracauer (1889–1966) and Ernst Jünger (1895–1998); see Bures, "Fantasies of Friendship." The theme of friendship in the Middle Ages is discussed in Classen and Sandidge, eds., *Friendship in the Middle Ages and Early Modern Age*, which contains an essay by C. Stephen Jaeger ("Friendship of Mutual Perfecting") that tacitly supports Perry's stress on Augustine's abiding influence on Arendt.

If the linearity of large-scale epochal narratives are open to contestation, perhaps even turning preposterous in their reframing, the same can be said of the narratives of parallel lives on a micrological level, as we can see by turning to Anna Kelner's essay on Simone Weil and medieval mysticism. Arendt and Weil were remarkable women of the same generation – the former born in 1906, the latter in 1909 – into European Jewish families, and were both directly affected by the rise of fascism. Although they never met and Weil was to die before Arendt's work was widely known, Arendt knew and admired at least some of Weil's.[48] Their ideas about politics have often been discussed together, perhaps most recently in two recent books, Robert Esposito's *The Origin of the Political: Hannah Arendt or Simone Weil* and Deborah Nelson's *Tough Enough*.[49] Indeed, both Arendt and Weil focused on the meaning(s) of love, often drawing on Augustine for inspiration.[50]

But in many respects, their parallel lives radically diverged. Not only did Weil convert from Judaism to Catholicism and, much to the discomfort of her later admirers, adopt anti-Semitic arguments to justify her self-hatred, but she also pursued the radical self-abnegation modeled on the lives of holy women who martyred themselves for their faith. Whereas both she and Arendt rejected the modern ideal of selfish, bourgeois individualism, the latter did so in order to love the world, whereas the former strove to escape it. Arendt also understood the value of creating institutions to provide the space for the political interaction she identified with freedom, while Weil saw them, including the established Church, as obstacles to the achievement of a higher goal.

As Kelner shows us, that higher goal was unity with divinity in the manner of medieval mystics, who sought to efface any trace of their individual egos and capacity to exert their will. Taking asceticism to an extreme – her death may have been accelerated by her refusal to take nourishment after being diagnosed with tuberculosis – Weil's martyrdom has invited a comparison with Bataille's notion of a sovereignty that required the violent dissolution of the self in a sacred community.[51] Whether admired as heroic or lamented as self-deluded, Weil's self-conscious appropriation of the experiential rather than theological legacy of medieval Christianity – or,

---

[48] See, for example, the glowing reference to Weil's *La condition ouvrière* in *The Human Condition*, 340.
[49] However, the comparison is made in terms not of their debts to the Middle Ages, but for Esposito of their responses to Homer's *Iliad* (eighth century BCE) and the relationship between war and politics and for Nelson of their attitudes towards suffering.
[50] A recent collection of Weil's writings is called *Love in the Void*.
[51] See Irwin, *Saints of the Impossible*.

more precisely, of one of the many experiential as opposed to a number of possible theological legacies[52] – shows that those who turned to the Middle Ages in the mid-twentieth century had considerable leeway in the choice of what they celebrated as alive and what they discarded as dead in the tradition.

The word "tradition," in fact, may not convey the most accurate relationship between the medieval legacy and its mid-twentieth-century appropriation. It suggests a smooth continuity – the word comes from the Latin *tradere*, which means hand over or hand down – that bridges the ruptures in the transfer and the temporal complexities we have seen manifested in "afterness." Both Clare A. Lees's survey of the role played by Old English literature in midcentury British scholarship, fiction, and poetry and Benjamin A. Saltzman's account of four major hermeneuticians and their interpretation of the medieval world acknowledge the insufficiency of presenting the relationship between past and present in simplistic traditionalist terms.[53]

Lees show us the rich and often contradictory variety of British responses to the quickening of interest in so-called "Anglo-Saxon" literature and culture after World War II. Against the earlier appropriation of Old English literature in the service of an imperialist and racist agenda, she argues that it was often transgressive modernists who found inspiration in the recovery and retelling of *Beowulf* and other Old English texts. The scholarly influence of J. R. R. Tolkien (1892–1973) was not as immense as his impact on popular culture, but along with the work of Gavin Bone (1907–1942) it created opportunities for a new appreciation not only of the literary merits of the texts, but also their cultural implications for the present. These were teased out by several postwar novelists, the most fascinating of whom was Bryher (1894–1983), the companion of H. D. (Hilda Doolittle, 1886–1961), whose 1948 novel *Beowulf* provided a realistic portrayal of life during the Blitz filtered through a queer sensibility.

Interestingly, neither Bryher nor the Scottish poet Edwin Morgan (1920–2010), who was also gay and much influenced by Old English literature, makes an appearance in Glenn Burger and Stephen F. Kruger's

---

[52] It might be possible, for example, to explore the links between apophatic theology, which denies the possibility of positively describing or conceptualizing God, and mystical experiences inexpressible in language.

[53] There have been, of course, non-simplistic notions of tradition, for example, in T. S. Eliot's famous essay "Tradition and the Individual Talent" (1919) or F. R. Leavis's (1895–1978) *The Great Tradition* (1948), but this is not the place to do them justice. For a discussion of some of the issues, see Phillips and Schochet, eds., *Questions of Tradition*.

pioneering 2001 collection of essays on *Queering the Middle Ages*. The introduction to that volume begins, however, with a section called "History and the Logic of the Preposterous," which cites Lee Edelman's argument for a literalization of "preposterous" as "the practice of giving precedence to the posterior and thus as confounding the stability or determinancy of literary or erotic positioning."[54] They then follow with a discussion of the challenge to temporal unidirectionality posed by queer theorizing, which anticipates the more general problematizing of "afterness" informing the Afterword you are now reading.

If Lees's essay thus fits well with the other essays in this collection in terms of temporal dislocation, it stands alone in another respect. Bryher may have been a cosmopolitan figure with considerable experience on the continent and friendships with figures such as Adrienne Monnier (1892–1955) and Walter Benjamin (1892–1940), and her *Beowulf* may have first appeared in French translation rather than in English. But the larger British postwar appropriation of "Anglo-Saxon" literature stands out for its insularity. There is no trace of the theological echoes we have heard resounding in the contributions of scholars trained in Central Europe and spending much of their career in American exile; nor any hint of the existential anguish suffered by a mystical seeker after martyrdom such as Simone Weil or political courage showed by Kantorowicz during the Berkeley loyalty oath controversy.

Absent as well from the British debate is sustained methodological self-reflection of the kind that inspired Paul Zumthor (1915–1995), the noted Swiss-born scholar of the medieval French romance, discussed by Saltzman. Focusing on a late career rumination on the state of his field, *Parler du moyen age*, Saltzman situates Zumthor at the crossroads of continental debates about hermeneutics, involving Hans-Georg Gadamer (1900–2002), Hans Robert Jauss (1921–1997), and, in a somewhat more adversarial way, Roland Barthes (1915–1980). Rather than looking for eternal verities in the medieval past or diluted secular equivalents of its robust religious life, Zumthor took from the hermeneuticians a keen awareness of, as it were, the need to mind the gap between past and present. To mind, that is, in the British sense of being cautiously aware about, not resenting it. For Zumthor appreciated the challenges of an ongoing "dialogue" between different epochs, one that involved keeping the horizon of each open to the other, without collapsing them, *pace* Gadamer, into an

---

[54] Burger and Kruger, eds., *Queering the Middle Ages*, xi. This exhortation may not have been as pertinent for lesbians such as Bryher.

integrated whole (as a naïve notion of tradition might assume). From Jauss in particular, he seems to have acquired a certain skepticism about the harmonious fusion of horizons and an awareness of the necessity of rupture in our contact with a past as remote as the Middle Ages.

Significantly, Zumthor's appreciation of the inevitability of differentiated horizons was tied up with his understanding of the performative dimension of medieval literature, which he called its "theatricality."[55] By recalling the gestural, corporeal, and oral quality of medieval literature, he shifted the emphasis away from pure textuality, and with it the assumption that the meaning of a text can be interpreted through retrospective linguistic analysis alone. Our reading, in other words, is never the same as their performing. The interference of intervening noise over the years also makes it more difficult to enjoy, in Barthes's sense, the immediate pleasure of the text. Or rather what pleasure it may give is through the stimulation of encountering an alterity that cannot easily be domesticated and made familiar.

For all his appreciation of the insights contained in Zumthor's hermeneutics of differentiation, Saltzman also notes in passing the Eurocentricism he shared with virtually all medievalists before the rise of what has come to be called in the past decade "the global Middle Ages."[56] D. Vance Smith's penetrating essay on Frantz Fanon's (1925–1961) nuanced approach to the legacy of Augustine's critique of the Manichean heresy – or, more precisely, the syncretic religion developed by the third-century Persian prophet Mani – shows how much is lost by ignorance of the larger story. Although Manichean dualism has been a foundational concept of postcolonial studies, at least since Abdul R. JanMohamed's 1983 *Manichean Aesthetics*, Smith convincingly shows that Fanon's understanding of its complexities was far more dialectical than previously understood. Rather than merely inverting the hierarchical terms of a simple opposition, he nimbly applied it to the complicated relations, economic, racial, psychological, and cultural, that entangled colonizers and colonized.

Smith, moreover, shows that Fanon was a serious student of the most illustrious son of the North Africa he was to adopt as his own homeland, Augustine, whose initial attraction to and ultimate critique of Manicheanism gain new relevance in the context of postcolonial studies. In so doing, Smith not only adds another layer to Andrew Cole's account

---

[55] See Zumthor's discussion with Solterer, "Performing Pasts."
[56] See, for example, Heng and Ramey, eds., *The Global Middle Ages*; and Holmes and Standen, eds., *The Global Middle Ages*.

of the anticipations of dialectical theory in medieval theology.[57] He also shows the value of integrating what seems peripheral to the central story of the Christian Middle Ages, an integration that would also have to overcome what we might call the simplistic Manicheanism emblematized by the Crusades and integrate Islam more prominently into the story as well.[58] That such an integration was already underway in the mid twentieth-century reevaluation of the Middle Ages is shown by the interest that a figure absent from the collection, the political philosopher Leo Strauss (1899–1973), had in the legacy of the tenth-century philosopher Al-Fararbi, whose reading of Plato's (*c*. 427 BCE–*c*. 347 BCE) *Laws* he much admired.[59]

The unexpected engagement of Fanon with Augustine is matched by the hitherto underappreciated interest that W. E. B. Du Bois (1868–1963) had in the Middle Ages, explored by Cord Whitaker, who argues it was present in all periods of his career. Whitaker's earlier work focused on the origins of contemporary racial stereotypes in medieval Europe at least since the time of the Crusades,[60] and he claims that Du Bois was himself well aware of this lamentable legacy. But he also argues that in both his creative and theoretical writings, Du Bois drew on the Middle Ages as a positive inspiration. Building on Cole's reading of the medieval sources of Hegelian dialectics, Whitaker claims that the lord/bondsman section of *The Phenomenology of Spirit* in particular suggested to Du Bois an alternative to the class and racial inequalities of modern society: "In Du Bois's prewar period, when his medievalism was shaped mainly by his encounters with [G. W. F.] Hegel [1770–1831], including the extended encounter that informed [*The*] *Souls* [*of Black Folk*], as well as by his knowledge of popular medievalist literature, the Middle Ages and its denizens exhibit a god-like freedom that is not yet available to regular humans."[61]

Du Bois, as Whitaker reads him, thus joins other Marxists who have dissented from Karl Marx's (1818–1883) own essentially linear notion of historical development to find in the Middle Ages unexpected resources

---

[57] Cole, *The Birth of Theory*, 202; Fanon only merits a brief reference for noting the limits of applying the Hegelian lord–bondsman relation in the context of colonial relations.
[58] Islamic Aristotelians, of course, are often acknowledged for their transmission and development of classical thought, and the achievements of Islamic scientists in such fields as optics, astronomy, medicine and mathematics have been recognized.
[59] Strauss, *What Is Political Philosophy?* chapter 5. For a discussion of his larger debts, see Perins, *Leo Strauss*.
[60] Whitaker, *Black Metaphors*. For other comparable assessments, see Heng, *The Invention of Race*; and Vernon, *The Black Middle Ages*.
[61] Chapter 2 in this volume, Whitaker, "The Noblest Blood God ever Made," 75.

for an alternative to modern capitalism.⁶² There is much to recommend this counterintuitive lineage, but closer attention to Hegel's attitude towards the Middle Ages would be necessary for it to be fully persuasive. *Pace* Cole, Hegel cannot be characterized as having been immersed in a still essentially medieval world in his youth. The Duchy of Württemberg where he was born was Protestant and imbued with a spirit that has been called that of "civil piety."⁶³ It owed much to the "second Reformation" tradition of Protestant *Bildung* promulgated by theologians such as Johann Albrecht Bengel (1687–1752), whose influence remained strong in the Stuttgart Gymnasium and Tübingen Stift where Hegel was educated. It is true that interpretations of Hegel that stress only his debts to classical Greek thought are one-sided, but his interest in Christian theology did not automatically imply that he was a closet champion of medieval ideas.

Similarly, however much his depiction of the lord/bondsman dialectic may have owed to his understanding of feudal relations, it should be remembered that Hegel was also an enthusiastic reader of the new science of economics developed at the time by Scottish scholars such as James Steuart (1712–1780) and Adam Smith (c. 1723–1790). Although his concept of "civil society" went beyond a bourgeois notion of market relations based on the exchange of commodities, he understood the latter as a valid element in the complexly articulated world of modernity. Hegel was, in fact, never nostalgic for feudal society as a whole way of life. By the time he wrote his *Philosophy of History*, Hegel could bemoan the collapse of the Carolingian empire into "that infinite falsehood which rules the destinies of the *Middle Ages* and constitutes their life and spirit."⁶⁴ The disappearance of a universal state meant the dependence of defenseless individuals on the protection of feudal lords. Hegel, to be sure, understood the value of a functional equivalent of medieval corporations against a state that would be only abstractly universal, but as Shlomo Avineri showed many years ago, his theory of the modern state with its enlightened bureaucracy was anything but a regressive celebration of premodern political arrangements.⁶⁵ Those of his contemporaries who yearned for their return – historicists such as

---

⁶² See, for example, Delany, "Marxist Medievalists." Marxist philosophers have also found inspiration in medieval philosophy, for example, Ernst Bloch's (1885–1977) celebration of Avicenna (c. 970–1037) and what he called "the Aristotelian Left" and Alain Badiou's location of redemptive universalism in St Paul (c. 5 CE–c. 67 CE). There have also been claims that Marx did not have a linear notion of historical development, but this is not the place to litigate them.
⁶³ See Dickey, *Hegel*.
⁶⁴ Hegel, *The Philosophy of History*, 366.
⁶⁵ Avineri, *Hegel's Theory of the Modern State*.

Karl von Savigny (1779–1861), Adam Müller (1779–1829), and Ludwig von Haller (1768–1854) – he explicitly disdained.

It would also be helpful to investigate more extensively Du Bois's education at the University of Berlin in 1892–94, or what has been called his "love affair with Imperial Germany."[66] He attended the seminars of Heinrich von Treitschke (1834–1896), Adolf Wagner (1890–1944) and Gustav von Schmoller (1838–1917), all nonliberal nationalist stalwarts of the Bismarckian *Kaiserreich*. It is significant, according to the historian Kenneth Barkin that Du Bois "chose to study not with philosophers, as he had as a Harvard undergraduate, or with professional historians, as in his graduate years. Berlin was full of Hegelians, but he chose to study political economy, or what would evolve into the discipline of sociology."[67] Even if he had focused on philosophy, moreover, Du Bois would have not had the benefit of reading Andrew Cole's exploration of the medieval echoes in Hegelian dialectics, but would have more likely read him as a defender of the modern bureaucratic state.

Awareness of the shortcomings of straightforward, progressive temporality can lead to a full-throated call for a reduced chronology that denies any "afterness" at all. Thus, it is not surprising to find a recent issue of the *Romanic Review* devoted to the importance of Bruno Latour (b. 1947) for medieval studies introduced by an essay provocatively titled "We Have Always Been Medieval."[68] Latour's controversial critique of the rigid dualisms – subject/object, nature/culture, real/constructed, and so on – underlying modernity's self-understanding implies, the essay suggests, a reappraisal of the medieval alternative in which hybridized, intersecting, fluid mediations of apparent binaries prevailed. This does not warrant a simple reversal of the normative hierarchy of modern and medieval, which would be a nostalgic exercise that inadvertently replicates the dichotomizing it purports to overturn (as we have seen D. Vance Smith also argue in his reading of Fanon's dialectical anti-Manicheanism). It means instead effacing the boundary

---

[66] Barkin, "W. E. B. Du Bois' Love Affair with Imperial Germany."
[67] Barkin, "Berlin Days," 92.
[68] Desmond and Guynn, "We Have Always Been Medieval." The title plays on Latour's provocative *We Have Never Been Modern*, and was already employed in passing in the introduction to Cole and Smith, eds., *The Legitimacy of the Middle Ages*, 24. In that latter collection, Ethan Knapp ("Medieval Studies") remarks, "much of the most innovative work of the past few decades has been generated by calls for medievalists to abandon their institutionally powerful sense of their professional alterity and acknowledge that, in some way or other, they and their objects of study have always been modern" (160). Whatever the direction of the conflation, it undermines not only the alterity of the two epochs, but also the sense of afterness, however understood, that relates one to the other.

between the two allegedly distinct historical epochs and acknowledging how stubbornly intertwined they remain.

Helen Brookman's spirited exploration of Dorothy Sayers's (1893–1957) intense relationship with Dante, whose work she translated in the 1940s and 1950s, reveals the performative effects of this putative intertwining. Sayers's desire for an "I–Thou" intimacy with Dante led her not merely to want to "speak with the dead," to borrow Stephen Greenblatt's familiar phrase, but somehow to sleep with one of them. Or at least the fantasy of an amorous affair with the great poet seems to have motivated a number of Sayers's transgressive readings of his poetic legacy. Brookman makes an intriguing case for the benefits of Sayers's unabashedly erotic involvement with Dante, which challenged normative masculinist interpretative approaches based on the familial model of the poet as paternal authority. Rather than dismissing Sayers's musings as the acting out of a troubled woman over her head in the world of professional scholarship, a woman whose claim on our attention resides solely in her popular detective fiction, Brookman offers a strong feminist reading of Sayers's disruption of traditional academic protocols of disinterested distance and genealogical influence. And in the process, she shows that Sayers helped us understand Dante's own advanced attitudes towards the legitimate erotic desires of women.

It is nonetheless worth pondering the costs of collapsing the distance between past and present and sacrificing the strangeness or otherness of a past whose inhabitants may not be as anxious to sleep with us as we might be with them. A transferential projection often occurs between present readers and historical figures, as the intellectual historian Dominick LaCapra has frequently argued.[69] But as Sigmund Freud (1856–1939) understood it, transference implies a delayed imposition of an unresolved emotion onto a current object, who serves as a screen for its projection. In therapy, it involves the reactivation of a past feeling in the present, but in historical interactions, time's arrow goes in the opposite direction. The historian transfers current feelings onto a lost object of desire. All of this might suggest an affective version of Latour's intertwining of medieval and modern. But what is absent is the possibility of countertransference, which in the therapeutic situation involves the analyst's feelings towards the patient. Dante's erotic investment in Sayers is, of course, an impossibility; his "thou" is never really an "I" to hers. The stubbornness of before and after cannot be entirely undone. Nor should it be, if we honor the psychoanalytic model

---

[69] See, for example, LaCapra, "Is Everyone a *Mentalité* Case?"

of working through transference, rather than wallowing in it, as a means to resolving symptomatic behavior.

A similar conclusion follows if we substitute "feudal" for "medieval" in the title of the *Romanic Review* issue called "We Have Always Been Medieval." Doing so would make it impossible, among other things, to read Marx's *Capital* as a meaningful depiction of an economic system with its own logic of reproduction and crisis that came after the "primitive accumulation" that occurred in the early modern period. Nor could we draw on Max Weber's (1864–1920) ideal typical distinction between "traditional" and "rational-legal" modes of authority, which is both an analytic and an historical distinction, albeit without a simple narrative of ascent (as shown by Weber's famous lamenting the "iron cage" of modernity). And perhaps even more troubling in the wholesale erasure of the epochal threshold would be the implicit denial of the possible advent of any radical newness in history, which is reduced instead, as we saw in the case of Curtius's adoption of Jungian archetypes, to repetitive figural synchronicity.[70]

We have, I think, learned two somewhat different lessons from the essays in this collection. The first is that although time's arrow rarely flies on a straight or unidirectional course, we cannot entirely dispense with the sense of before and after that orients us in the historical world. However arbitrary the alleged thresholds between putative epochs, however porous their boundaries, however entangled the threads of their stories, they cannot be entirely effaced. A night in which all cows are piebald is as ahistorical as one in which they are all black. The simple fact that medieval men and women could never have called themselves denizens of "the Middle Ages" and modernity could not have defined itself self-consciously as such without contrasting itself with a prior premodern epoch suggests that the two cannot be simply conflated.

Many in the Middle Ages, it should be recalled, were themselves acutely aware of their coming after a pagan, classical past. They were often ambivalent about its legacy, which at certain times they sought to recover and appropriate, while at others preferred to denigrate as a remnant of a bypassed era before the arrival of "the good news."[71] The carrying over of the Roman Empire and much of its culture into Christendom – the *translatio imperii* – was begun as early as Eusebius (*c.* 263-*c.* 339) and

---

[70] For a consideration of this issue, see Jay, "Historical Explanation and the Event."
[71] Ironically, this term (from the Greek *euangelian*) had been introduced during the reign of Emperor Augustus and acquired religious significance in the cult that surrounded him.

Augustine.[72] But with due respect to Curtius, it need not be understood as the affirmation of the normative superiority of the classical world to the medieval. And of course, the supersessionist logic that turned the Hebrew Bible into an "Old Testament" as opposed to a "New" one – a distinction often traced to Tertullian (c. 155-c. 220) in his *Against Praxeas* in the early third century – drew on both a sense of temporal progress and prefigurative anticipation. The BC/AD distinction, which turned the Incarnation into a radical rupture in secular as well as sacred history, is normally understood to have gained popularity only in the ninth century after Charlemagne adopted the system for dating acts of government throughout Europe.[73]

If medieval culture was aware of both continuity and discontinuity, it would be wrong to deny the same insight to the epoch that claimed to replace it. As Blumenberg has noted, the modern age continued to grapple with perennial questions pondered by ancient and medieval thinkers, albeit without satisfactorily resolving them. But at the same time, he insisted, modernity "in contrast to the Middle Ages is not present in advance of its self-interpretation, and while its self-interpretation is not what propelled the emergence of the modern age, it is something that the age has continually needed in order to give itself form."[74] The very concept of epochal rupture was, in other words, a sign of the new epoch, even if at times it overestimated the complete novelty of the *Neuzeit*.

We have also learned to be wary of the assumption that epochal differentiation necessarily brings with it an implicit judgment about the superiority of one period over the other, whether situated in a triumphalist or declension narrative. It is always possible to recall Leopold von Ranke's (1795–1886) familiar words from his 1854 lectures to King Maximilian of Bavaria: "every epoch is immediate to God, and its worth is not at all based on what derives from it but rests in its own existence, in its own self."[75] What comes after, in other words, is not necessarily better than what precedes it (including the Afterword to a stimulating collection of essays!).

On a more proximate level, the authors in our collection are fully aware that they come after the mid-twentieth-century interpretations of the Middle Ages, which can now be treated as historical moments in their own right. Similarly, this Afterword has had to register its composition in

---

[72] Pocock, "The Historiography of the *Translatio Imperii*."
[73] It might also be noted for those in the Middle Ages who followed the Jewish calendar, the birth of Jesus occurred in the ordinary year 3757 and did not signify an epochal shift.
[74] Blumenberg, *The Legitimacy of the Modern Age*, 468.
[75] von Ranke, "On Progress in History," 21.

the midst of the pandemic and racial justice crisis of 2020, which infuses it with a certain awareness not yet available when the essays were written. In one sense we may be feel closer to a past that haunts us or returns in uncanny ways, but in another we become more conscious of the need, as Zumthor suggested, to mind the gap. The very scandal of preposterous temporality is, after all, premised on the assumption that the default position is to distinguish between predecessor and posterity, however much we may then problematize it.

The second lesson is that we homogenize "the Middle Ages" into a coherent and uniform epoch with its own integral, immanent logic at our peril.[76] Here the concept of "*mouvance*" introduced by Paul Zumthor in his *Essai de poétique médiévale* of 1972 is especially suggestive. Contrasting the relatively fixed texts found in manuscripts of certain late-medieval French poets with the much more common earlier medieval combination of authorial anonymity and textual variation, he realized that any attempt to fix an "authentic" or "original" text was often deeply problematic. Combined with the oral nature of medieval literary performances, noted in Saltzman's treatment of Zumthor in his essay on hermeneutics, the mobility of texts complicates any attribution of ownership to a single proper name, even if we often use them as what Lacan would have called *points de capiton* (upholstery buttons) to fix moments in an infinite signifying chain.

The same caution is necessary when we unreflectively adopt the historical proper name "the Middle Ages" as if it referred to a coherent, unified, singular epoch, rather than a convenient term of art used by postmedieval observers to homogenize what was such a complex, heterogeneous, and even contradictory millennium of history. It is prudent to recall, returning to Jameson's notion of our "Imaginary" of the Middle Ages, that at least in Lacan's use of that term it connotes a problematic misrecognition of reality tied to the "mirror stage" of psychic development. The periodization that draws on it relies on a dubious notion of the "essence" of an

---

[76] For a nuanced discussion of the issue of epochs, which argues for a modified realist rather than fully nominalist position, based on new answers to perennial questions whose previous answers have failed, see Blumenberg, *The Legitimacy of the Modern Age*, part 4, chapter 1. Blumenberg's argument is aimed at both modernity's claim that it has wiped the slate clean and started ex nihilo and the secularization theorists' counterclaim that modernity merely recycles the substantive wine of theology in new bottles. For a critique of his position, which, however, flattens out some of its complexities, see Davis, "The Sense of an Epoch."

However persuasive Blumenberg's analysis might be, it is important to note that he relies on a notion of an epoch that is entirely cultural in definition. A materialist might wonder how reoccupied answer positions fit with transformations in the mode of production.

age, which can be easily summarized or epitomized.[77] Not only have we encountered fundamental variations in theological, political, and aesthetic attitudes, but we have also confronted the imperative to break down traditional boundaries and be more inclusive in our reckoning of whose stories are being told. And perhaps most striking of all, focusing on a previous generation of medieval scholars, acknowledging both their insights and their limits, has made it clear that "afterness," whether understood linearly or preposterously, is an ongoing dimension of any self-reflective attempt to write the history of a past epoch. For we too are upholstery buttons in a chain of meaning – or, better put, links in a tangle of multiple chains – that is destined to continue uncoiling and retangling for a very long time to come. However great the wisdom of our hindsight, we are denied the vantage point of that mythical last historian, who putatively will come after all.

[77] For a critique of essentializing the Middle Ages, see Rasula, "Medusa's Gaze," 235.

Bibliography

Agamben, Giorgio. *Homo Sacer: Sovereign Power and Bare Life.* Translated by Daniel Heller-Roazen. Stanford: Stanford University Press, 1998.
Albin, Andrew, Mary C. Erler, Thomas O'Donnell, Nicholas L. Paul, and Nina Rowe, eds. *Whose Middle Ages?: Teachable Moments for an Ill-Used Past.* New York: Fordham University Press, 2019.
Alighieri, Dante. *De Monarchia.* Translated by Richard Kay. Turnhout: Brepols, 1998.
Alighieri, Dante. *Hell: The Divine Comedy.* Vol. 1. Translated by Dorothy L. Sayers. London: Penguin Classics, 1949.
Alighieri, Dante. *Paradise: The Divine Comedy.* Vol. 3. Translated by Dorothy L. Sayers and Barbara Reynolds. London: Penguin Classics, 1962.
Alighieri, Dante. *Purgatory: The Divine Comedy.* Vol. 2. Translated by Dorothy L. Sayers. London: Penguin Classics, 1955.
Alighieri, Dante. *The Inferno.* Edited by Hermann Oelsner. Translated by John Carlyle. London: J. M. Dent and E. P. Dutton, 1900.
Allen, Diogenes, and Eric O. Springsted. "The Baptism of Simone Weil." In *Spirit, Nature, and Community: Issues in the Thought of Simone Weil.* 3–18. Albany: State University of New York Press, 1994.
Alloa, Emmanuel. "Could Perspective Ever Be a Symbolic Form? Revisiting Panofsky with Cassirer." *Journal of Aesthetics and Phenomenology* 2, no. 1 (2015): 51–72.
Altieri, Charles. "The Sensuous Dimension of Literary Experience: An Alternative to Materialist Theory." *New Literary History* 38, no. 1 (2007): 71–98.
Amato, Joseph. *Mounier and Maritain: A French Catholic Understanding of the Modern World.* Tuscaloosa: University of Alabama Press, 1975.
Amis, Kingsley. "Anglo-Saxon Platitudes." Review of *Beowulf: A Prose Translation,* by David Wright. *The Spectator,* April 5, 1957: 17.
Amis, Kingsley. "Beowulf." In *A Case of Samples: Poems, 1946–1956.* 14. London: Victor Gollancz, 1956.
Amis, Kingsley. "Beowulf." In *Collected Poems, 1944–79.* 18. London: Hutchinson, 1979.
Amis, Kingsley. "Beowulf." *Essays in Criticism* 4, no. 1 (1954): 85.
Amis, Kingsley. *Bright November.* London: Fortune Press, 1947.

Amis, Kingsley. "Dodos Less Daring." Review of *Anglo-Saxon Attitudes*, by Angus Wilson. *The Spectator*, June 1, 1956: 764–65.
Amis, Kingsley. *Lucky Jim*. London: Victor Gollancz, 1953.
Amis, Kingsley. *Memoirs*. London: Hutchinson, 1991.
Amis, Kingsley. *The Letters of Kingsley Amis*. Edited by Zachary Leader. London: Harper Collins, 2000.
Amis, Kingsley, Dick Clement, and Ian Le Frenais. *The Further Adventures of Lucky Jim*. TV. British Broadcasting Corporation, 1967.
Amis, Kingsley, Patrick Campbell, and John Boulting. *Lucky Jim*. DVD. Charter Film Productions, 1957.
Anderson, Amanda. *Bleak Liberalism*. Chicago: University of Chicago Press, 2016.
Anderson, Kevin. *Lenin, Hegel, and Western Marxism: A Critical Study*. Chicago: University of Illinois Press, 1995.
Anderson, Perry. *Passages from Antiquity to Feudalism*. New York: Verso, 2013.
Anievas, Alexander, and Kerem Nişancioğlu. *How the West Came to Rule: The Geopolitical Origins of Capitalism*. London: Pluto Press, 2015.
Arendt, Hannah. *Eichmann in Jerusalem: A Report on the Banality of Evil*. New York: Penguin, 1994.
Arendt, Hannah. *Lectures on Kant's Political Philosophy*. Edited by Ronald Beiner. Chicago: University of Chicago Press, 1982.
Arendt, Hannah. *Love and Saint Augustine*. Edited by Joanna Vecchiarelli Scott and Judith Chelius Stark. Chicago: University of Chicago Press, 1996.
Arendt, Hannah. *On Revolution*. New York: Penguin, 2006.
Arendt, Hannah. *On Violence*. New York: Harcourt, 1960.
Arendt, Hannah. "Organized Guilt and Universal Responsibility." In *Essays in Understanding, 1930–1954: Formation, Exile, and Totalitarianism*, edited by Jerome Kohn. 121–32. New York: Schocken Books, 2005.
Arendt, Hannah. "Preface." In *Between Past and Future*. 3–15. New York: Penguin, 2006.
Arendt, Hannah. "Reflections on Little Rock." *Dissent Magazine* (Winter, 1959): 45–56.
Arendt, Hannah. "The Aftermath of Nazi Rule: Report from Germany." *Commentary* 10 (1950): 342–53.
Arendt, Hannah. *The Human Condition*, 2nd ed. Chicago: University of Chicago Press, 1998.
Arendt, Hannah. *The Life of the Mind*, one volume edition. New York: Harcourt, 1981.
Arendt, Hannah. "The Meaning of Love in Politics: A Letter by Hannah Arendt to James Baldwin." *HannahArendt.net: Zeitschrift für Politisches Denken* 2, no. 1 (2006). www.hannaharendt.net/index.php/han/article/view/95/156.
Arendt, Hannah. *The Origins of Totalitarianism*. New York: Harvest, 1979.
Arendt, Hannah. *The Portable Hannah Arendt*. Edited by Peter Baehr. New York: Penguin Books, 2000.
Arendt, Hannah, and Martin Heidegger. *Letters: 1925–1975*. Edited by Ursula Ludz. Translated by Andrew Shields. New York: Harcourt, 2003.

Aristotle. *Categories.* Vol. 1 of *The Complete Works of Aristotle.* Translated by J. L. Ackrill. Edited by Jonathan Barnes. 3–24. Princeton: Princeton University Press, 1991.
Aristotle. *Catégories.* Translated by J. Tricot. Paris: J. Vrin, 2004.
Arthos, John. "'The Word Is not Reflexive': Mind and Word in Aquinas and Gadamer." *American Catholic Philosophical Quarterly* 78, no. 4 (2004): 581–608.
Asad, Talal. *Formations of the Secular: Christianity, Islam, Modernity.* Stanford: Stanford University Press, 2003.
Ashley, Kathleen, and Véronique Plesch. "The Cultural Processes of 'Appropriation'." *Journal of Medieval and Early Modern Studies* 32, no. 1 (2002): 1–15.
Assmann, Jan. *Herrschaft und Heil: Politische Theologie in Altägypten, Israel und Europa.* Munich: Carl Hanser Verlag, 2000.
Aston, T. H., and C. H. E. Philpin, eds. *The Brenner Debate: Agrarian Class Structure and Economic Development in Pre-Industrial Europe.* Cambridge: Cambridge University Press, 1985.
Auden, W. H. *Another Time: Poems.* London: Faber and Faber, 1940.
Auerbach, Erich. *Die Teilnahme in dem Vorarbeiten zu einem neuen Strafgesetzbuch.* Berlin: Juristische Verlagsbuchhandlung Dr. jur. Frensdorf, 1913.
Auerbach, Erich. "Epilegomena zu *Mimesis.*" *Romanische Forschungen* 65, no. 1/2 (1953): 1–18. Reprinted as "Epilegomena to Mimesis." Translated by Jan M. Ziolkowski. Appendix to *Mimesis.* 559–74. Princeton: Princeton University Press, 2003.
Auerbach, Erich. "*Figura.*" In *Gesammelte Aufsätze zur Romanischen Philologie.* 55–92. Bern: Francke, 1967. Translated as "*Figura.*" In *Time, History, and Literature: Selected Essays of Erich Auerbach*, edited by James I. Porter. Translated by Jane O. Newman. 65–113. Princeton: Princeton University Press, 2014.
Auerbach, Erich. *Introduction aux Études de Philologie Romane.* Frankfurt: Klostermann, 1949. Translated as *Introduction to Romance Languages and Literature: Latin, French, Spanish, Provençal, Italian.* Translated by Guy Daniels. New York: Capricorn Books, 1961.
Auerbach, Erich. *Literary Language and its Public in Late Latin Antiquity and the Middle Ages.* Translated by Ralph Manheim. Princeton: Princeton University Press, 1993.
Auerbach, Erich. *Mimesis: Dargestellte Wirklichkeit in der abendländischen Literatur.* Tubingen and Basel: A. Francke, 2001. Translated as *Mimesis: The Representation of Reality in Western Literature.* Translated by Willard R. Trask. Princeton: Princeton University Press, 2003.
Auerbach, Erich. *[Renaissance Novellas] Zur Technik der Frührenaissancenovelle in Italien und Frankreich.* Heidelberg: Carl Winter, 1921.
Auerbach, Erich. "Romantik und Realismus." In *Erich Auerbach: Geschichte und Aktualität eines europäischen Philologen.* Edited by Martin Treml and Karlheinz Barck. 426–38. Berlin: Kulturverlag Kadmos, 2007. Translated as

"Romanticism and Realism." In *Time, History, and Literature: Selected Essays of Erich Auerbach*, edited by James I. Porter. Translated by Jane O. Newman. 144–56. Princeton: Princeton University Press, 2014.

Auerbach, Erich. "Über die ernste Nachahmung des Alltäglichen." In *Erich Auerbach. Geschichte und Aktualität eines europäischen Philologen*, edited by Martin Treml and Karlheinz Barck. 439–65. Berlin: Kulturverlag Kadmos, 2007.

Augustine of Hippo. "Against the Epistle of Manichaeus Called Fundamental." In *The Works of Aurelius Augustine*, Vol. 5, edited and translated by Marcus Dods. 6–144. Edinburgh: T. & T. Clark, 1872.

Augustine of Hippo. *City of God, Vol. 4, Books 12-15*. Translated by Philip Levine. Cambridge, MA: Harvard University Press, 1966.

Augustine of Hippo. *Contra epistulam Manichaei quam uocant fundamenti*. Edited by Josephus Zycha. Corpus Scriptorum Ecclesiasticorum Latinorum 25. 193–248. Vienna, 1891.

Augustine of Hippo. *Contra epistulam Manichaei quam uocant fundamenti*. In *Sancti Aurelii Augustini Opera Omnia*, edited by Jacques-Paul Migne. Patrologia Latina 42. 173–206. Paris, 1841.

Augustine of Hippo. *De libero arbitrio libri III*. Edited by W. M. Green. In *Aurelii Augustini Opera*, pars II, 2. Corpus Christianorum Series Latina 29. 205–321. Turnhout: Brepols, 1970.

Avineri, Shlomo. *Hegel's Theory of the Modern State*. Cambridge: Cambridge University Press, 1972.

Baeumer, Max L., ed. *Toposforschung*. Darmstadt: Wissenschaftliche Buchgesellschaft, 1973.

Badiou, Alain. *Saint Paul: The Foundations of Universalism*. Translated by Ray Brassier. Stanford: Stanford University Press, 2003.

Bahti, Timothy. "Auerbach's *Mimesis*: Figural Structure and Historical Narrative." In *After Strange Texts: The Role of Theory in the Study of Literature*, edited by Gregory S. Jay and David L. Miller. 124–45. Tuscaloosa: University of Alabama Press, 1985.

Bajohr, Hannes. "The Unity of the World: Arendt and Blumenberg on the Anthropology of Metaphor." *The Germanic Review* 90, no. 1 (2015): 42–59.

Bambach, Charles R. *Heidegger, Dilthey, and the Crisis of Historicism*. Ithaca, NY: Cornell University Press, 1995.

Bandmann, Günter. *Mittelalterliche Architektur als Bedeutungsträger*. Berlin: Gebr. Mann, 1951.

Barclay, Fiona, Charlotte Ann Chopin, and Martin Evans. "Introduction: Settler Colonialism and French Algeria." *Settler Colonial Studies* 8 (2018): 115–40.

Bardy, Gustave. *Saint Augustin: l'homme et l'œuvre*. Paris: Desclée de Brouwer, 1940.

Barkat, Sidi Mohammed. *Le corps d'exception: Les artifices du pouvoir colonial et la destruction de la vie*. Paris: Editions Amsterdam, 2005.

Barkin, Kenneth D. "'Berlin Days', 1892–94: W. E. B. Du Bois and German Political Economy." *boundary 2* 27, no. 3 (2000): 79–101.

Barkin, Kenneth. "W. E. B. Du Bois' Love Affair with Imperial Germany." *German Studies Review* 28, no. 2 (2005): 285–302.

Baron, Salo W. "Germany's Ghetto, Past and Present: A Perspective on Nazi Laws Against the Jews." *Independent Journal of Columbia University* 3, no. 3 (1935): 1–4.

Baron, Salo W. "The Eichmann Trial: European Jewry before and after Hitler." *American Jewish Year Book* 63 (1962): 3–53.

Barthes, Roland. *Le Plaisir du texte*. Paris: Éditions du Seuil, 1973. Translated as *The Pleasure of the Text*. Translated by Richard Miller. New York: Hill and Wang, 1975; *The Pleasure of the Text*. Translated by Richard Miller, with a Note on the Text by Richard Howard. London: Jonathan Cape, 1976.

Bassnett, Susan. *Comparative Literature: A Critical Introduction*. Cambridge: Blackwell, 1993.

Bataille, Georges. *L'expérience intérieure*. Paris: Gallimard, 1954. Translated as *Inner Experience*. Translated by Stuart Kendall. Albany: State University Press of New York, 2014.

Beaumont, Matthew. "Introduction: Reclaiming Realism." In *Adventures in Realism*, edited by Matthew Beaumont. 1–12. Oxford: Blackwell, 2007.

Beckwith, Sarah. "Preserving, Conserving, Deserving the Past: A Meditation on Ruin as Relic in Postwar Britain in Five Fragments." In *A Place to Believe in: Locating Medieval Landscapes*, edited by Clare Lees and Gillian R. Overing. 191–210. University Park: Pennsylvania State Press, 2006.

Bédé, Jean-Albert. "Alain, pseud. of Emile Chartier." In *Columbia Dictionary of Modern European Literature*, edited by Jean-Albert Bédé and William B. Edgerton. 10–11. New York: Columbia University Press, 1980.

BeDuhn, Jason David. *Augustine's Manichaean Dilemma, 1: Conversion and Apostasy, 373–388 C.E.* Philadelphia: University of Pennsylvania Press, 2010.

BeDuhn, Jason David. *Augustine's Manichaean Dilemma, 2: Making a 'Catholic' Self, 388–401 C.E.* Philadelphia: University of Pennsylvania Press, 2013.

Belkacem, Krim. "Frantz Fanon, notre frère." *El Moudjahid* 88 (December 21, 1961). Reprint, *El Moudjahid* 3: 646–51.

Benhabib, Seyla. *Exile, Statelessness and Migration: Playing Chess with History from Hannah Arendt to Isaiah Berlin*. Princeton: Princeton University Press, 2018.

Benjamin, Walter. *Origin of the German Trauerspiel*. Translated by Howard Eiland. Cambridge, MA: Harvard University Press, 2019.

Benjamin, Walter. "Theses on the Philosophy of History." In *Illuminations: Essays and Reflections*, edited by Hannah Arendt. Translated by Harry Zohn. 253–64. New York: Harcourt Brace, 1968.

Benson, Larry D. *The Loyalty Oath Controversy: A Bibliography*. Monticello, IL: Vance Bibliographies, 1990.

Bergson, Henri. *Les deux sources de la morale et de la religion*. 4th ed. Paris: Librarie Félix Alcan, 1933. Translated as *The Two Sources of Morality and Religion*. Translated by R. Ashley Audra and Cloudesley Brereton. Westport: Greenwood Press, 1974.

Bernstein, J. M. "Promising and Civil Disobedience: Arendt's Political Modernism." In *Thinking in Dark Times: Hannah Arendt on Ethics and Politics*, edited by Roger Berkowitz, Jeffrey Katz, and Thomas Keenan. 115–28. New York: Fordham University Press, 2010.
Bernstein, J. M. *Why Read Hannah Arendt Now*. Cambridge: Polity Press, 2018.
Biddick, Kathleen. *The Shock of Medievalism*. Durham, NC: Duke University Press, 1998.
Bjork, Robert E., ed. and trans. *Old English Shorter Poems*, Vol. 2. Dumbarton Oaks Medieval Library 11. Cambridge, MA: Harvard University Press, 2014.
Blanton, C. D. "Medieval Currencies: Nominalism and Art." In *The Legitimacy of the Middle Ages: On the Unwritten History of Theory*, edited by Andrew Cole and D. Vance Smith. 194–232. Durham, NC: Duke University Press, 2010.
Bloch, Ernst. *Avicenna and the Aristotelian Left*. Translated by Loren Goldman and Peter Thompson. New York: Columbia University Press, 2019.
Bloch, Ernst. *Heritage of Our Times*. Translated by Neville Plaice and Stephen Plaice. Oxford: Polity Press, 1991.
Bloch, Marc. *Feudal Society*. Translated by L. A. Manyon. Chicago: University of Chicago Press, 1968.
Bloch, Marc. *Les rois thaumaturges: Étude sur le caractère surnaturel attribué à la puissance royale, particulièrement en France et en Angleterre*. Paris: Gallimard, 1924.
Bloom, Harold. *The Anxiety of Influence: A Theory of Poetry*. New York, Oxford: Oxford University Press, 1997.
Blumenberg, Hans. *The Legitimacy of the Modern Age*. Translated by Robert M. Wallace. Cambridge, MA: MIT Press, 1983.
Bober, Harry. "Gothic Architecture and Scholasticism by Erwin Panofsky." *The Art Bulletin* 35, no. 4 (1953): 310–12.
Bois, Guy. "Against the Neo-Malthusian Orthodoxy." In *The Brenner Debate: Agrarian Class Structure and Economic Development in Pre-Industrial Europe*, edited by T. H. Aston and C. H. E. Philpin. 107–18. Cambridge: Cambridge University Press, 1985.
Bone, Gavin. *Anglo-Saxon Poetry*. Oxford: Clarendon Press, 1943.
Bone, Gavin. *Beowulf in Modern Verse with an Essay and Pictures*. Oxford: Basil Blackwell, 1945.
Botshon, Lisa, and Meredith Goldsmith. *Middlebrow Moderns: Popular American Women Writers of the 1920s*. Boston: Northeastern University Press, 2003.
Bourdieu, Pierre. "Postface to Erwin Panofsky, *Architecture Gothique and Pensée Scolastique*." Translated by Laurence Petit. In *The Premodern Condition: Medievalism and the Making of Theory*, by Bruce Holsinger. 221–42. Chicago: University of Chicago Press, 2005.
Boureau, Alain. *Histoires d'un historien: Kantorowicz*. Paris: Gallimard, 1990.
Bourg, Julian. "The Red Guards of Paris: French Student Maoism of the 1960s." *History of European Ideas* 31, no. 4 (2005): 472–90.
Brabazon, James. *Dorothy L. Sayers: A Biography*. New York: Avon Books, 1981.
Bradbury, Malcolm. "Wilson, Sir Angus Frank Johnstone (1913–1991), Novelist and Biographer." In *Oxford Dictionary of National Biography*. https://doi.org/10.1093/ref:odnb/50701

Branner, Robert. "Review of *The Church of St. Martin at Angers* by G. H. Forsyth, Jr.; *L'Abbaye royale de Saint-Denis* by Sumner McK. Crosby; *Gothic Architecture and Scholasticism* (Wimmer Lecture 1948) by Erwin Panofsky." *Journal of the Society of Architectural Historians* 13, no. 1 (1954): 28–31.
Brient, Elizabeth. "Hans Blumenberg and Hannah Arendt on the 'Unworldly Worldliness' of the Modern Age." *Journal of the History of Ideas* 61, no. 3 (2000): 513–30.
British Library. "Anglo-Saxon Kingdoms: Art, Word, War." October 19, 2018–February 19, 2019. www.bl.uk/events/anglo-saxon-kingdoms
British Library. "Windrush: Songs in a Strange Land." June 1, 2018–October 21, 2018. www.bl.uk/events/windrush-songs-in-a-strange-land
Brooks, Francesca. *Poet of the Medieval Modern: Reading the Early Medieval Library with David Jones*. Oxford: Oxford University Press, 2021.
Brown, Bill. "Textual Materialism." *PMLA* 125, no. 1 (2010): 24–28.
Brown, Bill. "The Dark Wood of Postmodernity (Space, Faith, Allegory)." *PMLA* 120, no. 3 (2005): 734–50.
Brown, Wendy. *Edgework: Critical Essays on Knowledge and Power*. Princeton: Princeton University Press, 2005.
Brown, Wendy. *Manhood and Politics: A Feminist Reading in Political Theory*. Totowa, NJ: Rowman & Littlefield, 1988.
Brown, Wendy. *Undoing the Demos: Neoliberalism's Stealth Revolution*. New York: Zone Books, 2015.
Bryher, Winifred. *Beowulf: A Novel*. New York: Pantheon Press, 1956. Translated as *Beowulf: roman d'une maison de thé dans Londres bombardé*. Translated by Hélène Malvan. Paris: Mercure de France, 1948.
Bryher, Winifred. *The Days of Mars: A Memoir, 1940–1946*. London: Calder & Boyars, 1972.
Bryher, Winifred. *The Fourteenth of October: A Novel*. London: Collins, 1954.
Buchanan, Peter. "*Beowulf*, Bryher, and the Blitz: A Queer History." In *Dating Beowulf: Studies in Intimacy*, edited by Daniel C. Remein and Erica Weaver, 279–303. Manchester: Manchester University Press, 2019.
Burckhardt, Jacob. *The Civilization of the Renaissance in Italy*. Translated by L. Goldscheider. London: Phaidon Press Limited, 1995.
Bures, Eliah Matthew. "Fantasies of Friendship: Ernst Jünger and the German Right's Search for Community in Germany." PhD diss., University of California, Berkeley, 2014.
Burger, Glenn, and Stephen F. Kruger, eds. *Queering the Middle Ages*. Minneapolis: University of Minnesota Press, 2001.
Burke, Peter. *The French Historical Revolution: The "Annales" School, 1929–89*. Stanford: Stanford University Press, 1990.
Burroughs, Michael D. "Hannah Arendt, 'Reflections on Little Rock', and White Ignorance." *Critical Philosophy of Race* 3 (2015): 52–78.
Burrow, Colin. "Introduction to the 2013 Edition." In *European Literature and the Latin Middle Ages*, by Ernst Robert Curtius. xi–xx. Princeton: Princeton University Press, 2013.
Bursill-Hall, G. L., ed. and trans. *Thomas of Erfurt: Grammatica Speculativa*. London: Longmans, 1972.

Butler, Judith. "Hannah Arendt's Death Sentences." *Comparative Literature Studies* 48, no. 3 (2011): 280–95.
Butler, Judith. *Notes Towards a Performative Theory of Assembly*. Cambridge, MA: Harvard University Press, 2015.
Butler, Judith. *Parting Ways: Jewishness and the Critique of Zionism*. New York: Columbia University Press, 2012.
Butorac, Sean Kim. "Hannah Arendt, James Baldwin and the Politics of Love." *Political Research Quarterly* 71, no. 1 (2018): 1–12.
Bynum, Caroline Walker. *Holy Feast and Holy Fast: The Religious Significance of Food to Medieval Women*. Berkeley: University of California Press, 1987.
Cabaud, Jacques. *Simone Weil: A Fellowship in Love*. London: Harvill Press, 1964.
Cabrol, Fernand, and Henri Leclerc, eds. *Dictionnaire d'archéologie chrétienne et de liturgie*. Paris: Letouzey et Ane, 1928.
Caciola, Nancy. *Discerning Spirits: Divine and Demonic Possession in the Middle Ages*. Ithaca, NY: Cornell University Press, 2003.
Calhoun, D. H. "Review of J. R. R. Tolkien, *Lord of the Rings*." *Princeton Alumni Weekly* 58, no. 9 (1957), special insert 4.
Cameron, J. M. "The Life and Death of Simone Weil." *New York Review of Books* 24, no. 3 (March 3, 1977): 3.
Campbell, Joseph. *The Hero with a Thousand Faces*. 2nd ed. Bollingen Series 17. Princeton: Princeton University Press, 1972.
Cantillon, Alain. "Ernst Kantorowicz: personne ou personnage? Entretien avec Alain Boureau." *Esprit* 184, no. 8/9 (1992): 54–59.
Cantor, Norman F. *Inventing the Middle Ages: The Lives, Works, and Ideas of the Great Medievalists of the Twentieth Century*. New York: William Morrow and Company, 1991.
Cantor, Norman F. *Medieval History: The Life and Death of a Civilization*. New York: Macmillan, 1963.
Cardona, J. Aurell, ed. *Rewriting the Middle Ages in the Twentieth Century*. 3 vols. Turnhout: Brepols, 2005–2015.
Cassiodorus. *Expositio psalmorum*. Edited by M. Adriaen. Corpus Christianorum Series Latina 97 and 98. Turnhout: Brepols, 1958.
Cassirer, Ernst. *Das Erkenntnisproblem in der Philosophie und Wissenschaft der neueren Zeit*. 3 vols. Berlin: Bruno Cassirer, 1906–1920. Continued, though not translated, as *The Problem of Knowledge: Philosophy, Science, and History Since Hegel*. New Haven: Yale University Press, 1950.
Cassirer, Ernst. *Philosophy of Symbolic Forms, Vol. 3: The Phenomenology of Knowledge*. Translated by Ralph Manheim. New Haven: Yale University Press, 1957.
Cassirer, Ernst. *Philosophy of Symbolic Forms, Vol. 4: The Metaphysics of Symbolic Form*. Edited by John Michael Krois and Donald Phillipe Verene. Translated by John Michael Krois. New Haven: Yale University Press, 1996.
Cassirer, Ernst. *Zur Einsteinschen Relativitätstheorie*. Berlin: Bruno Cassirer, 1921. Translated as *Einstein's Theory of Relativity*. Chicago: Open Court, 1923.
Caver, Martin. "A Different Price for the Ticket: Hannah Arendt and James Baldwin on Love and Politics." *Polity* 51, no. 1 (2019): 35–61.

Césaire, Aimé. *Discourse on Colonialism*. Translated by Joan Pinkham. New York: New York University Press, 2000.
Chaganti, Seeta. "Choreographing *Mouvance*: The Case of the English Carol." *Philological Quarterly* 87, no. 1/2 (2008): 77–103.
Chance, Jane. *Women Medievalists and the Academy*. Madison, WI: University of Wisconsin Press, 2005.
Chance, Jane, ed. *Tolkien the Medievalist*. London: Routledge, 2002.
Chatterjee, Partha. "Reflections on 'Can the Subaltern Speak?': Subaltern Studies After Spivak." In *Can the Subaltern Speak?: Reflections on the History of an Idea*, edited by Rosalind Morris. 81–86. New York: Columbia University Press, 2010.
Cheetham, Mark. *Kant, Art, and Art History: Moments of Discipline*. Cambridge: Cambridge University Press, 2001.
Chenaux, Philippe. *Entre Maurras et Maritain: Une génération intellectuelle Catholique (1920–1930)*. Paris: Les Éditions du Cerf, 1999.
Chesnutt, Charles W. *The House Behind the Cedars*. Boston: Houghton, Mifflin & Company, 1900.
Chiba, Shin. "Hannah Arendt on Love and the Political: Love, Friendship and Citizenship." *The Review of Politics* 57, no. 3 (1995): 505–35.
Clarke, Catherine A. M. "Re-Placing Masculinity: The DC Comics Beowulf Series and its Context, 1975–6." In *Anglo-Saxon Culture and the Imagination*, edited by David Clark and Nicholas Perkins. 165–82. Cambridge: Boydell & Brewer, 2010.
Classen, Albrecht, and Marilyn Sandidge, eds. *Friendship in the Middle Ages and Early Modern Age: Explorations of a Fundamental Ethical Discourse*. Berlin: De Gruyter, 2011.
Coates, Ta-Nahisi. "The Case for Reparations." *The Atlantic* (June 2014). www.theatlantic.com/magazine/archive/2014/06/the-case-for-reparations/361631.
Coffman, George R. "The Mediaeval Academy of America: Historical Background and Prospect." *Speculum* 1, no. 1 (1926): 5–18.
Cohen, Hermann. *Das Prinzip der Infinitesimal-Methode und seine Geschichte: Ein Kapitel zur Grundlegung der Erkenntnisskritik*. Berlin: Dümmler, 1883.
Cohen, Hermann. *Kants Theorie der Erfahrung*. Berlin: Harrwitz und Gossmann, 1885.
Cohen, Hermann, and Paul Natorp. "Zur Einführung." *Philosophische Arbeiten* 1, no. 1 (1906): i–iii.
Cohen, Jeffrey Jerome, and Karl Steel. "Race, Travel, Time, Heritage." *postmedieval* 6, no. 1 (2015): 98–110.
Cole, Andrew. *The Birth of Theory*. Chicago: University of Chicago Press, 2014.
Cole, Andrew, and D. Vance Smith. "Introduction: Outside Modernity." In *The Legitimacy of the Middle Ages: On the Unwritten History of Theory*, edited by Andrew Cole and D. Vance Smith. 1–36. Durham, NC: Duke University Press, 2010.
Cole, Andrew, and D. Vance Smith, eds. *The Legitimacy of the Middle Ages: On the Unwritten History of Theory*. Durham, NC: Duke University Press, 2010.

Colledge, Edmund, and Bernard McGinn, trans. "The Bull 'In agro dominico' (March 27, 1329)." In *Meister Eckhart: The Essential Sermons, Commentaries, Treatises, and Defense*, edited by Edmund Colledge and Bernard McGinn. 77–81. Mahwah, NJ: Paulist Press, 1981.

Colored Tournament Club, "Grand Tournament Will Be Given by the Colored Tournament Club (Aiken, SC, 1879)." Box 2, No. 4. Miscellaneous Print Collection. Kislak Center for Special Collections. Philadelphia: University of Pennsylvania.

Constable, Giles. "Forgery and Plagiarism in the Middle Ages." *Archiv für Diplomatik, Schriftgeschichte, Siegel- und Wappenkunde* 29 (1983): 1–41.

Conway, Michael A. "With Mind and Heart: Maurice Blondel and the Mystic Life." In *Mysticism in the French Tradition: Eruptions from France*, edited by Louise Nelstrop and Bradley B. Onishi. 17–37. Farnham: Ashgate Publishing, 2015.

Cooke, Gordon. "Bone, Sir Muirhead (1876–1953), Printmaker and Draughtsman." In *Oxford Dictionary of National Biography*. doi.org/10.1093/ref:odnb/31957

Critchley, Simon. *The Faith of the Faithless: Experiments in Political Theology*. New York: Verso, 2014.

Crossley, Paul. "Medieval Architecture and Meaning: The Limits of Iconology." *The Burlington Magazine* 130, no. 1019 (1988): 116–21.

Crow, Thomas. *The Intelligence of Art*. Chapel Hill: University of North Carolina Press, 1999.

Cucullu, Lois. *Expert Modernists, Matricide and Modern Culture: Woolf, Forester, Joyce*. Basingstoke: Palgrave Macmillan, 2004.

Cummings, David. "Civilising the Settler: Unstable Representations of French Settler Colonialism in Algeria." *Settler Colonial Studies* 8, no. 2 (2018): 175–94.

Curtius, Ernst Robert. *Deutscher Geist in Gefahr*. Stuttgart: Deutsche Verlags-Anstalt, 1932.

Curtius, Ernst Robert. "Goethe oder Jaspers," *Die Tat*, April 2, 1949.

Curtius, Ernst Robert. *Europäische Literatur und lateinisches Mittelalter*. Bern: A. Francke, 1948. Translated as *European Literature and the Latin Middle Ages*. Translated by Willard R. Trask. Princeton: Princeton University Press, 1953. Reprinted with an afterword by Peter Godman. Princeton: Princeton University Press, 1990.

Dagenais, John, and Margaret R. Greer. "Decolonizing the Middle Ages: Introduction." *Journal of Medieval and Early Modern Studies* 30, no. 3 (2000): 431–48.

Davies, Joshua. *Visions and Ruins: Cultural Memory and the Untimely Middle Ages*. Manchester: Manchester University Press, 2018.

Davis, Creston, John Milbank, and Slavoj Žižek, eds. *Theology and the Political: A New Debate*. Durham, NC: Duke University Press, 2005.

Davis, Kathleen. *Periodization and Sovereignty: How Ideas of Feudalism and Secularization Govern the Politics of Time*. Philadelphia: University of Pennsylvania Press, 2008.

Davis, Kathleen. "The Sense of an Epoch: Periodization, Sovereignty, and the Limits of Secularization." In *The Legitimacy of the Middle Ages: On the Unwritten History of Theory*, edited by Andrew Cole and D. Vance Smith. 39–69. Durham, NC: Duke University Press, 2010.

Davy, Mary-Magdeleine. *The Mysticism of Simone Weil*. Translated by Cynthia Rowland. London: Salisbury Square, 1951.

De Angelis, Elio. "Sognando Gli Archetipi: Jung, Curtius, e i Segni Dei Tempi." *Medicina Nei Secoli: Arte e Scienza/Journal of the History of Medicine* 21, no. 2 (2009): 551–72.

de Beauvoir, Simone. *Ethics of Ambiguity*. Translated by Bernard Frechtman. New York: Philosophical Library, 1948.

de Beauvoir, Simone. *The Second Sex*. Translated by Constance Borde and Sheila Malovany Chevallier. New York: Vintage, 2010.

de la Salle, Antoine. *Sa vie et ses ouvrages d'apres des documents inedits: Suivi du Reconfort de Madame du Fresne d'apres le manuscrit unique de la Bibliotheque Royale de Belgique, du Paradis de la Reine Sibylle, etc. Par Antoine de La Salle*. Edited by Joseph Nève. Paris: Champion, 1903.

De Simone, Daniel, and Ali Winston. "Neo-Nazi Militant Group Grooms Teenagers," *BBC*. June 22, 2020. www.bbc.com/news/uk-53128169?pianomodal

de Vries, Hent, and Lawrence E. Sullivan, eds. *Political Theologies: Public Religions in a Post-Secular World*. New York: Fordham University Press, 2006.

Decret, François. *L'Afrique manichéenne (IVe-Ve siècles): Étude historique et doctrinale*. 2 vols. Paris: Études augustiniennes, 1978.

Delacroix, Henri. *Essai sur le mysticisme spéculatif en allemagne au quatorizième siècle*. Paris: F. Alcan, 1900.

Delacroix, Henri. *Études d'histoire et de psychologie du mysticisme: Les grands mystiques Chrétiens*. Paris: F. Alan, 1908.

Delany, Sheila. "Marxist Medievalists: A Tradition." *Science and Society* 68, no. 2 (2004): 206–15.

Delfino, Robert A. "Mystical Theology in Aquinas and Maritain." In *Jacques Maritain and the Many Ways of Knowing*, edited by Douglas A. Ollivant. 166–81. Washington, DC: The Catholic University of America Press, 2002.

Denifle, Heinrich. "Acten zum Processe Meister Eckeharts." *Archiv für Litteratur- und Kirchengeschichte des Mittelalters* 2 (1886): 616–40.

Desmond, Marilynn, and Noah D. Guynn. "We Have Always Been Medieval: Bruno Latour and Double Click, Metaphysics and Modernity." *Romanic Review* III, no. 1 (2020): 1–7.

Dickey, Lawrence. *Hegel: Religion, Economics and the Politics of Spirit, 1770–1807*. Cambridge: Cambridge University Press, 1987.

Dickson, Caitlin. "The Neo-Nazi Has No Clothes: In Search of Matt Heimbach's Bogus 'White Ethnostate'." *HuffPost*. February 2, 2018. www.huffpost.com/entry/neo-nazi-matthew-heimbach-bogus-white-ethnostate_n_5a745c5fe4b01ce33eb1d720

Dide, M., and P. Guiraud, *Psychiatrie du Médecin Praticien*. Paris: Masson et Cie, 1922.

Diebold, William J. "The Nazi Middle Ages." In *Whose Middle Ages? Teachable Moments for an Ill-Used Past*, edited by Andrew Albin, Mary C. Erler, Thomas O'Donnell, Nicholas L. Paul, and Nina Rowe. 104–15. New York: Fordham University Press, 2019.

Dinshaw, Carolyn. *How Soon Is Now: Medieval Texts, Amateur Readers, and the Queerness of Time*. Durham, NC: Duke University Press, 2012.

Dobb, Maurice. *Studies in the Development of Capitalism*. New York: International Publishers, 1947.

Dougherty, Richard J., ed. *Augustine's Political Thought*. Rochester Studies in Medieval Political Thought. Rochester: Boydell & Brewer, 2019.

Downing, Crystal. *Subversive: Christ, Culture, and the Shocking Dorothy L. Sayers*. Minneapolis, MN: Broadleaf Books, 2020.

Downing, Crystal. *Writing Performances: The Stages of Dorothy L. Sayers*. Basingstoke: Palgrave Macmillan, 2004.

Drabble, Margaret. *Angus Wilson: A Biography*. London: Secker & Warburg, 1955.

Dubilet, Alex. *The Self-Emptying Subject: Kenosis and Immanence, from Medieval to Modern*. New York: Fordham University Press, 2018.

Du Bois, W. E. B. "Close Ranks." *The Crisis* 16, no. 3 (July 1918): 111.

Du Bois, W. E. B. "Color and Democracy, November 20, 1947." W. E. B. Du Bois Papers (MS 312). Special Collections and University Archives, University of Massachusetts Amherst Libraries. credo.library.umass.edu/view/full/mums312-b199-i008

Du Bois, W. E. B. "Criteria of Negro Art." *The Crisis* 32 (October 1926): 290–97.

Du Bois, W. E. B. "Letter from W. E. B. Du Bois to the World Tomorrow, June 24, 1930." W. E. B. Du Bois Papers (MS 312). Special Collections and University Archives, University of Massachusetts Amherst Libraries. credo.library.umass.edu/view/full/mums312-b057-i144

Du Bois, W. E. B. "The African Roots of War." *The Atlantic Monthly* 115, no. 5 (May 1915): 707–14.

Du Bois, W. E. B. "The Black Man and the Wounded World: A History of the Negro Race in the World War and After." *The Crisis* 27, no. 3 (January 1924): 110–14.

Du Bois, W. E. B. *The World and Africa and Color and Democracy*. The Oxford W. E. B. Du Bois. Vol. 9. Edited by Henry Louis Gates, Jr. Oxford: Oxford University Press, 2007.

Du Bois, W. E. B. "The Princess Steel." Edited by Adrienne Brown and Britt Rusert. *PMLA* 130, no. 3 (2015): 819–29.

Dumitrescu, Irina. "Introduction." In *Rumba under Fire: The Arts of Survival from West Point to Delhi*, edited by Irina Dumitrescu. xiii–xxiii. Earth: Punctum Books, 2016.

Edwards, A. S. G. "Gavin Bone and his Old English Translations." *Translation and Literature* 30 (2021): 147–69.

Efal, Adi. "Reality as the Cause of Art: Riegl and Neo-Kantian Realism." *Journal of Art Historiography* 3, no. 2 (2010): 1–22.

Ekwall, Eilert. *The Concise Oxford Dictionary of English Place-Names*. 4th ed. Oxford: Oxford University Press, 1960.

Elias, Norbert. *The Civilizing Process*. Rev. ed. Translated by Edmund Jephcott. Oxford: Blackwell Publishers, 2000.

Eliot, T. S. "Preface." In *The Need for Roots: Prelude to a Declaration of Duties Toward Mankind*, by Simone Weil. Translated by Arthur Wills. v–xii. New York: Octagon Books, 1979.

Eliot, T. S. "Reflections on Contemporary Poetry." *The Egoist* 6, no. 3 (July 1919): 39–40.

Eliot, T. S. "Tradition and the Individual Talent." *The Egoist* 6, no. 4 (September 1919): 54–55.

Ellard, Donna Beth. *Anglo-Saxon(ist) Pasts, Post Saxon Futures*. Santa Barbara: Punctum Books, 2019.

Elsner, Jaś, and Katharina Lorenz. "The Genesis of Iconology." *Critical Inquiry* 38, no. 3 (2012): 483–513.

Elsner, John. "Review of Whitney Davis, *Masking the Blow: The Scene of Representation in Late Prehistoric Egyptian Art*." *The Art Bulletin* 76, no. 3 (1994): 535–36.

English, James. *Comic Transactions: Literature, Humor, and the Politics of Community in Twentieth-Century Britain*. Ithaca, NY: Cornell University Press, 1994.

"Erich Auerbach Collection." Catalogue list. Harry Ransom Center.

Ericksen, Robert P. *Complicity in the Holocaust: Churches and Universities in Nazi Germany*. Cambridge: Cambridge University Press, 2012.

Esposito, Roberto. *The Origin of the Political: Hannah Arendt or Simone Weil?* Translated by Vincenzo Binetti and Gareth Williams. New York: Fordham University Press, 2017.

Evans, Arthur R. "Ernst Robert Curtius." In *On Four Modern Humanists: Hofmannstahl, Gundolf, Curtius, Kantorowicz*, edited by Arthur R. Evans. 85–145. Princeton: Princeton University Press, 1970.

Evans, R. J. W., and Guy P. Marchal, eds. *The Uses of the Middle Ages in Modern European States: History, Nationhood and the Search for Origins*. New York: Palgrave Macmillan, 2011.

"Excerpt from Regents' Executive Session Minutes of February 24, 1950." University of California Archives. oac.cdlib.org/ark:/13030/hb8t1nb9fk/?brand=oac4

Fanon, Frantz. *Les damnés de la terre*. Paris: Éditions La Découverte & Syros, 2002. Translated as *The Wretched of the Earth*. Translated by Constance Farrington. New York: Grove Press, 1963. Newly translated by Richard Philcox. New York: Grove Press, 2004.

Fanon, Frantz. *Peau noire, masques blancs*. Paris: Editions du Seuill, 1952. Translated as *Black Skin, White Masks*. Translated by Charles Lam Markmann. London: Pluto, 1986.

Felski, Rita. "Context Stinks!" *New Literary History* 42 (2011): 573–91.

Ferguson, Wallace K. *The Renaissance in Historical Thought: Five Centuries of Interpretation*. Boston: Houghton Mifflin, 1948.

Fetterley, Judith. *The Resisting Reader: A Feminist Approach to American Fiction*. Bloomington: Indiana University Press, 1978.

Ficek, Douglas. "Reflections on Fanon and Petrification." In *Living Fanon: Global Perspectives*, edited by Nigel C. Gibson. 75–84. New York: Palgrave, 2011.

Fiedler, Leslie A. "Introduction." In *Waiting for God*, by Simone Weil. Translated by Emma Craufurd. 3–43. New York: Harper Colophon, 1973.

Fiori, Gabriella. *Simone Weil: An Intellectual Biography*. Translated by Joseph R. Berrigan. Athens: University of Georgia Press, 1989.

Fischer, Humbertus. "Ernst Kantorowicz und die deutsche Mediävistik." In *Ernst Kantorowicz (1895–1963): Soziales Milieu und Wissenschaftliche Relevanz*, edited by Jerzy Strzelczyk. 103–18. Poznań: Instytut Historii UAM, 1996.

Forrest, Martin. "The Abolition of Compulsory Latin and Its Consequences." *Greece and Rome* 50, no. 2 (2003): 42–66.

Foucault, Michel. *Discipline and Punish: The Birth of the Prison*. Translated by Alan Sheridan. New York: Pantheon Books, 1977.

Fredrick, Candice, and Sam McBride. *Women among the Inklings: Gender, C.S. Lewis, J. R. R. Tolkien, and Charles Williams*. Westport, CT: Greenwood Press, 2001.

Freud, Sigmund. *Civilization and Its Discontents*. Edited and translated by James Strachey. New York: Norton, 1989.

Friedman, Michael. *A Parting of the Ways: Carnap, Cassirer, and Heidegger*. Chicago: Open Court, 2000.

Fulk, R. D., Robert E. Bjork, and John D. Niles, eds. *Klaeber's "Beowulf."* 4th ed. Toronto: University of Toronto Press, 2008.

Gabriele, Matthew, and Mary Rambaran-Olm. "The Middle Ages Have Been Misused by the Far Right. Here's Why It's So Important to Get Medieval History Right." *Time*. November 21, 2019. time.com/5734697/middle-ages-mistakes/.

Gadamer, Hans-Georg. "On the Problem of Self-Understanding." Translated by David E. Linge. In *Philosophical Hermeneutics*. 44–58. Berkeley: University of California Press, 1976.

Gadamer, Hans-Georg. *Wahrheit und Methode*. Tübingen: J. C. B. Mohr, 1960. Translated as *Truth and Method*. 2nd rev. ed. Translated by Joel Weinsheimer and Donald G. Marshall. New York: Continuum, 2013.

Gall, Ernst. "Review of Erwin Panofsky, *Gothic Architecture and Scholasticism*." *Kunstchronik* 6 (1953): 42–49.

Galvin, Rachel. *News of War: Civilian Poetry 1936–1945*. Oxford: Oxford University Press, 2017.

Garrison, Eliza. "Ottonian Art and Its Afterlife: Revisiting Percy Ernst Schramm's Portraiture Idea." *Oxford Art Journal* 32, no. 2 (2009): 205–22.

Geréby, György. "Political Theology versus Theological Politics: Erik Peterson and Carl Schmitt." *New German Critique*, no. 105 (2008): 7–33.

Gilbert, Felix. *History: Politics or Culture Reflections on Ranke and Burckhardt*. Princeton: Princeton University Press, 1990.

Gilbert, Sandra M., and Susan Gubar. *The Madwoman in the Attic: The Woman Writer and the Nineteenth-Century Literary Imagination*. New Haven: Yale University Press, 1979.

Gilbert, Sandra M., and Susan Gubar. *No Man's Land: The Place of the Woman Writer in the Twentieth Century, Vol. 1: The War of the Words*. New Haven: Yale University Press, 1989.

Gillespie, Michael Allen. *The Theological Origins of Modernity*. Chicago: University of Chicago Press, 2008.

Gilmore, Janet. "Fifty Years after Cold War Suspicions Spawned a University Loyalty Oath, UC Berkeley Hosts Gathering on Topic." *University of California, Public Affairs*. 4 October 1999. www.berkeley.edu/news/media/releases/99legacy/10-8-1999.html

Gilroy, Paul. *Against Race: Imagining Political Culture beyond the Color Line*. Cambridge, MA: Harvard University Press, 2002.

Gombrich, Ernst. "I Think Art Historians are the Spokesman of Our Civilization; We Want to Know More About our Olympus." *The Art Newspaper* 19 (1993): 18–19.

Goodman, Nelson. *Languages of Art*. Indianapolis: Hackett, 1976.

Gordon, Peter E. *Continental Divide: Heidegger, Cassirer, Davos*. Cambridge, MA: Harvard University Press, 2012.

Gordon, R. K. *Anglo-Saxon Poetry*. London: J. M. Dent & Sons, 1926.

Goudsblom, Johan. "Norbert Elias and American Sociology." *Sociologia Internationalis* 38, no. 2 (2000): 173–80.

Gramsci, Antonio. *Further Selections from the Prison Notebooks*. Translated and edited by Derek Boothman. Minneapolis: University of Minnesota Press, 1995.

Greenhalgh, Michael. *The Military and Colonial Destruction of the Roman Landscape of North Africa, 1830–1900*. Leiden: Brill, 2014.

Gregory the Great. *Moralia in Iob*. Edited by Marc Adriaen. 3 vols, Corpus Christianorum Series Latina 143, 143a, 143b. Turnhout: Brepols, 1979.

Guha, Ranajit. *A Rule of Property for Bengal: An Essay on the Idea of Permanent Settlement*. Durham, NC: Duke University Press, 1996.

Gumbrecht, Hans Ulrich. "'Zeitlosigkeit, die durchscheint in der Zeit': Ernst Robert Curtius' unhistorisches Verhältnis zur Geschichte." In *Vom Leben Und Sterben Der Grossen Romanisten*. 49–71. Vienna: Carl Hanser, 2002.

Guy-Bray, Stephen. *Loving in Verse: Poetic Influence as Erotic*. Toronto: University of Toronto Press, 2006.

Hahn, Thomas. "Medievalism, Make-Believe, and Real Life in Wilson's 'Anglo-Saxon Attitudes'." *Mosaic: An Interdisciplinary Critical Journal* 12, no. 4 (1979): 115–34.

Hamacher, Werner. "The Gesture in the Name: On Benjamin and Kafka." In *Premises: Essays on Philosophy and Literature from Kant to Celan*, translated by Peter Fenves. 294–336. Stanford: Stanford University Press, 1996.

Hart, Joan. "Erwin Panofsky and Karl Mannheim: A Dialogue on Interpretation." *Critical Inquiry* 19, no. 3 (1993): 534–66.

Hart, Mitchell B. "'Modern and Genuine Mediaevalism': Guido Kisch's Romance with the German Middle Ages." *postmedieval* 5, no. 3 (2014): 295–307.

Harvey, David. *Spaces of Global Capitalism: A Theory of Uneven Geographical Development*. New York: Verso, 2006.
Hasenmueller, Christine. "Panofsky, Iconography, Semiotics." *Journal of Aesthetics and Art Criticism* 36, no. 3 (1978): 289–301.
Hathaway, Neil. "*Compilatio*: From Plagiarism to Compiling." *Viator* 20 (1989): 19–44.
Haverkamp, Anselm. "Richard II, Bracton, and the End of Political Theology." In *Shakespearean Genealogies of Power: A Whispering of Nothing in Hamlet, Richard II, Julius Caesar, and The Winter's Tale*. 47–56. London: Routledge, 2011.
Heaney, Seamus. *Beowulf: A Verse Translation*. Edited by Daniel Donoghue. New York: W. W. Norton, 2002.
Hegel, G. W. F. *Phänomenologie des Geistes*. Bamberg, 1807. Translated as *Phenomenology of Spirit*. Translated by A. V. Miller. Oxford: Oxford University Press, 1977.
Hegel, G. W. F. *Philosophie der Kunst oder Ästhetik. Nach Hegel. Im Sommer 1826. Mitschrift Friedrich Carl Hermann Victor von Kehler*. Edited by A. Gethmann-Siefert and B. Collenberg-Plotnikov. Munich: Wilhelm Fink Verlag, 2004.
Hegel, G. W. F. *Science of Logic*. Translated by A. W. Miller. New York: Routledge, 2002. Also translated by George di Giovanni. Cambridge: Cambridge University Press, 2010.
Hegel, G. W. F. *The Philosophy of History*. Translated by J. Sibree. New York: Colonial Press, 1900.
Heidegger, Martin. *Die Kategorien- und Bedeutungslehre des Duns Scotus*. Tübingen: J. C. B. Mohr, 1916. Translated as *Duns Scotus' Theory of Categories and of Meaning*. Translated by Harold J. Robbins, PhD diss., DePaul University, 1978.
Heng, Geraldine. *Empire of Magic: Medieval Romance and the Politics of Cultural Fantasy*. New York: Columbia University Press, 2003.
Heng, Geraldine. "The Global Middle Ages: An Experiment in Collaborative Humanities, or Imagining the World, 500–1500 C.E." *English Language Notes* 47, no. 1 (2009): 205–16.
Heng, Geraldine. *The Invention of Race in the European Middle Ages*. Cambridge: Cambridge University Press, 2018.
Heng, Geraldine, and Lynn Ramey, eds. "The Global Middle Ages." Special Issue, *Literature Compass* 11, no. 7 (2014).
Herrero, Montserrat. "Acclamations: A Theological-Political Topic in the Crossed Dialogue between Erik Peterson, Ernst H. Kantorowicz and Carl Schmitt." *History of European Ideas* 45, no. 7 (2019): 1045–57.
Herrero, Montserrat. "On Political Theology: The Hidden Dialogue between C. Schmitt and Ernst H. Kantorowicz in *The King's Two Bodies*." *History of European Ideas* 41, no. 8 (2015): 1164–77.
Hoban, Russell. *Riddley Walker*. London: Jonathan Cape, 1980.
Hobbes, Thomas. *The Leviathan: With Selected Variants from the Latin Edition of 1668*. Edited by Edwin Curley. Indianapolis: Hackett, 1994.

Hobsbawm, Eric. *Interesting Times: A Twentieth-Century Life*. New York: Pantheon Books, 2007.
Holly, Michael Ann. "Panofsky, Erwin (1892–1968)." In *The Encyclopedia of Aesthetics*, edited by Michael Kelly. Oxford: Oxford University Press, 1998. www.oxfordreference.com/view/10.1093/acref/9780199747108.001.0001/acref-9780199747108-e-549
Hollywood, Amy. "Bataille and Mysticism: A 'Dazzling Dissolution.'" *Diacritics* 26, no. 2 (1996): 74–85.
Hollywood, Amy. *The Soul as Virgin Wife: Mechthild of Magdeburg, Marguerite Porete, and Meister Eckhart*. Notre Dame: University of Notre Dame Press, 1995.
Holmes, Catherine, and Naomi Standen, eds. "The Global Middle Ages." *Past & Present* 238, no. S13 (2018).
Holsinger, Bruce. "Medieval Studies, Postcolonial Studies, and the Genealogies of Critique." *Speculum* 77, no. 4 (2002): 1195–227.
Holsinger, Bruce. *The Premodern Condition: Medievalism and the Making of Theory*. Chicago: University of Chicago Press, 2005.
Horkheimer, Max, and Theodor W. Adorno, *Dialectic of Enlightenment: Philosophical Fragments*. Translated by Edmund Jephcott. Stanford: Stanford University Press, 2002.
Howe, Nicholas. "Review of Norman F. Cantor, *Inventing the Middle Ages*." *Studies in the Age of Chaucer* 15 (1993): 180–85.
Hsy, Jonathan. "Antiracist Medievalisms: Lessons from Chinese Exclusion." *In the Middle*. February 16, 2018. www.inthemedievalmiddle.com/2018/02/antiracist-medievalisms-lessons-from.html.
Hugenholtz, F. W. N. "The Fame of a Masterwork." In *Johan Huizinga, 1872–1972: Papers Delivered at the Conference, Groningen 11–15 December, 1972*, edited by W. R. H. Koops, E. H. Kossmann, and Gees Van Der Plaat. 91–103. The Hague: Martinus Nijhoff, 1973.
Huizinga, Johan. "Burgund: Eine Krise des romanisch-germanischen Verhältnisses." *Historische Zeitschrift* 148 (1933): 1–28.
Huizinga, Johan. "Das Problem der Renaissance." In *Parerga*. 87–146. Basel: Pantheon Verlag, 1945. Translated as "The Problem of the Renaissance." In *Men and Ideas: History, the Middle Ages, the Renaissance*, translated by James S. Holmes and Hans van Marle. 243–87. New York: Meridian Books, 1959.
Huizinga, Johan. *Herbst des Mittelalters*. Munich: Drei Masken Verlag, 1924. Translated as *The Autumn of the Middle Ages*. Translated by Rodney J. Payton and Ulrich Mammitzsch. Chicago: University of Chicago Press, 1996.
Huizinga, Johan. "My Path to History." In *Dutch Civilization in the Seventeenth Century and Other Essays*, selected by Pieter Geyl and F. W. N. Hugenholtz. Translated by Arnold J. Pomerans. 244–76. New York: F. Ungar, 1968.
Huizinga, Johan. "Renaissance and Realism." In *Men and Ideas: History, the Middle Ages, the Renaissance*, translated by James S. Holmes and Hans van Marle. 288–309. New York: Meridian Books, 1959.

Humble, Nicola. *The Feminine Middlebrow Novel, 1920s to 1950s: Class, Domesticity, and Bohemianism*. Oxford: Oxford University Press, 2001.
Hutchings, Robert. "Introduction." In *Truth to Power: A History of the U. S. National Intelligence Council*, edited by Robert Hutchings and Gregory F. Treverton. 1–22. Oxford: Oxford University Press, 2019.
Huyssen, Andreas. *After the Great Divide: Modernism, Mass Culture, Postmodernism*. Bloomington: Indiana University Press, 1986.
Hyman, Arthur and James J. Walsh. *Philosophy in the Middle Ages: The Christian, Islamic, and Jewish Traditions*. New York: Harper and Row, 1967.
Hyppolite, Jean. *Genesis and Structure of Hegel's Phenomenology of Spirit*. Translated by Samuel Cherniak and John Heckman. Evanston: Northwestern University Press, 1974.
Ingham, Patricia Clare. *The Medieval New: Ambivalence in an Age of Innovation*. Philadelphia: University of Pennsylvania Press, 2015.
Irigaray, Luce. *Speculum of the Other Woman*. Translated by Gillian C. Gill. Ithaca, NY: Cornell University Press, 1985.
Irwin, Alexander. *Saints of the Impossible: Bataille, Weil, and the Politics of the Sacred*. Minneapolis: University of Minnesota Press, 2002.
Jaeger, C. Stephen. "Ernst Robert Curtius: A Medievalist's Contempt for the Middle Ages." *Viator* 47, no. 2 (2016): 367–79.
Jaeger, C. Stephen. "Friendship of Mutual Perfecting in Augustine's Confessions and the Failure of Classical *amicitia*." In *Friendship in the Middle Ages and Early Modern Age: Explorations of a Fundamental Ethical Discourse*, edited by Albrecht Classen and Marilyn Sandidge. 185–200. Berlin: De Gruyter, 2011.
Jakobson, Roman. "On Realism in Art." In *Readings in Russian Poetics: Formalist and Structuralist Views*, edited by Ladislav Matejka and Krystyna Pomorska. 38–46. Cambridge, MA: MIT Press, 1971.
James, William. *The Varieties of Religious Experience: A Study in Human Nature*. New York: Modern Library, 1936. Reprint, 1994.
Jameson, Fredric. "Afterword: On the Medieval." In *The Legitimacy of the Middle Ages: On the Unwritten History of Theory*, edited by Andrew Cole and D. Vance Smith. 243–46. Durham, NC: Duke University Press, 2010.
JanMohamed, Abdul. *Manichean Aesthetics: The Politics of Literature in Colonial Africa*. Amherst: University of Massachusetts Press, 1983.
Jaspers, Karl. "Unsere Zukunft und Goethe," *Die Wandlung*, 2 (1947).
Jauss, Hans Robert. *Ästhetische Erfahrung und literarische Hermeneutik*. 1st ed. Munich: W. Fink, 1977. *Ästhetische Erfahrung und literarische Hermeneutik*. 2nd ed. Frankfurt: Suhrkamp, 1982. Translated as *Aesthetic Experience and Literary Hermeneutics*. Translated by Michael Shaw. Minneapolis: University of Minnesota Press, 1982.
Jauss, Hans Robert. *Alterität und Modernität der mittelalterlichen Literatur: Gesammelte Aufsätze 1956–1976*. Munich: W. Fink, 1977. Translated as "The Alterity and Modernity of Medieval Literature." Translated by Timothy Bahti. *New Literary History* 10, no. 2 (1979): 181–229.

Jauss, Hans Robert. "Horizon Structure and Dialogicity." In *Question and Answer: Forms of Dialogic Understanding*, edited by Michael Hayes. 197–231. Minneapolis: University of Minnesota Press, 1989.

Jauss, Hans Robert. "Littérature médiévale et expérience esthétique: Actualité des *Questions de littérature* de Robert Guiette." *Poétique* 31 (1977): 322–36.

Jay, Martin. "Against Rigor: Hans Blumenberg on Freud and Arendt." *New German Critique* 44, no. 3 (2017): 123–44.

Jay, Martin. "Historical Explanation and the Event: Reflections on the Limits of Contextualization." *New Literary History* 42, no. 4 (2011): 557–71.

Jay, Martin. *The Dialectical Imagination: A History of the Frankfurt School and the Institute of Social Research 1923–1950*. Berkeley: University of California Press, 1996.

Jay, Martin. "The Reassertion of Sovereignty in a Time of Crisis: Carl Schmitt and Georges Bataille." In *Force Fields: Between Intellectual History and Cultural Critique*. 49–60. New York: Routledge, 1993.

Jefferess, David. *Postcolonial Resistance: Culture, Liberation, and Transformation*. Toronto: Toronto University Press, 2008.

Jefferies, Richard. *After London, or Wild England*. London: Cassell, 1885.

Johnson, Hannah, and Nina Caputo. "The Middle Ages and the Holocaust: Medieval Anti-Judaism in the Crucible of Modern Thought." *postmedieval* 5, no. 4 (2014): 270–77.

Johnson, Pauline. "An Aesthetics of Negativity/An Aesthetics of Reception: Jauss's Dispute with Adorno." *New German Critique*, no. 42 (1987): 51–70.

Jones, Chris. *Fossil Poetry: Anglo-Saxon and Linguistic Nativism in Nineteenth-Century Poetry*. Oxford: Oxford University Press, 2019.

Jones, Chris. *Strange Likeness: The Use of Old English in Twentieth-Century Poetry*. Oxford: Oxford University Press, 2006.

Jones, Chris. "While Crowding Memories Came: Edwin Morgan, Old English and Nostalgia." *Scottish Literary Review* 4, no. 2 (2012): 123–44.

Jones, David. *The Anathemata*. London: Faber and Faber, 1952.

Jordan, William Chester. "Preface to the 1997 Edition." In *The King's Two Bodies: A Study in Medieval Political Theology*, by Ernst H. Kantorowicz. ix–xv. Princeton: Princeton University Press, 1997.

Juminer, Bertène. "Hommages à Frantz Fanon." *Présence Africaine* 40 (1962): 118–41.

Jung, Carl. G. *Memories, Dreams, Reflections*. Rev. ed. Recorded and edited by Aniela Jaffé. Translated by Richard and Clara Winston. New York: Vintage, 1989.

Jung, Carl. G. *Synchronicity: An Acausal Connecting Principle*. Translated by R. F. C. Hull, with a new foreword by Sonu Shamdasani. Princeton: Princeton University Press, 2010.

Jung, Carl. G. *The Archetypes and the Collective Unconscious*. 2nd ed. Translated by R. F. C. Hull. Princeton: Princeton University Press, 1969.

Jung, Carl. G. *Two Essays on Analytical Psychology*. 2nd ed. Translated by R. F. C. Hull. Collected Works of C. G. Jung, Vol. 7. Princeton: Princeton University Press, 1966.

Justice, Steven. "Who Stole Robertson?" *PMLA* 124 (2009): 609–15.
Kabir, Ananya Jahanara. "Analogy in Translation: Imperial Rome, Medieval England, and British India." In *Postcolonial Approaches to the European Middle Ages: Translating Cultures*, edited by Ananya Jahanara Kabir and Deanne Williams. 183–204. Cambridge: Cambridge University Press, 2005.
Kaegi, Walter. *Muslim Expansion and Byzantine Collapse in North Africa*. Cambridge: Cambridge University Press, 2010.
Kahn, Victoria. "Political Theology and Fiction in *The King's Two Bodies*." *Representations* 106, no. 1 (2009): 77–101.
Kahn, Victoria. *The Future of Illusion: Political Theology and Early Modern Texts*. Chicago: University of Chicago Press, 2014.
Kant, Immanuel. *Sein Leben in Darstellungen von Zeitgenossen*. Berlin: Deutsche Bibliothek, 1912.
Kantorowicz, Ernst H. "*Deus Per Naturam, Deus Per Gratiam*: A Note on Mediaeval Political Theology." *The Harvard Theological Review* 45, no. 4 (1952): 253–77.
Kantorowicz, Ernst H. *The Fundamental Issue: Documents and Marginal Notes on the University of California Loyalty Oath*. San Francisco: Parker Printing Company, 1950. www.lib.berkeley.edu/uchistory/archives_exhibits/loyaltyoath/symposium/kantorowicz.html
Kantorowicz, Ernst H. *Kaiser Friedrich der Zweite*. Berlin: Georg Bondi, 1927.
Kantorowicz, Ernst H. *The King's Two Bodies: A Study in Medieval Political Theology*. Princeton: Princeton University Press, 1957. Reprinted in 1997 with a Preface by William Chester Jordan. Reprinted in 2016 with a Preface by William Chester Jordan and an Introduction by Conrad Leyser.
Kantorowicz, Ernst H. *Laudes Regiae: A Study in Liturgical Acclamations and Mediaeval Ruler Worship*. Berkeley: University of California Press, 1946.
Kantorowicz, Ernst H. "Mysteries of State: The Absolutist Concept and Its Late Medieval Origins." *Harvard Theological Review* 48, no. 1 (1955): 65–91.
Kantorowicz, Ernst H. "*Pro patria mori* in Medieval Political Thought." *The American Historical Review* 56, no. 3 (1951): 472–92.
Kantorowicz, Ernst H. *Selected Studies*. Locust Valley, NY: J. J. Augustin, 1965.
Kantorowicz, Ernst H. *Die zwei Körper des Königs: Eine Studie zur politischen Theologie des Mittelalters*. Translated by Walter Theimer und Brigitte Hellmann. Munich: Klett-Cotta, 1994.
Katz, Claudio J. "Karl Marx on the Transition from Feudalism to Capitalism." *Theory and Society* 22, no. 3 (1993): 363–89.
Kaufman, Amy S., and Paul B. Sturtevant. *The Devil's Historians: How Modern Extremists Abuse the Medieval Past*. Toronto: University of Toronto Press, 2020.
Keita, Maghan. "Race: What the Bookstore Hid." In *Why the Middle Ages Matter: Medieval Light on Modern Injustice*, edited by Celia Chazelle, Simon Doubleday, Felice Lifshitz, and Amy G. Remensnyder. 130–40. New York: Routledge, 2012.
Kemble, John Mitchell, trans. *A Translation of the Anglo-Saxon Poem of "Beowulf."* London: William Pickering, 1837.

Kennedy, Emmet. "Simone Weil: Secularism and Syncretism." *The Journal of the Historical Society* 5, no. 2 (2005): 203–25.
Kervégan, Jean-François. *Que faire de Carl Schmitt?* Paris: Gallimard, 2011.
Khalfa, Jean. "Frantz Fanon's Library." In *Frantz Fanon, Alienation and Freedom*, edited by Jean Khalfa and Robert J. C. Young. Translated by Steven Corcoran. 719–78. London: Bloomsbury, 2018.
Kidson, Peter. "Panofsky, Suger and St Denis." *Journal of the Warburg and Courtauld Institutes* 50 (1987): 1–17.
Kim, Dorothy. "White Supremacists Have Weaponized an Imaginary Viking Past. It's Time to Reclaim the Real History." *Time*. April 15, 2019. time.com/5569399/viking-history-white-nationalists/
Knapp, Ethan. "Medieval Studies, Historicity, and Heidegger's Early Phenomenology." In *The Legitimacy of the Middle Ages: On the Unwritten History of Theory*, edited by Andrew Cole and D. Vance Smith. 159–93. Durham, NC: Duke University Press, 2010.
Kojève, Alexandre. *Introduction à la lecture de Hegel*. Paris: Gallimard, 1979. Translated as *Introduction to the Reading of Hegel*. Translated by James H. Nichols, Jr. Edited by Allan Bloom. Ithaca, NY: Cornell University Press, 1980.
Kolodny, Annette. "The Influence of Anxiety: Prolegomena to a Study of the Production of Poetry by Women." In *A Gift of Tongues: Critical Challenges in Contemporary American Poetry Redefined*, edited by Marie Harris and Kathleen Aguero. 112–41. Athens: University of Georgia Press, 1987.
Konuk, Kader. *East–West Mimesis: Auerbach in Turkey*. Stanford: Stanford University Press, 2010.
Köster, Kurt. *Johan Huizinga, 1872–1945, mit einer Bibliographie*. Oberursel (Taunus): Verlag Europa-Archiv, 1947.
Koyré, Alexander. *From the Closed World to the Infinite Universe*. Baltimore: Johns Hopkins Press, 1968.
Krause, F., ed. "Kleine Publikationen aus der Auchinleck-hs, XI: *The King of Tars*." *Englische Studien* 11 (1888): 1–62.
Krijnen, Christian, and Andrzej Noras. *Marburg versus Südwestdeutschland: Philosophische Differenzen zwischen den beiden Hauptschulen des Neukantianismus*. Würzburg: Köningshausen and Neumann, 2012.
Kristeller, Paul Oskar. "Review of *Europäische Literatur und lateinisches Mittelalter*." *Annali della Scuola Normale Superiore di Pisa. Classe di lettere e filosofia*. Ser. 2. 19 (1950): 205–8.
Kristeva, Julia. *Hannah Arendt*. Translated by Ross Guberman. Ross Guberman. New York: Columbia University Press, 2001.
Krois, John Michael. *Cassirer: Symbolic Forms and History*. New Haven: Yale University Press, 1987.
Krul, Wessel. "In the Mirror of van Eyck: Johan Huizinga's *Autumn of the Middle Ages*." *Journal of Medieval and Early Modern Studies* 27, no. 3 (1997): 353–84.

Krumm, Christian. *Johan Huizinga, Deutschland und die Deutschen: Begegnungen und Auseinandersetzung mit dem Nachbarn*. Münster: Waxman, 2011.

La Piana, George. "Theology of History." In *The Interpretation of History*, edited by Joseph R. Strayer. 151–87. Princeton: Princeton University Press, 1943.

Lacan, Jacques. *The Seminar of Jacques Lacan, Book XX, Encore 1972–73: On Feminine Sexuality the Limits of Love and Knowledge*. Edited by Jacques-Alain Miller. Translated by Bruce Fink. New York: Norton, 1998.

LaCapra, Dominick. "Is Everyone a *Mentalité* Case? Transference and the 'Culture' Concept." *History and Criticism* 23, no. 3 (1984): 296–311.

Lange, Wolf-Dieter, ed. *"In Ihnen begegnet sich das Abendland": Bonner Vorträge zur Erinnerung an Ernst Robert Curtius*. Bonn: Verlag, 1990.

Lanser, Susan Sniader. *Fictions of Authority: Women Writers and Narrative Voice*. Ithaca, NY: Cornell University Press, 1992.

Latour, Bruno. *We Have Never Been Modern*. Translated by Catherine Porter. Cambridge, MA: Harvard University Press, 1993.

Lausberg, Heinrich. *Ernst Robert Curtius (1886–1956)*. Edited by Arnold Arens. Stuttgart: F. Steiner, 1993.

Lawson, Bill E. "Afterword: *Stormy Weather* and Afromodernism." In *Afromodernisms: Paris, Harlem, and the Avant-Garde*, edited by Fionnghuala Sweeney and Kate Marsh. 232–42. Edinburgh: Edinburgh University Press, 2013.

Leader, Zachary. "Amis, Sir Kingsley William (1922–1995), Writer." In *Oxford Dictionary of National Biography*. doi.org/10.1093/ref:odnb/60221.

Leader, Zachary. *The Life of Kingsley Amis*. London: Jonathan Cape, 2006.

Lees, Clare A. "Women Write the Past: Medieval Scholarship, Old English and New Literature." *Bulletin of the John Rylands Library* 93, no. 2 (2017): 3–22.

Lees, Clare A., and Gillian R. Overing. *The Contemporary Medieval in Practice*. London: UCL Press, 2019.

Lefebvre, Henri. *The Production of Space*. Translated by Donald Nicholson-Smith. Oxford: Blackwell, 1991.

Lefort, Claude. *The Political Forms of Modern Society: Bureaucracy, Democracy, Totalitarianism*. Edited by John B. Thompson. Cambridge, MA: MIT Press, 1986.

Lerner, Robert E. *Ernst Kantorowicz: A Life*. Princeton: Princeton University Press, 2017.

Lerner, Robert E. "Kantorowicz and Continuity." In *Ernst Kantorowicz: Erträge der Doppeltagung*, edited by R. L. Benson and J. Fried. 104–23. Stuttgart: Franz Steiner, 1997.

Levinas, Emmanuel. *Difficult Freedom: Essays on Judaism*. Translated by Seán Hand. Baltimore: John Hopkins University Press, 1990.

Levine, Emily J. *Dreamland of Humanists: Warburg, Cassirer, Panofsky, and the Hamburg School*. Chicago: University of Chicago Press, 2013.

Lewis, C. S. "A Panegyric for Dorothy L. Sayers." In *"On Stories" and Other Essays in Literature*, edited by Walter Hooper. 91–95. London: Harcourt Brace Jovanovich, 1966.

Lewis, Wyndham, ed. *BLAST: The Review of the Great English Vortex*. London: John Lane, 1914.

Leyser, Conrad. "Introduction to the Princeton Classics Edition." In *The King's Two Bodies: A Study in Medieval Political Theology*, by Ernst H. Kantorowicz. ix–xxiii. Princeton: Princeton University Press, 2016.

Locherbie-Cameron, Margaret A. "'Anglo-Saxon Attitudes': The Visual Nature of Some Poetic Narrative Structures." *Parergon* 10, no. 2 (1992): 71–82.

Locke, Alain. "Art or Propaganda?" *Harlem* 1, no. 1 (November 1928): 12–13.

Loerzer, Barbara. "William James, the French Tradition, and the Incomplete Transposition of the Spiritual into the Aesthetic." In *William James and the Transatlantic Conversation: Pragmatism, Pluralism, and Philosophy of Religion*, edited by Martin Halliwell and Joel D. S. Rasmussen. 65–80. New York: Oxford University Press, 2014.

Lomuto, Sierra. "Antiracism or Appropriation?: Performing Diversity Work in Medieval Studies." Unpublished presentation. RaceB4Race™ "Appropriations." January 17–18, 2020. https://youtu.be/-SuzQ5A85Jo.

Lomuto, Sierra. "Becoming Postmedieval: The Stakes of the Global Middle Ages." *postmedieval* 11, no. 4 (2020): 503–12.

Lomuto, Sierra. "Public Medievalism and the Rigor of Anti-Racist Critique." *In The Middle*. April 4, 2019. www.inthemedievalmiddle.com/2019/04/public-medievalism-and-rigor-of-anti.html.

Lomuto, Sierra. "White Nationalism and the Ethics of Medieval Studies." *In the Middle*. December 5, 2016. www.inthemedievalmiddle.com/2016/12/white-nationalism-and-ethics-of.html.

Löwith, Karl. *Meaning in History: The Theological Implications of the Philosophy of History*. Chicago: University of Chicago Press, 1949.

"The Loyalty Oath Controversy: University of California, 1949–1951." University of California History Digital Archives. www.lib.berkeley.edu/uchistory/archives_exhibits/loyaltyoath/index.html

Luft, Sebastian. "Philosophical Historiography in Marburg Neo-Kantianism: The Example of Cassirer's *Erkenntnisproblem*." In *From Hegel to Windelband*, edited by Gerald Hartung and Valentin Pluder. 181–205. Boston: De Gruyter, 2015.

Lye, Colleen. "Maoism and the Air We Breathe." *Commune Magazine*. November 29, 2018. communemag.com/maoism-and-the-air-we-breathe/.

Macaulay, Rose. *Pleasure of Ruins*. London: Weidenfeld and Nicolson, 1953.

Macaulay, Rose. *The World My Wilderness*. London: Collins, 1950.

Macey, David. *Frantz Fanon: A Biography*. 2nd ed. London: Verso, 2012.

Magennis, Hugh. *Translating "Beowulf": Modern Versions in English Verse*. Cambridge: D. S. Brewer, 2011.

Maitland, Frederic William, and Frederick Pollock. *The History of English Law Before the Time of Edward I*. 2 vols. Cambridge, 1895.

Mâle, Émile. *Religious Art in France, XIII Century: A Study in Mediaeval Iconography and Its Sources of Inspiration*. Translated by Dora Nussey. New York: E.P. Dutton & Co., 1913.

Mandel, Maud S. "Simone Weil (1909–1943): A Jewish Thinker?" In *Makers of Jewish Modernity: Thinkers, Artists, Leaders, and the World They Made*, edited by Jacques Picard, Jacques Revel, Michael P. Steinberg, Idith Zertal. 466–79. Princeton: Princeton University Press, 2016.

Mandelbaum, Maurice. *The Anatomy of Historical Knowledge*. Baltimore: Johns Hopkins University Press, 1977.
Mandouze, André. *Mémoires d'outre-siècle, tome 1: D'une résistance à l'autre*. Paris: Hamy, 1998.
Mandouze, André. *Prosopographie de l'Afrique chrétienne*. Paris: Centre nationale de la Recherche scientifique, 1982.
Mandouze, André. *Saint Augustin: L'aventure de la raison et de la grâce*. Paris: Études augustiniennes, 1968.
Männig, Maria. *Hans Sedlmayrs Kunstgeschichte: Eine kritische Studie*. Cologne: Wien Böhlau Verlag, 2017.
Manuellan, Marie-Jeanne. "Dans l'ombre de Fanon." *Le Monde*, September 12, 2017.
Marcus, Sharon. "Erich Auerbach's *Mimesis* and the Value of Scale." *Modern Language Quarterly* 77, no. 3 (2016): 297–319.
Marichal, Robert. "L'écriture latine et la civilisation occidentale du Ier au XVIe siècle." In *L'écriture et la psychologie des peuples. XXIIe semaine de synthèse*, compiled by Centre international de synthèse. 199–247. Paris: Armand Colin, 1963.
Maritain, Jacques. *Distinguer pour unir, ou les degrés du savoir*, 4th ed. Paris: Desclée De Brouwer & Cie, 1946. Translated as *Distinguish to Unite, or The Degrees of Knowledge*. Translated by Gerald B. Phelan. The Collected Works of Jacques Maritain, Vol. 7. Notre Dame: University of Notre Dame Press, 1995.
Marrou, Henri-Irénée. "France, ma patrie…" *Le Monde*, April 5, 1956.
Martel, James. "Amo, Volo ut Sis: Love, Willing and Arendt's Reluctant Embrace of Sovereignty." *Philosophy and Social Criticism* 34 (2008): 287–313.
Marx, Karl. *Grundrisse: Foundations of Political Economy*. Translated by Martin Nicolaus. New York: Penguin, 2005.
Matthews, David. "From Medieval to Medievalism: A New Semantic History." *Review of English Studies* 62 (2011): 695–715.
Mbembe, Achille. *Critique of Black Reason*. Translated by Laurent Dubois. Durham, NC: Duke University Press, 2017.
Mbembe, Achille. *Necropolitics*. Durham, NC: Duke University Press, 2019.
McGuire, William. *Bollingen: An Adventure in Collecting the Past*. Princeton: Princeton University Press, 1982.
Meaney, Marie Cabaud. *Simone Weil's Apologetic Use of Literature: Her Christological Interpretation of Classic Greek Text*. Oxford: Oxford University Press, 2007.
Meinecke, Friedrich. *Die deutsche Katastrophe: Betrachtungen und Erinnerungen*. Zurich: Eugen Rentsch Verlag, 1946.
Meister Eckhart. "Predigt 48." In *Meister Eckharts Predigten*, edited by Josef Quint. *Meister Eckhart: Die deutschen und lateinischen Werke 2*. 712–13. Stuttgart: W. Kohlhammer Verlag, 1971. Translated as "Sermon 48." In *Meister Eckhart: The Essential Sermons, Commentaries, Treatises, and Defense*. Translated by Edmund Colledge and Bernard McGinn. 197–98. New York: Paulist Press, 1981.
Mellino, Miguel. "The *Langue* of the Damned: Fanon and the Remnants of Europe." *South Atlantic Quarterly* 112, no. 1 (2013): 79–89.

Milch, Werner. "Goethe, Curtius, Jaspers und die Öffentlichkeit." *Archiv der Hessischen Nachrichten*, June 3, 1949.
Miles, Margaret. "Volo ut Sis: Arendt and Augustine." *Dialog* 41 (2002): 221–30.
Mills, Robert. *Derek Jarman's Medieval Modern*. Cambridge: D. S. Brewer, 2018.
Mittleman, Alan. *Hope in a Democratic Age: Philosophy, Religion, and Political Theory*. Oxford: Oxford University Press, 2009.
Miyashiro, Adam. "Appropriating the Crusades: Were the Crusades a Form of Medieval Colonialism?" Unpublished presentation. RaceB4Race[tm] "Appropriations." January 17–18, 2020. youtu.be/dcI7vOSmqVg.
Miyashiro, Adam. "'Our Deeper Past': Race, Settler Colonialism, and Medieval Heritage Politics." *Literature Compass* 16, no. 9/10 (2019): 1–11.
Momma, Haruko. *From Philology to English Studies: Language and Culture in the Nineteenth Century*. Cambridge: Cambridge University Press, 2012.
Moore, Brenna. *Sacred Dread: Raïssa Maritain, The Allure of Suffering, and the French Catholic Revival (1905–1944)*. Notre Dame: University of Notre Dame Press, 2012.
Morgan, Benjamin. *The Outward Mind: Materialist Aesthetics in Victorian Science and Literature*. Chicago: University of Chicago Press, 2017.
Morgan, Edwin, trans. *Beowulf: A Verse Translation into Modern English*. Manchester: Carcanet Press, 2002.
Morris, William. *News from Nowhere*. London: Commonweal, 1890.
Moten, Fred. *The Universal Machine*. Consent Not to Be a Single Being 3. Durham: Duke University Press, 2018.
Motion, Andrew. *Philip Larkin: A Writer's Life*. London: Faber and Faber, 1993.
Moulakis, Althanasios. *Simone Weil and the Politics of Self-Denial*. Translated by Ruth Hein. Minneapolis: University of Missouri Press, 1998.
Moulton, Mo. *The Mutual Admiration Society: How Dorothy L. Sayers and Her Oxford Circle Remade the World for Women*. London: Corsair, 2019.
Moxey, Keith. "Perspective, Panofsky, and the Philosophy of History." *New Literary History* 26, no. 4 (1995): 775–86.
Moyn, Samuel. "Hannah Arendt on the Secular." *New German Critique* 35, no. 3 (2008): 71–96.
Natorp, Paul. "Kant und die Marburger Schule." *Kant-Studien* 17, no. 3 (1912): 193–221.
Nava, Alexander. *The Mystical and Prophetic Thought of Simone Weil and Gustavo Gutiérrez: Reflections on the Mystery and Hiddenness of God*. Albany: State University of New York Press, 2001.
Nelson, Deborah. *Tough Enough: Arbus, Arendt, Didion, McCarthy, Sontag, Weil*. Chicago: University of Chicago Press, 2017.
Nelstrop, Louise. "Acting and Enacting: Mystical Theology and its Reception in France." In *Mysticism in the French Tradition: Eruptions from France*, edited by Louise Nelstrop and Bradley B. Onishi. 1–17. Farnham: Ashgate Publishing, 2015.
Newlyn, Lucy. *Reading, Writing, and Romanticism: The Anxiety of Reception*. Oxford: Oxford University Press, 2000.

Newman, Jane O. "Figural Passion: Auerbach's Racine and the (Un)Timing of (Early) Modernity." Paper presented at the Renaissance Society of America Conference, Boston, MA, April 2, 2016.

Newman, Jane O. "The Gospel According to Auerbach." *PMLA* 135, no. 3 (2020): 455–73.

Newman, Jane O. "'The Present Confusion Concerning the Renaissance': Burckhardtian Legacies in the Cold War United States." In *Other Renaissances: A New Approach to World Literature*, edited by Brenda Deen Schildgen, Gang Zhou, and Sander L. Gilman. 243–68. New York: Palgrave Macmillan, 2006.

Newton, Lloyd A., ed. *Medieval Commentaries on Aristotle's Categories*. Leiden: Brill, 2008.

Ney, Stephen. "Teleology and Secular Time in Armah and Ngũgĩ: Augustine, Manicheanism, and the African Novel." *Research in African Literatures*, 48, no. 2 (2017): 37–52.

Niell, Paul B., and Richard A. Sundt. "Architecture of Colonizers/Architecture of Immigrants: Gothic in Latin America from the 16th to the 20th Centuries." *postmedieval* 6, no. 3 (2015): 243–57.

Nirenberg, David. *Communities of Violence: Persecution of Minorities in the Middle Ages*. Princeton: Princeton University Press, 2015.

Nixon, Jon. *Hannah Arendt and the Politics of Friendship*. London: Bloomsbury Publishing, 2015.

North, Michael. "The Making of 'Make It New'." *Guernica*. August 15, 2013. www.guernicamag.com/the-making-of-making-it-new/

O'Donnell, C. Oliver. *Meyer Schapiro's Critical Debates: Art Through a Modern American Mind*. University Park: Pennsylvania State University Press, 2019.

O'Donnell, C. Oliver. "Two Modes of Mid-Century Iconology." *History of Humanities* 3, no. 1 (2018): 113–36.

Olschki, Leonardo. "Letter to Kantorowicz of 30 September, 1949." *Leonardo Olschki Papers*. Getty Research Institute.

Olschki, Leonardo. "Letter to the University of California Regents of 6 September, 1950." *Leonardo Olschki Papers*. Getty Research Institute.

Oosting, Jonathan. "FBI: Neo-Nazi Leader Sought 'White Ethno-State' in Michigan's Upper Peninsula." *Bridge Michigan*. May 17, 2021. www.bridgemi.com/michigan-government/fbi-neo-nazi-leader-sought-white-ethno-state-michigans-upper-peninsula

Oresme, Nicholas. *Questiones super Physicam*. Edited by Stefano Caroti, Jean Celeyrette, Stefan Kirschner, Edmond Mazet. Leiden: Brill, 2013.

Osborne, John. *Look Back in Anger*. Royal Court Theatre, 1956.

Oxford English Dictionary Online. Oxford: Oxford University Press. www.oed.com.

Paccagnella, Ivano, and Elisa Gregori, eds. *Ernst Robert Curtius e l'identità culturale dell'Europa: Atti del XXXVII Convegno Interuniversitario (Bressanone/Innsbruck, 13–16 luglio 2009)*. Padova: Esedra, 2011.

"Panofsky and Scholasticism." *The Vassar Chronicle*, December 9, 1944: 7.

Panofsky, Erwin. *Early Netherlandish Painting: Its Origins and Character*. Cambridge, MA: Harvard University Press, 1953.
Panofsky, Erwin. *Gothic Architecture and Scholasticism*. London: Thames and Hudson, 1957. Translated as *Architecture Gothique et Pensée Scolastique*. Translation and postface by Pierre Bourdieu. Paris: Les Éditions de Minuit, 1967.
Panofsky, Erwin. *Idea: Ein Beitrag zur Begriffsgeschichte der älteren Kunsttheorie*. Berlin: Bruno Hessling, 1960. Translated as *Idea: A Concept in Art Theory*. Translated by Joseph J. S. Peake. Columbia: University of South Carolina Press, 1968.
Panofsky, Erwin. *Meaning in the Visual Arts*. Garden City, NY: Doubleday, 1955.
Panofsky, Erwin. *Perspective as Symbolic Form*. Translated by Christopher Wood. New York: Zone Books, 1991.
Panofsky, Erwin. *Renaissance and Renascences in Western Art*. Stockholm: Almqvist & Wiksells, 1960.
Panofsky, Erwin. *Studies in Iconology: Humanistic Themes in the Art of the Renaissance*. New York: Harper & Row, 1972.
Pareles, Mo. "'What the Raven told the Eagle': Animal Language and the Return of Loss in *Beowulf*." In *Dating Beowulf: Studies in Intimacy*, edited by Daniel C. Remein and Erica Weaver. 165–85. Manchester: Manchester University Press, 2019.
Parker, Patricia. "Preposterous Events." *Shakespeare Quarterly* 43, no. 2 (1992): 186–213.
Pasnau, Robert. "Scholastic Qualities, Primary and Secondary." In *Primary and Secondary Qualities: The Historical and Ongoing Debate*, edited by Lawrence Nolan. 41–61. New York: Oxford University Press, 2011.
Patterson, Orlando. *Slavery and Social Death*. Cambridge, MA: Harvard University Press, 1982.
Pattison, George and Kate Kirkpatrick. *The Mystical Sources of Existentialist Thought: Being, Nothingness, Love*. New York: Routledge, 2019.
Pearl. Edited by Sarah Stanbury. Kalamazoo, MI: Medieval Institute Publications, 2001.
Peirce, Charles Sanders. "Fraser's *The Works of George Berkeley*." In *The Essential Peirce: Selected Philosophical Writings*. Vol. 1, edited by Nathan Houser and Christian Kloesel. 83–105. Bloomington: Indiana University Press, 1992.
Pels, Dick. *The Intellectual Stranger: Studies in Spokespersonship*. London: Routledge, 2000.
Perins, Joshua. *Leo Strauss and the Recovery of Medieval Political Philosophy*. Rochester: University of Rochester Press, 2016.
Perrin, J. M., and G. Thibon. *Simone Weil as We Knew Her*. Translated by Emma Craufurd. London: Routledge & Kegan Paul, 1953. Translation of *Simone Weil telle que nous l'avons connue*. Paris: La Colombe, 1952.
Pétrement, Simone. *Simone Weil: A Life*. Translated by Raymond Rosenthal. New York: Pantheon Books, 1976.

Phillips, Mark Salber and Gordon Schochet, eds. *Questions of Tradition*. Toronto: University of Toronto Press, 2004.

Pinnock, Sarah K. "Mystical Selfhood and Women's Agency: Simone Weil and French Feminist Philosophy." In *The Relevance of the Radical: Simone Weil 100 Years Later*, edited by A. Rebecca Rozelle-Stone and Lucian Stone. 205–20. New York: Continuum, 2010.

Pocock, J. G. A. "The Historiography of the *Translatio Imperii*." In *Barbarism and Religion: The First Decline and Fall*. 127–50. Cambridge: Cambridge University Press, 2003.

Porete, Marguerite. *The Mirror of Simple Souls*. Edited by Clare Kirchberger. London: Burnes Oates and Washbourne Ltd., 1927.

Porter, James I. "Erich Auerbach and the Judaizing of Philology" *Critical Inquiry* 35, no. 1 (2008): 115–47.

Porter, James I. "Old Testament Realism in the Writings of Erich Auerbach." In *Jews and the Ends of Theory*, edited by Shai Ginsburg, Martin Land, and Jonathan Boyarin. 187–224. New York: Fordham University Press, 2019.

Postan, M. M. *The Medieval Economy and Society: An Economic History of Britain, 1100–1500*. Berkeley: University of California Press, 1973.

Postan, M. M., and Eileen Power, eds. *Studies in English Trade in the 15th Century*. London: Routledge, 1933.

Pound, Ezra. *Ta Hio: The Great Learning*. Seattle: University of Washington, 1928.

Pugh, Tison, and Susan Aronstein, eds. *The Disney Middle Ages: A Fairy-Tale and Fantasy Past*. New York: Palgrave Macmillan, 2012.

Radkau, Joachim. *Max Weber: A Life*. Translated by Patrick Camiller. Cambridge: Polity Press, 2009.

Rambaran-Olm, Mary. "Misnaming the Medieval: Rejecting 'Anglo-Saxon' Studies." *History Workshop*. November 4, 2019. www.historyworkshop.org.uk/misnaming-the-medieval-rejecting-anglo-saxon-studies

Rasula, Jed. "Medusa's Gaze." In *The Legitimacy of the Middle Ages: On the Unwritten History of Theory*, edited by Andrew Cole and D. Vance Smith. 233–42. Durham, NC: Duke University Press, 2010.

Raulff, Ulrich. *Ein Historiker im 20. Jahrhundert: Marc Bloch*. Frankfurt am Main: S. Fisher, 1995.

Recht, Roland. *Believing and Seeing: The Art of Gothic Cathedrals*. Translated by Mary Whittall. Chicago: University of Chicago Press, 2008.

Redfern, Rebecca, and Joseph T. Hefner. "'Officially Absent but Actually Present': Bioarchaeological Evidence for Population Diversity in London during the Black Death, AD 1348–50." In *Bioarchaeology of Marginalized Peoples*, edited by Madeleine L. Mant and Alyson Jaagumägi Holland. 69–114. London: Academic Press, 2019.

Redfern, Rebecca, Michael Marshall, Katherine Eaton, and Hendrik N. Poinar. "'Written in Bone': New Discoveries about the Lives and Burials of Four Roman Londoners." *Britannia* 48 (2017): 253–77.

Reynolds, Barbara. *The Passionate Intellect: Dorothy L. Sayers' Encounter with Dante*. Eugene, OR: Wipf and Stock, 2005.

Richter, Gerhard. *Afterness: Figures of Following in Modern Thought and Aesthetics*. New York: Columbia University Press, 2011.
Rieff, Philip. *The Triumph of the Therapeutic: Use of Faith After Freud*. New York: Harper & Row, 1968.
Robb, David. "Scott, Alexander Mackie (1920–1989), Poet and Scholar of Scottish Literature." In *Oxford Dictionary of National Biography*. doi.org/10.1093/ref:odnb/60468.
Robbins, Harold J. "Duns Scotus' Theory of Categories and of Meaning." PhD diss., DePaul University, 1978.
Robertson, D. W., Jr. *Preface to Chaucer*. Princeton: Princeton University Press, 1962.
Rowlett, John. "Ralph Cohen on Literary Periods: Afterword as Foreword." *New Literary History* 50, no. 1 (2019): 129–39.
Rozelle-Stone, A. Rebecca, and Lucian Stone. *Simone Weil and Theology*. New York: Bloomsbury, 2013.
Ruehl, Martin A. "'In This Time Without Emperors': The Politics of Ernst Kantorowicz's *Kaiser Friedrich der Zweite* Reconsidered." *Journal of the Warburg and Courtauld Institutes* 63 (2000): 187–242.
Rush, Ormond. *The Reception of Doctrine: An Appropriation of Hans Robert Jauss' Reception Aesthetics and Literary Hermeneutics*. Rome: Gregorian University Press, 1997.
Rust, Jennifer. "Political Theologies of the *Corpus Mysticum*: Schmitt, Kantorowicz and de Lubac." In *Political Theology and Early Modernity*, edited by Graham Hammill and Julia Reinhard Lupton. 102–23. Chicago: University of Chicago, 2012.
Said, Edward. *Culture and Imperialism*. New York: Vintage Books, 1994.
Said, Edward. "Introduction to the Fiftieth-Anniversary Edition." In *Mimesis: The Representation of Reality in Western Literature*, by Erich Auerbach. ix–xxxii. Princeton: Princeton University Press, 2003.
Saltzman, Benjamin A. "Towards the Middle Ages to Come: The Temporalities of Walking with W. Morris, H. Adams, and Especially H. D. Thoreau." *postmedieval* 5, no. 2 (2014): 235–52.
Samuels, Andrew. "National Psychology, National Socialism, and Analytical Psychology: Reflections on Jung and Anti-Semitism, Part I." *Journal of Analytical Psychology* 37, no. 1 (1992): 3–28.
Santner, Eric L. *The Royal Remains: The People's Two Bodies and the Endgames of Sovereignty*. Chicago: University of Chicago Press, 2011.
Sayers, Dorothy L. "Are Women Human?" In *Are Women Human*, edited by Mary McDermott Shideler. 17–35. Grand Rapids: William B. Eerdmans, 1971.
Sayers, Dorothy L. "Charles Williams: A Poet's Critic." In *The Poetry of Search and the Poetry of Statement, and Other Posthumous Essays on Literature, Religion and Language*. 69–88. London: Victor Gollancz, 1963.
Sayers, Dorothy L. *Further Papers on Dante*. London: Methuen, 1957.
Sayers, Dorothy L. *Introductory Papers on Dante*. Preface by Barbara Reynolds. London: Methuen & Co., 1954.

Sayers, Dorothy L. "The Human-Not-Quite-Human." In *Are Women Human?*, edited by Mary McDermott Shideler. 37–47. Grand Rapids: William B. Eerdmans, 1941.

Sayers, Dorothy L. "The Poetry of the Image in Dante and Charles Williams." In *Further Papers on Dante*. 183–97. London: Methuen, 1957.

Sayers, Dorothy L. *The Letters of Dorothy L. Sayers, 1899–1936: The Making of a Detective Novelist*. Vol 1. Edited by Barbara Reynolds. London: Hodder, 1995.

Sayers, Dorothy L. *The Letters of Dorothy L. Sayers, 1944–1950: A Noble Daring*. Vol 3. Edited by Barbara Reynolds. London: Hodder, 1998.

Sayers. Dorothy L. "On Translating the *Divina Commedia*." In *The Poetry of Search and the Poetry of Statement, and Other Posthumous Essays on Literature, Religion and Language*. 91-126. London: Victor Gollancz, 1963.

Sayers, Dorothy L. "The 'Terrible' Ode." *Nottingham Medieval Studies* 9 (1965): 42–54.

Sayers, Dorothy L. "The Translation of Verse." In *The Poetry of Search and the Poetry of Statement, and Other Posthumous Essays on Literature, Religion and Language*. 127–53. London: Victor Gollancz, 1963.

Scanlon, Michael J. "Arendt's Augustine." In *Augustine and Postmodernism: Confession and Circumfession*, edited by John D. Caputo and Michael J. Scanlon. 159–72. Bloomington: Indiana University Press, 2005.

Schapiro, Meyer. "Philosophy and Worldview in Painting." In *Worldview in Painting: Art and Society*. 11–73. New York: George Braziller, 1999.

Schaub, Melissa. *Middlebrow Feminism in Classic British Detective Fiction: The Female Gentleman*. Basingstoke: Palgrave Macmillan, 2013.

Schmitt, Carl. *Der Begriff des Politischen*. Berlin: Duncker and Humblot, 1932. Translated as *The Concept of the Political*, expanded ed. Translated by George Schwab. Chicago: University of Chicago Press, 2007.

Schmitt, Carl. *Der Nomos der Erde im Völkerrecht des Jus Publicum Europaeum*. Berlin: Duncker & Humblot, 1950.

Schmitt, Carl. *Politische Theologie: Vier Kapitel zur Lehre von der Souveränität*. Berlin: Duncker & Humblot, 1922. Translated as *Political Theology: Four Chapters on the Concept of Sovereignty*. Translated by George Schwab. Chicago: University of Chicago Press, 2005.

Schramm, Percy Ernst. *Hitler: The Man and the Military Leader*. Translated by Donald S. Detwiler. Chicago: Academy Chicago Publishers, 1999.

Scott, Alexander. *The Latest in Elegies*. Glasgow: Caledonian Press, 1949.

Scragg, Donald G., ed. *The Battle of Maldon AD 991*. Oxford: Blackwell, 1991.

Sears, Elizabeth. "Panofsky on 'The Gothic Style'." Unpublished lecture at Zentralinstitut für Kunstgeschichte, Munich, July 3, 2019.

Sedlmeyer, Hans. *Die Entstehung der Kathedrale*. Zurich: Atlantis Verlag, 1950.

Sekyi-Otu, Ato. *Fanon's Dialectic of Experience*. Cambridge, MA: Harvard University Press, 1996.

Semper, Gottfried. *Style in the Technical and Tectonic Arts; or, Practical Aesthetics*. Translated by Harry Francis Mallgrave and Michael Robinson. Los Angeles: Getty Research Institute, 2004.

Shaw, Harry E. *Narrating Reality: Austen, Scott, Eliot*. Ithaca, NY: Cornell University Press, 1999.
Siemerling, Winfried. "W. E. B. Du Bois, Hegel, and the Staging of Alterity." *Callaloo* 24, no. 1. (2001): 325–33.
Skidelsky, Edward. "The Philosophy of Symbolic Forms." In *Ernst Cassirer: The Last Philosopher of Culture*. 100–27. Princeton: Princeton University Press, 2008.
Smalley, Beryl. "Review Article: *The King's Two Bodies*." *Past and Present* 20, no. 1 (1961): 30–35.
Smith, James McCune. "To the River Clyde (Scotland) (August, 1833)." Cassey & Dickerson Friendship Album Project. Philadelphia: Library Company of Philadelphia. lcpalbumproject.org/?page_id=344.
Solterer, Helen. "Performing Pasts: A Dialogue with Paul Zumthor." *Journal of Medieval and Early Modern Studies* 27, no. 3 (1997): 595–640.
Sorace, Christian, Ivan Franceschini, and Nicholas Loubere, eds. *Afterlives of Chinese Communism*. New York: Verso, 2019.
Sosnowska, Paulina. "The Reinforcement of Political Myth? Hans Blumenberg, Hannah Arendt and the History of the Twentieth Century." *Eidos* 3, no. 2 (2019): 51–61.
Spitzer, Leo. "Review of Ernst Robert Curtius, *Europäische Literatur und lateinisches Mittelalter*." *American Journal of Philology* 70, no. 4 (1949): 425–31.
Spitzer, Leo. "Zum Goethekult," *Die Wandlung*, 4 (1949).
Spivak, Gayatri Chakravorty. "Can the Subaltern Speak?" In *Marxism and the Interpretation of Culture*, edited by Cary Nelson and Lawrence Grossberg. 271–313. Urbana: University of Illinois Press, 1988.
Staley, Lynn. [As Lynn Staley Johnson]. "The Trope of the Scribe and The Question of Literary Authority in the Works of Julian of Norwich and Margery Kempe." *Speculum* 66 (1991): 820–38.
Staley, Lynn. *Margery Kempe's Dissenting Fictions*. University Park: Pennsylvania State University Press, 1994.
"Statement adopted by Regents June 24, 1949." University of California Archives. content.cdlib.org/view?docId=hb787011nc&brand=oac4
Steigmann-Gall, Richard. *The Holy Reich: Nazi Conceptions of Christianity, 1919–1945*. Cambridge: Cambridge University Press, 2003.
Stewart, Jeffrey C. *The New Negro: The Life of Alain Locke*. New York: Oxford University Press, 2018.
Strauss, Leo. "Notes on Carl Schmitt, *The Concept of the Political*." Translated by J. Harvey Lomax. In *The Concept of the Political*, expanded edition. 97–122. Chicago: University of Chicago Press, 2007.
Strauss, Leo. *What Is Political Philosophy?* Chicago: University of Chicago Press, 1988.
Stray, Christopher. "Sisam, Kenneth (1887–1971), Anglo-Saxon Scholar and Publisher." *Oxford Dictionary of National Biography*. doi.org/10.1093/ref:odnb/94507.
Strong, Tracy B. "Foreword: The Sovereign and the Exception: Carl Schmitt, Politics, Theology, and Leadership." In *Political Theology: Four Chapters on the Concept of Sovereignty*, by Carl Schmitt. vii–xxxv. Chicago: University of Chicago Press, 2005.

Sweeney, Fionnghuala, and Kate Marsh, eds. "Afromodernism: Modernity, Paris and the Atlantic World." Special Edition, *International Journal of Francophone Studies* 14, no. 1/2 (2011).

Sweezy, Paul. "A Critique." In *The Transition from Feudalism to Capitalism*. 33–56. London: NLB, 1976.

Symes, Carol. "The Middle Ages between Nationalism and Colonialism." *French Historical Studies* 34, no. 1 (2011): 37–46.

Tate, Claudia. *Psychoanalysis and Black Novels: Desire and the Protocols of Race*. Oxford: Oxford University Press, 1998.

Taylor, Charles. *A Secular Age*. Cambridge, MA: Harvard University Press, 2007.

Thibon, Gustave. "Introduction." In *La pesanteur et la grâce*, by Simone Weil. Paris: Librarie Plon, 1948. Translated as "Introduction." In *Gravity and Grace*, by Simone Weil. Translated by Emma Crawford and Mario von der Ruhr. vii–xl. New York: Routledge, 2002.

Thomas Aquinas. *Quodlibetal Questions I and II*. Translated by Sandra Edwards. Toronto: Pontifical Institute of Mediaeval Studies, 1983.

Thomas of Erfurt. *De modis significandi*. In *Thomas of Erfurt: Grammatica Speculativa*, edited and translated by G. L. Bursill-Hall. 127–322. London: Longman, 1972.

Thomson, Iain. "Thinking Love: Heidegger and Arendt." *Continental Philosophy Review* 50 (2017): 453–78.

Thornbury, Emily V. *Becoming a Poet in Anglo-Saxon England*. Cambridge: Cambridge University Press, 2014.

Tolkien, J. R. R. *The Fellowship of the Ring*. London: George Allen and Unwin, 1954.

Tolkien, J. R. R. *The Hobbit*. London: George Allen and Unwin, 1937.

Tolkien, J. R. R. *The Monsters and the Critics and Other Essays*. London: George Allen and Unwin, 1983.

Trigg, Stephanie. *Congenial Souls: Reading Chaucer from Medieval to Postmodern*. Minneapolis: University of Minnesota Press, 2002.

Ullyot, Jonathan. *The Medieval Presence in Modernist Literature: The Quest to Fail*. New York: Cambridge University Press, 2016.

van Deusen, Nancy. "Assembled in the Presence of God: Majestic Perseverance and the *cantus coronatus*." In *Mobs: An Interdisciplinary Inquiry*, edited by Nancy van Deusen and Leonard Michael Koff. 79–94. Leiden: Brill, 2012.

van Deusen, Nancy. "*Laudes regiae*, In Praise of Kings: Medieval Acclamations, Liturgy, and the Ritualization of Power." In *Procession, Performance, Liturgy, and Ritual: Essays in Honor of Bryan R. Gillingham*, edited by Nancy van Deusen. 83–118. Ottawa: Institute for Medieval Music, 2007.

van Deusen, Nancy, ed. *The Place of the Psalms in the Intellectual Culture of the Middle Ages*. Binghamton: State University of New York Press, 1999.

van Deusen, Nancy. "*Ubi Lex*? Robert Grosseteste's Discussion of Law, Letter, and Time and Its Musical Exemplification." *Dayton Philosophical Review* 22 (1994): 219–32.

van Engen, John. "The Christian Middle Ages as an Historiographical Problem." *The American Historical Review* 91, no. 3 (1986): 519–52.

van Oort, Johannes. *Jerusalem and Babylon: A Study into Augustine's City of God and the Sources of his Doctrine of the Two Cities*. New York: Brill, 1991.
van Oort, Johannes. *Mani and Augustine: Collected Essays on Mani, Manichaeism and Augustine*. Leiden: Brill, 2020.
van Wyk Smith, Malvern. *The First Ethiopians: The Image of Africa and Africans in the Early Mediterranean World*. Johannesburg: Wits University Press, 2001.
Vance, Eugene. "A Coda: Modern Medievalism and the Understanding of Understanding." *New Literary History* 10, no. 2 (1979): 377–83.
Verduin, Kathleen. "Sayers, Sex, and Dante." *Dante Studies* 111 (1993): 223–33.
Vernon, Matthew X. *The Black Middle Ages: Race and the Construction of the Middle Ages*. New York: Palgrave Macmillan, 2018.
Vessey, David. "Gadamer, Augustine, Aquinas, and Hermeneutic Universality." *Philosophy Today* 55, no. 2 (2011): 158–65.
Vessey, David. "Who Was Gadamer's Husserl?" *The New Yearbook for Phenomenology and Phenomenological Philosophy* 7 (2007): 1–23.
Vetö, Miklos. *The Religious Metaphysics of Simone Weil*. Translated by Joan Dargan. Albany: State University of New York Press, 1994.
Viola, Tullio. "Peirce and Iconology: Habitus, Embodiment, and the Analogy between Philosophy and Architecture." *European Journal of Pragmatism and American Philosophy* 4, no. 1 (2012): 1–28.
Viswanathan, Gauri. *Masks of Conquest: Literary Study and British Rule in India*. 25th Anniversary ed. New York: Columbia University Press, 2015.
von Ranke, Leopold. "On Progress in History (from the First Lecture to King Maximilian II of Bavaria, 'On the Epochs of Modern History', 1854)." In *The Theory and Practice of History*, edited by Georg G. Iggers. Translated by Wilma A. Iggers. 20–23. New York: Routledge, 2011.
von Simson, Otto Georg. "The Gothic Cathedral: Design and Meaning." In *Change in Medieval Society: Europe North of the Alps*, edited by Sylvia L. Thrupp. 168–87. New York: Appleton-Century-Crofts, 1964.
von Simson, Otto Georg. *The Gothic Cathedral: Origins of Gothic Architecture and the Medieval Concept of Order*. Princeton: Princeton University Press, 1987.
Waddell, Helen. *Poetry in the Dark Ages*. Glasgow: Jackson, Son & Company, 1948.
Waddy, Helena. *Oberammergau in the Nazi Era: The Fate of a Catholic Village in Hitler's Germany*. Oxford: Oxford University Press, 2010.
Wallace, David. "General Introduction." In *Europe: A Literary History, 1348–1418*, edited by David Wallace. xxvii–xlii. Oxford: Oxford University Press, 2015.
Wallace, David. "Medieval Studies in Troubled Times: The 1930s" *Speculum* 95, no. 1 (2020): 1–35.
Walwyn, K. S., and Clare L. Taylor. "Ellerman, (Annie) Winifred [pseud. Bryher] (1894–1983), Writer and Philanthropist." In *Oxford Dictionary of National Biography*. doi.org/10.1093/ref:odnb/31067.
Warner, Sylvia Townsend. *The Corner That Held Them*. New York: Viking, 1948.
Warren, Calvin. *Ontological Terror: Blackness, Nihilism, and Emancipation*. Durham, NC: Duke University Press, 2018.

Warren, Michelle R. *Creole Medievalism: Colonial France and Joseph Bédier's Middle Ages*. Minneapolis: University of Minnesota Press, 2010.

Wasianski, E. A. C. *Über Immanuel Kant. Immanuel Kant in seinen lezten Lebensjahren* 3. Königsberg: F. Nicolovius Königsberg, 1804.

Waters, Lindsay, and Wlad Godzich, eds. and trans. *Reading de Man Reading*. Minneapolis: University of Minnesota Press, 1989.

Watson, Nicholas. "The Middle English Mystics." In *The Cambridge History of Medieval English Literature*, edited by David Wallace. 539–65. New York: Cambridge University Press, 1999.

Weil, Simone. *Attente de Dieu*. Paris: Fayard, 1985. Translated as *Waiting for God*. Translated by Emma Craufurd. New York: Harper Colophon, 1973.

Weil, Simone. *Cahiers*. Edited by Alyette Degrâces, Marie-Annette Fourneyron, Flourence de Lussy, and Michael Narcy. Œuvres Complètes 6. Paris: Gallimard, 2002. Translated as *The Notebooks of Simone Weil*, 3 vols. Translated by Arthur Willis. New York: Routledge, 2004. Also translated as *First and Last Notebooks*. Translated by Richard Rees. Oxford: Oxford University Press, 1970.

Weil, Simone. *L'enracinement: Prélude à une déclaration des devoirs envers l'être humain*. Paris: Gallimard, 1949. Translated as *The Need for Roots: Prelude to a Declaration of Duties Toward Mankind*. Translated by Arthur Wills. New York: Octagon Books, 1979.

Weil, Simone. *Love in the Void: Where God Finds Us*. Edited by Laurie Gagne. New York: Plough Publishing House, 2018.

Weil, Simone. *La pesanteur et la grâce*. Paris: Librarie Plon, 1948. Translated as *Gravity and Grace*. Translated by Emma Crawford and Mario von der Ruhr. New York: Routledge, 2002.

Wellek, René. "Auerbach's Special Realism." *The Kenyon Review* 16, no. 2 (1954): 299–307.

Wellek, René, and Austin Warren. *Theory of Literature*. 3rd ed. New York: Harcourt, 1977.

Whalen, Brett Edward. "Political Theology and the Metamorphoses of *The King's Two Bodies*." *American Historical Review* 125, no. 1 (2020): 132–45.

Whitaker, Cord J. "B(l)ack Home in the Middle Ages: Medievalism in Jessie Redmon Fauset's 'My House and a Glimpse of My Life Therein'." *postmedieval* 10, no. 2 (2019): 162–75.

Whitaker, Cord J. *Black Metaphors: How Modern Racism Emerged from Medieval Race Thinking*. Philadelphia: University of Pennsylvania Press, 2019.

Whitaker, Cord J. "Race-ing the Dragon: The Middle Ages, Race and Trippin' into the Future." *postmedieval* 6, no. 1 (2015): 3–11.

Whitaker, Cord J. "'We Were Outside History': The Middle Ages in *Invisible Man* and the Struggle for Black Lives in 2020." *PMLA* 136, no. 3 (2021): 432–40.

White, Hayden. "Auerbach's Literary History: Figural Causation and Modernist Historicism." In *Literary History and the Challenge of Philology: The Legacy of Erich Auerbach*, edited by Seth Lerer. 124–39. Stanford: Stanford University Press, 1996.

Wilderson, Frank B. *Afropessimism*. New York: Liveright, 2020.
Williams, Chad L. "The Wounded World: W. E. B. Du Bois and the History of WWI." Lecture, Radcliffe Institute for Advanced Study, Harvard University, Cambridge. November 30, 2017. www.youtube.com/watch?v=8hpiK7gUf_c
Williams, Chad L. "World War I in the Historical Imagination of W. E. B. Du Bois." *Modern American History* 1, no. 1 (2018): 3–22.
Wilson, Angus. *Anglo-Saxon Attitudes*. London: Secker & Warburg, 1956.
Wilson, Angus. *Hemlock and After*. London: Secker & Warburg, 1952.
Wilson, Angus, Andrew Davies, and Diarmuid Lawrence. *Anglo Saxon Attitudes*. TV Miniseries. Euston Films Ltd., 1992.
Wilson, W. Daniel. *Das Goethe-Tabu: Protest und Menschenrechte im klassischen Weimar*. Munich: Deutscher Taschenbuch Verlag, 1999.
Wimmer, Mario. "Kantorowicz's Oaths: A Californian Moment in the History of Academic Freedom." *Österreichische Zeitschrift für Geschichtswissenschaften* 25, no. 3 (2014): 116–47.
Wimmer, Mario. "The Afterlives of Scholarship: Warburg and Cassirer." *History of Humanities* 2, no. 1 (2017): 245–70.
Wolin, Richard. *The Seduction of Unreason: The Intellectual Romance with Fascism from Nietzsche to Postmodernism*. Princeton: Princeton University Press, 2004.
Wood, Christopher. "Introduction." *Perspective as Symbolic Form*, by Erwin Panofsky. 7–24. New York: Zone Book, 1991.
Wood, Ellen Meiksins. *The Origin of Capitalism: A Longer View*. New York: Verso, 2002.
Woodson, Carter G. "Review of W. E. B. Du Bois, *Color and Democracy: Colonies and Peace*." *The Journal of Negro History* 30, no. 3 (July 1945): 342–43.
Woolf, Virginia. *Collected Essays*. 4 vols. London: Hogarth Press, 1966–1967.
Wrenn, C. L. "Review of Bone, *Anglo-Saxon Poetry*." *Medium Ævum* 13 (1944): 68–71.
Wuttke, Dieter, ed. *Erwin Panofsky Korrespondenz 1910 bis 1968*. 5 vols. Wiesbaden: Harrassowitz, 2001–2014.
Zakai, Avihu. *Erich Auerbach and the Crisis of German Philology: The Humanist Tradition in Peril*. Basel, Switzerland: Springer, 2017.
Zakai, Avihu, and David Weinstein. "Erich Auerbach and His 'Figura': An Apology for the Old Testament in an Age of Aryan Philology." *Religions* 3, no. 2 (2012): 320–38.
Zamir, Shamoon. *Dark Voices: W. E. B. Du Bois and American Thought, 1888–1903*. Chicago: University of Chicago Press, 1995.
Zemgulys, Andrea. "Review of Bryher, *Visa for Avalon*, ed. Susan McCabe." *Modern Language Studies* 35, no. 1 (2005): 91–93.
Žižek, Slavoj, Eric L. Santner, and Kenneth Reinhard. *The Neighbor: Three Inquiries in Political Theology*. Chicago: University of Chicago Press, 2006.
Zumthor, Paul. *Essai de poétique médiévale*. Paris: Éditions du Seuil, 1972. Translated as *Toward a Medieval Poetics*. Translated by Philip Bennett. Minneapolis: University of Minnesota Press, 1992.

Zumthor, Paul. "Médiéviste ou pas." *Poétique* 31 (1977): 306–21.
Zumthor, Paul. *Parler du moyen age*. Paris: Les Editions de Minuit, 1980. Translated as *Speaking of the Middle Ages*. Translated by Sarah White. Lincoln: University of Nebraska Press, 1986.
Zumthor, Paul, Annette Tomarken, and Edward Tomarken. "From Hi(story) to Poem, or the Paths of Pun: The Grands Rhétoriquers of Fifteenth-Century France." *New Literary History* 10, no. 2 (1979): 231–63.
Zumthor, Paul, and Betty R. H. Sapir. "Comments on H. R. Jauss's Article." *New Literary History* 10, no. 2 (1979): 367–76.
Zupitza, Julius. *Beowulf: Autotypes of the Unique Cotton MS Vitellius A xv*. Early English Text Society o.s. 77. London: 1882.

Index

a priori, the, 279
  for Kant, 170, 176
  for Marburg school, 170, 174
Aberdeen, University of, 147
Achard, Paul, 61–62
Adorno, Theodor, 2, 26, 64, 114n25, 262, 265
Afromedievalism, 70–71
  Black Madonnas, 86
  and Maurice, Saint, 86
  as modernist, 80–81, 85–87
  and *Parzival* (von Eschenbach), 86
Afromodernism, 78. *See also* modernism
Agamben, Giorgio
  "bare life," 114
  on *The King's Two Bodies* (Kantorowicz), 5
Algeria, 36–49, 56–62
  and Augustine, 41
  burial place of Fanon, 61
  French war in, 27, 40, 56, 58–59, 60
  independence from France, 20, 36, 57
  indigeneity in, 43, 61–62
  medieval landscape of, 46
  University of, 36
American Revolution, 288
Amis, Kingsley, 1
  on *Anglo-Saxon Attitudes* (Wilson), 150
  "Beowulf," 29, 149, 153–55
  and *Beowulf* (Bryher), 161
  Bright November, 149
  career of, 152
  Lucky Jim, 29, 150, 153, 161–63
Angry Young Men, 151
Annales School, 2n2, 21, 23, 26–27, 232
appropriation of medieval history, 6–10, 12–13, 28–29, 10n37, 106, 286, 290–91. *See also* history; medievalism
  and impact on Black people, 81, 85
  by Nazis, 6–7, 28, 106–107
  by white supremacists, 4, 13n46, 28, 87, 126, 286
Aquinas, Thomas, 55, 107, 122, 243, 269, 280, 283n28. *see also* Scholasticism

Summa Theologica, 178, 179
Arendt, Hannah, 1–4, 11, 17, 28–29, 106–27, 286–89
  on the Augustinian community, 115–16
  education of, 14
  on the Eichmann trial, 109n16, 118–19, 287
  and Fanon, 39–40, 125
  on freedom, 114
  Love in Saint Augustine, 107, 116–18, 124
  and Heidegger, 14, 109, 115n28, 120, 287
  on the Hobbesian individual, 111–12
  The Human Condition, 108–109, 287
  The Life of the Mind, 107, 109, 286
  on man's place in the world, 116–17
  on the Nazi problem, 109
  on neighborly love, 5–6, 108, 117–18, 124–27, 287–88
  The Origins of Totalitarianism, 17, 108, 110–18
  On Revolution, 288
  and Weil, 289
  on the will, 119–20
Aristotle, 54–55, 107
  Categories, 54
  Metaphysics, 122n38
  Poetics, 261
  Rhetoric, 277
asceticism, 239, 245
Ashley, William (economist), 15
Auden, W. H.
  In Memory of W. B. Yeats, 147
Auerbach, Erich, 2, 3, 17n61, 31, 255
  and comparative literature, 22
  and Curtius, 8–9
  and Huizinga, 227, 229, 276
  library of, 228
  Literary Language, 216, 221
  Mimesis, 13, 16, 131, 215, 276
  reception of, 218–19, 238
  and periodization, 217–19n20

Auerbach, Erich (cont.)
  Renaissance Novellas (*Zur Technik der Frührenaissancenovelle in Italien und Frankeich*), 226
  "Romanticism and Realism," 218–21, 230
  teaching at Marburg, 230
Augustine, Saint, 3, 6, 292, 297–98
  Against the Epistle of Manichaeus Called Fundamental, 49
  and Algeria, 35–36, 40–41, 58–61
  and Arendt, 6, 14, 28–29, 107–24, 127, 286–89
  The City of God, 49
  and Fanon, 27, 35–36, 40–41, 49–50, 58–65, 292–93
  and Gadamer, 269
  and Hobbes, 28, 107–108, 110–11, 113–18
  and Algeria, 35–36, 40–41, 58–61
  and Manicheism, 35, 59, 63
  Mandouze, as scholar of, 60
  on legal temporality, 90
  and the will, 90, 120
Avicenna, 107, 122n37, 294n62

Baidou, Alain, 294n62
Bandmann, Günter, 280n18
Balzac, Honoré de, 138
  as realist author, 218, 219
Barthes, Roland, 2, 191, 208, 262, 263, 291
  and Jauss, 262–63
Bataille, Georges, 2, 245n42, 284, 289
The Battle of Maldon (Old English poem), 147. *See also* Scott
Beauvoir, Simone de, 2, 17
  The Ethics of Ambiguity, 16
  The Second Sex, 16
Bengel, Johann Albrecht, 294
Benjamin, Walter, 15, 291
Berlin, University of, 15, 105, 276n6, 295
Bhabha, Homi, 39n16, 62
Black medievalism. *See* Afromedievalism
Blackness, 37, 41, 54–56, 63, 74, 85–87. *See also* whiteness
Bloch, Ernst, 2, 6, 14, 106–107, 294n62
Bloch, Marc, 88n2, 98, 232
Blumenberg, Hans, 4, 18–19, 273n1, 282–83, 286n40, 298–99
Bois, Guy (historian), 25
Bollingen Series, 144–45
Bone, Gavin, 29, 155–57, 290
  Anglo-Saxon Poetry, 155–56
  Beowulf in Modern Verse, 155–57
  contrast with Tolkien, 156
  impression on Amis, 149
  influence on Morgan, 156
  The Seafarer, 156

The Wanderer, 156
Bonn, University of, 105, 133, 135
Bourdieu, Pierre, 2, 30, 280
  and "habitus," 188–89
  and Panofsky, 4
  and reception of *Gothic Architecture and Scholasticism* (Panofsky), 169
  on superstructure and symbolic capital, 57
Bracciolini, Poggio, 278
Brenner, Robert (historian), 24–26
Bruno, Giordano, 19
Bryher (Annie Winifred Ellerman), 2
  and "Beowulf" (Amis), 161
  Beowulf, 29, 151, 153, 158–61, 164, 290, 291
    difficulty publishing, 158, 161
    and empire, 164–65
    reception of, 160
    writing of, 164
  career of, 152
  The Fourteenth of October, 152, 160
  reception of, 153–54
Burckhardt, Jacob
  The Civilization of the Renaissance in Italy, 216, 224, 276

California, University of, 28, 103
  Loyalty Oath Crisis, 89, 93–99, 282
Cambridge University, 191
  and women, 13
Cantor, Norman (historian), 2n2, 26–27, 279n13
Capitalism, 23–26, 46, 52, 80, 112–13, 294. *See also* Marxism
Carroll, Lewis, 150, 163
Cassiodorus
  Commentary on the Psalms, 91–92, 95, 281
Cassirer, Ernst
  and Panofsky, 30, 170–75, 279
  Philosophy of Symbolic Forms, 168, 172
  The Problem of Knowledge, 171
Catholicism, 14, 31, 106n1, 240, 289. *See also* Christianity
Césaire, Aimé, 20–21, 66
Charlemagne, 4–5, 107n4, 277, 298
Charles the Bold, 222–23
Chartier, Alain (medieval poet), 15
Chartier, Émile-Auguste (teacher of Weil), 15–16, 244
Chaucer, Geoffrey
  Man of Law's Tale, 76
  Treatise on the Astrolabe, 72
Cicero, 278
Cohen, Hermann, 170, 279
  revision of Kant, 170–71
Cold War, the, 11, 23–26
colonialism, 22n84, 60. *See also* decolonization
  and enslaved labor, 86

and indigineity, 61–63
justifications made for, 43
and manicheism, 36, 39–41, 43, 45–50, 58–60, 65
as medieval, 52–53, 85
narratives of legitimacy of, 62
and postcolonial studies, 27, 35, 36, 47, 68, 292
Columbia University, 6n20, 17
communism, 23, 96. *See also* Marxism
the "Constance" group (medieval romances), 76
Constance, University of, 258
Cortés, Juan Donoso, 285
Christianity, 62, 74–75, 191, 223, 241, 244, 248, 252–53, 286, 289–90. *See also* Catholicism; mysticism
Crusades, 10n37, 20, 223, 293
Cullen, Countee, 78
Curtius, Ernst Robert, 2, 255, 276–79
  and archetypes, 137–40
  and Auerbach, 8
  career of, 132–33
  on critics of Dante, 140
  on filling historical gaps, 256
  European Literature and the Latin Middle Ages, 7–8, 29, 131, 146
    English publication of, 144–45
  "The German Spirit in Peril," 133
  and Jung, 29, 131–46, 277–79
  on literature, 7–8, 29, 132, 143
    atemporality of, 140
    biology of, 139
    Divina Commedia (Dante) as representative of, 141–43
    inspirations of, 141
    reception of, 145
  on Roman antiquity, 137
  on translations of Homer, 141

Dante Alighieri
  for the common reader, 193
  De Monarchia, 56
  Divina Commedia, 30, 141–43, 190
  on female desire, 199–200
  modern relevance of, 191, 284
  sources for, 140, 203
  translators of, 210
  and violence and eroticism, 198, 209
  and Virgil, 203
  and whiteness, 55
  and women, 208
decolonization, 19–23, 61. *See also* colonialism
Delacroix, Henri, 242–43. *See also* Weil
Deor (Old English poem), 147. *See also* Scott
Derrida, Jacques, 2, 274
Dide, Maurice (psychologist), 48, 50
Dobb, Maurice (historian), 24–26
Dreyfus, Alfred, 40, 110

Du Bois, W. E. B., 2, 15, 28, 68, 293
  "The African Roots of War," 83
  on art, purpose of, 78–80
  on Black Americans in World War I, 81–82
  on the colonial rationale, 20
  "Color and Democracy" (speech), 85
  Color and Democracy, 84–85
  criticism of Dumbarton Oaks accords, 84
  Dark Princess, 28, 68, 75–78, 82–84
  on decolonization, 22
  on double consciousness, 69, 75, 81–83, 86
  education of, 15, 295
  on Greco-Roman antiquity, 73
  on human freedom, 84
  on human sovereignty, 75
  on the medieval as epistemic tool, 72, 87
  on the origins of war, 82
  political medievalism of, 68
  "The Princess Steel," 28, 68, 71–75, 76
  Souls of Black Folk, 69
  on tropes of medieval romance, 76
  The World and Africa, 85n54
  on the world in crisis, 19–20
Duns Scotus, John, 3, 107, 121–24, 286
Durkheim, Emile, 284n32

East Anglia, University of, 152
Eckhart, Meister, 250–51, 253–54
Eisenhower, Dwight D., 23
Elias, Norbert, 21
Eliot, T. S., 1, 156, 277
  on the presence of the past, 17
  "Tradition and Individual Talent," 203, 290
  The Waste Land, 1, 80
  on Weil, 239
Ellerman, Annie Winifred. *See* Bryher
eschatology, 18, 49–50, 77
Eucharist, the, 281
Euclid, 171
Eusebius, 297

Fanon, Frantz, 2, 23, 27, 292, 295
  on the Algerian war, 27
  and Arendt, 39, 125
  and Augustine, 58
  Black Skin, White Masks, 35–39, 47–48, 50–51, 58–59, 63
  on *Categories* (Aristotle), 54–55
  colonial inheretence in urban and rural distinctions, 45–46
  on decolonization, 21–22
  as Hegelian, 37–38, 47, 50–52, 56
  on manicheism, 35–67
    as domination, 47

Fanon, Frantz (cont.)
    as pathology, 48
    as psychosis, 50
    definition of, 41
    on "primitive Manicheism," 42
    reception of, 36–37n8, 41n26
    The Wretched of the Earth, 21–22, 35–49, 53–57, 59, 63–67
Fanon, Josie, 36
fascism, 17, 60, 106, 110, 197, 289. See also Nazism; white supremacy
Fauset, Jessie Redmon, 78
Febvre, Lucien, 232–33
feminism, 30, 159, 194–97, 207, 210, 296
    "immasculation," 200–201
Ferguson, Wallace K.
    The Renaissance in Historical Thought, 216
feudalism, 21, 23–25, 28, 46, 57, 68–71, 294–95
Foucault, Michel, 286n37
Frankfurt School, the, 17, 101, 105
French Revolution, 288
Freud, Sigmund, 76n19, 117n34, 277n7, 296
Friedländer, Paul, 237n71

Gadamer, Hans-Georg, 2, 32, 255, 257–58, 264–69, 291
    on dialogue, 265
    on hermeneutics, 258, 264, 268
    and Jauss, 257–58, 268
    medieval influence on, 269
    on temporal distance, 269
    Wahrheit und Methode, 257
Gall, Ernst
    objections to *Gothic Architecture and Scholasticism* (Panofsky), 186
Gawain and the Green Knight (Middle English poem), 76
genealogies, intellectual, 3–4
    of Fanon, 40, 63
    literary, 207–8, 210, 220
    of manicheism, 50
    in Marburg school, 170
    of midcentury German intellectuals, 14–15
    in the study of hermeneutics, 255
genealogy, concept of
    of Dante, 194, 206–8
    European inheritance, 217
    and indigeneity, 43
    isolation of, for enslaved people, 81
George, Stefan, 13, 101, 285
Glasgow, University of, 147, 148, 153
Global Middle Ages, 11, 270, 292
Goethe, Johann Wolfgang von, 277
Gombrich, Ernst, 279
Gothic architecture, 21, 30, 176–88, 280–81

Gramsci, Antonio, 2, 23, 25
Gregory the Great, 263
Greifswald, University of, 226
Guiraud, Paul (psychologist), 48, 50

H. D. (Hilda Doolittle), 152, 158–60, 290
Habermas, Jürgen, 274n5
Haller, Ludwig von, 295
Harlem Renaissance, 78
Harvard University, 15, 68, 295
Heaney, Seamus, 153
Hegel, Georg Wilhelm Friedrich, 2, 28, 37, 264, 293–95. See also Du Bois; Fanon; Panofsky
    on bondsman-master dialectic, 37–38, 49–57, 68–70
    on the concept of history, 170
    on determination, 47, 63
    on "drama of alterity," 81
    medievalism of, 68, 87, 177, 293–95
    Phenomenology of Spirit, 38, 66, 68, 293
Heidegger, Martin, 2
    and Arendt, 14, 109, 120, 287
    Duns Scotus's Theory of the Categories and of Meaning, 14
    and Gadamer, 265
    skepticism of individual will, 124
    will-to-not-will, 109
Heidelberg, University of, 94, 226, 257
Hildegard of Bingen, 247
historicism
    and Curtius, 141
    as naive historicism, 3, 6, 256
    and Zumthor, 4
historiography, 21, 23–24, 44–45, 53, 57, 141, 160–61, 224, 260
history, 2–3, 6, 14, 18–23, 27, 32, 68–71, 74, 84–85, 87, 106–107, 110, 119, 131–32, 140–43, 161–63, 215–38, 275–76, 285, 297–300. See also appropriation of medieval history; Latinity; periodization
    of art, 6, 30, 132, 167–89
    construction of, 4
    economic, 15, 25–27
    and Fanon, 35–67
    of ideas, 89
    of London, 151
    of medieval studies, 255–63, 269–72
    and the modern era, 17
    of mysticism, 243
    of Scotland, 148
    of the United States, 27–28, 80–81
Hobbes, Thomas, 110–15, 285, 287–88
    and Arendt, 110–15
    and Augustine, 28, 107–108, 113–18

on individual interest, 124
Leviathan, 100, 102
Honnecourt, Villard de, 186
Horkheimer, Max, 64, 114n25
Hughes, Langston, 78
Huizinga, Johan, 2, 31, 217, 276
   and Auerbach, 276
   Autumn of the Middle Ages, 217, 227, 231–34
      reception of, 221, 232–33
   "Burgundy: A Crisis," 221–24
   on Charles the Bold, 222
   "My Path to History," 224
Hyppolite, Jean, 50–51

identity
   authorial, 194, 208–209, 246–47
   and colonialism, 43, 292
   corporate, 92, 284
   exploitative, 42
   gendered, 134n16, 197–98, 200–203, 208–209
      masculine, 76, 151, 153–55, 197, 209
   as judgement, 210
   in postwar England, 164
   production of, 51, 58
   racial, 37, 63 (*see also* Blackness, whiteness)
      for Black Americans, 71n13, 81–82
   in romance, 70
   and Zumthor, 257
India
   and colonialism, 20, 83
indigeneity, 45n34, 61–63
Inklings, the (Oxford intellectual group), 206
Interwar Period, 152. *See also* World War I, World War II, World Wars
Islam, 62, 72, 75, 293
Istanbul University, 227, 228, 230

James, William, 134, 246
Jameson, Fredric, 3, 56, 273, 299
Jaspers, Karl, 107, 277n8
Jauss, Hans Robert, 2, 32, 255, 291
   "The Alterity and Modernity of the Middle Ages," 269
   Ästhetische Erfahrung und literarische Hermeneutik, 261, 268
   and Barthes, 262–63
   and Gadamer, 257–58, 268
   on hermeneutic distance, 265–66, 268–70
   Kleine Apologie der ästhetischen Erfahrung, 262
   on literature, 265
   Literaturgeschichte als Provokation, 257, 258
   Poetik und Hermeneutik, 258
   reader response theory, 258
   on the "surprise of alterity," 265
   Weltmodell, 270

   and Zumthor, 257, 260–61, 265, 267, 269, 272
Joan of Arc, 249
John of the Cross, Saint, 249
Joyce, James, 277
Judaism, 8n31, 241, 289
Julian of Norwich, 70
Jung, Carl, 2, 29, 133–40, 142–46, 277
   on *anima*, concept of, 134, 137, 138, 142
   on archetypes, 137–39, 277
   collected works of, 144
   on the human psyche, 144
   and racism and anti-Semitism, 277
   problems with theory of, 136
   on the unconscious, 132, 135–36
Jünger, Ernst, 288n47

Kafka, Franz
   The Castle, 80
Kant, Immanuel, 169, 279
   on the *a priori*, 170, 174
   and Panofsky, 175–76
Kantorowicz, Ernst, 2, 13, 28, 285, 291
   career of, 105
   The Fundamental Issue, 95–96, 98
   The King's Two Bodies, 99, 281
      as medieval composition, 103
      reception of, 88
   and Maitland, 89n5, 92, 95, 103
   on medieval canon law, 96
   and Panofsky, 5
   and Radin, 101
   reception of, 3
   scholars' sovereignty, 95, 97, 284
Kempe, Margery, 247
King of Tars, 73–74, 76
kingship, 28, 91–92, 104, 223, 281
knowledge
   accumulation of, 72
   and feminism, 195
   and free will, 122
   of identity, 63, 87
   and Manicheism, 63
   Marburgian definition of, 171–75
   and medievalism, 71
   and the medieval, 16, 72, 87, 150
   and mysticism, 243–44, 248
   neo-Kantian, 30, 170
   symbolized in cathedrals, 178
Kojève, Alexandre, 27, 69
   Introduction a la lecture de Hegel, 38
Kracauer, Siegfried, 288n47

Lacan, Jacques, 2, 47, 262n18, 274, 299
Latinity, 8, 29, 142, 274, 278, 297
  assimilation through education, 144
  and Curtius, 144
  legacy of, 7
  in Sayers, 196
Latour, Bruno, 295–96
Lefebvre, Henri, 2, 25
Lefort, Claude, 285
Lenin, V. I., 24
Lewis, C. S.
  discomfort with women, 206
  on Sayers, 201
literature, 78–80, 131–46, 265, 270–71, 290–91.
    See also Auerbach; Curtius; Harlem
    Renaissance; Jauss; medievalism;
    modernism; Zumthor
  as atemporal, 140–41, 204, 237, 255n1, 259
  comparative, 23, 277
  French, 227
  medieval, 80, 147–49, 152–61, 191, 257, 265, 292
  medievalist, 293
  popular fiction, 192–93
Locke, Alain LeRoy (philosopher, activist, art patron)
  "Art or Propaganda?" 79
Löwith, Karl, 4, 18–19
Lukács, György, 14

Macaulay, Rose
  Pleasure of Ruins, 152
  The World My Wilderness, 151
Macron, Emmanuel, 59
Mâle, Émile (art historian), 178
Mandouze, André (scholar of Augustine and colleague to Fanon), 36, 61
Manhattan, University of (fictional), 76
Manicheism, 27, 35–36, 40, 48, 59, 64, 253.
    See also Augustine; Fanon
  and colonialism, 61
  as distinct from manicheism, 35n3
  as historical phenomenon, 50
  as North African phenomenon, 61–63
Mannheim, Karl, 277
Marburg University, 30, 170, 221, 226, 228, 230
  hiring of Auerbach, 221
  Huizinga lecture at, 221, 226, 228
Marichal, Robert (paleographer)
  and Panofsky, 188
Marinetti, Filippo Tommaso, 16
Maritain, Jacques (Catholic philosopher), 243–44
Marrou, Henri Irénée (scholar of Augustine, colleague to Fanon), 59–60
Marx, Karl, 2, 52, 57, 69, 293

Capital, 297
Grundrisse, 23
  precapitalist moment, 57
Marxism, 23–27, 46, 53, 56–59, 113
Mary, Queen of Scots, 148
Mayflower Compact, 288
Mbembe, Achille, 47
McCarthyism, 26
medievalism, 1n1, 9–11, 68–87, 106, 153, 225–26, 293. See also Afromedievalism; appropriation of medieval history; Black medievalism
  and hermeneutic distance, 269–70
Milton, John, 205–6
Modernity
  as "blind modernism," 256
  and capitalism, 57, 293–94
  and colonialism, 46, 57–58, 61, 63–64, 67
  failure and bleakness of, 17–18, 28, 80
  and fascism, 106–9
  and Hegel, 69
  and history, 74
  and individualism, 107–8, 111, 124, 224, 289 (see also Hobbes)
  legitimacy of, 18–19, 282–83 (see also secularization thesis; periodization; Blumenberg)
  literary modernism, 151–53, 192–94, 290
  and politics, 68, 106–9, 286–87
  and progress, 16, 282
  and race, 71, 77–81, 85–86, 293 (see also Afromodernism)
  in relation to the medieval, 14, 28–29, 31, 57, 70, 72, 80–81, 86–87, 154, 209–210, 257, 273–76, 295–98
  renaissance as birth of, 217, 276–78
  and technology, 16, 77–78, 85
Monnier, Adrienne, 291
Morgan, Edwin (poet and translator), 153, 290
  Beowulf, 148
  and Bone, 156
  The Ruin, 152
Müller, Adam, 295
mysticism. *See also* Weil
  as anachronistic, 241
  censorship of, 247
  as divine encounter, 242, 245, 248
  and divine knowledge, 243–44
  and Kantorowicz, 92n14
  and mental illness, 241–42
  and organized religions, 242–43
  and Scholasticism, 242

naive historicism. *See under* historicism
nationalism, 6–9, 42, 46–47, 87, 116, 131–33, 224–25, 277, 295
Nazism, 4–6, 8, 18, 28, 95, 105–107, 109, 118, 133, 136, 159, 166, 282
Nicholas of Cusa, 19, 269
Nietzsche, Friedrich, 109, 268n41, 276n6

Olschki, Leonardo, 90, 94–95, 103. *See also* Kantorowicz
Oresme, Nicholas, 55
Oxford University, 12, 29, 100, 149, 153, 155, 161, 191, 206
  "language men," 154
  and women, 12

Panofsky, Erwin, 2, 167–89, 280
  American phase, 173
  and Bourdieu, 188–89
  and Cassirer, 174, 279
  Gothic Architecture and Scholasticism, 30, 169, 176–89
    justification of analogy, 176
    objections to, 186–88
  Idea, 172–73
  on habitus, 4
  and Kantian thought, 30, 175–76
  and Kantorowicz, 5
  and Marichal, 188
  on Plato's theory of art, 172–73
  reception of, 167–68
  and Schramm, 5
  Studies in Iconology, 173–74
Pearl (Middle English poem), 56
Peirce, Charles Sanders (American philosopher), 167
periodization, 176, 215–18, 224–28, 230–38, 276. *See also* Auerbach
  anachronism in, 31
  projection, 264
  terms for, 221, 226, 227, 232
  transcended by realism, 237
Perrin, Joseph-Marie (Dominican friar), 240. *See also* Weil
Peterson, Erik, 105, 283, 285
Petrarch, 273, 278
Pizan, Christine de, 16
Plato, 55, 141, 172–73, 263, 280–81, 293
Porete, Marguerite, 247
Postan, Michael (historian), 25
Pound, Ezra, 77, 153, 156
Power, Eileen (historian), 26
Princeton University, 26, 98, 103
  Institute for Advanced Study, 5, 144
  Press, 144

Protestantism, 14, 294
Psalms, Book of, 91
Pseudo-Dionysius the Areopagite, 280

Radin, Max (legal scholar), 101
reader resonse theory. *See under* Jauss
realism
  creatural/creaturely, 235–37
  existential, 238
  and naturalism, 233
  transcending periodization, 237
renaissance, 278. *See also* periodization
  and Auerbach, 230–38
  and Hegel, 177
  and Huizinga, 230–38
  Italian, 173, 175, 208, 225
  and Olschki, 95
  and periodization, 31, 215–18, 224–28
  and realism, 230–38
Riegl, Alois, 279n14
Robertson, D. W., 108n9
Roma aeterna, 134–35, 142, 278
Rome, University of, 94
The Ruin (Old English poem), 152. *See also* Morgan

Said, Edward, 145, 219
Sartre, Jean-Paul, 27
  on Fanon, 39–40
Savigny, Karl von, 295
Sayers, Dorothy L., 2, 30, 296
  on authority, 193–94, 207, 211, 296
  The Burning Bush, 203
  career of, 191, 210–11
  and Dante, 205–206
    Dante and his Daughter Bice, 208
  on female desire, 199–200
  translation of *Divina Commedia*, 191
  and feminism, 194–97
  gender performance of, 200–203, 209
  "The Human-Not-Quite-Human", 196–97
  and Milton, 206
  on political movements, 197
  on superiority, 205–206
  on Williams, 202–205
  "Are Women Human?", 195–96
Schapiro, Meyer, 187
Schmitt, Carl, 2, 28, 89, 101–102, 282, 285. *See also* Kantorowicz
  conception of friend and enemy, 113
  and the Nazi party, 105
  "political theology," 99–101, 103
  reception of, 283–84
  "secularization thesis," 282

Schmitt, Carl (cont.)
  on sovereignty, 99, 285
  training of, 104
Schmoller, Gustav von (economist), 15, 295
Scholasticism, 177, 243, 283n28. *See also*
    Aquinas; Panofsky
  and architecture, 169, 186–87
  conception of whiteness, 55–56
  concordatia, 178–79
  law of the excluded middle, 187–88
  manifestatio, 177–78
  and mysticism, 242
Scholem, Gershom, 287
Schramm, Percy Ernst (historian), 4–5
Scott, Alexander, 29
  career of, 147
  The Latest in Elegies, 147, 164
  recognition, 149
  Sang for a Flodden, 148
  Scottish literature, 147, 153
  Seaman's Sang, 148
The Seafarer (Old English poem), 147, 156.
    See also Bone; Scott
secularization thesis, 18–19, 282, 284, 299n76
Sedlmayr, Hans, 4n10, 280n18
Semon, Richard, 277
Semper, Gottfried (art critic), 167
Shakespeare, William, 199, 204, 274
  Richard II, 89, 284
Simmel, Georg, 14
Simson, Otto von, 280–81, 283
Smith, Adam, 294
Socrates, 55
Sorbonne University, 59, 242
Sorel, Georges (right-wing intellectual), 40
Spivak, Gayatri Chakravorty, 22
Stendhal (Marie-Henri Beyle, French author),
    218, 219
Steuart, James, 294
Strauss, Leo, 111, 293
Strayer, Joseph R., 26
Structuralism, 189
subaltern studies, 23
Suger (Abbot), 280–81
Swansea, University of, 152
Sweezy, Paul (historian), 24

Tempier, Étienne, 283n28
Tertullian, 298
Thibon, Gustave (Catholic philosopher), 240,
    243–47, 253. *See also* Weil
Thierry of Chartres, 280
Thomas of Erfurt, 14
Thorkelin, Grímur Jónsson, 154
Tolkien, J. R. R., 29, 149, 290

"*Beowulf*: The Monsters and the Critics," 149,
    154–55, 157
  Inklings, 206
Toronto, University of, 15
Totalitarianism, 6–7, 106, 110–19, 124, 285–88
Townsend Warner, Sylvia
  The Corner that Held Them, 151
Treitschke, Heinrich von, 295

university. *See* individual universities under
    respective names
  access to, 12, 13
  corporate identity of, 97–98, 284
  critique of, 164
  in *Lucky Jim*, 150, 161
  medieval, 12, 285

violence, 23, 39–40, 57, 59–60, 63, 65–67, 131n3,
    198, 209, 232, 233
Virgil
  and Dante, 141–43, 203
  and *Roma aeterna*, 142

Waddell, Helen
  Poetry in the Dark Ages, 151
Wagner, Adolf, 295
Wallace, William (Scottish hero), 148
The Wanderer (Old English poem), 156.
    See also Bone
Warburg, Aby, 277, 279
The Warburg Library, 4, 172
Weber, Max (sociologist), 14, 64, 297
Weil, Simone, 2, 15, 31, 291
  and affliction, 249–52
  and Arendt, 289
  and the Catholic Church, 240–41
  on Christian exclusion, 253
  on Eckhart, 250–51, 253–54
  education of, 15, 244
  and her editors, 240
  Gravity and Grace, 240, 245–47, 253
  and mystic authenticity, 245–46
  and mystical experiences, 251–52
  political engagement by, 245
  and readings in mysticism, 248–49
  Waiting for God, 240, 241, 247–50, 253
Wellek, René, 131, 238
whiteness, 41, 53–57, 63, 81. *See also*
    Blackness
  as grounds for ethnostates, 87
  as a medieval abstraction, 55–56
William of Ockham, 283, 286n40
Williams, Charles (writer and theologian)
  and Sayers, 202–205
Wilson, Angus, 2, 29

Anglo-Saxon Attitudes, 29, 150–51, 153, 161–62
  as social critique, 163–64
  career of, 152
Windrush, HMT Empire, 165–66
Woolf, Virginia, 196, 200, 216, 219, 238, 278n12
World War I, 16–17, 75. *See also* Interwar Period, World War II, World Wars
  and the Black American identity, 81–82
  as the end of the "gentleman," 201
  as extension of earlier French-German conflict, 222
  origins of, 82
World War II, 1, 9, 12, 17, 23. *See also* Interwar Period, World War I, World Wars
  academic exodus during, 227
  Dumbarton Oaks accords, 84
  effect on colonized people, 84, 165
  effect on literature, 132, 147
  and French refugees, 246
  origins of, 84
  and the resulting displacement of people, 114
  and Sayers, 190
  and Winston Churchill, 159
World Wars, 122–23, 192, 275. *See also* Interwar Period, World War I, World War II

Zedong, Mao, 24
Zumthor, Paul, 2, 4, 32, 291–92, 299
  on dialogue, 263–64
  Essai de poétique médiévale, 257–58, 264–67, 270–72
  on historical distance, 266–67
  on identity, 257
  and Jauss, 257, 260–61, 265, 267, 269, 272
  on medieval alterity, 269–70
  on *mouvance*, 271–72, 299
  on reading, 259–60
  Speaking of the Middle Ages, 6, 255–56, 258–62, 266–72, 291–92
Zupitza, Julius (philologist), 155

For EU product safety concerns, contact us at Calle de José Abascal, 56–1º,
28003 Madrid, Spain or eugpsr@cambridge.org.

www.ingramcontent.com/pod-product-compliance
Lightning Source LLC
LaVergne TN
LVHW020340260326
834688LV00045B/1457